THE
SECRETS
OF
ROME

THE
SECRETS
OF
ROME

LOVE & DEATH
IN THE ETERNAL CITY

CORRADO AUGIAS

TRANSLATED FROM THE ITALIAN BY
A. LAWRENCE JENKENS

First published in the United States of America in 2007 by
Rizzoli Ex Libris
An Imprint of Rizzoli International Publications
300 Park Avenue South
New York, NY 10010

Edited by Julie Di Filippo and Alta L. Price
Jacket design: Gabriele Wilson
Typesetting: Tina Henderson

2007 2008 2009 2010 2011 / 10 9 8 7 6 5 4 3 2 1

Printed in the United States of America

ISBN-10: 0-8478-2933-2
ISBN-13: 978-0-8478-2933-0

Library of Congress Catalog Control Number: 2007920511

CONTENTS

C'est ici un livre de bonne foy, lecteur. . . . Je veus qu'on m'y voie en ma façon simple, naturelle et ordinaire. . . . Ainsin, lecteur, je suis moi-mesmes la matière de mon livre.

Montaigne, *Essais*, «Avertissement au lecteur»

To the Reader
You have here, Reader, a book whose faith can be trusted. . . . Here I want to be seen in my simple, natural, everyday fashion. . . . And therefore, Reader, I myself am the subject of my book.

Montaigne, *The Complete Essays*

EDITOR'S NOTE

This book was written, and will ideally be read, more as a novel than an essay; it's simply a series of stories about Rome. Each of the world's great cities has it's own saga, and this book aims to recount the saga of Rome—one of the longest, most dramatic, and most fascinating in world history. Where possible, the sources of quotes and anecdotes have been included for those interested in finding out more, and readers are invited to contact the publisher should they have information for future editions of this book. That said, the sheer richness of Rome's history, characters, and chroniclers has brought forth stories that can't always clearly be traced back to the source. Hopefully these tales—which resemble Rome in all its beauty, chaos, and timelessness—will unfold like a stroll through the city itself.

PREAMBLE IN TWO SCENES

WHERE CAN WE BEGIN the story of the universe that is Rome? In a city as contradictory as this, filled with all the glory, ruins, and dust left behind by past centuries, it's possible to see traces of every human event and sentiment in its history—the bravery and cowardice, the generosity and indolence, the resourcefulness and louche limpness of the lazy. There's not a single event in its past that hasn't left a sign, scar, or scratch on its hide. Rome will never be a city of order, symmetry, events that unfold according to plan, or the coherent result of urban planning. If human history is nothing but violence and tumult, then Rome has been its mirror over the centuries, capable of reflecting each and every detail with painful fidelity, including those from which we would willingly look away.

So where can we begin, then? Every respectable story should start at the beginning, *ab ovo* as the Romans said, referring to the *ovo* or egg of Leda, which she laid after being seduced by Jupiter in the form of a swan. It was from this egg that Helen, the woman of such fatal beauty, was born. So let us, too, start *ab ovo* then, not just for chronological convenience, but also because the story, the myth of Rome's origins, seems to contain a basic trait still recognizable after all the city's adventures and misadventures; put simply, its destiny. So from which of its origins shall we start? Everyone knows the legend of Romulus and Remus, but not everyone remembers the various versions of how these two legendary twins came into the world. It seems their mother was Rhea Silvia, a princess of Alba Longa who was forced to become a nun (as they'd have said in the seventeenth century) and enter the sacred college of the Vestal Virgins, whose members, among other duties, took a vow of absolute chastity. She was forced into this by her uncle, usurper of the throne, to prevent her from bearing any heirs who might jeopardize his dynasty.

Instead, one day the young woman found herself pregnant, supposedly at the hands of a deity (an oft-repeated explanation), perhaps Mars himself. Following these branches of the family tree, this version leads us to Ascanius, son of Lavinia and the pious Aeneas. Can we believe this? Virgil did, or so he wrote, in his epic poem on the nation's foundation, *The Aeneid*.

This legend, built up little by little, is known in other, more embarrassing versions recounted by Plutarch in his *Life of Romulus*. One day King Tarchetius of Alba Longa, a cruel man, witnessed the astonishing appearance of a gigantic male member that descended through the chimney and began to flutter around the house. The Etruscan oracles, even without having read Freud, explained that this was the spirit of Mars who, irritated with the king, wanted to produce a successor for him. To appease the irate god the king had to offer him a virgin; Tarchetius ordered his daughter to satisfy the thing that continued to flit about, but the girl, understandably, refused. A slave girl, who didn't have the option to say no, was called as a substitute.

These are the rather dishonorable events that led, nine months after the surreal encounter, to the birth of two boys whom the evil king, to avoid all risk, ordered to be murdered. Abandoned in a basket along the banks of the Tiber (like Moses), the twins were saved because the waters receded, and because a she-wolf, driven down from the nearby mountains by thirst, nourished them by offering her own breasts. But was she really a wolf? In his history of Rome, Livy insinuates that it wasn't a real wolf, but rather a woman, Larenzia, whom the local shepherds called "she-wolf," another name for prostitute, because she so often sold herself to those rude men: "Sunt qui Larentiam volgato corpore lupam inter pastores vocatam putent." [There are those who think that Larentia was called a she-wolf by the shepherds because she was a prostitute.] When twentieth-century Italian Fascists thought of giving the nickname "children of the she-wolf" to the children inducted into the party's youth organization they didn't realize, in their ignorance of history, the unintentional humor of that name.

The two boys, of less-than-flawless lineage, grew up revealing distinctly different temperaments. Remus was the more resolute, and seemed more suited to command. Romulus appeared physically weaker than his brother, but was also much more astute. When it came time to found the city, Romulus tricked his brother with a bet over which of them would first spot vultures in the Murcia Valley, where the Circus Maximus would later rise. The bet degenerated; Romulus reneged, and Remus was enraged. To provoke his brother, he jumped the furrow being dug to outline the city's perimeter, and was struck down by a blow from the hoe of an Etruscan assassin. With his brother gone, Romulus, consumed with fury, cried out, "Sic deinde, quicumque alius transiliet moenia mea" [The same will happen to anyone else who dares to trespass my walls].

Might the city's name derive from Romulus? It's possible, but by no means certain. Other hypotheses include the Etruscan word *rumon*, or river, and thus the "city of the river," or the Oscan *ruma*, or hill. So the origin of the city's name is as uncertain as the lineage of its founding twins.

Romulus brought together a bunch of misfits from all over to populate his city. According to Plutarch, each of them brought a handful of earth from his own country to throw into the pit, or *mundus*, that had been dug at the center of the walled enclosure. At the same time, Plutarch adds, they also tossed in the first fruits "of all things deemed good according to custom, and necessary for human life according to nature." In this village of villains there was just one thing among all life's necessities still missing—women. The young women of neighboring villages were invited to settle in the new city but, horrified, they refused the offer. In short, the Romans resorted to the extreme measure of kidnapping women from the nearby Sabine nation, thus allowing Rome to truly begin to live.

It took a lot to ennoble this grim story of rape and murder. Because the story of Mars siring the twins seemed tenuous, someone wisely thought of rooting the new city in another illustrious myth, the Trojan War, somehow transforming Pious Aeneas, son of Venus, into the father of Romulus. Virgil refined this new legend by linking it, during the golden age of Augustus, directly to Homer, and by way of the *Iliad* gave both himself and his story a grand literary pedigree.

There's a grain of truth in every legend, and in the case of Rome that grain tells us that its beginnings were turbulent, most likely because of its inhabitants' aggressiveness. They made a name for themselves through violence in the new settlement, strategically located on the border between two cultures—Etruscan and Italic—

and at the crossroads of the important commercial roads connecting Etruscan Tuscany and Greek Campania. It took centuries to create not only the city's mythology, but also a system of laws and social norms that insured some fairness in communal life in a city whose beginnings had been so adventurous. These norms were respected for centuries, and with regard to bona fide jurisdiction Roman law remains in many ways unsurpassed to this day, as we hear in the vehement formulae that sum up some of its principle tenets: *Unicuique suum* (to each his own), *Neminen laedere* (injure no one), *Dura lex sed lex* (the law is harsh but it is the law), *Ne bis in eadem* (no one should be punished twice for the same thing), *Nemo ad factum cogi potest* (no one can be forced into a deed), and so on.

Although it took centuries to perfect, the light of the law began to shine in Rome. Numa Pompilius, second king of the city (sometime between 700 and 600 BC), came from the Sabine region and was the son-in-law of King Titus Tatius. When Romulus died, the Romans chose Numa Pompilius as their sovereign. Pious and pacific, he maintained good relationships with the city's neighbors and thus guaranteed a long period of peace. In recounting the story of his life, Plutarch passes a memorable judgment on Numa's reign that has persisted to the present day:

> And yet as someone will say, did not Rome progress and advance thanks to war? This is a question which would require a long response for some people who reckon progress in terms of money, luxury, and in supremacy rather than in security, kindness, independence from others and justice towards others.

King Numa was especially dedicated to the religious life of the city, and knew that divine assistance and a fear of the hereafter were both very useful in educating a primitive population about respecting the law. "Numa's muse," wrote Plutarch, "was gentle and humane; he converted the city to peace and justice by placating its unrestrained and fiery habits." Remembering the outrageous behavior of the first Romans toward the women of his own nation, Numa was particularly careful to devise a restrained code of sexual behavior, reprimanding men, and especially women. "He required of [women] a great reserve and forbade them any role in public life, and he admonished them to moderation and silence." Roman women married at a very early age, "at twelve or even younger because then they brought their husbands their bodies and souls pure and intact." The modesty imposed on all young women became the stringent duty of the order of Vestal Virgins, which Numa founded. The goddess Vesta, virgin guardian of the flame, symbolized the eternity of Rome. Her priestesses were selected from amongst Roman girls of patrician families between the ages of six and ten. They were obliged to maintain their virginity for thirty years, after which they were allowed to marry. Other than tending the flame, they also became responsible, over time, for keeping watch over the Palladium, praying for the public's health, and guarding wills and other important documents. Great honors were reserved for them: magistrates made way for them, and the consular fasces were lowered as they passed. They had the right to be escorted by lictors, and anyone who insulted them was punished by death. A vestal virgin who violated her vow of chastity was considered guilty of *incestum*; her seducer was flogged to death, and she was taken to the Campus Sceleratum where she suffered a terrible punishment that Plutarch described in great detail:

But she that has broken her vow is buried alive near the gate called Collina,

> where a little mound of earth stands inside the city, reaching some little distance, called in Latin agger; under it a narrow room is constructed, to which a descent is made by stairs; here they prepare a bed, and light a lamp, and leave a small quantity of victuals, such as bread, water, a pail of milk, and some oil; that so that body which had been consecrated and devoted to the most sacred service of religion might not be said to perish by such a death as famine. The culprit herself is put in a litter, which they cover over, and tie her down with cords on it, so that nothing she utters may be heard. They then take her to the forum; all people silently go out of the way as she passes, and such as follow accompany the bier with solemn and speechless sorrow; and indeed, there is not any spectacle more appalling, nor any day observed by the city with greater appearance of gloom and sadness. When they come to the place of execution, the officers loose the cords, and then the high priest, lifting his hands to heaven, pronounces certain prayers to himself before the act; then he brings out the prisoner, being still covered, and placing her upon the steps that lead down to the cell, turns away his face with the rest

of the priests; the stairs are drawn up after she has gone down, and a quantity of earth is heaped up over the entrance to the cell, so as to prevent it from being distinguished from the rest of the mound. This is the punishment of those who break their vow of virginity.

In 1972 Mario Praz published his wonderful book *Il patto col serpente*. Amongst the many essays in the book, one—"La Roma dannunziana" or "D'Annunzio's Rome"—contains this evocative passage: "Sometimes I pass by a house on Via Varese adorned with *sgraffito* decorations, its shutters usually closed, and made sad by happy trees, pines and palms, which here seem mournful and solemn, like northern trees. No other scene I know is a more appropriate setting for a detective novel." When the daily newspaper *La Repubblica* moved its editorial offices to a building on the Piazza Indipendenza, where they stayed for some thirty years, the sentence quoted above came back to me. I worked at the paper's offices, and Via Varese was around the corner. The mysterious house was (and still is) there, halfway up the street, on the left as you come from the square. Praz was right— the house is mysterious, but even more strikingly, it seems to have nothing to do with the neighborhood (once called Macao) around it, at least as we now see it with its "dreary and melancholy streets, a derelict residential district whose villas have been converted into inexpensive hotels, schools, and offices, its decayed Corinthian columns and small parks choked by modern boxes. [Here I think Praz was referring to the building that later became *La Repubblica's* offices.] Here and there, though, there is a corner that has kept some mark of distinction."

We need only look more carefully, however, and the marks that Praz noted become clearly visible. These streets were once at the heart of a life that, although it has since disappeared, did leave behind a memory of itself. The sparse architectural remains, certain friezes, and a few views glimpsed through tall gates are its witnesses. There are a few books, too, which almost no one reads, that make reference to life there. They don't include *Il piacere* (D'Annunzio's *The Pleasure*), the most important work in the period immediately after 1870, which we will return to later, nor the journal *Cronaca bizantina* in its fleeting moment of aestheticism when D'Annunzio himself was its director (1885–1886). They do, on the other hand, include the slim volume by the antiquarian Alberto Arduini with the winning title *Dame al Macao*, first published in 1945 and never reprinted. But why the name Macao? What does Rome have to do with the former Portuguese colony in the South China Sea, long considered a place of "belle dame sans merci" and exotic adventures? The neighborhood's name was actually taken from a Jesuit seminary built on a part of the Castro Pretorio where, from the end of the sixteenth century on, missionaries destined to serve in the Far East were educated.

It was here that the Piemontese—the new administrators of the recently united nation, from the Northern region of Piedmont—decided to build a residential neighborhood and the headquarters for the important ministries of the newly formed Kingdom of Italy. One of the principal reasons for this choice was the convenience of having the railway station close by. Its elevation, too, was important; this is the highest part of Rome, dubbed *alta semita* in ancient times, and its air is healthier, thanks to the 80 to 100 meters it has over the insalubrious lowlands encircled by the river bend. Here the new administrators planned a modern, rational, secular neighborhood with houses and apartment buildings for the new managerial class, the highest hierarchs of the state. It had not one single church (making Macao unique in all Rome, with only one exception we'll discuss in the last chapter).

Statesmen and literary figures, financiers and journalists, and the "belles dames" of Arduini's title all roamed the streets of Macao.

> In the morning the lazy neighborhood awakens late. There are waiters in striped uniforms, coachmen who wash the carriages with great torrents of water, and gardeners armed with shears and watering cans. Later, ladies and gentlemen on horseback with riding hats, and parliamentarians in furs. After midday, pathetic departures for the Pincio. At five o'clock a passerby might glimpse, behind balconies draped with lace curtains, soft lights which silhouette women with bustles, pale, well-brought-up girls, and elegant gentlemen in the most restrained frock coats. Tea is served in winter gardens . . . in an atmosphere that is perfumed but never without a slight odor of gas.

The Macao described by Arduini probably never really existed. Some of its small, elegant villas are still there, but the ambience he described has more a feeling of fantasy or desire than of reality. Rome never resembled Bloomsbury, nor the small quiet streets of Paris's Neuilly or the Sixteenth Arrondissement. Its appearance is different; it can be indolent or tragic, and has always been that way. (Arduini himself met a violent end, murdered by an American officer in the months after the liberation over a quarrel that perhaps had to do with a relationship gone bad.) Yet even if Arduini's Macao never was, the new Kingdom of Italy did try, in part with neighborhoods like it, to link Rome to the great metropolises of Europe—Paris, London, Berlin—finally freeing it from political and social isolation.

The ancient Rome of Romulus and Remus, as well as the Rome that disappeared with the end of the nineteenth century, were both swallowed by the vortex and dust of history. If I had to note just one feature of the city, I would point to the simultaneous presence of many cities, each locked inside the other, overlaid in three, four, or five layers ready to reveal themselves as soon as you look beyond the noisy exterior of the present.

In the Fora, after a day of heavy rain, one can see a myriad of small stones glimmering on the ground. These are fragments, little more than dust, of the multicolored marbles that over the centuries were brought here from every corner of the earth. Every excavation in the historic center of the city—be it for a building's foundations or a subway tunnel—invariably reveals the remains of an earlier life. Renzo Piano found this out during the construction of the new Auditorium and Parco della Musica, and Federico Fellini imagined it in his film *Roma*, where a Roman fresco is brought to light in the bowels of a tunnel, but that same light, in mere moments, burns its delicate surface, erasing it forever.

Only in Rome could Nero's Domus Aurea, one of the greatest royal palaces ever constructed, be buried after just a few years of splendor to serve as the foundations of a new emperor's baths. Only in Rome could the entrance of an apartment building constructed in 1909 be supported by a buttress belonging to the Circus of Nero, or the columns in a Christian church be taken from a temple dedicated to Venus. These multiple stratifications document an uninterrupted history all across the city, erasing and then adding, with a stubborn-ness that switches from gentle to violent—like the waves that relentlessly batter the same stretch of coastline. In his novel *Rome*, Émile Zola understood this aspect of the city perfectly. His protagonist reflects:

> [Pierre] was again becoming absorbed in the idea he had formed of pagan Rome resuscitating in Christian Rome and turning it into Catholic Rome, the new political, sacerdotal, domineering centre of earthly government. Apart from the primitive age of the Catacombs, had Rome ever been Christian? The thoughts that had come to him on the Palatine, in the Appian Way, and in St. Peter's were gathering confirmation. Genius that morning had brought him fresh proof. No doubt the paganism which reappeared in the art of Michael Angelo and Raffaelle was tempered, transformed by the Christian spirit. But did it not still remain the basis? Had not the former master peered across Olympus when snatching his great nudities from the terrible heavens of Jehovah? Did not the ideal figures of Raffaelle reveal the superb, fascinating flesh of Venus beneath the chaste veil of the Virgin? [1]

This layering is part of Rome's fascination, but also its burden. Encumbered by its own past, it has never been, nor will it ever be, easy for the city to free itself from its own ghosts. New York, which is constantly redefining itself, is not a good comparative example, but even Paris does not have the same dense ties to its own past. Until almost the year 1000 the French capital, Lutetia Parisiorum as the Romans called it, was little more than a fortified village on the Ile de la Cité, important only because of its location below the confluence of the Seine and Marna rivers. Paris is seventeen hundred years younger than Rome—seventeen hundred visible, palpable years.

This book is neither a history of nor a guidebook to Rome, rather it is a collection of events tied to a certain street, palace, monument, or in some cases to my own life—in other words, to encounters and combinations that I hope are meaningful, but that are also, like life itself, often accidental. These are places I lived, places I saw differently from the way they are now—because even Rome changes— or places I took from books and neighbors' stories. Describing some places of the city, it was inevitable that I'd have to review parts of its troubled history, a history that has never really settled down, even after 1870, the year Rome became part of the Kingdom of Italy. Sometimes I catch myself imagining what Rome might have become had it—in other centuries, such as the fifteenth and sixteenth—been the center of a kingdom freed of papal domination, able to transform itself into a truly modern capital. In those two centuries the Italian peninsula benefited from an economic and cultural energy unparalleled in all of Europe. If Machiavelli and Giucciardini's dreams of unification had come true back then, Rome's destiny would certainly have been different, and probably better. Their goal, however, was slowed by a complex articulation of local and regional interests and egos. Rome did become the capital, but only at the end of the nineteenth century, when Italy was experiencing a period of cultural, social, and industrial stagnation, and when it counted for very little on the international radar—even this continues to be a burden.

In this book, however, I will tell of at least two instances when the city seems to have thrown off the cloak of centuries past. The first—which erased the humiliation suffered after the fall of the Empire, the bloody battles of the Middle Ages, and the repressions following the Protestant Reformation—was the glorious and futile attempt in 1849 to found a democratic republic based on the rule of law. The second, which redeemed the outrageous vulgarity of the Fascist period, was the resistance that rose up during the nine months of Nazi occupation. You'll find stories and summaries, personalities and episodes meant to restore the comprehensive picture of a city that has had to confront its (perhaps overly) demanding legacy—the Roman Empire, Jewish monotheism later revised by Christianity, and centuries of social inertia, ferocious anarchy, and acquiescence to the rules of those in power. Yet even this spinelessness, this resignation that often turned into indifference, has probably contributed to the fact that so many have experienced Rome as their own home—Belisarius and Totila, the Ostrogoth kings, Theodoric the Barbarian, Charlemagne and Otto the Emperor, Goethe and Montaigne, Dumas and Zola, Stendhal and Gogol, Henry James and Corot, as well as hordes of tourists, pilgrims, and artists. Of all the great cities of antiquity—Niniveh, Babylon, Alexandria, Tyre, Athens, Carthage, Antioch—Rome is the only one that has existed continuously without ever having been reduced to a semi-abandoned village. Instead it was often the epicenter of events of global significance, and often paid a hefty toll. For more than twenty-seven hundred years Rome has stood on the banks of its muddy river, at times embellished by the melancholy appeal of its ruins, at others spoiled by the sloth of its citizens. Repeatedly violated by foreign armies, destination of disorganized immigration, sometimes protagonist, sometimes slave, Rome has always managed to preserve some small trace of each passage and every period. Despite its many travails, or perhaps because of them, Rome retains its immense illusionistic, theatrical capacity.

1. Émile Zola, *Rome*, http://www.gutenberg.org/dirs/etext05/rome610.txt

I

BETWEEN SPACE AND TIME

IN 1957 A POETRY COLLECTION that became an immediate sensation was published—Pier Paolo Pasolini's *The Ashes of Gramsci*. For the first time a poet who declared himself a communist sympathizer challenged the leftist political culture by issuing a call for justice that went beyond mere economic disparities. In his wonderful biography of the poet, Enzo Siciliano writes, "Within the framework of leftist ideology, which Pasolini shared, the demand for an ethics of the person—a new morality whereby the individual would be salvaged in his entirety, in his specificity—went completely unheeded."[1] Pasolini's "specificity" was his homosexuality and the fact that it caused him, as a Catholic, both guilt and remorse. He asked the left—cried out to it, even—for this new morality.

In those years there were things no one spoke of, even if it seems almost unthinkable now. No one talked about gay pride, and homosexuality was an illness, something to be ashamed of, to hide. Pasolini was the first to painfully put his orientation on display, to proclaim it in his writings. He was showered with scorn by the bourgeois conformists (their abuse would follow him throughout his life), but he was also a real embarrassment to the left, just as he would be again in 1968 when he defended the police, the "sons of the people," who had been attacked in the Valle Giulia by the students, the "sons of the bourgeoisie."

Fellow writer and critic Cesare Garboli was one of the first to see a parallel between Pasolini's subversive experience in Rome and Caravaggio, who was also Roman by adoption, and also a subversive. Pasolini expressed his experience in his films and novels, while the painter did it in his images of youthful Bacchus figures and studio apprentices who brazenly look back at those who gaze at them. They bare themselves not with the innocence of angels, but with the winking shrewdness of those who knew the street value of their own bodies.

Additionally, and for the first time ever, Pasolini's *Ashes of Gramsci* (which gave its title to the entire collection) transformed the so-called Protestant Cemetery, near the Pyramid of Cestius, into an intensely poetic place, a Père Lachaise in miniature, contained and severe in its modesty, both neoclassical and romantic, set like a gem into the edge of baroque and Catholic Rome:

> Inside the ancient walls
> The autumnal May diffuses a deathly
> Peace, disquieting like our destinies,
> and holds the whole world's dismay,
> the finish of the decade that saw
> the profound naïve struggle to make
> life over collapse in ruins . . .[2]

It was May, although it felt like autumn, when Pasolini stopped for the first time in front of Antonio Gramsci's urn, which bears the simple inscription, *Cinera Antonii Gramscii* (Antonio Gramsci's Ashes). The dreariness of the day revealed just how "profound" and "naïve" was the attempt to "to make life over." There were the ashes of the great political thinker, on a narrow plot of the "waxen earth" whose boundaries are marked by two gnarled butter-bushes. The Latin inscription on the urn is wrong (it should read *cineres*, not *cinera*). The distant ideal pointed to by Gramsci's "thin hand" (as Pasolini describes it elsewhere in the poem) no longer illuminates the silence, and all that survives are the emotions that real politics can provoke:

> A scrap of red cloth, like those the Partisans
> Knotted up around their necks
> and, near the urn, on the waxen earth,
> a different red, of two geraniums.[3]

Then there is the cemetery itself and beyond its walls the neighborhood of Testaccio with its workshops and mechanics. The waves of noise from their shops lap up against the tomb:

> And the only sound that reaches you
> is the faded hammer blow on an anvil

from the workshops of Testaccio, drowsy
in the evening, with its shacks of poverty, its
naked piles of tin cans and scrap iron, where
singing, leering, an apprentice already is
ending his day, while the last raindrops fall.[4]

That poem, for many of my generation, represented both the discovery of a great poet and a new way of fostering political ideals without the ideological baggage so common back then. Pasolini quarreled
ceaselessly with the left, he protested, he fought, and he brought to
light the ways it lagged behind the times; yet he always remembered
the ideals that kept the movement going in the politically backward
Italy of his day. Some of his verses in *The Ashes of Gramsci* have an
almost nineteenth-century sense of identifying with the people.

The Ashes of Gramsci also led many of us to discover one of the
most fascinating corners of Rome. The area around the Pyramid of
Cestius—the somewhat ostentatious monument the Roman tribune
Gaius Cestius Epulo had built to his own memory—was, until the
beginning of the nineteenth century, nothing but fields—the famous
prati del popolo romano, or common meadows, where the people of
Rome grazed their flocks. Little by little it also became the place
where non-Catholics—Germans and the English for the most
part—were buried, since they were forbidden, as were prostitutes,
from being interred in consecrated ground. Funerals were allowed
only after dark, probably to avoid igniting popular fury at seeing a
man of the cloth who was not Catholic. When Sir Walter Synnod
was given permission in 1821 to bury his daughter in broad daylight,
the police commissioner arranged for mounted police to accompany
him "to protect him from any possible harm." And because the
cemetery was near the taverns of Testaccio, it wasn't unusual for
drunks and the occasional fanatic to stop by at night and vandalize
its tombs.

In 1817 the representatives of Prussia, Russia, and the Electorate
of Hannover sought permission from Cardinal Consalvo, the secretary of state, to build walls around the cemetery at their own
expense. It took four years and some pointed criticism from the
British parliament before the cardinal finally considered the request.
He explained his reluctance to approve the proposal by saying that

he was afraid the walls would block access to the pyramid. He was willing, however, to give them the area next to the ancient structure, and the expense of the walls built around this space was covered by the Papal States. It took several more years to secure the old part of the cemetery. A large section of the ancient Roman Via Ostiensis was unearthed when the walls were being built, and some of it can still be seen in the furrow between the pyramid and the cemetery. The cemetery was enlarged to its present size after 1870. As long as the grounds were under the jurisdiction of the papal authorities, there were strict rules that governed graves in the cemetery: inscriptions could not make any reference to eternal happiness because salvation was reserved for Catholics alone; crosses were forbidden on tombs; and even inscriptions suggesting divine benevolence—"God is Love," for example, or "Hier ruht in Gott"—were prohibited.

Two great English poets, Shelley and Keats, are among those buried here. Keats's grave is marked with a stone, but there is no mention of his name. Its famous inscription is a masterpiece of romantic sentiment:

> This Grave / contains all that was Mortal / of a / YOUNG ENGLISH POET, / Who, / on his Death Bed, / in the Bitterness of his Heart / at the Malicious Power of his Enemies, / Desired / these Words to be engraven / on his Tomb Stone / "Here lies One / Whose Name was writ in Water" / Feb 24th 1821.

A second inscription on a nearby wall answers the poet: "Keats! If thy cherished name be 'writ in water' / Each drop has fallen from some mourner's cheek." This moving dialogue between people long since passed away occurs in one of the rare places in Rome, especially the older part of the cemetery, where there is a fusion between the flourishes of romanticism and the attempts at simplicity and decorum that symbolized the neoclassical movement.

I spent much of my youth not far from the Protestant Cemetery, near the Porta Latina and the ancient Via Appia. Did playing amongst the Roman tombs dull the carefree delight of children's games? No more, I suppose, than playing with unexploded hand grenades or artillery shells. The countryside all around Rome was littered with them for some time after the war, and it was good fun to empty the explosive charge out of the large caliber shells. Yet even the small calibers (from pistols and muskets) gave some satisfaction to restless boys, myself included. We took the shell casings, emptied of their explosives and projectiles, and put them in a line on the tram tracks; when it passed they exploded, creating an exciting noise that sounded like a volley of shots, greatly startling the passengers. This added to the amusement of the little ruffians hidden around the tracks. The news these days often shows children in war-torn countries doing more or less the same kind of thing, and I imagine their reactions aren't too different from ours back then.

The Via Appia was a popular place in those days, and going there had all the characteristics of an adventure. It was easy to ride as far as the tomb of Cecilia Metella on a bicycle; there were very few cars, and a deep silence enveloped the occasional building, the ruins, the rows of cypress trees, and the large paving stones where, if you looked carefully enough, you could see the ruts made by cart wheels centuries before. Cecilia Metella sounded like such a mysterious name, and the gigantic tomb, shaped like a cylinder or drum crowned with crenellations, seemed to us like a fairy-tale castle, tall and mysterious.

The road stretched into the distance straight as an arrow. If you squinted it seemed like you could follow that straight line all the way to the bluish bumps of the faraway hills. The Via Appia also offered a myriad of fascinating detours, meandering paths, and the unexpected apparition of a funerary marker behind an elder tree, an inscription only a few words long that seemed to elude translation.

It was the gravestones themselves, more than the surrounding landscape or even the engineering miracle of the Appia itself, that gave me the first keys to an understanding of the place where we were living. There was, for example, an inscription set into the wall of the portico of the tiny, Early Christian church of San Giovanni a Porta Latina. It said, with a terse beauty, "Titiena uxor viro" [Titiena, the wife, to her man/husband]; the Latin *viro*, like the German *mein Mann*—my man and my husband—has a dual meaning, permitting this inscription to say everything in three words. I read another inscription on the tomb of a child, and its modest brevity was even more moving, "Terra sis illi laevis / fuit illa tibi" [O Earth be gentle on her / as she was on you]. The Romans were capable of extraordinary expressiveness even in their funerary rhetoric. There is an inscription on the tomb of a dog, "Raedarum custos, numquam latravit inepte; nunc silet et cineres vindicate umbra suos" [Guardian of the carts, he never barked in vain; now silent, a friendly shade watches over his ashes].

The Via Appia begins just outside the Porta San Sebastiano at a sarcophagus that now serves as the basin of a small fountain. You can drink from it, rinse your hands, and play at splashing your friends with the water in it, all under the watchful worn marble faces of a deceased couple. This husband and wife were most likely thinking about their eternal health as their portraits were sculpted, and certainly not the frivolous pastimes of passersby. In other cases it was precisely the passersby who were the much-considered audience. Tombs lined the roads outside the city walls, and were exposed to both public viewing and to vandalism, since miscreants are present in every society. One monument carries a dire and very specific threat: "Qui hic minxerit aut cacarit habeat deos Superos et Inferos iratos" [Whoever comes here to piss or crap will face the wrath of the gods above and below]. Trimalchio, in Petronius's *Satyricon*, has similar concerns. After drinking too much wine he starts to dictate plans for his funeral in the middle of the banquet. With the refreshing frankness of a drunk, he declares at one point, "I'll see to it in my will that my grave is protected from damage after my death. I'll appoint one of my ex-slaves to act as custodian to chase off the people who might come and crap on my tomb."[5]

The Via Appia has, over the centuries, endured dangers much greater than just a little bit of excrement. Robbed of its monuments, desecrated by inane vandalism in the postwar period, hemmed in by illegal construction, and plagued by traffic, the most glorious road in the world is now a mere shadow—not only of what it once was, but also of what it could have been even today. In the middle of the fifteenth century, Aeneas Sylvius Piccolomini (the future Pope Pius II) scolded a peasant who was breaking up the ancient stones to build himself a house. In the middle of the following century the Roman Senate gave Ippolito d'Este permission to demolish the tomb of Cecilia Metella for raw materials with which to build his villa (the famous Villa d'Este) at Tivoli—a crime on a completely different level than the peasant with his wretched pickaxe. Fortunately the capitol's enlightened conservator, Paolo Lancellotti, rescinded this permission, but the travertine revetment at the base of the tomb had already been removed, leaving it as we see it today.

The Via Appia was commissioned by the censor Appio Claudius (Claudius the Blind), who was also famous for having built the first aqueduct. This magnificent arterial began at the Tiber Island in the heart of Rome, crossed the valley of the Circus Maximus, and exited the city through the Republican-era walls at the Porta Capena. It then followed what is now called the Archaeological Promenade and then, just after Piazzale Numa Pompilio, it branched off from the Via Latina (this intersection, although unimpressive to see, is still there) and continued, by way of later additions, all the way to Brindisi. I have already noted that the Via Appia was a miracle of engineering, and indeed this road was built with the precision of a highway—long straight stretches which head directly to their destination, stepping over valleys and avoiding populous town centers. The so-called "fettuccia di Terracina"—dozens of kilometers of straight road without a single curve—is a perfect example; it was constructed because it was necessary, for military as well as commercial reasons, to reach Capua as quickly as possible. A traveler could cover almost 200 kilometers in five days of walking, which was an excellent pace. Pliny the Elder was able to say, with some pride, in his discussion of the glories of Egyptian and Greek architecture, "We Romans excel in three things which the Greeks neglected: the construction of aqueducts; sewers; and, above all, roads."

For a better idea of what it meant to travel from Rome to Brindisi along the Via Appia, read Horace's *Satire* I.5, which gives a vivid description of the journey. The first day covered the 25 kilometers or so from Rome to Ariccia; the second covered the following 40 to Forappio; and so on and so forth, through a hundred tawdry and mischievous adventures punctuated by the occasional moment of enchantment. Hearing these verses, "Iam nox inducere terries / umbras et coelo diffundere signa parabat" [The night had wrapped its robe around the earth and sown the sky with stars], one might imagine the opening lines of some lyrical nocturne.[6] Not quite—it's only a rhetorical trick interrupted immediately by a crude argument between servants and sailors. Ah, magnificent Horace!

The Via Appia has been trod by kings and emperors, and by all kinds of armies in every century, up until the armored vanguard of the American Fifth Division arrived in Rome on June 4, 1944, and put an end to the Nazi occupation of the city. Ottorino Respighi imagined Roman legions marching along it, their weapons clanging as they returned from some victory in the East, when he wrote the fourth movement of his symphonic poem *The Pines of Rome*. The composer evoked the pine trees of the Via Appia with a strong marching tempo, introduced by a description as clear as the music that expresses it: "A grey dawn on the Via Appia. Solitary pines watch over the tragic countryside. The poet's fantasy creates a vision of past glories. Trumpets blaze, and the consular army floods in, in the radiance of the newly risen sun, moving toward the Via Sacra and their triumph on the Capitoline Hill."

I could devote the whole of this chapter, and perhaps the entire book, to the ancient and modern tales of this mythical road. Yet Rome is big, and so I will point out only three of the evocative places along its length. Less than a kilometer from the Porta San Sebastiano, on the right side of the road, we come across a former paper mill, the former Cartiera Latina, which is a remarkable example of industrial archaeology. Until the last war it used the water of the Almone, the small river that ran beside and under it (today you have to stand directly over it to see the modest stream sunk deep in its bed). The Romans identified the river with a divine spirit, the god Almon, the central divinity in an important Eastern cult. As the Germans were retreating from Rome in 1944 they blew up the short stretch of road that bridged the stream in order to slow down the advancing Americans. I was there, a small boy holding his father's hand, and I watched wide-eyed as the Allies' enormous, clattering tanks advanced. They stopped at the small chasm, and a little while later an excavator carrying two steel rails that looked like folded-up claws appeared from the back of the column. It lifted them up, rotated them, and then dropped them over the hole created by the explosion. A few minutes later the column was moving again. The tank drivers (the majority of whom were African American) were leaning out of the turrets, and, amused, threw us candies—strange sweets with a hole in the middle and gummy strips that we would quickly learn to chew. These are the minute details that clog the memory and populate dreams, and grow more acute as the years pass—the wrinkled soldering on the plates of armor, a peeling white star on the side of one of the tanks, the deep tread marks on a clump of earth, and a tank driver, glad to be in Rome, alive. The people watching, thin and poor like me, applauded with tears in their eyes.

A few hundred meters beyond there is a sort of intersection of three streets: the Via Ardeatina on the right; the Via Appia straight ahead; and to the left, somewhat smaller than the other two, the Via della Caffarella. Just at that crossroads there is a small, round chapel. It looks neglected, but its appearance is deceptive. It was built in the middle of the sixteenth century by the English cardinal Reginald Pole, to give thanks on the exact spot where he escaped from an ambush set for him by assassins sent by King Henry VIII. A jealous guardian of the newly founded Anglican Church, the arrogant king could not abide that an English subject had become a Roman Catholic cardinal. (I will return to the extraordinary figure of Reginald Pole and the role he played in Michelangelo's affairs in the chapter dedicated to that artist.)

Continuing along the Via Appia, about 300 meters before reaching the tomb of Cecilia Metella, we come to the Circus of Maxentius, one of the most impressive Roman buildings. Immense in size, with seats for ten thousand spectators and a field 300 meters long, the structure was about half a kilometer in length; a hill had to be moved to fill in a hollow on the site where it was built. The obelisk Bernini used in his Fountain of the Four Rivers in Piazza Navona was found at this site—a curious story featuring the erudite English adventurer William Petty. Petty spotted the obelisk in 1636; it lay in pieces and was half-hidden by vegetation. He bought it immediately from the papal authorities with the intention of taking it to England, where he had already found a passionate antiquarian to buy it. At the last minute, however, Pope Urban VIII (Maffeo Barberini) blocked its export, and then Bernini intervened. He saw the obelisk as the perfect centerpiece for his new fountain.

The pope's action was shrewd and provident, although it was not enough to stop the unfortunate habit of despoiling ancient monuments. More than a century later, in 1756, Giovan Battista Piranesi wrote in the preface to his *Antichità Romane*, "I decided to record the remains of the ancient buildings of Rome in my prints because, since they are scattered for the most part in gardens and other cultivated areas, they are diminished on a daily basis, whether by the harm done them by the weather or through the greed of their owners, who with barbarous license destroy them in secret and then sell the pieces to build modern buildings."

The ruins of Maxentius's residence rise up on the top of a small hill, and are connected to the circus by a portico. The tomb of the emperor's son, Romulus, is a little closer to the Via Appia. Everything here is grandiose—and tragic. Maxentius challenged Constantine in the famous battle of the Milvian Bridge in AD 312. He lost, and sought to save himself by jumping into the Tiber, where he either drowned or was stabbed to death. He left behind his basilica in the Forum and these impressive ruins as witnesses to the end of the pagan era.

The end of paganism can also be looked at from another vantage point, through the earliest traces of Christianity. Let's leave the Via Appia and move to the Aventine Hill. Even though there is no lack of early Christian basilicas in Rome, few (if any) of them capture the beginnings of the new religion like the churches on the Via di Santa Sabina, by far one of the most fascinating streets in the city. The Aventine, whose western end hangs over the Tiber, faces the Janiculum and shelters at its feet the basin where the oldest part of the city was laid out. Originally the Aventine was crowded with the houses of plebian Romans. The Latians, in the period of the kings, built a temple dedicated to Diana on this hill, and it is quite possible that the notorious abduction of the Sabine women took place not far from the Aventine, in the valley where the Circus Maximus was later constructed.

In the Middle Ages much of the Aventine was still cultivated land, but it also became a place for monasteries and churches. Traces of their imprint remain, but you need to know how to find them. Santa Sabina is the perfect example of a fifth-century basilica, and is the epitome of the early Christian concept of this type of building. Its columns are from an older Roman building, and the main door is made of finely carved cypress wood divided into square panels. The panel with a scene of the Crucifixion is one of the oldest representations of that subject. Inside the church a fragment of the ancient mosaics refer to the Council of Ephesus in AD 431.

The next church is dedicated to Sant'Alessio, and is also quite old, although not as ancient as Santa Sabina, as it dates back only to the eighth century. It was constructed on the site of an earlier sacred building that had been remodeled several times. The church has the only Romanesque crypt in the city, and the altar there contains holy relics underneath a baldachin. There are some who claim, although it is only a legend, that the column under the crypt is the one to which Saint Sebastian was bound when he was martyred.

The Via Santa Sabina ends in one of Rome's loveliest piazzas—beautiful for the dignity, ornamentation, and meditative spirit that characterize it. Dedicated to the order of the Knights of Malta, its wide end is closed off by a wall decorated with obelisks, niches, and stele bearing religious and nautical emblems—a precocious neoclassical vision designed by Giovan Battista Piranesi for Cardinal Rezzonico in 1764. The piazza is also famous for the portal and its celebrated keyhole that, if you peer through it, perfectly frames the dome of Saint Peter's at the end of a green garden path. A little beyond this portal is the gate to the knights' priory and the church of Santa Maria del Priorato, also designed by Piranesi, and which contains his tomb as well. The church is not particularly lovely; it has a single, stuccoed nave and contains several funerary monuments. The space around it is more beautiful—the carefully tended garden, the arrangement of the buildings, the thirteenth-century Templar well, and a small plaque marking Pius IX's visit there in 1854 to observe the restoration of the church after the damage caused by a French bombardment during the siege of 1849. The priory's villa was built in 939 as a Benedictine monastery (Oddo of Cluny was abbot here); it then passed to the Knights Templar, and finally to the Knights Hospitaler. The aura of its history and the echo of time still cling to the building, and it is easy to imagine what the city must have looked like from this dizzying perch over the valley. In this small space, between the piazza, garden, and church, Piranesi—sublime watercolorist and masterful recorder of classical antiquity—gave us his sole built work.

The church of Sant'Anselmo stands almost directly in front of the garden, on the Via di Porta Lavernale. With respect to the other churches here, it is a recent addition to the Aventine, since it was not built until the end of the nineteenth century. It is also an excellent place to hear Gregorian chants. The bastion beneath it was built by Giuliano da Sangallo for Pope Paul III in the middle of the sixteenth century as part of a larger, later abandoned project to reinforce the city's walls to better defend it against a possible Muslim attack.

At this point it is impossible not to point out another basilica—it dates back to the same period and is equally fascinating—not on the Aventine, but nearby on the Celian Hill. We take the Via San Paolo della Croce to get there, passing through the remarkable Arch of Dolabella, which dates back to the beginning of the Imperial era and was originally the Porta Celimontana in the city's Servian walls. This austere path brings us to the basilica of Santi Giovanni e Paolo. At the close of World War II New York's Cardinal Francis Spellman wanted to restore the church, which had been profoundly altered over the centuries, to its original appearance. This church has survived from very ancient times, and the John and Paul it was named for were two Christian officials murdered by Julian the Apostate during his brief reign as emperor of Rome. The first church was built in 398 but was damaged about a dozen years later when Alaric, King of the Visigoths, invaded Rome and allowed his troops to sack the city. The church was plundered again in 1084 by the Norman soldiers of Robert Guiscard, and was subsequently remodeled and altered to suit the tastes of later periods in the continuous series of vicissitudes that make up the history of Rome.

The church we see today is the result of this dramatic history. There is a door at the end of the right-hand nave that leads down some steps to a series of underground rooms discovered at the end of the nineteenth century. There are about twenty chambers, some of which are finely frescoed, spread over three levels that include the remains of both a pagan and a Christian building, as well as several oratories associated with the original cult of the two martyrs. A visitor here cannot help but be deeply moved; there are few other places in Rome where you can literally touch history as it unwinds over the course of long, turbulent centuries. But this venerable basilica is also extraordinary because it reveals in a very real, physical way how far the Catholic Church, with all its baroque splendor and ostentation, has come from the simple austerity of its origins. Whether this change has affected the spirituality of the church is a question each visitor must answer for himself.

You only have to cross the valley of the Murcia, also called the valley of Circus Maximus, to return to the Aventine Hill. In addition to the churches we have already discussed, the Aventine also has a magnificent terrace with a panoramic view over the city, its rooftops and domes, its covered terraces, and the turbid waters of the Tiber. There are two places in the city where the natural elevation allows an extraordinary vista of the city—the panorama on the Janiculum faces toward the east, while the one on the Aventine looks in the opposite direction. Personally, I prefer the latter, especially because of all that surrounds the viewer, and the many monuments that imbue this vision of the city with a sense of longing. If there is one place where Christianity first triumphed and then began to expand, it is here. The Emperor Constantine recognized Christianity as a *religio licita*—a legally tolerated religion—in Milan in 313, and in 350 his son Constantius made it the official religion of the Roman Empire. Another emperor, Theodosius, confirmed Christianity as the official religion of the state in 391, and banned every other cult, including the native cult of the *antenates*, or ancestors. In a little over sixty years the civilized world had passed from a mild and tolerant polytheism to an exclusive monotheism.

The oft-repeated story of how Christianity, in its Roman Catholic version, was slowly able to dominate every other religion, including the dozens of sects it spawned but then gradually crushed for being "heretical," is one of the most remarkable in all of human history. Its success lay perhaps in its unique combination of political cunning, an unbiased adaptation to the spirit of the times and scientific discoveries, as well as the suppression of its most dangerous enemies. These are the immutable rules that uphold every power, and there is no institution that can avoid them. In the Roman Catholic Church these rules were often mixed with a spiritual energy that was later reinforced by the buildings and images created for the new institution. The churches on the Aventine document those years, the institution's struggles, and its final victory. Furthermore, the highest terrace on this very hill allows you to see, on the distant horizon, the architectural icon that best encapsulates this sense of triumph—the superb dome of Saint Peter's. Nikolai Gogol, looking at it from the Alban Hills in the dying light of the day, described it in his story *Roma*: "The majestic cupola of Saint Peter's seems to get bigger the further away from it one gets, until it remains completely alone on the whole arc of the horizon, even when the city itself has disappeared."

In a city that has so often echoed with supplications and procla-mations, where there have been so many violent deaths, there is also no lack of places that evoke death or are dedicated to it. I don't mean the cemeteries, but more secluded and less well-known places, even though some of them were created by the most famous of artists. One example is the church of San Giacomo in Settimiana on the Via della Lungara. This little building contains a curious work by Gian Lorenzo Bernini just to the right of the presbytery. It is the funerary monument of the jurist Ippolito Merenda, and is distinguished by a hovering winged skeleton holding a commemorative plaque between his hooked fingers and his teeth. Bernini inserted a similar bit of macabre realism in the tomb of Pope Alexander VII (Fabio Chigi) in Saint Peter's. The pope is represented as humble and absorbed in prayer at the top of this elaborate, sumptuous creation. A precious shroud is spread out below him, and it only partially conceals the Door of Death at the center of the tomb, from which a skeleton emerges holding an hourglass to tell the pope that his time has come.

Bernini's tomb of Alexander VII is a complement to the tomb of Pope Paul III (Alessandro Farnese), which is on the left side of the tribune of Saint Peter's, behind the papal altar. Sculpted by Guglielmo della Porta, many consider it his masterpiece, and it is worth a brief digression from our subject here.

The effigy of Paul III, placed atop the tomb, is both majestic and absorbed in contemplation. At his feet are two statues of virtues (originally there were four); Justice is on the left, and Prudence on the right. Legend has it that the first is a portrait of Pope Paul III's sister, Giulia Farnese—who was also Pope Alexander VI's underage lover—and the other as Paul III's mother, Giovannella Caetani. The tomb encompasses a welter of emotion and ideal mirrored in Alexander VI's life—lust and sanctity, family affections and political gratitude. The dedication of the tomb in 1575 was attended by another Alessandro Farnese, nephew of the pope buried within it. Some years and five popes later, Clement VIII interpreted the nude figure of Justice as provocative, and made it the first battle in his righteous war to make all religious art created after the Council of Trent morally decent. He ordered that "the statues on the tomb of Pope Paul III, in glad memory, be either removed or covered in a more decent manner." The censorious order speaks of "nipples, breasts, and other parts which they say are too lascivious," noting especially "a thigh uncovered all the way to the edge of her 'natural vessel.'" In short, it was just too much.

There is more, and the legend becomes obscene as the rumor spread that a pilgrim or tourist, turned on by this indecent statue, had been caught masturbating. Giuseppe Gioacchino Belli took up that rumor again in a sonnet he wrote in May of 1833:

She's so beautiful that an English gentleman
Once surprised a church attendant
In the middle of a rude act, cock in hand.

Then the Pope who then was Pope
Had a camise made for her in bronze,
And you can still see it there to this very day.[7]

The historian Roberto Zappieri has studied Paul III and the period of his reign for many years. He suggests that Belli's true target may have been the English on the Grand Tour, who came to Rome and then left with their preexisting prejudices intact. But I don't want to digress too far from the point of the story. We need only know that in reality this gossip refers back to another legend, born from the "beauty of the members" of Praxiteles's *Venus of Cnidos*, a marble figure so perfect that a visitor had himself shut into her temple so that he could make love to it.

We will come back at some length to this in chapter ten, "The Most Beautiful Lady of Rome," but it is worth saying here that everyone talked about the loveliness of Giulia Farnese, the youthful lover of Alexander VI Borgia. It was thanks to her that her brother became cardinal. Luther made mention of this bargain in his pamphlet, writing "Pope Paul III had a sister who, before he became pope, he gave to a pope as lover, thus earning for himself the cardinal's hat." Antonio Soriano, the Venetian Ambassador to Rome, also knew of this, and reported back to his government that "his elevation to cardinal was not very honest, since it came about from an obscene act; that is, from the love and familiarity which Pope Alexander VI had for Signora Giulia, his sister; for this reason he was for a long time called Cardinal Fregnese (a play on the Farnese name which roughly translates to 'Cardinal Cunt')."[8] There is also an older, fifteenth-century source for this story. It comes from the list Stefano Infessura made in his *Cronaca di Roma* of the cardinals Alexander VI nominated on September 20, 1493, including "unum de domo Farnesia, consanguinem concubinae suae, Iuliae bellae" [one from the House of Farnese, related to his concubine, the beautiful Julia].

In 1595 the statue of Justice was covered with a metal sheath that was then painted to imitate marble. For a long time it was said that the basilica's custodians would, for a *zecchino* (i.e., for a farthing), briefly remove this cover to allow the visitor to admire the figure's underlying beauty. While we're on the subject, it's worth adding that a similar thing happened with the four Naiads Mario Rutelli cast in 1901 for the fountain in the Piazza della Repubblica (also called Piazza Esedra). It seems that the artist used a famous courtesan as his model for the florid opulence of their bodies. Here, too, the allusive realism of the figures fueled gossip and stirred desires. Since the Naiads couldn't be covered, the seminarians who had to cross the piazza every day were told to divert their gaze from those wet, voluptuous forms.

Let's return to the subject of death. The insistent representations of skeletons, some of them armed with hourglasses or scythes, is a stereotype of Counter-Reformation monuments in the seventeenth century. There are two of them, for example, in the left aisle of the church of San Pietro in Vincoli, both skillfully executed and impressive. Yet a visitor to almost any church of this period will have encountered death in the most lugubrious ways, dressed in black or brilliant in the whiteness of its naked bones, looking at him from the empty sockets of a skull, or even two skulls paired together, as we see in the church of Santa Maria del Priorato on the Aventine. Throughout the century of baroque mannerism and the Counter-Reformation, representations of death became the ubiquitous warning against the vanity of worldly things and the eternal punishments that awaited the sinner.

The height of macabre is reached when the skeletons are not just skillfully carved from marble but are made from the real bones of the dead, the miserable, grey remains of people who were once alive and, as Hamlet recalled, moved by emotions and desires, full of feelings and troubled by sorrows. The underground ossuary of the Capuchins on the Via Veneto is one of the most eloquent examples of this cult of death. To set the scene you must envision the Capuchin church (Santa Maria della Concezione) above the ossuary not at the foot of the street Fellini made famous, but as it was in its original setting. The Via Veneto is a recent creation; before it existed there was only a small square in front of the church, with a double row of elm trees that descended the hill toward the nearby Piazza Barberini, where Bernini's lovely Triton fountain stands. The Capuchin convent houses a Saint Francis by Caravaggio, but the church's biggest draw is its crypt, where the bones of about four thousand friars who died between the seventeenth and nineteenth centuries are amassed; they were disinterred by their brother monks, and here their bones were reassembled with a maniacal decorative genius. It took three hundred carts to bring this rather grim cargo from an ancient cemetery at the foot of the Quirinal Hill. The ossuary's admonitory purpose is summed up in a severe inscription: "You are what we were, and you will be what we are."

Another church that focuses with an exaggerated baroque sensibility on death is Santa Maria dell'Orazione e Morte on the Via Giulia. It is older than the Capuchin church (it dates back to the late sixteenth century) and it is still associated with the Compagnia della buona morte—a "volunteer" association, as we would call it today, in which pious people were dedicated to collecting unburied bodies both on the city streets and in the Roman countryside. Its crypts hold almost 8,000 people buried over the course of 350 years, up until the end of the nineteenth century, all now decorously arranged here.

Years ago, when I was doing some journalistic background research on the Quirinal Palace (which, with Versailles, is one of the loveliest royal residences in Europe), I discovered that the bodies of dead popes were eviscerated before they were embalmed and that this took place in the large reception hall behind the balcony overlooking the piazza. The viscera, which Romans rather unceremoniously called the "holy entrails," were sealed in canopic jars and then solemnly transported to the church of Santi Vincenzo ed Anastasio on the piazza in front of the Trevi Fountain at the corner of the Via del Lavatore. Sixtus V, the first pope to live in the Quirinal Palace, began this tradition, and it survived for almost three centuries, until the reign of Leo XIII. The church still preserves the entrails of twenty-two popes in an underground chapel that Pope Benedict XIV had constructed in 1757. A late-eighteenth-century chronicler described the embalming process in some detail: "Once the pope was dead, the apothecary and the aforementioned brothers of the bull blocked his mouth, nostrils and ears with myrrh, incense, and aloe, if they could get it, and finally his face was also rubbed, and oiled with a good balsam, followed by the hands."

This practice is the butt of jokes in a conversation the poet Belli imagined between two Romans in his sonnet "San Vincenz' e Ssatanassio a Ttrevi" (April 22, 1835):

> When a Pope dies, he's split open and embalmed,
> And the holy innards, in a jar,
> Are turned over to the curate.
>
> Then he and his good friars
> Put them in a kind of cellar,
> A museum of entrails and viscera.[9]

The church of Santi Vincenzo ed Anastasio has an interesting history. The building is very old, although it was almost completely rebuilt in the seventeenth century by Cardinal Giulio Mazzarini, who was originally from Abruzzo and would later go on, as Jules Mazarin, to become Minister of France. A man of extraordinary diplomatic skills, he was a cardinal despite the fact that he had never been ordained a priest; he was also the dowager Queen of France's lover, and perhaps secretly her husband. His rich coat-of-arms dominates the facade of the church, where it is carried not by two, but by four angels.

I can't conclude this brief excursus without mentioning another site, which is dedicated not so much to death as to the atrocity of suffering. The church of Santo Stefano Rotondo, an ancient but often remodeled church, stands on the slopes of the Celian Hill, and at the end of the sixteenth century Il Pomarancio and Antonio Tempesta decorated it with thirty-four frescoes representing the martyrdoms of the same number of saints during various periods of persecution. They were painted at the height of the Counter-Reformation, and the shocking exhibition of sadism was meant to serve the edifying purpose of preparing Catholic missionaries for their own possible martyrdom. In this sampler of tortures we see wretched people being torn apart by wild animals, drowned with rocks hung around their necks, burned alive, blinded, strangled, mutilated, and stoned. There is even an executioner who is slicing off the breast of a young virgin (a scene that is said to have upset even the Marquis de Sade when he saw it in 1775).

There is a neighborhood in Rome that has long been considered a typically working-class area, with its blocks of low-rent housing and small workshops of artisans who work in marble, iron, and now even plastic. It is called San Lorenzo, and is near Verano, the city's largest and oldest cemetery. Verano was founded in 1804, after Napoleon's famous edict establishing suburban cemeteries, and also inspired Ugo Foscolo's poetic work *I sepolcri*. The San Lorenzo neighborhood was named after its ancient church, one of Rome's five patriarchal basilicas. In July of 1943 the area was heavily bombed by British and American planes. Having arisen from its ashes, San Lorenzo today is almost fashionable, and has all the qualities of other European neighborhoods that are popular with young people. You can still see, however, some traces of the horrific event on its streets if you look carefully enough. There are variations in the height of the buildings, spaces left empty where houses once stood, mangled walls, and new construction next to structures that are clearly older. Then there are the memories of the old people who were there on the morning of the attack; they have repeated their stories of those moments so many times that even they are not sure what is true and what only imagined.

On July 10, 1943, the Americans came ashore in Sicily, encountering little resistance as they landed. Nine days later the bombing of Rome served a double purpose, one military and the other political, since hitting the nation's capital was a clear sign that the Fascist regime was all but completely defeated. The Allies assembled a gigantic squadron, the largest flotilla of airplanes ever seen in Italian skies—662 bombers escorted by 268 fighter planes. There were only slightly fewer than 1,000 planes, including the famous B-17 Flying Fortresses, B-24s, B-26 Marauders, Liberators, and P-38 Lightning Fighters, all of them the best that the United States war industry could churn out. They arrived over Rome at 20,000 feet (at "twenty angels," in code).

Monday, July 19, 1943—the 1,134th day of the war—was hot, bright, and clear, and there was no breeze at all. The temperature had risen steadily throughout the morning, and at two o'clock the thermometer hit 104° Fahrenheit. The first bomb fell on the railway yards of San Lorenzo at 11:03 A.M. It was dropped from a B-17 called Lucky Lady; she was the flight leader, the first of that terrible squadron, consisting of six waves of airplanes, which hammered Rome with more than one thousand tons of explosives, killing more than two thousand people and causing immense devastation, including the destruction of the basilica of San Lorenzo. The capital was bombed for 152 minutes, from 11:03 A.M. to 1:35 P.M. As the waves of bombers passed over, clouds of smoke and dust obstructed the aviators' view. In addition to the freight yard, hundreds of apartment buildings, the university, and nearby hospital were all hit. At the clinic, two teams of surgeons continued to operate even as explosions shook the building's walls. Dozens of flower vendors at the cemetery were blown away by the first blasts. Azolino Hazon, commanding general of the *carabinieri*, had come out to inspect the damage and was surprised by the second wave of bombers; he, his aide, and their driver were all killed in his car by an incendiary bomb.

The mission's military targets included the airports of Littorio (now called Urbe) on the Via Salaria and Ciampino on the Via Appia, as well as the railway yards at San Lorenzo. In their preflight briefings, the pilots were instructed categorically to hit only those targets, and the most fervent Protestants (and thus anti-Catholic) amongst them were exempted from the mission. For the opposite reasons, the commanders made it known that Catholic aviators who objected to the mission would be excused.

The strategic purpose of the bombing was to disrupt transportation systems in order to stop military replenishments from reaching Sicily, where fighting had continued since the day of the landing. The Italian forces in Rome had only one outdated anti-aircraft artillery, some parts of which dated back to World War I, and a handful of airplanes to counter the allies' 930 heavily armored and armed planes escorted by the most modern fighters. The Italian pilots, true heroes, took off knowing they might well never return. The Americans, who knew the Italian situation, had predicted their own losses at about one percent of the force; in the end they were much lower, at 0.26 percent. Asked about the mission when he returned, one of the commanders described it as "too easy."

Twice in the days before the bombardment American airplanes had flown over Rome dropping thousands of leaflets on the city. The second time was during the night of Saturday, July 17. The pamphlets were signed by Churchill and Roosevelt and said, "This is a message to the Italian people from the President of the United States and the Prime Minister of Great Britain. At this moment the allied forces of the United States, Great Britain, and Canada are bringing the war to the heart of your country. Mussolini dragged you into this war as the satellite of a brutal destroyer of peoples and liberty." Given that so many people had already read the leaflets, newspapers were allowed to print their text. Even though they came in the form of a message from the enemy, this was the first time in twenty years that headlines such as "The war is the direct result of the shameful policies that Mussolini and the Fascist regime imposed upon us," appeared in any Italian newspaper.

King Vittorio Emanuele III watched the bombing from the terrace of the Villa Savoia, often using a pair of Zeiss binoculars for a better view. Pope Pius XII saw the clouds of fire and smoke from a window in his apartment, and was joined there by the Assistant Secretary of State, Giovan Battista Montini (who was later elected Pope Paul VI). Mussolini was not in Rome on that Monday; instead he was at Feltre for a meeting with Hitler. He had promised his own staff that "this time I will speak clearly and frankly to him." In reality Hitler yelled the whole time, and Mussolini hardly opened his mouth.

Rome has been violated many times over the course of its history—by the Goths and the Huns, by Robert Guiscard and later the Imperial lansquenets in 1527, by the Americans on that morning in July, and then by the Germans on September 8, in that same terrible year of 1943. The attack of July 19 was successful on all counts. The freight yards were obliterated, and a week later, on the night between Saturday, July 24, and Sunday, July 25, the Fascist regime collapsed in on itself like a worm-eaten tree trunk.

For a long time after the war there was an oft-told tale in which an American soldier, aghast as he drove around the Coliseum, exclaimed to his companion, "My God, we even bombed this!" No one knows if that story is true. There are ruins in Rome that do look like someone had just bombed them, although this is not as true of the Coliseum as it is of the remnants of the Baths of Caracalla. These gigantic remains speak volumes about the engineering talent of the Romans as well as the ambitions of the young emperor who built them. They are nothing, however, but derelict ruins when you compare them to the splendor of the baths when they were first completed. The melancholy ruins still exude a certain fascination, but the wonder the baths inspired must have been completely different when they were at the height of their splendor. In his *The Revolt of the Masses*, José Ortega y Gasset wrote:

> When in the early stages of the Empire some cultured provincial—Lucan or Seneca—arrived in Rome, and saw the magnificent imperial buildings, symbols of an enduring power, he felt his heart contract within him. Nothing new could now happen in the world. Rome was eternal. And if there is a melancholy of ruins which rises above them like exhalations from stagnant waters, this sensitive provincial felt a melancholy no less heavy, though of opposite sign: the melancholy of buildings meant for eternity.[10]

Water for the baths was supplied by a branch of the Acqua Antoniana, an aqueduct that crosses the Via Appia at the so-called Arch of Drusus. Totila and his army of Goths cut off the aqueducts, making the area around the baths into a malarial swamp. For centuries afterward, the building was despoiled, stripped of everything and transformed into a giant quarry for construction materials. The granite column now standing in the Piazza della Santissima Trinità in Florence came from the Baths of Caracalla; it was removed by Duke Cosimo de'Medici in 1561. The two magnificent grey granite basins that are now the graceful fountains in the Piazza Farnese in Rome also came from the baths—stolen by Odoardo Farnese in 1612. Only at the beginning of the twentieth century did any real protection for this monument begin, when the Minister for Public Instruction, Guido Baccelli, created the *Passeggiata Archeologica* (or Archaeological Promenade).

Giosuè Carducci visited the Baths of Caracalla in the spring of 1887. These powerful stumps of a building dazzled him, and the huge ruins, standing in the midst of what was essentially a wild landscape, seemed finally to give muscle and bones to the ghost of the Roman spirit the poet had so long brooded over. The clear, solemn meter of his thundering *Odi Barbare* seemed the best way for him to recount that spirit. In a passage that is halfway between memory and fantasy, the poet described a stormy day in April at the baths: "Dark ran the clouds between the Coelian and the / Aventine: humid moves the wind from the sad plain: in the / background stand the Alban hills white with snow."[11]

I don't know if there was still snow on the hills that spring so long ago, but I am certain that you cannot see the Alban Hills from the Baths of Caracalla. The poet saw them with his mind's eye and he moved them there, dressed in snow, to complete a picture that he thought needed a bit of white. He also saw an English tourist intent on searching her Baedeker guide for some information about the ruins, ". . . a British / woman seeks in her guide-book these menaces of Roman / walls against the sky and time." He saw a flock of crows, "Continuous, thick, cawing," rise and fall in the sky. Most of all, though, he saw the impressive ruins, "Old giants—the angered prophetic flight of birds / seems to urge—why do you attempt the sky?—Heavy / through the breezes comes a sounding of bells from the / Lateran."[12]

I realize these are not sublime verses; if there is anything sublime about them it is the "barbaric"—that is, Greco-Roman—meter that so suited him. It came, however, from those old giants that reached for the sky, and the poet loved the ideas of grandiosity and of a civic religion behind them. Emperor Caracalla must have shared the same notion of grandeur when he opened his splendid baths in 217; the complex covered over twenty-seven acres and could accommodate 1,700 people. The baths included hot and cold pools, gymnasiums, libraries, ambulatories, mosaic floors, frescoed walls, sculpture (including the figure later known as the *Farnese Hercules*), and basements so vast that they were traversed with carts. There were also gardens around the complex, ornamental fountains, copses of trees, and altars.

In the brief period of his reign (211–217), Marcus Aurelius Antoninus Bassianus, called Caracalla because of the hooded Celtic tunic he wore, was grandiose in everything, including ferociousness. He was born in Lyon in 188 and rose to power, acclaimed by the legions, when he was only twenty-three years old. His father, Septimius Severus (who built the last triumphal arch in the Roman Forum), offered his sons, including Caracalla's younger brother Geta, only one piece of deathbed advice: "Make sure that the army is both strong and loyal; the rest you can forget about." The old emperor hoped, in vain as it turned out, that his sons would get along. Caracalla stabbed Geta to death as his mother tried to protect him; this was the first in a series of murders which would make him famous, feared, and of which he even bragged. Some have calculated that he sent 20,000 people to their deaths, some of whom were guilty only of grieving for Geta. But that is according to the historians, who, because they all belonged to the Senatorial class, may have been exaggerating. Bearing his father's advice in mind, Caracalla doubled the pay of his soldiers. To cover the additional burden on the public treasury, he increased the confiscation of the property and income of his political enemies and minted a new coin (the *Antoninianus*), which had a rather high silver content that the emperor was forced gradually to reduce, considering inflation.

Caracalla's most sensational political gesture, however, came in 212, when he granted Roman citizenship to all free men who lived in the Empire (the so-called *Constitutio antoniniana*). This was a revolutionary move, although it was likely inspired by cunning and convenience. The law increased what we would think of today as the empire's tax base, or at least this was the hypothesis of the historian Dio Cassius. But perhaps Caracalla risked so much for a different reason—by making all his subjects equal with respect to the monarchy, he inflicted another mortal blow to the senatorial aristocracy, with which he had a mutual distrust. As far as we know, Caracalla failed only once in obtaining something he really wanted, and that was in his quest to marry the King of Parthia's daughter. That union would have allowed him to fulfill Alexander the Great's ambitious dream of unifying East and West in a single empire. His potential father-in-law, the king of kings, did not favor the alliance, nor did he have any faith in Caracalla, and the marriage went up in smoke.

Caracalla depended on the army, yet it was a soldier who ended his reign and his life. He had departed for the East, again following Alexander's grand ambition, and there Macrinus, one of his legionnaires, ran him through with a sword. He was not yet thirty years old.

Here I owe the reader a brief explanation of why I chose, amongst many possibilities, to dedicate these few pages to Caracalla and his baths. The whole of the book, and the first chapter in particular, is largely based on choices dictated by my own life story—that is to say, the choices were arbitrary. As chance would have it, I spent much of my childhood exploring the Baths of Caracalla from one end to the other, above and below, including the basements, and my memory of them—endless hallways that were mostly dark, but occasionally interrupted by shafts of light streaming through holes in the ceiling—has remained vivid through the years. Living in the neighborhood, the baths were a natural playground for a group of children who in those unsettled years were growing from childhood into adolescence. There were rooms, some large and others smaller, that opened off the galleries; they were mysterious tunnels, recesses that ended in almost absolute darkness that we never dared enter. The walls often had holes in them at various heights, and it was only years later that I realized they were conduits for water. The bottoms of the conduits were covered in a yellowish dust that was finer than a woman's face powder. With the active imaginations of children, we believed it was the dust of the dead, and that it came from men killed in one of the many cruel games we saw depicted in our reading books. We learned later that those images were of early Christians who had been sacrificed in the bloody delirium of the circuses, and that we should not confuse the baths and the Coliseum.

One day, in the autumn I think, we came across a small group of men in one of those dark rooms. Some men were standing and some sitting, but all were intent on their discussion. There were only three or four of us, and we burst in suddenly from the corridor. We surprised them; they hadn't heard us coming, nor we their voices. A long moment of embarrassed silence followed, and then one of them took the initiative, nodded to the others and moved toward the exit. As he passed us he ruffled my hair with his hand, a gesture that was both rough and affectionate. For years I suppressed the memory, and when it came back to me I wondered if perhaps those men had been partisans intent on formulating some plan, and that they broke up the meeting when they saw us, either because they had finished talking or for the sake of caution. Who knows who they really were?

My love for Paris and France, which I consider my second home and where I hope to die, was born in Rome and nurtured by songs and books. The songs were mostly those of Georges Brassens, and the readings, at the beginning, were the memoirs of Chateaubriand, both of which opened the door for me to French literature and culture. When Einaudi-Gallimard published their splendid Italian version of his *Mémoires d'outre-tombe*, edited by Ivanna Rosi and Cesare Garboli, I finally understood the force behind Chateaubriand's spell. In their preface, the editors wrote, "To read is to be transported away, to change time and place and not be where you are. No one knows how to seize a reader and then plunge him into the facts of history like Chateaubriand." I, too, took the plunge, changing the space and time I inhabited. The few streets between the Piazza di Spagna and the Piazza del Popolo—the Via Margutta, Via del Babuino, and Via Condotti—became for me like certain street corners in Saint-Germain-des-Près, which was so in vogue at the time. My childish attempts at imitation pushed me all the way to smoking Gauloises *gros caliber*—the worst cigarettes, whose smoke could rip your chest open, but still unmistakable because Jean Gabin smoked them. The Via Margutta, a fundamental part of this illusory Paris, was originally just an alley behind the palaces on the Via del Babuino. It had stables, carriages were parked there, and simple artisans lived there before it became a popular place for atelier, just like some of the streets on the slopes of Montmartre. Then there was the Caffè Greco, too, on the Via Condotti. It was opened by a Levantine at the end of the eighteenth century, and is one of the few places to have preserved its eighteenth-century furnishings in a city that—even in its café décor—hasn't managed to keep much tradition alive.

The French have always had a strong presence in Rome. The Villa Medici, seat of the French Academy, has been the privileged residence of Prix de Rome winners since the sixteenth century; its rooms have housed Ingres, Bizet, Berlioz, and Debussy, to cite only a few of them. The Palazzo Farnese, now the French Embassy and the most beautiful diplomatic seat in the world, is impeccably maintained by the governments of both France and Italy. The French Cultural Center in Piazza Campitelli, now part of the University of Rome 3 (the most active in the city), was once an important place for French studies of all sorts, including music. And then there is San Luigi dei Francesi, the French national church where, after this short tour, we come right back to Chateaubriand. Pauline de Beaumont, Chateaubriand's lover, died in Rome of consumption at the age of thirty-six; she was buried at San Luigi, and her tomb was commissioned by Chateaubriand himself. It is worth repeating that author's description of their last outing together:

> One day I took her to the Coliseum, it was one of those October days like there only are in Rome. I was able to descend and I sat down on a stone facing one of the altars placed around the interior of the building. I lifted my eyes, moving them slowly over those dead porticoes which so many years ago witnessed so many deaths. The ruins were decorated with briar bushes and columbine turning yellow in the autumn air. They were flooded in light. Then my dying friend lowered her eyes, step by step, into the arena. Abandoning the sun, they fixed on the cross on the altar, and she said to me, "Let's go, I'm cold." I took her home. She went to bed then and never arose again.

Most of this book about Rome is organized like this chapter—a series of discoveries, surprises, and places tied to work, love, and above all to chance. Only when you have lived in a city for a long time, when it becomes part of your life, can you tell its story in such an arbitrary way. When we visit a foreign city, including those where we might have lived for years, our movements are guided by some precise goal, at least at the beginning; it directs our steps toward a certain neighborhood, monument, or street. In a foreign city you can also have the experience of not knowing where you are—it becomes a maze, an unknown universe, and even a jungle like the famous "asphalt jungle" in John Huston's unforgettable film of the same name.

It's curious how the metropolis, the epitome of civilized urban life, can also be a metaphor for the savage life, a place of snares and traps. On the one hand it's the incarnation of rationality, with its crowded and reassuring avenues, gardens, and piazzas, and on the other it's an irrational place full of loneliness and danger. The symbolist writers, especially Charles Baudelaire in his *Les Fleurs du mal*, clearly saw these opposites in an urban reality that made room for life in all its forms: "Fourmillante cité, cité pleine de rêves, / Où le spectre en plein jour raccroche le passant ! / Les mystères partout coulent comme des sèves / Dans les canaux étroits du colosse puissant. [City swarming with people, how full you are of dreams! / Here in broad daylight, surely, the passer-by may meet / A spectre,—be accosted by him! Mystery seem / To move like a thick sap through every narrow street.][13] Or, "Voici le soir charmant, ami du criminel; / Il vient comme un complice, à pas de loup; le ciel / Se ferme lentement comme une grande alcôve, / Et l'homme impatient se change en bête fauve." [Behold the sweet evening, friend of the criminal; / It comes like an accomplice, stealthily; the sky / Closes slowly like an immense alcove, / And impatient man turns into a beast of prey.][14]

It seems to me that Rome is only somewhat familiar with the ferociousness of the modern metropolis. Horrifying things obviously happen in Rome too, cruel acts and unsolved killings; these happen everywhere, and therefore happen here, too. But this type of ferociousness is not the predominate characteristic of the city. I would say instead that Rome swings between two very different qualities as a city—a neutrality caused by a sort of globalization in which so much is the same as what happens or exists in every city and, on the contrary, the weight of a past so old that it can only be told as a story. Then there are the clouds, cupolas, palm trees, columns, and the almost always troubled relationship with the present. Maybe this is why a sense of the "Roman spirit" exists today mostly as settings for novels or films. At the turn of the nineteenth century Rome was still seen, although I think for the last time, as an ideal civic, literary, and artistic model. Now the neoclassical period is spent, the last echoes of Romanticism have dissipated, and it seems we can only talk about Rome as a sort of literary fantasy. We can also see this, even if just because of the sharp contrast, in the Fascist experiment, which was a political attempt to recreate the myth of Rome, Empire included. The experiment ended as a ridiculous parody built with gilded cardboard and tin swords.

But perhaps reducing the city to its illusory dimensions is not such a bad thing. The quality of a place—its spirit or, as some say, its soul—is always a product more of the imagination than any reality. In a passage of his *Zibaldone* dated November 30, 1828, Giacomo Leopardi recorded a thought I have cited in other works but which I am always happy to return to: "For a sensitive and imaginative man who, like I, has lived for a long time but can still imagine and feel, the world and its things become in a certain sense double. He will see a tower or the countryside with his eyes, his ears will hear the sound of the bell, and at the same time he will see, with his imagination, another tower, another countryside, and hear another sound. In this second seeing lies all the beauty and pleasure of things."

This is always true when you really want to see something. I'll give just one example. This is how Nikolai Gogol, in love and somewhere between reality and imagination, saw Rome in that moment before sunset:

> The Eternal City lay before him in a prodigious and gleaming panorama. All that bright mass of houses, churches, domes and spires was illuminated by the glint of the setting sun. In groups and alone, one after the other, houses, rooftops, statues, airy terraces and galleries rose up; down there the iridescent mass of the city swarmed with bell towers with thin pinnacles and domes with capricious lanterns; down there the flat cupola of the Pantheon appeared; down there he could see the decorated top of the Column of Marcus Aurelius with its capital and statue of the Apostle Paul; a little to the right the tops of the buildings on the Capitoline pushed up with their statues of men and horses; a little further to the right the broad, dark bulk of the Coliseum rose, majestic and austere, above the shining mass of houses and rooftops; down there the multitude of walls, terraces and rooftops appeared again, this time glowing in the waning light of the setting sun. Above the brilliant mass of the city, in the distance, the greeny-black ilex trees of the Villa Ludovisi and the Villa Medici darkened, and then above them a whole line of Roman pines, their domed tops held up by tapering trunks, stood out against the sky. And then along the edges of the entire scene diaphanous, blue mountains rose up, as light as air and suffused with an almost phosphorescent light.

Villa Ludovisi was one of the marvels of Rome. In his 1865 guide to the city, Antonio Nibby described it like this: "In the garden there are statues, busts, bas-reliefs, urns, etc. Among these marbles there is a superbly sculpted satyr . . . and nearby two Eastern plane trees of extraordinary size." The Villa Ludovisi no longer exists; it was one of the first casualties of the new urbanism brought on by Italy's unification. Henry James, who came to Rome in time to see it, was awed and exclaimed, "I have never seen anything so beautiful." Marc Augé, in his lovely book *Le temps en ruines*, writes, "We find ourselves today needing to relearn to feel time in order to take back an awareness of history. While everything works to convince us that history is over and that the world is a spectacle that highlights that end, we need to find time to believe in history again. This may well be the pedagogic mission of ruins today." I'd like, and I hope I'm not fooling myself, for this to be the sense and, perhaps, usefulness of this book. Rome, at least in part, is still here—you need only know how to look at it.

---

1. Enzo Siciliano, *Pasolini*, trans. John Shepley (New York: Random House, 1982), 208–9.

2. Ibid., 3.

3. Ibid., 7.

4. Ibid., 5.

5. Petronius, *The Satyricon*, trans. William Arrowsmith (Ann Arbor: The University of Michigan Press, 1959), 71.

6. Horace, *Satire*, trans. William Matthews (New York: Ausable Press, 2002), I:5, 26.

7. Excerpt from "The Covered Statue," May 1833. Translated from the Italian by Daniel Seidel.

8. *Fregna*, in Roman slang, is the rough equivalent of "cunt" or "pussy"; this nickname combines *fregna* with the family name Farnese.

9. Excerpt from "San Vincenzo and Anastasio at the Trevi Fountain," April 22, 1835. Translated from the Italian by Daniel Seidel.

10. José Ortega y Gasset, *The Revolt of the Masses* (New York: W. W. Norton & Co., 1957), 33.

11. Giosuè Carducci, *Odi Barbare*, trans. William Fletcher Smith (New York: S. F. Vanni, 1950), 25.

12. Ibid.

13. George Dillon, *Flowers of Evil. From the French of Charles Baudelaire*, trans. Edna St. Vincent Millay (New York: Harper & Brothers, 1936), 183 ("The Seven Old Men").

14. William Aggeler, *The Flowers of Evil* (Fresno, CA: Academy Library Guild, 1954).

II

MY NATIVE LAND,
I DO THE WALLS BEHOLD

THIS CHAPTER SPANS MANY CENTURIES and recounts both the history of the loveliest gate in Rome's walls and the mysterious affair of the high-ranking Fascist official Ettore Muti, the end of whose story is now all but forgotten, and even a recent biography shows no sign of recalling it. This chapter takes its title from the first line of Giacomo Leopardi's canto *All'Italia*:

> My native land, I do the walls behold,
> The arches, columns, statues and deserted
> Towers by our forbears builded,
> But not the glory, not
> The laurel and the weapons that of old
> Our fathers bore . . .[1]

Many times throughout the history of Rome and Italy these lines have become less an invocation, and more actual fact. Later in the poem Leopardi laments, "How pale thou art! What blood streams from thy wounds!"; lines which set the tone for the story that follows.

The majestic gate where this tale begins takes its name from the basilica of San Sebastiano, which was first called the Porta Appia because it arches over the Via Appia, queen of all roads, and launches the historic route into the countryside. Its present name was first used in the Christian era, when custom preferred to name it after the nearby church. The Porta Appia is Rome's most beautiful gate, but such an adjective won't suffice, as it merely describes the external appearance. In reality this impressive structure, still a noble one despite the traffic that besieges it, has witnessed such an endless chain of events that it is, to those who know its history, something of a time machine to the past.

The history of the city walls is a strange one. The walls of the most ancient Rome—which really only encircled the Palatine Hill—have all but vanished, and are reduced to just a few isolated fragments. In the fourth century BC the Servian walls arose, named after King Servius Tullius, and were constructed largely of tufa blocks. By the Imperial period even these walls, however, had been partially demolished, cut, or used for other purposes. The Celimontana Gate (known as the Arch of Dolabella, mentioned in the last chapter) was part of these ramparts; they ran for 11 kilometers and enclosed the city's seven hills. The walls we see today were first planned by Emperor Aurelian in AD 270, built by his successor Marcus Aurelius Probus, and rebuilt and reinforced numerous times thereafter. The Aurelian walls are a remarkable feat of engineering; they wander for almost 19 kilometers, encircle the seven hills, and then cross the Tiber to include part of the right bank as well. The ramparts incorporate many imposing gates that correspond, for the most part, to the great consular roads. Every once in a while there is an opening in the walls for the *posterule*, smaller, easily defended gates that allowed local traffic to enter and exit the city.

Unique amongst ancient cities, Rome had no real need for ramparts except at the very beginning and end of its history—in its fragile youth and agonizing decline. For much of its history, though, the city's boundaries were those of the empire, and the latter was almost as vast as the known world, which the Romans dominated for more than six centuries. Frequent civil wars were fought either in some distant province or within the city itself and its buildings, and each war was a terrible sequence of assassinations, banishments, betrayals, and sequestering of goods. At the beginning of his *Histories* Tacitus sketches a harsh picture of the political atmosphere at the time. Beginning with an account of the reigns from Galba to Domitian (from 69 to 96 AD), he writes:

> The history on which I am entering is that of a period rich in disasters, terrible with battles, torn by civil struggles, horrible even in peace.... Rome was devastated by conflagrations, in which her most ancient shrines were consumed and the very Capitol fired by citizens' hands. Sacred rites were defiled; there were adulteries in high places. The sea was filled with exiles, its cliffs made foul with the

bodies of the dead. In Rome there was more awful cruelty. High birth, wealth, the refusal or acceptance of office—all gave ground for accusations, and virtues caused the surest ruin. . . . Slaves were corrupted against their masters, freedmen against their patrons; and those who had no enemy were crushed by their friends.[2]

In Tacitus's splendid Latin—which, incidentally, only Machiavelli would later be able to capture in Italian—the last phrase of the above passage resonates: "Et quibus deerat inimicus, per amicos oppressi." In this kind of war, when evil comes from within, no circuit of walls can offer protection, and thus ramparts serve no purpose.

The 19 kilometers of the Aurelian walls were erected quickly and skillfully. When the emperor died, in 275, the perimeter was almost complete. The walls' modest height and the unabashed incorporation of natural outcrops and pre-existing constructions contributed to the speed with which the enterprise was accomplished: from the Pyramid of Cestius to the arches of the aqueducts at Porta Maggiore and Porta Tiburtina, as well as sections of the walls around Castro Pretorio, not to mention a route that incorporated natural hills and ridges, many such supplements made the walls more imposing. Even the river became part of the fortifications; a stretch of wall ran along its left bank and then crossed over to include Trastevere, while remarkable triangular ramparts protected the Janiculum Hill. On the north side of the city, the retaining walls beneath the gardens of Domitian and the Acilii (today the Muro Torto) were also integrated into Aurelian's ramparts.

The masonry work follows a regular pattern; every three meters there is an arrow slit for archers, and about every 30 meters (100 Roman feet; the Anglo-Saxon foot still equals about 33 centimeters) is a massive square tower. These towers project three meters from the surrounding walls and allowed attacking soldiers to be fought with raking fire. The distance between each tower was based on the range of the machine that launched stone projectiles called *ballistae*.

The walls Aurelian built soon proved insufficient. No longer at the height of its power, threats to the former world capital were becoming more real. The German-born General Stilicho convinced Emperor Honorius (384–423 AD) to reinforce the walls, making them both taller and thicker. This work was quickly completed, but didn't do much to slow down the Visigoths, who sacked the city in 410 (one of the most disastrous dates in the history of Rome).

The intention was good, though, and the remodeling makes the walls even more interesting for us today. There is a path along the top of the ramparts from the Porta San Sebastiano, across the Viale Cristoforo Colombo, to Sangallo's mighty bastion. Walking along, it isn't too difficult to see, here and there, joints between the older and newer constructions, and the same is true for the height added to make a second, higher footpath for additional military patrols. There were many additions and alterations to the Aurelian Walls over the centuries, but the most troubling moment of their history remains the very earliest part. In the space of only a few years, in fact, Rome went from having no walls, to fortifications that were little more than symbolic, to powerfully fortified, yet nevertheless insufficient, ramparts. In the end they failed to hold back the tide of armies pushing toward the ancient capital from all parts of the Empire, driven by a desire for revenge, nascent "national" pride throughout the Roman provinces, and the promise of rich plunder. Yet the walls remain significant—not just because they're a powerful testimony of the past, but also because they demonstrate how the Romans, depleted as they were in those years of economic and political decline, managed to keep, up to the very end, their extraordinary capacity to organize and execute such a vast project.

A few decades before the walls were built, Aelius Aristides wrote in his *In Praise of Rome,* "For it was enough for his safety that he is a Roman, or rather one of those under you. And what was said by Homer, 'The Earth was common to all,' you have made a reality, by surveying the whole inhabited world, by bridging the rivers in various ways, by cutting carriage roads through the mountains, by filling desert places with post stations, and by civilizing everything with your way of life and good order."[3] While this tone may be typical of the encomiastic writing found in the traditional *Laudes Romae* repertory, the Greek author may also have exaggerated somewhat in so emphatically expressing his gratitude to the city that had taken him in.

There are, nevertheless, numerous texts that document just how serious the situation was at the end of the Empire, how alarmed and saddened were those who understood what was happening, and how the signs of decline grew more evident each year. In 415, five years after Alaric's army of Visigoths sacked the city—Aurelian's walls notwithstanding—Claudius Rutilius Namatianus, a pagan patrician who had held the office of *praefectus Urbi* (city prefect), decided to leave the decaying city and return to Gaul, to his home in Toulouse. In the small part of his oeuvre handed down to us (traditionally titled *De reditu suo*), the author makes it clear that he is consciously embarking on a voyage from which he will not return. Behind him Rome disappears into the distance forever, just as the civilization it embodied seems to be rapidly vanishing. The author noted that the Empire's generous tolerance of paganism, able to admit any cult into its temples, was being replaced by Christian monks whose faith, in his eyes, was a regression to a more primitive state. Having left the city he praised the greatness of Roman civilization, but in a different tone than Virgil's heroic epic, *The Aeneid*, that describes the founding of the city: "Tu regere imperio populos, romane, memento. Hae tibi erunt artes, pacisque imponere morem, parcere subiectis, debellare superbos." [But, Rome, 'tis thine alone, with awful sway, / To rule mankind, and make the world obey, / Disposing peace and war by thy own majestic way; / To tame the proud, the fetter'd slave to free . . .].[4] Choked with emotion, Rutilius's words echo with the foreboding of the Empire's impending end, and in his verses the *Laudes Romae* take on accents of sorrowful sincerity. The Latin authors of the decadent period are unjustly ignored; their sensibility—an inclination toward tenderness, openness to feelings, and understanding of human impulse—makes them seem quite close to our feelings and reactions. Their work reveals the same doubts and anguish that characterize our own terrible, empty years. Rutilius's farewell to Rome, his "prayer" for the city, is a magisterial passage in which skillful rhetoric and a sincerity of inspiration are perfectly blended in his memorable verses, "Fecisti partriam diversis gentibus unam . . . urbem fecisti quod prius orbis erat."

> O Rome, translated to the starry skies!
> Hear, Mother of Men, and Mother of the Gods!
> We, though thy temples, dwell not far from heaven.
> Thee sing we, and, long as Fate allows, will sing;

None can forget thee while he lives and breathes.
Sooner shall we be guilty of the crime
Of burying in oblivion the sun
Than from our heart shall fade thy meed of love.
Thy gifts thou spreadest wide as the sun's rays,
As far as earth-encircling ocean heaves.
Phoebus, embracing all things, rolls for thee;
His steeds both rise and sink in thy domains.
Thee not with burning sands could Libya stay,
Nor thee did Ursa armed with frost repel.
Far as the habitable climes extend
Toward either pole thy valour finds its path.
Thou hast made of alien realms one fatherland;
The lawless found their gain beneath thy sway;
Sharing thy laws with them thou hast subdued,
Thou hast made a city of the once wide world.[5]

The superintendent of the Museum of the Walls, whose offices are in the Porta San Sebastiano, showed me one day how to look at the masonry and make out the different hands that built the walls, as well as the varying skill levels of the workers. You can see it, for example, in the way the mortar beds were laid down, the thickness between brick courses, and the varying quality of the materials used. There are even idiosyncratic patterns in the masonry, little compositional games, which were the signatures of the various shops contracted to build a given section of the walls.

Inside the gate, about 10 meters away, an impressive ruin called the Arch of Drusus appears. This was actually a monumentally sized fornix in the aqueduct that crossed the Via Appia to supply the nearby Baths of Caracalla with water. Later on the arch was used as a second gate, creating a courtyard and transforming the space into a veritable fortress. Many other gates around Rome were similarly fortified, but San Sebastiano remains the most spectacular. The lower portion has been covered with a partial marble revetment made with marble taken from other monuments and tombs that had fallen into disuse along the neighboring Via Appia.

I won't dwell here on details that you can discover for yourself or find easily enough in a guidebook: the eloquent graffiti that record memorable events; the iron supports, also quite full of meaning, buried in the walls; and some spectacular and evocative carvings and figures. It is, however, worthwhile to describe the gate's interior, accessible through the museum entrance in the right bastion. Several flights of steps lead up to the first gallery, overlooking the street, where a number of surprises await us. What we first enter is actually the operations room, where the mechanisms that open and close the passageway below—a vertically mobile iron-grille gate and a gigantic double-door portal—are housed. A glass-covered opening in the floor of the gallery allows a glimpse of the grooves in the marble that guide the movement of the gate.

The museum's rooms are filled with detailed panels, models, and photographs accompanied by texts that provide a wealth of information about the walls, the phases of their construction, and other curiosities. What really attracts the visitor's eye, however, are two mosaics: a rectangular one set into the floor of the gallery, and a round one inside the bastion. These skillfully produced compositions are made with small black-and-white tesserae in the style of the ancient Romans. The round mosaic depicts a female deer about to be attacked by stalking tigers. The rectangular one in the gallery is larger, and its composition is dominated by a heroic knight figure at the center, surrounded by armed soldiers battling an enemy. The border is a frieze of swords and laurel branches.

Are these ancient Roman mosaics? They appear to be so, but because the august horseman's face bears a close resemblance to Mussolini any confusion is short-lived. The mosaics date back to the nineteen-thirties, and beg the question of why there are two Fascist works of art in a third-century building. The answer is simple: they're there because the Porta San Sebastiano was, during the Fascist period, the home of Ettore Muti, one of the highest-ranking officials of Mussolini's regime.

I have a vivid personal memory of Muti and his extravagant residence. On an autumn afternoon many years ago, when I was a child, a group of friends and I were playing around the Porta Latina. At a certain point we noticed that from the nearby Porta San Sebastiano there came a parade of people carrying all sorts of objects: one had a rolled-up rug over his shoulder, another held two chairs, yet another carried a bunch of pots and pans, and two or three people struggled to move a table. Our curiosity aroused, we went against the flow of people and quickly made our way to the gate. A small crowd had gathered in front of a tiny doorway located (as it still is today, though it's no longer used) in the left bastion of the gate as you look at it from inside the city walls. People rushed breathlessly back and forth, and were impeded in the narrow passageway as those already loaded down with booty were blocked by those frantically trying to get in to steal something for themselves. After a little while, before nightfall, a patrol of (perhaps German) soldiers arrived and put an end to the looting. Two soldiers took up positions beside the gate, and others went inside. The flow of looters stopped, and only one girl, after a murmured conversation with the sentry, was allowed to pass. Many in the crowd wondered in hushed voices why she got through and speculated, with malicious grins, about what might happen to her. Only several years later was I able to realize what had happened in that scene that, at the time, had only struck me with an oppressive sense of danger. The looting must have happened around September 8, 1943—that is, about ten or fifteen days after Muti had been killed in the pine forest of Fregene, under circumstances we're about to examine.

Ettore Muti was born in Ravenna in April 1902. His father was a humble civil servant, and the dominant family figure was his mother, Celestina, who may have been of noble birth and was certainly ambitious. She adored her restless, boastful son who stubbornly avoided his studies (and was therefore sent to a trade school rather than an academic high school) but was also courageous, tall, and robust, with a handsome face and easy, movie-star good looks. A popular children's weekly at the time, *L'Esploratore* (The Explorer), featured adventure stories about a boy called Gim (pronounced Jim). Muti chose this as his own nickname, and it stuck for the rest of his life—the poet Gabriele D'Annunzio created a more complete variation, and called him *Gim dagli occhi verdi* (Green-Eyed Jim).

When Italy entered World War I Muti fretted with impatience. School bored him, while the idea of war was thrilling. In the fall of 1917 he ran away from home and, lying about his age, enlisted in the elite corps of assault troops. His valor at the front earned him a recommendation for a silver medal, but he refused the honor, primarily to avoid having to reveal that he was only fifteen years old. When he returned home the newspaper *Il Resto del Carlino* ran a long feature on him, accurately titling the article "Italy's Youngest Soldier." He went back to school, but that didn't last long. When D'Annunzio and his band of Italian nationalists occupied Fiume—a city on the Istrian peninsula, the much-contested area between Italy and Croatia—Muti was immediately drawn to the chaos and disorder of that roguish adventure. With four or five other former commandos he left to join the poet's legionaries. That was the year he should have graduated from technical school, but by then another life already had him in its grip. Not a word is said about school ever again, and reading remains a rare activity throughout the rest of his life. The adventurous tales written by Emilio Salgari were an exception; Muti was so passionate about them that he named one of his daughters Jolanda—not as a tribute to the princess of the royal house of Savoy, but after the daughter of Salgari's Black Corsair.

A lot has been written about how the events in Fiume, cradle of Fascist belief, influenced the formation of Italian Fascism. Muti adhered to the model of a perfect Fascist so closely that he might easily be considered its prototype. In the turbulent months before the march on Rome he distinguished himself as a member of a Fascist action squad that carried out attacks on Socialist Party headquarters. Muti made a mockery of an adversary by forcing him to drink castor oil and then doubled over with laughter as he writhed with intestinal spasms; he attacked the *Case del Popolo*—Communist Party social centers—with a dagger at his belt, rounds of pistol shots, and hand grenades. A pure, impartial Fascist, Muti did these things not to further his career, but because his gut, aggressive nature, and vision told him to; he saw life as a heroic act, beautiful in itself, a bold wager that was its own reward.

But a character with such personality—irreverent, energetic, immensely likable, coarse yet genuine—embodied more than merely the ideal Fascist. For the women of his day, Ettore Muti represented the ideal man par excellence: the companion with whom to share the thrill of driving his Maserati 2300 at sixty miles per hour, a bottle of champagne, or a night at the Grand Hotel. He had married in Ravenna, had a daughter, separated from his wife, and come to Rome, where, among many loves, he had a more lasting one. Her name was Araceli Ansaldo y Cabrera, and she was an amateur soprano, cousin of the journalist Giovanni Ansaldo, and above all daughter of a Spanish grandee. When Araceli (Ara, for short) first saw Muti she was nineteen years old, and had a head full of dreams so typical at that age. In her diary she wrote a high-spirited description of that evening: "Leaving the Quirino Theater we went to have dinner at the Roma restaurant in Piazza Poli . . . when all of a sudden he came in. O Lord! It was as if some great magnetic power had entered. I was so shaken when he stared at me for a moment that I could not tell if it were his vibrations that shook within me, or mine within him. His face and figure had a classical beauty about them; he was like an Olympic god . . . " and so on.

Theirs was an affair worthy of the romance novels of Liala or Luciana Peverelli, which were just then becoming popular. Even the unpolished Muti, drunk with adventure, seemed to temper his usual arrogance with witticisms that were somewhere between a debased version of D'Annunzio's poetry and a paperback romance. "Our love is recorded in a celestial symphony, set within the altar made of crystal and moon that you offer me," or, "I made a silken knot from our two sobs." Ara matched his words with her own sugary lines. When the two lovers met in Trent, at the Hotel Aurora, Ara wrote, "One night—and I remember that my dressing gown was white—I went out onto the balcony to admire the play of bright moonlight on the flowers and water spouting from the putti . . . I did not hear him come in, and then just his voice, 'Divine! Luminous! Don't move, Juliette.' Playing along with the joke, I replied, 'Romeo, I awaited you on the balcony!' 'Of course; here I am.' If I hadn't stopped him he would have run down to the garden and climbed up on the balcony . . . " Araceli describes an almost cinematic scene, taken wholesale, it seems, from one of those films made soon thereafter that were nicknamed *telefoni bianchi*—"white telephone" films—after the props in their luxurious sets.

There are no doubts about Muti's military valor and willingness to brandish his fists. He was a daring pilot during the war in Africa, and later fought in the war in Spain, where the armored division he commanded was in the front line of Fascist troops entering Madrid. He fought again in Albania, where he was one of the first to land in Tirana. As soon as he touched down he left the plane, jumped into a car, rushed to the royal palace (King Zog had in the meantime fled), and practically captured it by himself. He then climbed the tower and planted the Italian flag at the top.

Toward the end of 1939 Mussolini appointed Muti to replace Achille Starace as Secretary of the National Fascist Party. Mussolini's letter to Starace informing him of "a changing of the guard" is remarkably terse: "Dear Starace, I have decided definitely on Muti . . . The last war, in Spain, earned him special recognition. You will go to the Army. Mussolini." There's not a single word of thanks for a man who, however awkward or even ridiculous he had been at times, had served him with blind loyalty for years. That, however, is another story.

Mussolini failed to understand that putting a man of Muti's restless temperament at the head of a complex and corrupt bureaucracy could only make things worse. Muti loved action, and was completely incapable of the reflection and cunning such politics required. His nomination was the idea of Galeazzo Ciano, Mussolini's Foreign Minister and son-in-law, who suggested Muti would be the best choice. On October 4, 1939, Ciano wrote in his diary, "Mussolini spoke to me for the first time in six years about replacing Starace. I encouraged him in this good idea, and Muti's name was brought up as successor. Muti is both courageous and loyal, and although he is still inexperienced in public administration, he is strong-willed and full of talent. If he were nominated, he'd do well. Whoever it might be, though, Starace's successor will be an immediate success—if for no other reason than he is not Starace, whom the Italian people so hate." A few days later, on October 7, "I gave Muti's c.v. to the Duce [Mussolini], and he was impressed. He is worthy of comparison to a medieval knight."

Many of Ciano's friends and favorites made it into the new cabinet, but it was precisely as a creature of the young and ambitious Foreign Minister that Muti proved to be a disappointment. He acted of his own accord and was overconfident, which often made his actions counterproductive and even eccentric, and he didn't respect the rules of the game or the established hierarchies and privileges. As if this weren't bad enough, he made it worse by doing things thoughtlessly, instinctually, and without any plan.

Giuseppe Bottai, the national Minister of Education, immediately disliked the new party secretary. Director of the journal *Critica Fascista*, Bottai was a refined, educated man who would also soon show a certain temperament. On the night of July 24, 1943, he helped bring Mussolini's government down and immediately afterward, to avoid retribution, he made a daring escape from Italy and joined the

Foreign Legion. Bottai had real contempt for Muti, and found his coarseness and modest intellect irritating. On January 11, 1940, he notes in his diary, "Muti received me in his office, which was very hot and oppressive, in shirt sleeves. We had an incoherent and inconclusive discussion about the problems raised by the Centers for the Preparation of Youth. . . . Muti is a hero, not a soldier. He sympathizes with acts of valor but not the shaping of social values."

One day, while Bottai was visiting Palermo, Muti suddenly arrived, cheerful as ever, the eternally rambunctious boy. "I have been in Palermo since yesterday for a conference on rural schools. Muti appeared from nowhere. At breakfast he said to me, 'I didn't know you would be here. It will not surprise you, but I do not read the newspapers. Once, when I was a boy in Romagna, one fell under my glance, but it was so boring that I never read one again.'" One can only imagine the effect such stupidity had on a man such as Bottai. His feelings about Muti were so negative that in August of 1943 he offered this remarkable description of the man: "On his small, solid, round head his hair cropped like that of Germans and boxers; the gaze that emerges from those sunken eye sockets is so destitute of any power of reflection, observation or comprehension that his eyes seem to have no color, they are neutral, a mimetic grey, and that forehead of his is so remarkably low that it immediately seems, upon first meeting him, to be a sinister sign."

In August of 1940 Bottai was at the beach in Fregene with Ciano. One evening he reports in his diary, "At the beach with Galeazzo and Starace. Our aversion for Muti is growing; we are near the limit of our hatred and scorn for him . . . they showed me, between the pine forest at Castel Fusano and the sea, a large and luxurious colonial-style bungalow with a sloping thatched roof and a pretty English veranda; they tell me that it was built, furnished, and landscaped with palms and flowerbeds for Muti at the expense of the Governor's office, and that he brings his merry band of clients and women here. In return the Governor's membership card in the PNF (the National Fascist Party) was backdated to 1919. These two have behaved scandalously, and they tell me Mussolini knows of their suspicious doings." This is the first reference by a significant individual to the small villa, the "luxurious bungalow" which would, as we will see, provide the backdrop to this story's grand finale.

Muti, the "executioner's assistant," as Bottai and Ciano mockingly called him because of his proud and coarse appearance, did not last long in his new job. As secretary of the party he behaved the same way he had as a soldier, impetuously and with daring, but also without worrying too much about the consequences of his decisions, or whom they might annoy. He had accepted the job declaring a desire to "clean out every little corner," and acted accordingly. He removed many mid-level bureaucrats, he discovered and reported their corruption to the magistrates, he ignored the personal recommendations of powerful officials, and he declared that working for the party was incompatible with accepting other remunerative activities. It didn't take long for dissatisfaction to spill forth from the ranks of the ineffective bureaucracy, where many people viewed an appointment the equivalent of a lucrative, comfortable sinecure.

Muti most likely could've endured the growing irritation he caused amongst the party's petty bureaucrats and mid-level managers had he known to maintain a solid rapport with the man who had given him his job. Whether it was out of ignorance, naïveté, or arrogance, he ignored Galeazzo Ciano, and this proved to be his downfall. Initially, Ciano had carefully and consistently praised Muti in front of Mussolini, but once he understood he could expect very little from the appointee, Ciano did his best to end his career. He wrote, "Muti has more pluck than brains. . . . He acts of his own accord and listens less and less to me." Later, on October 4, he noted with some satisfaction, "[Had] a long conversation with the Duce on the train. He will soon remove Muti because he is inept and unscrupulous." So much for being party secretary.

Other events had also become pressing—the disastrous course of the war and the allied bombings of important cities, including Rome, had worn down the national morale. On the night between July 24 and 25, 1943, the Fascist Grand Council presented Mussolini with a resolution put forth by the president of the Chamber of Deputies, Dino Grandi, which requested that he "beseech his Majesty the King to take control of the armed forces—that supreme prerogative that our institutions have conferred upon him." This effectively ended the Duce's government, and it was a carefully crafted blow the dictator essentially had to deliver himself. To be relieved of supreme command of the military was, for Mussolini, the equivalent of admitting he had mismanaged the war he had wanted and called for at any cost, regardless of the fact that the country was not prepared for it or that he was determined to stand by the wrong allies.

Muti was in Spain with Araceli, who was by then his second wife, when this happened. The week before, in Rome, he had not hidden his disillusionment with Mussolini. Learning of the resolution being prepared in the Grand Council, he exclaimed with his usual impetuousness, reverting to his native Romagnolo dialect, "Ma quale Ordine del giorno, se volete il Duce a l'amazz me!" [What resolution? If you want the Duce, I'll kill him for you!] He knew the situation was heating up, and he tried to return to Rome from Spain on an Ala Littoria flight (the forerunner to Alitalia). Enemy planes, however, forced the aircraft to land at Marseilles. Muti continued his journey on the train, but it was not an easy trip, as the train was shot at, attacked by air, and several railway bridges had been blown up. He stopped in Bologna and made a quick trip to Ravenna to see his first wife and then, on the morning of the 24th, he left for Rome. The meeting of the Grand Council was set for six o'clock that evening, but the trip from Bologna to Rome was so slow that Muti did not arrive in the capital until Sunday morning. By then the die had been cast, and Mussolini was preparing to go to the Villa Savoia to meet with the king who would then have him arrested.

How would Muti have voted, had he been present? This has always been a controversial question. After the war, and given his tragic end, the neo-Fascists made him the first martyr of their cause. In reality, the events can be interpreted several different ways. If we believe his exclamation that Mussolini wanted him dead, it seems likely that Ettore Muti would also have signed Grandi's famous resolution, bringing the final vote in its favor to twenty of twenty-nine (the official result was nineteen of twenty-eight).

After Mussolini's arrest the conspirators were overcome with fright, fearing they, too, might be arrested or perhaps killed by the soldiers of Battalion M—the troops that remained loyal to Mussolini, at least on paper, until his death. Muti took the coup's leader, the terrified Grandi, and sheltered him first in his residence at the Porta San Sebastiano, then in his luxurious bungalow in Fregene.

It was in that same villa that the rest of Muti's story played itself out. He spent the summer months in that pleasant resort, so close to

Rome yet cooled by the sea's breeze and the magnificent surrounding pine forest. With him was an attendant, a maid, and an old friend from Ravenna. He was also entertained by the company of a Czech actress known as Dana Havlowa (née Edith Fischerowa on May 4, 1921) who spent her holiday with him after appearing in a theatrical review (*Mani in tasca, naso al vento*) with Odoardo Spadaro's company.

According to unconfirmed sources, this young woman was also a German spy. After September 8 she fled to Spain, and was shot to death in the 1960s; some believed she was murdered by the last of her many lovers. Others maintain that she'd betrayed so many Jews during the Occupation that the Israeli secret service hunted her down in revenge.

Why was Muti, amongst all the high-ranking Fascist officials, some of whom fled to Portugal while others sought refuge in Germany or went underground, the one whose end was so inexplicable and tragic? Two versions of his murder began to circulate as soon as it all happened. Since both were politically motivated and neither offered a complete accounting of the events, the mystery of this death, like so many others, is destined to remain unsolved. However, the facts surrounding the event, or, more precisely, the bits of them that have surfaced, can be summarized.

After the sudden coup of July 25, while Mussolini still believed he could take his family and retire as a peaceful pensioner at Rocca delle Caminate, rumors began to circulate about a plot to restore him to power. Muti seems to have given it little thought. From time to time he went to Rome where he was spotted in the bars along the Via Veneto. He behaved with his usual confidence, as if nothing had happened. He believed he'd been spared, and was unaware that his days were already numbered. Pietro Badoglio, the new Prime Minister of Italy, was informed by General Giacomo Carboni, head of the secret service, that there might be a plot afoot to restore Mussolini to power. Who would've benefited from starting such an unfounded rumor? It has been suggested that Badoglio himself, who feared the king wanted to be rid of him, had it circulated because he believed it would make his own position more secure. Or perhaps it was General Carboni's initiative, an attempt to frighten Badoglio, push him out of office, and take his job.

It is impossible to know with any certainty what was going through Muti's mind in those few days. Some have said he was tired of Fascism and Mussolini, and was in any case eager to get out of politics, while others say he had a cordial meeting with Badoglio. Others maintain (General Carboni) that Badoglio saw Muti both as the ringleader of the plot to restore Mussolini and as a threat to his physical safety. Some have suggested that it was Badoglio who ordered Muti's arrest, and that his execution was entrusted to Giovanni Frignani, a lieutenant colonel in the *carabinieri* who was particularly suited to such a delicate assignment (he was the official who had arrested Mussolini at the Villa Savoia). Just for the record, we might add that Frignani later joined the Resistance and was arrested in January of 1944 by a German squadron commanded by Captain Priebke. He was then murdered in the infamous Nazi reprisal killings at the Fosse Ardeatina outside of Rome.

Was Muti merely supposed to be arrested, or was he really to be executed immediately? As with all other aspects of this story, the sources also differ on this point. On the night of August 23–24, a squadron of *carabinieri* commanded by Lieutenant Enzo Taddei, a robust and quick man, arrived at Muti's house at Via Palombina 12. The former secretary of the Fascist Party opened the door wearing only his pajama bottoms. When the lieutenant explained that he had a warrant for his arrest, an annoyed Muti replied that it was against regulations to send a lieutenant to arrest a colonel. He also tried to stop Taddei from going into the bedroom where Dana, who had been awakened by the ruckus, was trying her best to get dressed. Facing a group of armed and menacing soldiers, Muti finally relented and, after he had dressed in his summer air force uniform, he left with them, displaying an ostentatious tranquility. His calm demeanor, the worrying circumstances of his arrest notwithstanding, may have been the result of the several assurances about his safety he had recently received from Carmine Senise, the chief of Rome's police. As he left the house Muti put on his uniform beret, cocking it at the usual eleven o'clock angle, a detail that, as we shall see, is more important than it might seem.

Instead of taking the road to Fregene, where the squadron had parked its vehicles, the group went instead toward the woods. Attilio Contiero, a former *carabiniere* who took part in the mission, later described where the various individuals were: "Muti was in front with the commander of the special squad on his right and Frau Salvatore, a *carabinieri* officer from the Maccarese barracks, on his left. Behind him was the famous man dressed in khaki overalls. The group I was in was about ten or fifteen paces further behind, with Lieutenant Taddei and Brigadier Barolat at the center." The mysterious man in khaki, who was holding a submachine gun, stood out amongst the group of men on the left; he was a short, balding man, about forty years old, who spoke with a Neapolitan accent (he was later identified as a certain Abate). His group was the first to enter the dark pine forest (the reports said that it was a moonless night) on a badly marked path. From this moment on we know only what some of the eyewitnesses told the judges during the various investigations of the incident, which were all given later. Contiero, for example, was interrogated both during and after the war, and gave two rather different versions of his story.

As the group moved forward they heard gunshots coming from the bushes. They feared an attack, as everyone said that a company of German paratroopers was camping nearby, or perhaps the shots came from gunners at the coastal battery. The *carabinieri* fired back but, fearing it might instigate friendly fire, Lieutenant Taddei immediately ordered them to stop. According to those who were there, Muti immediately started to run as if he were trying to escape; he was stopped dead by a burst of gunfire. According to a second version, Muti didn't try to escape at all, and was instead shot only at the end of the first brief burst of gunfire, which had been a pretext to cover the shots fired at the official taken hostage. He was seen falling to the ground, dead, at about three o'clock in the morning on August 24.

Which version should we believe? Colonel Antonio Quartulli, a high-ranking military judge, was called to examine Muti's body at the Celio military hospital the next morning. He reported, "Two projectiles from a submachine gun passed through his cranium, entering from below and moving upward, joining trajectories as they did so, making a single tunnel through the brain. They exited together from his forehead, leaving a large hole about ten centimeters across and causing multiple fractures to the bones of the face and the base of the skull, with traumatic injury to the brain." It was also noted that the bullets made holes in his beret. Major Moci, a friend of Muti's, gave that beret to his wife, Fernanda, who had rushed to Rome and was staying at the Hotel Plaza. "Keep it forever," the major said as he gave it to her. She did, and it became something of a relic. There is an entry hole in the back of the beret and, in the front, an exit hole. There is no trace of the residual halo of powder characteristic of point-blank shots, but the precision of the aim is surprising, and quite difficult to reconcile with the image of shots taken at a man running in the almost total blackness of a moonless night.

Was this a premeditated murder, or a situation that somehow got out of hand? The presence of the man in khaki gives some added weight to the first hypothesis, since the *carabinieri* would have been reluctant to take part in any execution. Colonel Frignani, questioned by magistrates on September 7, said that he had received an order to arrest Muti, but not to kill him. Did Muti himself provoke the fatal shot by trying to flee? Judge Quartulli accepted this version and closed the case, "given that, by the royal decree of June 18, 1941, the use of arms is authorized if caused by the necessity of stopping a prisoner from escaping."

The neo-Fascist version of the story suggests that the murder (whatever the circumstances, it was certainly murder) made Muti into the first martyr of Salò after Mussolini's fall, and that the so-called civil war that bloodied the nation until April of 1945 began with his death.

Police chief Carmine Senise insisted after the war that it was only an accident, maintaining that he could not believe the *carabinieri* would have made such a mess if indeed they had been ordered to eliminate the ringleader of a plot against the state. He then added, "there were a thousand other ways that would've been more convenient, less noisy, and infinitely surer."

On the morning of August 24 the Stefani press agency published the following laconic dispatch: "Last night Ettore Muti, the former secretary of the now disbanded Fascist Party, died near Rome. He had been awarded the Gold Medal for Military Valor during the war in Spain." Several other sources reported that "Marshall Badoglio gave signs of great satisfaction" when he learned the news, while others said it was more like great joy. The Republic of Salò, formed as a puppet regime of the Germans on September 24, badly needed symbolic figures, and it turned Muti into a mythical hero. His remains were exhumed from the cemetery of Verano in January of 1944 and transported to Ravenna, where they were entombed in the church of San Francesco—where Dante is also buried—in a grandiose public ceremony. Alessandro Pavolini, secretary of the Republican Fascist Party, said in his eulogy that Muti had been "the bravest of our soldiers, the most handsome warrior of our race . . . an officer and a member of the Fascist action squads, he bore innumerable signs of death defied in combat." A military brigade was formed and named after Muti in the region of Piedmont, but it was full of criminals, and ruined its reputation by helping the Nazis in the most ferocious rounding up and repression of Resistance fighters.

In 1951 a new investigation ended with the judgment that General Carboni had stoked Badoglio's fear of a possible coup attempt, and although the magistrates didn't specify why, the motives are fairly clear. In any case, the court found that Badoglio had not ordered Colonel Muti's death, since it was Carboni rather than the Prime Minister who had ordered his arrest. Did Carboni also order the assassination? With the facts we have, it's impossible to answer this question with any certainty.

On August 26, forty-eight hours after the fact, Bottai noted in his diary, "Two days ago, on Tuesday, Ettore Muti was assassinated in the pine forest of Fregene. Whether this is the right verb, I don't know, and we won't know for a while. It is certain that he was killed by a squadron of *carabinieri* that had gone to arrest him at one of his seaside homes. Was it the justified killing of a man trying to escape? This seems to be the most probable hypothesis. Already, though, other rumors are circulating that he was killed either for what he 'knew,' or because he may have been implicated in the financial scandals swirling around AGIP [the state oil company], where his followers worked, or because he was the leader of a plot. . . . I remember him in Africa, an aviator at the air base in Mek'ele. I met him there for the first time, and my contact with that group of killers was only occasional, and filled with mutual distrust. Even down there, their way of waging war repulsed me. They acted as if it were a sporting event, with a bravado that so perverted normal human feelings that it obliterated all traces of emotion, religious 'suffering,' or surprise in the face of the deaths they caused or suffered. . . . Now Muti is dead. I think about his tragic end with melancholy." A hard eulogy for a man who, according to Bottai, had—in the mindless heat of action and with unquestionable courage—lost sight almost completely of every other human value.

While working on this chapter I visited Muti's tomb in the cemetery of Ravenna. It's modest grave, made of gray stone, and its simple inscription reads, "Ettore Muti, Gold Medal for Military Valor – 22.5.1902 / 24.8.1943." Beneath it is the outline of a three-engine airplane. It also has a small marble plaque with a dedication that reads, "[From the] Italian assault soldiers to this unforgettable hero." Muti's tomb is right behind the Gardini family chapel, which, being the essence of discretion, has no inscription on its exterior. Raul Gardini and his father-in-law Serafino Ferruzzi were argricultural entrepreneurs; Gardini became CEO of the Montedison group, which in the early 1990s was involved in a scandal that led to Gardini's 1993 suicide. Gardini was also a major wind sailor who raced in the America's Cup.

And what of Porta San Sebastiano? At a certain point in his career, Muti wanted a residence appropriate to the status he had achieved in his tumultuous life. He chose the ancient gate in the Aurelian walls for its numerous advantages, including the extraordinary view from its high towers, still partially visible today. Aside from the panorama, this exceptional residence also provided the discretion essential to a well-known man who had a significant number of lovers, a situation Mussolini was regularly informed of. For the gate's renovation Muti sought the assistance of one of the great twentieth-century architects, Luigi Moretti (1907–1973). Moretti was a cultured man, passionate bibliophile, and an erudite connoisseur of ancient and modern art; he died of a heart attack at sixty-six while sailing his boat off the island of Capraia.

Some of Moretti's works, to name just a few, include the Gil House in Trastevere, the Casa delle Armi, and Mussolini's gymnasium at the Foro Italico. The Casa delle Armi—also known as the Palazzina della Scherma, for the fencing tournaments held inside—was destroyed in the nineteen-seventies when it was converted into a courtroom for high-profile trials. The numerous protests, imprecations, and reminders that the building was one of the masterpieces of twentieth-century Italian architecture were all for naught. Finally, in the first years of this century, there has been some talk of restoring it.

After a period when he was largely ignored because of his strong ties to the Fascist regime, Moretti began to build again, thanks in part to his real estate connections and ties to the Vatican. He created some masterpieces and even worked abroad; his designs include the Watergate Hotel in Washington, D.C., so famously linked to Richard Nixon's political downfall. The most important part of Moretti's career, however, unfolded during the period of Fascist rule in Italy. He often met with Mussolini, who was fond of him and made him the technical director of the Opera Nazionale Balilla. He and Muti became friends because of that job and, perhaps just for amusement, Moretti agreed to furnish his friend's strange residence.

After Muti's death and the looting described above, there is obviously no trace left of the genial architect's plan. Today the walls of the Porta San Sebastiano are bare, but luckily the photographs in the State Archives survive, some of which are included in this book. Two characteristics of Moretti's work emerge from the photos and in loco descriptions. Firstly, the architect did as little as possible to alter its basic spaces, and the little that he did do, just to make them inhabitable, was done in such a way as to minimize any changes to the tower walls. Amongst the rare exceptions are the still-visible plumbing pipes that he tried to hide, at least partially, in a recess in the wall. Secondly, the furnishings in the apartment seem to have been planned to underscore, perhaps a bit ironically, the adventurous and fatuous character of the man who would inhabit the space. There were sumptuous, heavy drapes and large beds covered with tiger pelts; a style so pompous it seems more like a movie set than a private residence. Bottai called Muti's home at Porta San Sebastiano a "garçonnière," or bachelor pad. Although he designed it in an elegant and amusing, rather than a scornful way, Moretti seems to have gone in the same direction.

Neither Muti nor his architect knew, on the day of the residence's completion, how briefly its tenant would enjoy it. They could never have guessed at the sinister end he would meet with, and the horrors that would stain his memory, perpetrated by those who claimed to be fighting in his name.

1. Geoffrey L. Bickersteth, ed. and trans., *The Poems of Leopardi* (New York: Russell & Russell, 1973), 137.

2. Tacitus, *The Histories*, trans. Clifford H. Moore (New York: G. P. Putnam's Sons, 1925), 1:5, 7.

3. Aelius Aristides, *The Complete Works, Orations XVII–LIII,* trans. Charles A. Behr (Leiden: E. J. Brill, 1981), 2:95.

4. Virgil, *The Aeneid*, trans. Robert Fitzgerald (New York: Random House, 1983), 190.

5. Claudius Rutilius Namatianus, *De reditu suo, The Home-coming of Rutilius Claudius Namatianus from Rome to Gaul in the Year 416 A.D.,* ed. Charles H. Keene, trans. George F. Savage-Armstrong (London: G. Bell, 1907), lines 47–66.

III

TWENTY-THREE THRUSTS
OF THE DAGGER

ROME HAS WITNESSED its share of political murders ever since the very first one, committed by Romulus, gave rise to the city itself. Daggers in dark corridors, poison in cups of precious metals, surprise attacks on palace steps, and public executions legitimized by the presence of powerful men—in togas, ermine, and scarlet cardinal's robes—all of them unmoved, all protected by verdicts, holy texts, or official seals. Christians, slaves, and prisoners of war were torn to pieces by wild beasts at the circus. All the murders perpetrated to hold the government's line, reinforce the popular appeal of a leader, or distract the people from other, perhaps more pressing concerns, were political killings. Rome's soil is soaked with that blood. Yet of all these murders there is one that has become the prototype for all other political assassinations, and that, of course, is the assassination of Julius Caesar.

Each time I visit the Roman Forum I wonder if there is any other place like it—any place that for so many centuries represented the umbilicus of the world, and evoked even from a geographic, physical point of view the fact that Rome truly was the center of the universe, and that the Forum was the center of Rome. On this same ground, beneath all the temples and statues, at the foot of two fateful hills—the Palatine and the Capitoline—the great axes of human civilization and the triumph of law intersected. Near the Arch of Septimius Severus there is still the base of a circular column that once supported the *umbilicus Urbis*, the navel of the city and, therefore, of the entire world. Not far from it was the *miliarium aureum*, a column sheathed in bronze and referred to as the golden milestone, which marked the start of all the great Imperial roads that radiated from the Forum in all directions—to the frozen forests of the north, the blazing deserts of Africa, and the vast Asian steppes that led into the great unknown—an eternal challenge to the legions that seemed to question even the size of the planet.

Today the Forum is a collection of mangled remains that have survived the destruction of invaders, natural disasters, and the sackings carried out by its own citizens. Its statues have been smashed, its columns knocked down, its streets torn up; its magnificent buildings have been reduced to ruins, their marble burned for lime, and their decorations and ornaments stolen and scattered round the world. All that remains are ashes, the walls' nude masonry, and miniscule, multicolored debris—a single coin, a pair of dice, a small jewel. The Forum contains not only these simple remains, but also precise signs of time and place, and specific references to the affairs of men, including those who, in the past, held the fate of the world in their hands. Julius Caesar was one such man, and the last day of his life began right here; here he took the first steps toward that fatal appointment with his assassins.

When all is said and done, the Forum is a relatively small place, and its appearance is far from monumental—it's a low-lying plain, a swamp drained centuries before Christ by means of the impressive hydraulics of the *cloaca maxima*. The crowds and closely packed monuments, basilicas, and temples impart a feeling of near suffocation, and give us a good sense of what daily life in ancient Rome must have been like, full of clamor and chaos. It was here that most things in Rome eventually converged—its citizens as well as its political, bureaucratic, and commercial machinery. Here democracy was exercised (for as long as it lasted in Rome), business deals were done, friends arranged appointments, and chance meetings were made. Horace described it well in his *Satire* I.9, "Ibam forte via sacra, sicut meus et mos, nescio quid meditans, nugarum, totus in illis," [I went for a stroll along the Via Sacra, as I always do, totally absorbed in its nonsense]. Solemn religious processions and military triumphs passed along the Via Sacra before ascending to the temple of temples, dedicated to Jupiter Optimus Maximus, atop the Capitoline Hill, where it all began. The Temple of Antoninus Pius and Faustina (today the church of San Lorenzo in Miranda) is, along with the Curia, one of the most imposing buildings belonging to the Forum, and has an interesting history. Antoninus built this magnificent temple to honor his wife, Faustina, whom he had deified after she died. Antoninus himself died in AD 161. He earned the nickname Pius because he had aspired to be just, and had one adoptive son, Marcus Aurelius, who also became a great emperor, and married his daughter. In the seventh century the temple of Antoninus Pius and Faustina was transformed into a church, but in 1536 Pope Paul III ordered the Christian revetment removed because he wanted to impress Emperor Charles V with what remained of the glories of ancient Rome. Charles was in Rome on a solemn mission of reconciliation nine years after his troops had sacked the city. Like Mussolini, who built a new train station (Ostiense) to welcome Hitler, Paul III stripped a church, and where there had been little more than a path among the ruins he built the striking Via San Gregorio, all to impress the Holy Roman Emperor.

The grandeur of the impressive Temple of Antoninus Pius and Faustina is clearly visible from the outside. Perhaps an even better example of the sheer power of Roman architecture can be found on the other side of town, at the Mausoleum of Costanza on the Via Nomentana. Built at the beginning of the fourth century for Helena and Constantina, Emperor Constantine's daughters, it has preserved the structure (and luminosity) of a Roman temple, even though a few centuries later it was converted into a church. Those entering for the first time are treated to an extraordinarily powerful experience— its circular plan, its dome, and the space itself, which is metered by twelve pairs of granite columns with magnificent capitals. Then there is the ambulatory that encloses the entire interior, its walls and vaults covered with some of the oldest and most beautiful mosaics in Rome, which date back to the fourth century, as does the church. They have a white ground and are filled with decorative motifs, intertwined vines and leaves, figures of small animals and, at each end, images of Constantina and her husband, Hannibalianus. The whole complex is exceptional. A few steps away is the basilica of Sant'Agnese (with extensive catacombs beneath it), an important example of early Christian architecture with Byzantine influences.

Getting back to the Forum, there's yet another curiosity worth mentioning; there are two key buildings, each with a pair of magnificent bronze doors. The first pair secures the entrance to the Curia (next to the Arch of Septimius Severus), though the one visible there today is a copy of the original, which Francesco Borromini moved to the church of San Giovanni in Laterano, where it can still be seen.

The second pair was on the Temple of Romulus, also known as the Temple of the Penates, next to the Temple of Antoninus Pius and Faustina. The Romulus to whom the temple was dedicated is not to be confused with the city's founder, but was the son of the Emperor Maxentius who died in 307, whose father buried him on the Via Appia in a mausoleum across the road from his circus. It's amazing to think that these two enormous doors were cast in bronze, decorated, and installed so long ago—and above all to think that they somehow miraculously survived centuries of pillaging and neglect.

Among the many places in the Forum that commemorate Caesar and his death is the so-called altar of Octavian (who later took the title Augustus Caesar) dedicated to him in 29 BC. Built on a terrace in front of the Temple of Romulus, not far from the lovely House of the Vestals, Octavian had it decorated with the prows—*rostra*—of the Egyptian ships he had captured at Aktion two years earlier. The dictator's body had been cremated on that site, as the Greek historian Appianus described several centuries later in his *Roman History*: "... they placed [his body] again in the forum where stands the ancient palace of the kings of Rome. There they collected together pieces of wood and benches, of which there were many in the forum, and anything else they could find of that sort, for a funeral pile ... Then they set fire to it, and the entire people remained by the funeral pile throughout the night. There an altar was first erected, but now there stands the temple of Caesar himself, as he was deemed worthy of divine honours. . . ."[1] In his *Lives of the Caesars*, Suetonius added, "His friends raised . . . a gilded shrine on the Rostra resembling that of Mother Venus. In it they set an ivory couch, spread with purple and gold cloth, and from a pillar at its head hung the gown in which he had been murdered."[2]

Not far from the altar are the ruins of Caesar's residence, the Domus Publica. After living for many years in a modest house in the Suburra, a neighborhood outside the city center, the dictator moved here and remained until he finally met with destiny. The last days of his life were restless, full of projects and promises (just as his entire existence had been), but also of sinister omens.

The night of March 14–15 Julius Caesar barely slept, and as soon as he arose he had an attack of vertigo, an ailment he had long suffered and that had recently become increasingly frequent and bothersome. That morning he was supposed to preside over the senatorial assembly in the Curia but he had no desire to go, and not just because of the unusual dizzy spell. Over the last few days he'd had strange premonitions, and even though he was not particularly superstitious, the signs had been numerous and strangely unambiguous. As a young man, as he was assiduously climbing the *cursus honorum* (the ancient Roman political ladder), he had scoffed at omens. Every time some new project was begun, or a new appointment was to be made, the heavens were expected to give some kind of sign— perhaps an unexpected flash of lightning or a flicker of light—and Caesar had somehow seen to it that these signs appeared. Priests and zealous officials did their best to satisfy him. If the sign, for example, was a propitious flash of light, there was always someone afterward who swore to have seen it precisely where it had been predicted.

But now these were different; men were seen engulfed in flames but not burned, a small bird with a laurel branch in its beak was attacked and ripped apart by a bird of prey, and the shields of Mars fell over, creating an ominous bronze clanging throughout the palace where they were kept. And there was more: a few days earlier Spurinna, a soothsayer Caesar detested, had paid him a visit, and this time she had spoken powerfully, as if her words, rather than being dictated by divine inspiration, were instead dictated by concrete information. "Beware, Caesar, the Ides of March," she had said. As soon as Spurinna left, Cornelius Balbo broached the same topic: "I beseech you, Caesar, when you go to the Curia be sure to have your loyal Spanish guards with you." At the feet of the statue of Lucius Brutus someone had left a scrap of paper that read, "If you were alive, O Brutus, you would kill the tyrant." With this the other Brutus, Caesar's adopted (or perhaps illegitimate) son, was reminded that he was descended from the great Brutus who, for love of the Republic, had assassinated King Tarquinius. Troublesome rumors were heard all over town claiming that Caesar preferred the Barbarians to the Romans, that he was going to concede the political privilege of the Laticlave to the Gauls, and above all that he wanted to attack the institutions of the state and crown himself king. That would constitute a coup d'état punishable by the death. "The people hate even the idea of a monarchy," his counselors repeated, and he listened patiently to their annoying droning. It would have been an effort made in vain to explain that the Republic was already dead, that only vestiges, its husk, remained, and that these too should be disposed of. And then there was Calpurnia, Caesar's fourth wife, who humbly loved him and forgave him everything; for several nights her sleep had been restless, punctuated by worrisome moans.

The previous evening Caesar had gone to dinner at the house of Marcus Lepidus. Reclining on the triclinium, he allowed himself the rare luxury of drinking wine. Amongst the other guests was Decimus Brutus Albinus, one of Caesar's enemies who, had he the courage, would have revealed himself straightway. Instead he raised his calyx in a gesture of greeting, and at the same time posed an oblique, somewhat philosophical question: "What sort of death do you think is the best, Caesar?" He promptly replied, as was his custom, "I read in Xenophon that King Cyrus, when he knew he was gravely ill, made all the arrangements for his own funeral. I do not want a death for which I have time to prepare. The best death is an unexpected one." All conversation in the room came to a halt, not just because it was Caesar who was talking, but because this brief exchange resounded with a troubling echo. Caesar took advantage of the silence that followed, got up, and left. Now it was morning, the senatorial assembly was approaching, and perhaps it would indeed be best not to go.

Who was this man who tortured himself over such troubling omens? He's a nearly omnipotent man, lord of Rome and therefore the world, still vigorous for his fifty-six (perhaps fifty-seven) years. He'd spent most of his life in combat, from the frozen wastelands of Britain to the African deserts, on land and on sea, was endowed with an indomitable physical energy, and had a mental agility that allowed him to dictate four or five important letters simultaneously to his scribes. He was bold and defiant, a dandy who loved to spend freely even when there wasn't any money. He wasn't handsome, and the soldiers even mocked him for his baldness, but he nevertheless had an aura capable of subjugating any and everyone. He had the style of a great statesman, and emanated a regal charisma. Yet some also wrote (Cicero, for example) that he was capable of trampling all principles, be they human or divine. Cato of Utica wrote that for the sake of his own ambitions he would break any law. Certainly he had trampled the institutions of Rome; he'd conquered Gaul but then, for personal reasons, inspired a civil war there that caused great grief and ruin. In a word, Caesar was a man who, sixteen centuries before Machiavelli theorized any such practice, had successfully separated the great politician from the moral codes of his time.

The moral autonomy of the politician doesn't mean he can pocket money from the public treasury, but rather that he must establish goals in the general interest and pursue them even at the price of overcoming obstacles along the way. There wasn't a single provincial governor in all of Rome who hadn't stolen from those he governed, Caesar included, but he did so with such grandiosity and design that it inspired fear. With an arrogant and absolute serenity he ignored the law and then focused, serious and implacable, on expanding the boundaries of the state by crossing the Rubicon. He became an enemy of the Republic because when he had the choice of bringing about change through reform or revolution, he chose the latter—it was a calculated decision born also of sheer impatience. His immorality consisted of granting himself freedom from the same moral expectations that bound the Roman aristocracy both in the name of law and tradition. Caesar's greatness lay not in a sense of obedience, but rather in the fact that he was almost always successful in furthering the interests of the state without neglecting his own.

His political career was a succession of skillfully calculated moves that were also often blessed by pure luck. Right from the start he chose to ally himself with the plebeians and the army. He thought what everyone thought about the masses—that they had no more discernment than that of a child, and therefore needed someone to guide them. He was an aristocrat, scion of one of Rome's most illustrious families, which counted Ascanius, son of Aeneas and Creusa, grandson of Venus, amongst its ancestors. In delivering the funerary oration for his aunt, Julia, Caesar declared, in no uncertain terms, "On my mother's side my family descends from royalty; my father's side traces its origins to the immortal gods." By the time he was thirty he'd already determined that, in political life, the bolder a lie is, the more useful it is, provided it was told with the necessary nerve. In any case, between the patricians and the plebeians he chose the latter, which had become what we would now call the urban proletariat—a restless hoard that had to be distracted by games and held at bay by public gifts within a patronage system.

On his career path Caesar ran across two other influential men, Gnaeus Pompey and Marcus Licinius Crassus. The first was a high general, as great as Caesar and six years his senior. When pirate raids on grain shipments became bad enough to threaten famine, Pompey was charged with driving them off. These criminals were both daring and provocative; they attacked convoys of ships and raided the coasts, sacked villages, raped and assaulted the inhabitants. Pompey gave them no respite, and within three months he routed them: 10,000 were killed, and 20,000 captured, along with 800 of their ships. He enjoyed the same success in the war he waged against Mithridates, King of Pontus, an ardent enemy of Rome, defeating his army and forcing the king first to flee, and then to commit suicide.

Crassus was an equally impressive man. He was enormously wealthy, having obtained concessions that allowed him to run the public mines, and with those earnings invested in real estate speculation. When Caesar ran for the office of Pontifex Maximus, Crassus almost single-handedly bankrolled his campaign, helping him to a landslide victory. Crassus was also an excellent general, and subdued Spartacus's slave rebellion, which was no small task. It took two years and between six and eight legions to quell the revolt led by men willing to die for their cause. Crassus defeated them on the battlefield and then crucified the survivors along the Via Appia. Thousands suffered in great agony for days on those terrible crosses, so that no one would again dare to challenge Rome, its social order, or its economy.

Pompey and Crassus were both elected consuls in 70 BC. Crassus was forty-five and wealthy, Pompey thirty-six and laden with glory. Caesar was only thirty then, but was already keeping his eye on them. He knew that, despite their formal alliance, the two of them hated each other, and that the oligarchs were playing one against the other even though they feared both. He liked the possibility of allying himself with them and becoming the balancing factor. Crassus needed Pompey's enormous popularity, and the other two needed the influence Crassus's wealth bought in the Senate. Caesar was popular with Rome's restless plebeians and adored by the soldiers who'd fought under him.

The so-called Catiline conspiracy illuminates both the flavor of Roman public life and Julius Caesar's complex personality. The event unfolded like a political thriller with protagonists of enormous stature: Caesar; Cicero; Cato; and, playing the part of the villain, Lucius Sergius Catilina. The most mysterious of the four is surely the last, but Caesar played the most ambiguous role. Marcus Porcius Cato of Utica was the great grandson of the other Cato, nicknamed the Censor because of the severity of his wardrobe and stubborn conviction that Carthage must be destroyed (he coined the famous phrase saying just that, "Carthago delenda est"). Marcus Porcius defended republican ideals and the Senate's role with that same sense of conviction. Anyone who attacked the institutions of the state was his enemy, including Silla, Cataline, and the first triumvirate (Caesar, Crassus, and Pompey). When civil war erupted between Pompey and Caesar, Cato sided with Pompey, believing he was less dangerous to the Republic. Once the battles began he stopped cutting his hair and beard as a sign of mourning for his wounded homeland. When Pompey and his followers were defeated, Cato was exiled to Utica, where he committed suicide.

Cato of Utica is a magnificent figure about whom, unfortunately, little is known. Ezio Raimondi attributed to him the traits "of a Roman hero added to those of a Biblical patriarch." Dante placed him on the shore outside purgatory, custodian of places, his face illuminated by the "four sacred lights," the cardinal virtues (Prudence, Justice, Fortitude, and Temperance) that he possessed even without the grace of revelation. In introducing him to the poet, Virgil describes him this way:

> Now may it please you to approve his coming;
> his goal is liberty, and one who has
> forfeited life for that knows how dear it is.

> You know, for whom death tasted not bitter
> In Utica where you laid aside the clothing
> That on the great day will give off such shining.[3]

Dante made Cato into a symbol of moral freedom, strength of character, a sense of justice, and dedication to the common good. In the face of his great morality the fact that he was also a pagan and a suicide could justifiably be overlooked. In his *Convivio* he wrote:

> There were then very ancient philosophers, the first and most important of whom was Zeno, who perceived and believed that the end of human life consisted solely of strict integrity—that is, in strictly, unreservedly following truth and justice . . . They and their sect were called Stoics, and to them belonged that glorious Cato . . .[4]

Yet even Cato could earn a rebuke. It came from Mommsen, who deemed him a conservative, one of those who "wanted to conserve the Republic principally to let it die."

How and why did this conspiracy come about? Thrice Catiline ran for consul and each time, with excuses and gerrymandering, and in part also due to Cicero's own astute maneuvering, he was defeated. In the election of 64 BC Cicero was a candidate as well, and was the most likely to win. He ran on what we might today call the aristocrat's ticket, and he was up against Catiline and Caius Antonius Hybrida, both of whom were supported (officially) by the plebeians and assisted by the important influence exercised by Caesar and the wealthy Crassus. Hybrida was the weaker of the two popular candidates, and for that reason Cicero secretly promised to swing some of his votes to him. He did, and Hybrida was elected. Catiline came in third and was, in contemporary jargon, first among the excluded.

What role did Caesar and Crassus play in this affair? It seems likely that they assisted Hybrida, assuming that, once elected, he would be a more docile instrument than the restless and energetic Catiline, a man of sly charm and broad appeal among the masses. This brings us to the point—who was Catiline, really? Was he an unscrupulous rebel who plotted against the state, or an ardent reformer detested by Cicero and the conservative party? It seems most likely that he was what we might today call a populist demagogue, a figure who was able to simultaneously attract the interest of both progressive and conservative elements. One of his campaign promises was to cancel debts, which would've been a popular proposal for a society in which money lending typically entailed usurious interest rates. Rich and poor alike were often heavily in debt, and if you wanted to run for public office—especially for re-election—you could not afford to be stingy. This particular plank in his election platform, as we'd call it today, may have pushed Crassus to oppose Catiline, since Crassus was one of the biggest moneylenders of that period. Catiline's platform also included the redistribution of land, a proposal that would have impacted large landholders, and the granting of certain rights to women and slaves. These may all have been sorely needed reforms, but in a society as conservative as ancient Rome they could also cause social instability. Catiline used his proposals to seek the support of small businessmen on the verge of bankruptcy, outcasts, and the plebian class. Cicero and Sallust did everything they could to paint his supporters as the dregs of society. Nor is there any doubt that Catiline also attracted adventurers and the kind of hothead who's always present whenever there's the promise of a fight. But if they had only been the dregs of Roman society the end of the story would have been different.

Catiline ran for office again in 63 BC on a decidedly leftist platform. He was an aristocrat of minor nobility, but was nonetheless a Roman patrician who sided openly with the plebeians. We mustn't, however, think of him as an idealist, or prophet of nineteenth-century socialism a bit ahead of his time. Catiline was an ambitious man who was even ready to kill in his quest for power; he was fiercely determined and courageous (as he would demonstrate), but also as capable as anyone else of seeking his own advantage in every possible maneuver. His campaign was probably awkward and conducted with excessive vehemence, without the political and strategic ability Caesar would display a few years later when he played essentially the same electoral game. Catiline was deemed guilty of extremism, and this allowed Cicero some room to maneuver. Taking advantage of his position as Consul, he was once again able to draw away some of Catiline's supporters.

Naturally the other two candidates, supported by Caesar and Crassus, won the election, and Catiline again found himself relegated to the position of first runner up. His plot started at that moment, and at that moment he decided it was worth risking his own life, thus transforming himself into a revolutionary idealist. In a certain sense this redeemed him, at least in the eyes of the historians who accept this hypothesis of the events. It was a woman, Fulvia, who was the first to reveal the plot. Entrusted with (or perhaps worming out) the secrets of her lover, she thought she might profit from taking the information to Cicero. Sallust wrote in his *De coniuratione Catilinae*, "She decided that such a serious danger to the state must not be concealed."[5] In reality the reason for the betrayal was much less noble; her lover was short of cash, and to jumpstart a languid relationship he alluded to future riches. Her curiosity aroused, Fulvia badgered him with questions until he confessed everything. Thus she learned that the conspirators were planning a few murders in the city and would be supported by rebellious troops. Caesar was able to furnish additional information, since he operated at the margins of the plot, waiting to see what happened but careful not to be too involved, in case things went badly. Even Crassus helped, and turned over threatening letters that were considered convincing evidence, despite the fact that they were anonymous and likely penned by him or his followers.

Cicero, as Consul, was granted complete authority by the Senate to deal with the crisis. But because he was not a courageous man, he also kept a phalanx of bodyguards so large that according to Plutarch, in his biography of Cicero, "when he came into the Forum it was filled almost entirely by his entourage." On November 8 the Senate met at the highly fortified Temple of Jupiter Stator, at the foot of the Palatine Hill. Whether as an insolent gesture, or to belie any accusation that he was complicit in the revolt taking place in Etruria, Catiline appeared at this meeting, although he sat apart from the other senators. He was still unaware that Cicero, who would soon take the floor, was prepared to accuse him, in one of the best political and legal orations of all time, of crimes that would be punished by *damnatio memoriae*, expunging his name from all public records. Cicero asked him, rhetorically, "Quo usque tandem abutere, Catilina, patientia nostra? Quam diu etiam furor iste tuus nos eludet? Quem ad finem sese effrenata iactabit audacia?" [When, O Catiline, do you mean to cease abusing our patience? How long is that madness of yours still to mock us? When is there to be an end of that unbridled audacity of yours, swaggering about as it does now?]⁶ Memorable words indeed, but Catiline seemed impervious enough to them that the Consul ordered his arrest, perhaps for breach of the peace. If Sallust is to be believed, the rebel answered this charge with a direct challenge: "Since I am encompassed by foes and hounded to desperation, I will check the fire that threatens to consume me by pulling everything down about your ears."⁷ He then left the Senate to join his troops in Fiesole.

In the meantime the conspirators faithful to Catiline set their coup d'état for December 17, first day of the Saturnalia. Catiline behaved as if he were unaware that the Roman legions were marching against his troops and that a plot like his, unveiled so publicly, is no longer of any value—and is no longer even a conspiracy, but merely a prelude to massacre. Why was his behavior so seemingly illogical? We have no answer, and any attempt at one remains speculative, leaving each of us to imagine whatever seems most convincing. One of the possibilities, though, is that the rebel knew that if he stayed in Rome he would certainly be assassinated. Leaving as if he wanted to go into exile may have offered him a greater chance for survival.

The end of this was both pitiful and epic. The five conspirators who stayed in Rome were arrested and strangled in prison after a lively debate in the Senate. A few days later, on a cold morning in January of 62 BC, Catiline confronted the praetorians in Tuscany, near Pistoia. The battle was ruthless and drawn out; at the end the rebel's body was found, still palpitating, amidst a pile of cadavers, and his decapitation swiftly ordered. According to Sallust, "Only when the battle was over could the daring and ferocity with which Catiline's troops had fought be fully appreciated. Practically every man lay dead in the battle station which he had occupied while he lived."[8]

And what of Caesar? The fact that his behavior was ambiguous was evident as early as December 5, as the Senate was debating what to do with the five conspirators locked up in the Mamertine prison. In his position as Praetor Elect, he took the floor and, according to Sallust, began by condemning Catiline and his followers in no uncertain terms. He then continued by saying that there was no punishment sufficient for their crime, and that in any case the Senate's decisions were absolute. At that point, and with a subtle sophistry, he suggested that the immortal gods had conceived of death not as a punishment, but as a natural end to life. Thus the lives of Catiline and his co-conspirators should be spared, since death would finish both their lives and their punishments. He drew the assembly's attention to the very real danger that any executions would be followed by rioting and unrest, and concluded by saying that there was a punishment much harsher than death—life in prison.

His discourse is still thought of as an oratorical masterpiece. Even if there was no certain proof that Caesar was involved in the conspiracy, everyone knew that he was at least watching it with great interest. His position in the chamber that day was difficult; had he supported the death penalty, he would have repudiated members of the party he traditionally relied on for support, and had he opposed it he would have fueled the suspicions already harbored against him. He extricated himself from this difficulty with great skill, avoiding the problem by suggesting, amongst other things, that it was unconstitutional to condemn a Roman citizen to death without guaranteeing him the right to appeal to the people. His skill lay in supporting a penalty so severe that it made death seem inadequate. On one hand he recognized the Senate's right to condemn the guilty to death, and on the other hand, arguing against it, he stressed the danger of popular uprisings to an audience of timorous men (beginning with Cicero). He was able to confuse their verdict, extinguishing the apparent determination with which the meeting opened. Only he could have succeeded in such a delicate task. Crassus, for example, was also suspected of being sympathetic to the plot, but he didn't even appear that day. The speech's effect was extraordinary. Everyone who spoke afterward gave his support to the proposal, and one senator was so moved by his words that he suggested capturing Catiline alive and bringing him back to the Senate for examination.

At this point, however, there was a coup de théâtre. Rising up from one of the back benches, Marcus Cato, Tribune of the Plebians Elect, began to speak. He was thirty-two, five years younger than Caesar, and his discourse had all the greatness of his rival's. He criticized Caesar and the cowardliness of the Senate, saying that with such a grave conspiracy there could be no hesitation, that death was the only punishment that fit the dimension of the crime, and that any penalty inflicted with a trembling hand would be ruinous for the Republic. Speaking thus, he stirred the conscience of the senators, riling them such that, one by one, they stood up to join him, revealing how they intended to vote. The passion that resonated through the room with his words was broken only when Cato, who noticed that a message had been delivered to Caesar, took the occasion to accuse him of communicating with enemies of the state even in the Senate chambers. This was a misstep that allowed Caesar to score a small point against him as he revealed the note, which turned out to be a love letter from Servilia, his lover as well as Cato's half-sister.

This was the first time that Caesar and his more important adversary tangled. Despite his gaffe, Cato prevailed, although no one understood that with his victory he had also sealed his own destiny. Sallust put the two rivals on almost the same level of oratorical skill and *magnitudo animi*, proclaiming their greatness of spirit:

> Caesar was esteemed for the many kind services he rendered and for his lavish generosity; Cato, for the consistent uprightness of his life.

The former was renowned for his humanity and mercy; the latter had earned respect by his strict austerity. Caesar won fame by his readiness to give, to relieve, to pardon, Cato by never offering presents. The one was a refuge for the unfortunate, and was praised for his good nature; the other was a scourge for the wicked, admired for his firmness.[9]

A few years later, in 59 BC, Caesar, who had been elected Consul with Marcus Calpurnius Bibulus, proposed a land reform that would reapportion land in favor of Pompey's veterans and Rome's poor. Bibulus, a close friend of Cato's, tried to oppose him by rallying senators against the proposal. Caesar bypassed his co-consul and took his reform bill directly to the popular assembly. The night before the vote Caesar's followers occupied the Forum, and the next morning when Bibulus arrived he could just barely make his way through the crowd, amid many insults. He tried to speak but they wouldn't let him, and the fasces carried by his lictors, symbols of his consular authority, were broken. The next day the Consul went to the Senate to report this violence, but nothing happened. Their indignation was great, but the senators' fear was even greater. The meeting served only to demonstrate that the old order of the Republic could no longer control the difficult demands of these new times. Infuriated, Bibulus withdrew to his own house and announced he wouldn't leave it again. His intent was a dramatic gesture to show that law was dead and liberty no longer existed in Rome, but given the circumstances he succeeded only in proving his own impotence. The people asked that the agrarian legislation be approved, and the Senate conceded. Caesar's enemies spread the cynical joke that the Consuls were no longer Caesar and Bibulus, but rather Julius and Caesar.

Years passed, and things ended as they did with Pompey because not even Rome was large enough for both men. Crassus died fighting the Parthians, and Caesar suffered a moment of weakness after the unsatisfactory result of his British expedition. His old enemy Marcus Porcius Cato insisted that he be charged, at the end of his commission in Gaul, with breaking Roman law for his behavior. Pompey was now quite close to the oligarchs; his wife Julia, who was also Caesar's daughter, had died, and this further weakened the bonds between them, as if their respective ambitions—now in open conflict—weren't enough to break all ties. Caesar was in Gaul; he was asked to return, but had no intention of doing so as a simple general. He feared Cato and the Senate, and wanted an elected post that would guarantee him immunity and shelter him from their attacks. There was no solution to this problem, and no one in Rome tried much to find one. As tensions continued to rise, things began to happen, propelled in part by inertia. When the *Optimate*, the aristocratic party, convinced Pompey to side openly with them against Caesar, the Senate got its resolve back. When all attempts at negotiations failed, it ordered the rebellious general to lay down his arms.

In January of 49 BC, Caesar camped out, awaiting the outcome of the debate, along the banks of a small river, the Rubicon. Though it may have been an insignificant stream, it nevertheless marked the insuperable border of the Republic. The general had to make a decision, and in doing so left us yet another of his striking slogans, "Alea iacta est" ("the die is cast"). The civil war had begun, and it would be fought over a vast territory, first in Spain, then Greece, and finally in Africa. The decisive moment of the war occurred in Thessaly, at the Battle of Pharsalus. Seventy thousand men met in battle, and Caesar won thanks to impeccable military tactics that forced his rival to flee. Pompey requested asylum in Egypt, but the Pharaoh, Ptolemy XIII, instead ordered him assassinated in order to ingratiate himself with the victor. When Caesar arrived in Alexandria on October 2, 48 BC, he found his rival's body and was not pleased. The treacherous pharaoh had misjudged the situation; he wanted to offer Caesar Pompey's head, but was unaware of the complex emotions that had bound the two Romans before their final conflict. Nor could he imagine that his sister, Cleopatra, would spark the strongest passions of the general's life.

Caesar's physical vigor included an almost insatiable energy for lovemaking. Suetonius attempted a list of all the Roman matrons he had seduced; although far from complete, it includes: Postumia, wife of Servius Sulpicius; Lollia, wife of Aulus Gabinius; Tertulla, wife of Marcus Crassus; and Mucia, Pompey's wife. It doesn't include all the virgins, slaves, and foreign women he bedded, nor the two or perhaps three great loves of his life. First amongst them was Servilia, who, in the twenty years of their relationship, Caesar showered with gifts— including an almost priceless pearl—worth some six million sesterces.

Servilia was Marcus Brutus's mother, and it is not impossible that Caesar was his father, or at least that was the rumor that was whispered around Rome for a long time. When Servilia noticed her lover might be tiring of her, she pushed her young daughter Terzia into his bed, thus doubling his familial ties with Brutus, who had Caesar as both father and a brother-in-law.

Then there was Cleopatra—legend, the East, lust, and politics all mixed with love—a love lived as an explosion of sensuality in which reciprocal ambition and common interests doubled the pleasure of the lovers' embraces. When Caesar arrived in Alexandria and met Cleopatra, he was already a mature man of fifty-two. She was only twenty, but what she already knew of love could be compared with the knowledge of Venus herself. Cleopatra and her brother, Ptolemy XIV, were fighting over succession to the throne. The Ptolomies were the exhausted heirs to Pharaonic Egypt, a family that had no scruples about resorting to intermarriage and incest in order to guarantee its hold on power. Ptolemy X married his daughter Berenice after she had been married to his brother, Ptolemy XI. At twenty Cleopatra married her brother when he was just thirteen. Suicide was also common in the family, and Cleopatra died, it seems, by letting an asp bite her after she had been the lover of Caesar and Mark Antony and had tried, in vain, to seduce Octavian as well. It is true that her charms were no longer what they had once been, but it was also true that Octavian Augustus had an ironclad list of priorities and Cleopatra was just not one of them.

When Caesar arrived in Alexandria he found another royal sister, Arsinoe, who was no less power-hungry than the other Ptolomies. He tried unsuccessfully to reconcile the quarrelsome siblings by offering each a share of power. Instead he barely escaped an attempted assassination; his enemies had been able to poison the water in his residence. He was thus forced to confront Ptolemy and rout him from the field. Arsinoe was taken to Rome in chains, and Cleopatra, now sure of the throne, gave her victorious lover the best honeymoon a man has ever enjoyed. According to Suetonius (perhaps spitefully written) Caesar was so enamored of her charms and her inexhaustible ability to inflame his lust that he might have followed her all the way to Ethiopia, had he not noticed that his soldiers wouldn't follow him. He was limited to sailing on the Nile with her on a ship gently propelled by oarsmen. The whole of its stern had been transformed into a magnificent bridal chamber. It was April of 47 BC, the air stirred with refreshing breezes, and the verdant banks of the great river were dotted with palm trees, wells, small villages and the impressive gilt piers of ancient temples, vestiges of a mysterious religion. A small flotilla of boats escorted the flagship, allowing for periodic replenishments and for its passengers to go ashore for brief hunting trips. Two months passed under the spell of this enchantment, and later Cleopatra would say that her son, whom she named Caesarion, was conceived during those weeks.

This idyll ended, however, with troubling news that required an urgent response from Caesar. King Pharnaces of Pontus (modern Turkey), son of Mithridates and sworn enemy of Rome, had defeated Caesar's lieutenant on the battlefield. This defeat had to be redressed immediately, as Pontus was a Roman province its loss would be a dangerous sign of weakness—a possibility far worse than the fact that Pharnaces was executing Roman citizens in horrendous ways. Caesar slipped away from Cleopatra's embraces and marched his army directly to Pontus, where he set up camp less than a mile away from Zela, the stronghold were Pharnaces had barricaded himself. He soon realized that the petty despot was an incompetent strategist whose poorly led troops were easily slaughtered. Caesar promised his soldiers all the city's plunder, and took Zela in less than five days. Afterward he sent Rome the briefest, proudest dispatch ever issued by a general, "Veni, vidi, vinci" [I came, I saw, I conquered].

This legendary dispatch brings us to another of Caesar's characteristics, the geniality of his communications and his extraordinary ability to project an ever-positive image of himself, underscoring each favorable circumstance and disguising the negative. His literary works and the accounts of his military campaigns were masterpieces not only for the quality of the writing but also for the ability with which he could bend history to suit his own needs. Only Napoleon could do better—he always offered the most flattering accounts of himself, sending notices to his government of resounding victories even when his armies were devastated by dysentery and the battles were in reality skirmishes with some small band of marauders. Caesar didn't behave much differently. In 61 BC he left to govern Western Hispania, knowing that such a post would provide him with enough money to pay off his enormous debts. But he wanted something else from the assignment—the military glory that would make him Pompey's match on the battlefield. He thus began to wage war, sometimes for valid reasons, more often based on mere pretext, as was the case when he ordered the mountain people of the Sierra Estrella to relocate en masse to the lowlands. He had no valid reason, and when they refused he attacked, slaughtering them, and even pursuing them as far as the coast.

Upon Pompey's death, the war against his followers continued until their final defeat at the Battle of Thapsus (now in Tunisia) in 46 BC. Cato, who was not yet fifty years old, took refuge in Utica, but when he realized that all was lost he committed suicide. Dante's melancholy verses come to mind:

> His goal is liberty, and one who has
> forfeited life for that knows how dear it is.
> You know, for whom death tasted not bitter
> In Utica . . .[10]

The Senate granted unprecedented honors to the victor. For days on end ceremonies were held in Rome, and there were at least four triumphal processions put on for Caesar—for his victories in Gaul, Egypt, Pontus, and Africa. In the first, chained up behind Caesar's chariot, was Vercingetorix, the young nobleman who had successfully united the Gallic and Averni tribes and then, in 52 BC, engaged Caesar in what would be one of his hardest-won battles. Caesar held him captive for more than six years before putting him on display at his triumph, and had him executed afterward. Cleopatra, official mother of his only son, was invited to the second triumph, and her greatest joy was seeing her sister and rival, Arsinoe, paraded about in chains. The processions left from the Campus Martius, skirted the Circus of Flaminius, crossed the Velabrum, and then followed the Via Sacra up to the temple of Jupiter Optimus Maximus on the Capitoline Hill. The streets overflowed with a noisy, excited, undulating crowd, and long lines passed by displaying booty and panels painted with scenes from this or that battle, or illustrating the places they were fought (popular tally claimed that Caesar had fought in fifty battles and killed more than a million enemies). The prisoners followed, carrying their own chains. The presence of Arsinoe, a woman, was a scandalous novelty (even if Caesar spared her life, and had Vercingetorix strangled as rebel and traitor). The lictors came next, carrying the fasces decorated with laurel branches, and only then did the victor's chariot appear, drawn by pairs of white horses and greeted by the joyous shouts of the crowd. The triumphant general wore a scarlet toga and a laurel wreath on his head. His face was painted red because he was meant to represent Jupiter, whose protection was credited for his victory. He held a scepter crowned with a Roman eagle in his right hand, and a slave stood behind him holding a gold crown over his head, whispering constantly in his ear, "Remember that you are a man." Caesar's chariot was followed by the legionnaires who fought with him, and who were now briefly allowed to utter comments making fun of their leader.

In Caesar's case their mocking focused on his baldness, as well as his fame as a womanizer: "Citizens, watch your womenfolk. We're following the bald-headed lover." Another taunt, which this time annoyed Caesar enough that he forbade it, regarded a youthful lapse in Bythnia. In one of his first foreign missions, Caesar was sent to Asia Minor as ambassador to Nicomedes III, the cultured king who ruled Bythnia, a strip of land that bordered both the Black Sea and the Sea of Marmara. His mission was to convince the king to supply ships to assist the Roman blockade of Mytiline. Nicomedes agreed, but he hesitated, and the ships were late to arrive. Caesar was finally able to get them to depart, but in the time he spent in the kingdom he and Nicomedes were lovers. Roman merchants who had been there then spread the news at home that Caesar had become the Queen of Bythnia. The soldiers recited an irreverent and satirical couplet that went, more or less, "Caesar triumphs in subduing the Gauls; Nicomedes did not triumph in subduing Caesar." Even Cicero reproached him with that.

Magnificent spectacles in the circuses and theaters followed the triumphal processions. Famous gladiators fought in the arenas, while both comedies and tragedies were staged all over town, in every language of the empire. A system of curtains covered the whole of the Via Sacra, shielding the public from the fierce rays of the sun, and twenty thousand tables had been laid out so that everyone would have enough to eat. For five days there were fights to the death amongst prisoners and inmates condemned to the death penalty. The festivities included a thousand men, sixty horsemen, forty elephants, and the greatest curiosity—a giraffe, an animal never before seen in Rome, which inspired screams of admiration and great applause. The Campus Martius was flooded to create an artificial lake on which two groups of ships fought a mock naval battle. Suetonius recounts that so many people came to Rome that many were sleeping in improvised tents or even on the streets, and that "often the pressure of the crowd crushed people to death. The victims included two senators."[11] At the end of all of it, the booty was divvied up, and it's been estimated that in the two-year period from 46 to 44 BC Caesar had about twenty million gold coins minted from war plunder. Veterans received generous sums, and smaller amounts were distributed to the masses of disinherited people.

In March of 45 BC the last of Pompey's supporters were crushed in Munda, Spain, and from that time on Caesar had no rivals. The Senate was excessive in its recognitions—Caesar's person was declared inviolable, and it conferred on him the title of dictator, with the power to nominate candidates for the highest offices, for ten years. Freed from any military responsibilities, he was able to dedicate himself to public life, which he conducted at his usual frenetic pace. The overall goal of his legislative agenda was to reduce or eliminate the disparities created by the oligarchs at the expense of the plebian class. He promulgated one law that forbade overly ostentatious displays of wealth, and had it enforced so rigorously that even tables already set for banquets were commandeered. He strove to find work for his veterans, established that provincial commands were to be limited to two-year periods in order to contain corruption, and at the same time fought the electoral favoritism and corruption that had been useful to him in the past. He commissioned building projects meant to reduce chaos in the capital, championed land reclamation in the swamps south of Rome, began building new roads and bridges, and undertook the planning of an enormous theater. Caesar never saw the last project to completion; it was left to Augustus to finish, and he called it the Theater of Marcellus. Until that time the Romans had followed a lunar calendar, so that every two years they had to add a month in the middle, and often this adjustment was carelessly done with regard to the movement of the heavenly bodies. Caesar instituted a solar year with 365 days and a leap year every fourth year.

One can only imagine what sort of day a man like Caesar had—involved as he was in so many grandiose projects—the sort of atmosphere that must've surrounded him, and the pace at which his secretary and chancellor's office had to work. It is said that he read even at the theater, and that he responded quickly and apparently effortlessly to letter, petitions, and supplications. He was absorbed by his work, and each day grew more aware of the stature he was assuming. He considered the institutions of the Republic to be obstacles. For this reason, probably, he increased the number of senators from six hundred to nine hundred; he wanted them bogged down in debates, leaving him both the task and joy of making decisions and putting them into action. It's true that he valued some of their advice as individuals; what he found intolerable was the institution as a whole, a body that several times over the course of his life had close brushes with cowardice and uselessness.

Caesar was beset by a single worry—the Parthian Kingdom, beyond the Euphrates River, bordering the province of Syria. In 53 BC Crassus had gone there to fight the Parthians, who defeated and subsequently killed him. Now the situation had worsened, and Syria was in the hands of a Pompeian rebel. It was said that the plan Caesar was hatching was grandiose, and that he wanted an expedition so audacious that it would seem like a dazzling burst of fire capable of overshadowing the fame of Alexander the Great. On January 1, 44 BC, Caesar declared that before he left Rome he would relinquish each of his offices. He was unaware that he had less than eighty days to live.

His final testament was recorded in September of 45 BC. His principal heir was his eighteen-year-old great nephew, who was a very promising lad despite his sickly disposition. His name was Gaius Octavius, and Caesar left him both his name and a good part of his estate. Once again his foresight would prove accurate; this ailing youth would become Caesar Augustus, the first and perhaps greatest of the Roman emperors. At the end of 45 and the beginning of 44 BC, the Senate conferred on Caesar a series of new honors that were now unjustified by any military victories. He was given the right to wear triumphal garb all the time and his lictorial fasces were always to be decorated with laurel leaves. He received the title of *pater patriae*, "Father of his Country," his birthday was made a public holiday, and the month of his birth was renamed—*Julius*, July—in his honor. His statue had to decorate every temple, and during Senate meetings he could sit upon a golden seat and wear the golden crown of the Etruscan kings. Last but not least, his dictatorship was extended for the rest of his lifetime. His rule had become, in effect, a monarchy, and even more than that, a cult. That particular kind of administration, Ceasarism, is named after him.

As a leader he was greater than all other warriors and politicians, and only Napoleon, Augustus, Alexander the Great, and a very few others can be compared to him. The massive scope of his undertakings, his fulminating genius, his gifts as a writer, and the luck that seemed to accompany him throughout his life all helped him reach that height. But his conception of public affairs and power was so flexible and ambiguous that it also took a weighty toll.

It is possible that the accusation that he wanted to be named King of Rome was unjustified. It hardly seems likely that Caesar aspired to the throne, and certainly not because he considered himself unworthy of it; there was, rather, a practical reason. He preferred to keep the title of dictator for life because it allowed him to exercise absolute power without the obligations and encumbrances of a dynasty. Together with his power, he wanted to keep the affection of the people. He liked the skilful interweaving he was able to create between control of the army, mild police repression, and populism— a dangerous form of authority founded on demagoguery and personal charisma that has been imitated in every period, including our own, and which is, at its core, anti-democratic. A so-called democratic dictator does not govern against the people, although he certainly needs a loyal police force, a secret service whose eyes and ears can reach where needed, money to bribe with, and informers to know what is happening. Such a dictator must also be a man capable of appearing in public without fear, sure enough to receive the ovation from the crowd he so enjoys saluting from a tribune, balcony, or TV screen with a broad, calm gesture. The democratic dictator is not the watchful, circumspect tyrant who mercilessly eliminates his adversaries, about whom imprecations are uttered from the corner of men's mouths, nor the leader who, as he passes, is followed by a chorus of curses. His power lies somewhere between repression and consensus, the imposition of his will and listening to the real concerns of the people, a cult of personality and the total identification (or confusion) of his personal interests with those of the state. The functioning of democracy is complicated, slow, and expensive. The democratic dictator cuts the costs, accelerates decision making by eliminating any balance of powers, and offers certain advantages. In exchange he is free to limit liberties and impose his will as the only legitimate power. He wants to be feared, but won't give up being loved. The democratic dictator sees himself as the father of his people, and like a father he reserves the right to reward or punish at his discretion. His reign is the exact opposite of democracy.

It's perfectly understandable that Caesar might have taken pleasure in the extra honors bestowed upon him in the last months of his life. It's harder to imagine the reasons the Senate prostrated itself in such a way. Was it simply an excess of cowardliness on the part of the senators, or was it an underhanded way to ruin him? In antiquity no one really knew where to draw the line between men and the gods. By making Caesar more like a god than a king, did the senators perhaps hope to push him to such vertiginous heights that a ruinous fall was more than likely? The higher the dictator went, the more frequent were the signs of impatience, not so much among the people, who were kept giddy with generous gifts and spectacles, as among the nobility and intellectuals. It is always a minority who first notice the signs that the state is yielding, and they suffer from it by adding the inevitable problems of the future to the woes of the present. This was also the case with Caesar. Few worried, and most focused on enjoying the lavish beneficence of the democratic dictator. At the height of the Republic, the *populus* was one of the two pillars—the Senate being the other—of established power. This was no longer true, and there was little left of that conscience and function. The *populus* was for the most part reduced to the uninformed masses.

Only one title was missing to complete Caesar's pile of honors— that of king. There were repeated indications that, in one way or another, it would eventually be granted him. One day his statue on the tribune of the orators was decorated with a crown. In January, as he was entering the city on horseback, there were shouts of "Rex, rex!" ("King, king!") from the crowd that had gathered to greet him. He responded that his name was Caesar not Rex, even though that was, in effect, his grandmother's family name. Having made the distinction, he also made sure that those people in the crowd who were immediately stopped by the police were not punished. A more significant episode came, however, in the middle of February, a month before his assassination, during the festival of the Lupercalia. The priests of the ancient cult of Faunus Lupercus celebrated rites favoring female fertility that were rooted in the myth of Romulus, Remus, and the legendary she-wolf who suckled them. Caesar presided over the festivities wrapped in a purple mantle. While he sat on a gilded seat, his consular colleague, Mark Antony, who had taken part in the traditional run of the Luperci (priests of the cult), dressed only in a loin cloth made of goatskin, tried twice to place a crown on his head, and twice Caesar pushed away both the symbol and recognition he carried.

What did that gesture mean? And what can be made of Caesar's refusal of the crown? There have been many different interpretations. Had Mark Antony, one of Caesar's most loyal confidants, made a spontaneous gesture? Or, sensing the danger, did he want to provoke the dictator to test his will? Or was it Caesar who suggested the gesture to gauge what the reaction might be among the crowd? Perhaps Caesar asked his colleague to play that role so he could publicly refuse the crown and thus allay suspicions of his ambition. We must not forget that in the Republic the death penalty was prescribed for anyone who tried to make himself king. At that moment Caesar already had regal powers, and a formal recognition of them would have made little difference in the reality of his authority. But it would have been important from a dynastic point of view, and this was the issue of particular concern to his allies. Cleopatra was in Rome at that time, staying in Caesar's gardens across the Tiber, and she had Caesarion with her. He was the only son the dictator would ever have, if we exclude the possibility that he fathered Brutus. This gesture and its refusal were the subject of lively commentary. It was repeated over and over that what happened at the Lupercalia was just a trial run, that the real offer would come a month later, at the meeting of the senators on the Ides of March.

Not all the motivations behind Caesar's assassination are clear, nor is his behavior in the last days of his life. This is part of the fascination that this murder continues to exercise; crimes with aspects that have never been, nor can ever be, fully explained are always the most intense from a narrative point of view.

Is it plausible that a politician as astute as Caesar, expert in any possible maneuver, would not have understood that the recognitions showered upon him were making him the target of public hate? Even if he did not seek out such recognition, why did he allow it to be given? Does it seem reasonable that a man of his experience, now growing fairly old, would so completely have lost his sense of perspective? Was he intoxicated by all the honors, or did he think that they would bring him a permanent place in the memory of the Roman people, the only real kind of immortality he still believed in? Might not his behavior offer the ultimate proof that the vanity of men knows no bounds?

And what if, of all these possibilities, the real reason was something unconscious in his temperament, a hidden drive or instinct? Was it a completely existential motivation in a man now worn down by a life lived at a pace no one else could have sustained? It seems clear that he was not feeling well, that he was tired. According to Cicero, he, like Crassus, would never have returned from a war against the Parthians. Perhaps he was aware of this, or at least suspected it; in those last days he seemed to behave with an almost Eastern sort of fatalism. He knew he was surrounded by dangers, and yet he dismissed the loyal Spanish guards who escorted him when he moved around in public—unless going out unescorted in a dangerous place was meant as a challenge, a contemptuous gesture aimed at the conspirators, as if he wanted to say to them, "let's just see if you dare."

About sixty people took part in the conspiracy. There was, as with any political plot, all sorts of men among them—former followers of Pompey who wanted to avenge their leader, former partisans of Caesar who had abandoned him for personal grudges, professional plotters, and defenders of the Republic. Cassius Longinus and Marcus Brutus had become its leaders. The latter was Cato's nephew, and perhaps Caesar's own son. In any case his mother had for years been Caesar's favorite, and it was his sister's turn afterward; it's only understandable that Brutus's feelings about the dictator must have been complex. Dante confines him to hell (*Inferno*, Canto XXXIV, 64–65), placing him amongst the worst traitors. Shakespeare, on the other hand, makes him a great hero of freedom. Emotions aside, we can say that the conspirators were all upright men who were moved by a sincere love for the Republic, even if Cicero, in his cynical wisdom, wrote that they acted "with virile spirits but infantile intelligence." Their idea was that, once the tyrant was dead, the Republic would be restored to its ancient splendor, austere habits, and the intransigent, rustic morality that had made Rome great. Caesar had more foresight; he understood that that Republic could never return, and that there was much to be gained from entrusting Rome to men who were in themselves great—he himself, for example, and his adopted son Gaius Octavian (Caesar Augustus).

The conspirators were not necessarily shortsighted, but they were driven by political as well as military calculations. Caesar's supporters included Mark Antony, who was Consul, and Lepidus, his representative as dictator. Together they had several legions at their disposal, even without counting the veterans upon whom Caesar had bestowed such lavish gifts of land and money. Because in political calculations only the final result counts, it must be said that the outcome of Caesar's assassination (which would later be judged more of a mistake than a crime) was another fifteen years of civil war for Rome that ended only in 27 BC, when Octavian was granted the title of Augustus.

Perhaps Caesar foresaw all this on that March morning in 44 BC— certainly not the course of events or even his approaching death, but he probably foresaw his solitude, the weight of his existence, and the tremendous war he was setting off for in a few days. While his slaves were dressing him, Calpurnia came in and embraced him; she held him close, and was upset and trembling. She had dreamed—and not for the first time—that the roof of their house had been blown off in a storm, and she saw her husband's body covered in blood. Perhaps just then Caesar was considering not going to the Senate, but then Decimus Brutus interrupted, exhorting him not to insult the senators again by ignoring a meeting he himself had called. Then he ordered his litter to be brought, and was gone. Perhaps bumped by a passing slave, his statue next to the door fell over and shattered. Calpurnia screamed; Caesar ignored her and ordered his slaves to continue. For one last time he passed through the streets of Rome that Jérôme Carcopino so vividly evoked in his book *Daily Life in Ancient Rome*: "The *tabernae* were crowded as soon as they opened and spread their displays into the street. Here barbers shaved their customers in the middle of the fairway. . . . Elsewhere the owner of a cook-shop, hoarse with calling to deaf ears, displayed his sausages piping hot in their saucepan. . . . On the one hand, a money-changer rang his coins on a dirty table . . . and the quavering voices of beggars rehearsed their adventures and misfortunes to touch the hearts of the passers-by. . . . In sun or shade, a whole world of people came and went, shouted, squeezed, and thrust through the narrow lanes unworthy of a country village."[12]

Caesar glimpsed from behind the curtains of his litter the city he'd had such a large part in shaping. Those who recognized him shouted, "Imperator! Dictator!" A man approached him and thrust a parchment at him, saying that his master, Artemidorus of Cnidos, asked that he read it. When Caesar made a gesture that it should be given to a secretary, the man insisted, "Read it immediately and alone!" It was an exhortation to be vigilant, and went unheeded. Caesar's route took him across what is today the area of Piazza Venezia, proceeded along a street where the Via delle Botteghe Oscure now runs, and arrived at Largo di Torre Argentina, at the Curia of Pompey (whose statue he had ordered not be removed) at the edge of the piazza where today we can see the excavations with their impressive ruins. He saw Spurinna, the soothsayer who had warned him of the Ides of March in her lugubrious manner, turned toward her, and said jokingly, "You spoke to me of the Ides of March, and as you can see they have arrived." She replied, in a sinister voice, "But they have not yet passed."

Senators crowded the hemicycle of the curia dressed in white togas, a fearsome crowd, had they not been so amiable, of nine hundred people, almost all of whom were present for the occasion. While entering solemnly and approaching the statue of Pompey, Tullius Cimber appeared in front of Caesar and kneeled, taking hold of his toga and begging for a pardon for his brother. Caesar turned and was then surrounded by Cassius, Brutus, Casca, Trebonius, and Pontius Aquila. Tullius Cimber grabbed his arms; his act was no longer one of supplication, but one of violence. At first slowly, then with increasing fury, the others drew their blades and began to strike. Caesar attempted to react, but he had only a stylus in his hand. He planted that in someone, but it was not enough. He felt his blood flowing, the pain of the wounds on his back, neck, and groin. He huddled by the statue of Pompey to protect at least one of his flanks, and from there he saw his son, Brutus, as he was raising his knife. He had just enough time to pronounce the last of his messages, which would go down in history with the others: "Tu quoque, fili mi" [You, too, my son]. He then covered his face with his toga and collapsed.

An inspection of his corpse allowed the number of stab wounds to be confirmed—twenty-three in total—and established that only one of them, to the chest, was fatal; he would have survived the rest. Suetonius recorded the scene:

> Twenty-three dagger thrusts went home as he stood there. Caesar did not say a word after Casca's first blow had drawn a groan from him. . . . The entire Senate then dispersed in confusion, and Caesar was left lying dead for some time until three of his household slaves carried him home in a litter, with one arm hanging over the side. . . . He was fifty-five years old when he died, and he was deified immediately. . . . Very few of the assassins outlived Caesar for more than three years, or died naturally . . . some [used] the very daggers with which they had treacherously murdered Caesar to take their own lives.[13]

1. Appianus of Alexandria, *Roman History*, trans. Horace White (New York: The MacMillan Co., 1913), 501.

2. Suetonius, *Lives of the Caesars*, trans. Robert Graves (Baltimore: Penguin Books, 1957), 46–47.

3. Dante Alighieri, *Purgatorio*, trans. W. S. Merwin (New York: Alfred A. Knopf, 2000), canto 7, lines 70–75.

4. Dante Alighieri, *Convivio*, trans. Richard Lansing, 1988, bk. 4, ch. 6.

5. Sallust, *The Jugurthine War and The Conspiracy of Catiline*, trans. S. A. Handford (Baltimore: Penguin Books, 1957), 192.

6. Cicero, *Against Catiline*, ed. C. D. Yonge (http://perseus.uchicago.edu/hopper/text.jsp?doc=Perseus:text:1999.02.0019:text=Catil.)

7. Sallust, *The Jugurthine War*, 198–99.

8. Ibid., 233.

9. Ibid., 226.

10. Extract from Dante's *Purgatory*.

11. Suetonius, *Lives of the Caesars*, 27.

12. Jérôme Carcopino, *Daily Life in Ancient Rome. The People and the City at the Height of the Empire*, ed. Henry T. Rowell, trans. E. O. Lorimer (New Haven: Yale University Press, 1940), 48–49.

13. Suetonius, *Lives of the Caesars*, 46, 48–49.

IV

THE OTHER MICHELANGELO

ONE OF THE PRIVILEGES of living in Rome is the chance to freely admire, just as if they were any other regular church decoration, some of Caravaggio's greatest masterpieces—all you have to do is walk in and look. Anywhere else in the world, this alone would be enough to make a city famous. In Rome, on the other hand, the six gratis works by Caravaggio (I'm not counting the ones in various museums and galleries) get mixed right in with the rest of the city's marvels. Our tour of Caravaggio's work can begin in the Piazza del Popolo. Just inside the eponymous city gate is the church of Santa Maria del Popolo. According to legend, it was founded in 1099 to exorcise the ghost of Nero, which was apparently wandering restlessly near his family tomb. Santa Maria del Popolo houses works by Bramante, Pinturicchio, Raphael, Sebastiano del Piombo, Bernini, and Sansovino, among many others. Today, though, we'll only have eyes for Caravaggio's two canvases in the Cerasi Chapel, just to the left of the high altar. They represent *The Crucifixion of St. Peter* and *The Conversion of St. Paul*. Look at Saint Peter—he is old, but still vigorous even though he's had a trying life. Notice his executioners—they work like dogs to hoist the weight of the oppressive wooden cross and its burden. They're just poor devils with dirty feet who happen to make their living as jailors, and could just as well be construction workers or farmers. The year is 1601; the artist, in his thirties by now, was finally enjoying some success, and this painting was a harbinger of a new style in his work. Look at Saint Paul in the other painting— he lies flat on his back, his arms raised toward the heavens, terrified, and conquered by faith. His horse, one of the most beautiful in the history of painting, towers over him.

For the next stop I suggest we go to the sixteenth-century church of San Luigi dei Francesi. This is yet another church with no shortage of masterpieces (works by Domenichino, Guido Reni, and others), but we'll go straight to the Contarelli Chapel, which has three Caravaggios—*St. Matthew and the Angel*, *The Calling of St. Matthew*, and *The Martyrdom of St. Matthew*. These images are made powerful by the brutal realism of the martyrdom, the magic of the composition accentuated by a dramatically angled light, and the emotional presence of the figures—starting with Matthew himself, who is shown right at the moment when he abandons his job as tax collector to become a disciple of Christ. Caught at the decisive moment, stupefied, he points to himself with his finger, asking, "Me? You really want me, Lord?"

Our last stop is the church of Sant'Agostino, just a few feet from the Piazza Navona, whose facade is made of travertine blocks lifted from the Coliseum. Here we can admire the *Madonna di Loreto* (also called *Madonna of the Pilgrims*) one of the master's most moving and perplexing works. Even for a layman the extraordinary image of the Virgin, in reality just an ordinary Roman mother with her child in her arms, takes your breath away. She's a rather common beauty, as was Lena, the model who posed for this picture. The Virgin stands just above the two pilgrims kneeling in front of her; she is a slender figure, perhaps a little out of proportion, and listens intently to the travelers' prayers, her head inclined toward them. The coarse-looking youth on his knees is seen from behind, his large rear and big, dirty peasant feet facing the viewer. Next to him is a poor, wrinkled old woman, her hair held back in a dirty rag. Not until the nineteenth century would this type of realism, intense to the point of being visionary and yet quite stark, leave its imprint on an entire artistic current.

There could have been a seventh work by this extraordinary artist in yet another church, Santa Maria della Scala in Trastevere. Yet things happened differently, and today this supreme masterpiece is in Paris, at the Louvre.

To explain why Caravaggio painted the way he did, and how he arrived at his style, means exploring one of the most interesting moments in all of art history. The story's setting is Rome on the cusp between the sixteenth and seventeenth centuries—a time of disorder, savagery, miracles, and atrocities committed in the name of faith. In short, a city in perpetual turmoil, wracked by a hundred practical and religious problems, and full of risks; the life of Michelangelo

Merisi, called Caravaggio, became its mirror. The evidence we have highlights the artist's intemperance, arrogance, unsteadiness, and sudden outbursts. Might his nasty reputation come from the fragmentary nature of the news available to us, or is it instead shaped by the quality of his painting itself, from the dark depths of its realism? The Catholic Church had been badly shaken by the spread of Protestantism, and in response it tried to impose edifying, idealizing, and strongly ideological principles on art. Caravaggio painted as if the crude truths of life were revealing themselves for the first time—the saints and virgins don't stare rapturously toward the heavens, are not accompanied by garlands of angels, nor do they clasp their hands together in ecstatic prayer. Whether they reside in glory or are being gruesomely martyred, they remain human beings; their bodies show the signs of exhaustion, old age, illness, misery, and the weight of the flesh. There is torture and death in these pictures; victims fall to the ground in pools of their own blood, and their assassins stand over them, knife in hand, ready to deliver the final blow.

When Caravaggio arrived in Rome, in the autumn of 1592, he was barely twenty years old and totally unknown. A barber named Luca described him as "a large youth of twenty or twenty-five with a sparse black beard, chubby, with dark eyes and long eyelashes. He dresses untidily in black, his black socks are slightly ragged, and he wears his hair long in front." These words come from a police report, the inevitable result of one of the brawls the young painter was involved in—a hasty scuffle or sudden attack followed by a breathless chase, stifled cries in the Roman night, a yell, dark alleys with crumbling walls marred by trickling liquids of suspicious origin. Caravaggio's dark complexion has often been remarked on, and some have exaggerated its importance, attributing to his "long lashes and dark eyes" the character of his works. Giovan Pietro Bellori, an intellectual and art connoisseur who lived just after Caravaggio, from 1613 to 1696, wrote in his *Lives of the Modern Painters, Sculptors, and Architects*, "Caravaggio's manner corresponded to the appearance of his face. He had a dark complexion and dark eyes, his eyebrows and hair were black, and that color was reflected in his paintings."

Michelangelo Merisi was born in 1571, the fateful year in which the navy of the Holy League crushed the myth of Turkish invincibility at Lepanto. He trained in Milan and perhaps visited Venice, but by the time he was little more than twenty years old he was already in Rome, the mecca for every talented artist, just as Paris was at the end of the nineteenth century, and New York at the end of the twentieth century. He began as an apprentice in the shop of Giuseppe Cesari, known as Cavalier d'Arpino, and it's hard to imagine two more different personalities. The two men were almost the same age—Arpino was only about three years older than Caravaggio. Arpino had had a poor childhood, and was the son of a mediocre ex-voto painter. Because he knew how to find the right favors, including papal favors, he reached quick success. His paintings were elegant, decorative, facile, and therefore much in demand. Success kept him in good health, making him "happy, witty, and free of sentimentality." He did seem to succumb to melancholy at the end of his long life, which lasted from 1568 to 1640, but such things, among the old, aren't surprising.

Arpino had a lively workshop in the area around Piazza della Torretta, and many apprentices and young artists from Italy and Northern Europe worked there. Taking his cue from Raphael's workshop organization, Arpino meted out tasks to his studio assistants—an ornamental frame for one, some less important finishing work for another, a few flowers here, some fruit there. Twenty-year-old Caravaggio was part of this workshop, and was also lodged there, though his accommodations seem to have been scarce—little more than a pallet in a corner. He also painted flowers and fruit; according to Bellori, "he was set to painting flowers and fruits so well rendered that many others came to repeat those same charms that are so popular today." This lasted for about nine months, until there was an incident or some scuffle that left him with a badly wounded leg. He was sent to recover at the Ospedale della Consolazione, and upon leaving the hospital he wanted nothing more to do with the Cavalier d'Arpino or his shop. Traces of all the fruits and flowers he'd painted for Arpino can be found in his *Sick Bacchus* and *Boy with a Basket of Fruit*. The character of these two pieces, however, comes from the figures, and the contours of these two youths contain all of Caravaggio's later work.

Exactly which Rome did this clever, restless twenty-year-old get to know? The capital of the Catholic Church was, at the end of the sixteenth century, little more than a village crossed by wandering flocks of animals and strewn with majestic ruins. Its princely palaces rose up against an expanse of small houses. Most were only two stories, built of poor materials, and inhabited by even poorer people. The population was just over one hundred thousand, and outside the walls, as well as in parts of the city itself, were vast open areas with dense vegetation interrupted here and there by a buttress or the peak of some ancient ruin. Some Catholics were cheered by this landscape of ruin; the Jesuit Gregory Martin wrote in a letter dated 1581, "Where there was so much beauty on the seven hills, what is there now but desolation and solitude? Not a dwelling, not a house, only here and there good and holy churches of great piety . . . the kingdom of Christ has overturned the empire of Satan."

The abundance of holy buildings notwithstanding, Rome was as turbulent and dangerous as it always had been. In the classical period Juvenal had warned in one of his satires, "He who goes out at night goes to his death," and the poet Belli, in the nineteenth century, used that line as a title for one of his sonnets. In the sixteenth century venturing out into the dark and deserted streets after sunset could become a fatal adventure. Those who could defend themselves went out armed with a sword or a rapier even though they were officially banned. Respectable people, young women, and the elderly avoided going out at all after sunset. But there were, of course, those who did go out looking for adventure, including sexual adventure, in the dark of the night, regardless of the risk. Among them were many artists, including a hoard of foreigner painters attracted to Rome by the transparency of its incomparable light. They gathered in the taverns around the Platea Trinitatis (today the Piazza di Spagna), dominated by the Trinità dei Monti, the church that looked down on the square from the top of a steep, grassy slope. Here they held noisy parties and dinners that went on and on amidst jokes, laughter, vulgarities, and dares, all in an atmosphere of apparent camaraderie that often hid bitter feelings. Competition among artists was fierce, and often caused jealousy, disagreements, cheating, and swift exchange of accusations, including one of the most frequent and slanderous (as well as fraught with possible legal consequences)—sodomy.

Another densely populated area of the city lay on the slopes of the Capitoline Hill, including the Jewish Ghetto, extending to the edges of the Theater of Marcellus. Here you could go to places with names like the Taverna del Moro, del Lupo, dell'Orso, della Torre, or del Turco (Tavern of the Moor, Wolf, Bear, Tower, and Turk, respectively) and drink late into the night. It was also easy to find female companionship here, and women could be seen hurrying their clients along, sometimes toward home, sometimes straight to the nearest secluded corner. Bordellos were also densely packed in the area around the Mausoleum of Augustus.

The overabundance of priests, soldiers, adventurers, and pilgrims—all of them officially celibate or at least deprived of female company—meant that prostitutes flocked to Rome from all over, certain of secure earnings. It has been estimated that there were at least 13,000 prostitutes in Rome at the beginning of the seventeenth century, or eighteen for every hundred female residents of the city, including old women and children. Pope Leo X had turned prostitution into a source of income for the papal treasury, levying a special tax on them to pay for the construction of the Via di Ripetta. Rome is still today one of the few cities in the world where there is a square named after a famous courtesan, dubbed an honest courtesan, or high-class kept woman, as we might call her today. The Piazza Fiammetta, near the Via dei Coronari, gets its name from Fiammetta Michaelis, whose many lovers included Cesare Borgia, the illegitimate son of Pope Alexander VI, better known as Valentino, the nickname Machiavelli gave him. Fiammetta lived at Via Acquasparta 16, just at the corner of the little square that now carries her name. Like most of her colleagues, she went to the nearby church of Sant'Agostino to confess and pray, and also left generous gifts there on behalf of the souls in purgatory. She was buried there, although all traces of her tomb have long since disappeared.

Another salient characteristic of seventeenth-century Rome was the vast quantity of beggars who crowded the city's every street and intersection. For the most part they were professional mendicants—gypsies who were considered the epitome of poverty, or quintessential cheats, and they were often stereotyped in the collective imagination as shrewd thieves or kidnappers of children—or poor pilgrims looking for a little money so they could go home. According to the chronicler Camillo Fanucci, "in Rome you see nothing but beggars, and so many that it is impossible to walk without being surrounded by them." Pope Sixtus V branded them with very harsh words, saying that they wandered around like wild animals disturbing the meditations of the faithful with their lamentations. Caravaggio represented mendicants and cheats at work in some of his paintings. In *The Fortune Teller* a gypsy woman steals from her witless victim while reading his palm, and in *The Card Sharps* two picturesque swindlers are fleecing an inexperienced young man.

There were also those who treated the poor and marginalized with compassion. These included Saint Philip Neri, one of the most affable figures in Catholic tradition, who the people of Rome called Pippo Buono, or Pippo the Good. Neri spent his time in the poorest neighborhoods, prisons, and hospitals, paying special attention to the ubiquitous abandoned children who were destined for a life of crime or prostitution. With a mix of his native Florentine humor and his acquired Roman common sense, he entertained the children, made them sing, play, and smile, and at the same time tried to teach them something, keep them off the streets, and prevent them from going hungry.

The streets of Rome were a veritable theater, sometimes merry, sometimes sinister, and almost always unpredictable. In considering the spectacles played out there we mustn't exclude the public executions held in the square at the end of the Ponte Sant'Angelo (a convenient spot since it was close to the Tor di Nona prison), the Piazza del Popolo, and the Campo de'Fiori. In November of 1825, Angelo Targhini and Leonida Montanari were executed in the Piazza del Popolo "by order of the Pope," as the commemorative plaque records; the two *carbonari*, or members of a secret revolutionary society, had been convicted of high treason and assault with the intent to injure. The next year saw the last execution carried out there—Giuseppe Farina was bludgeoned to death for having killed a priest who robbed him. Public executions were so frequent that, according to Ferdinand Gregorovius in his monumental *History of the City of Rome in the Middle Ages*, guests at the Locanda del Sole, an inn on the Campo de'Fiori, complained that "they witnessed the spectacle of torture or watched people dangling from the gallows in the area every day."

But one of the most famous places of execution was the Ponte Sant'Angelo, originally the Pons Aelius, built by Hadrian as the monumental approach to his mausoleum. The bridge continued to be called the Ponte Elio until the seventh century, when Pope Gregory the Great had a vision of an angel sheathing his sword, thus signaling the end of a devastating plague. From then on both the bridge and the castle were renamed Sant'Angelo after the vision of the holy angel. The bridge became very important in 1300, when Boniface VIII declared the first Holy Year. Miniscule shops were built on the bridge; they served a commercial purpose, and also divided the flow of pilgrims into those going to Saint Peter's and those coming back. In 1488 the bridge became a showcase for the heads of decapitated prisoners and the bodies of those who had been hanged. The ten lovely statues that now decorate it, making it something of a Via Crucis, were based on designs by Bernini and sculpted by his assistants. The master only carved two of them himself—the one holding the crown of thorns and the one with a scroll. After a series of interesting vicissitudes those two ended up where they are now, in the church of Sant'Andrea delle Fratte. Regarding our story, there was one particularly memorable and horrifying execution in the Piazza di Ponte Sant'Angelo that's worth a little digression here because of its impact on those who witnessed it, including Caravaggio.

On September 11, 1599, a sweleteringly hot day, Beatrice Cenci, her stepmother Lucrezia, and her brother Giacomo were all put to death in the Piazza di Ponte Sant'Angelo. This was the final chapter in a criminal case so famous that it took on mythic proportions and inspired artists like Stendhal, Shelley, Dumas, Guido Reni, Delaroche, and Moravia, as well as several film directors. A number of the circumstances of this murky affair caught people's attention and fired their imaginations, including Beatrice's tender age (she was barely twenty), the sexual violence she endured, the legal controversies, and remote motives for the crime. Thus Beatrice has understandably become a symbol of youthful rebellion against parental tyranny, of bewitching beauty, of innocence punished, and of an oppressed woman who sought independence at any cost.

Beatrice was the daughter of Francesco Cenci, a depraved and tyrannical man whose economic fortunes were on the decline. Married for the first time at fourteen, Francesco fathered twelve children, seven of whom survived to adulthood. When his first wife, Ersilia Santacroce, died, he married Lucrezia Petroni, a well-to-do widow who bore three of his children. Beatrice grew up in the ancient Palazzo Cenci, which stood in the old ghetto in front of the

Isola Tiberina. She grew into a lovely young woman, open-minded and in love with life, perhaps too much so, at least in her father's eyes. He imprisoned her and Lucrezia in the fortress of Petrella Salto, which stood just outside the confines of the Papal States, toward the Abruzzi, in the Kingdom of Naples. Cenci sent Beatrice away in an attempt to separate his children and thereby stop them from making any joint claim on his almost exhausted resources. "I want you to die out here," he told Lucrezia as he accompanied her to the desolate fortress in the feudal territory of Marzio Colonna, who'd granted him permission to use the castle.

A pair of servants were assigned to guard the women, including Marzio Floriani, called Il Catalano, who was later identified as one of the men who carried out the crime, and Olimpio Calvetti, Colonna's faithful castellan and an energetic fifty-year-old who was described as "a large and handsome man." He also had a heroic past, as he had served with Marcantonio Colonna in the legendary Battle of Lepanto in 1571. A relationship, probably manipulated by Beatrice, developed between the girl and Olimpio, who was married to Plautilla Gasparini. She began to beg Olimpio to help her kill her father, hiring, if possible, one of the many bandits wandering around in that area. In the end the crime was carried out differently, and it was Giacomo who organized delivery of a fatal dose of opium and other soporific drugs to his restless sister.

At dawn on September 9, 1598, Francesco Cenci's body was found with its head split open in the garden beneath the castle's balcony. The balcony's railing was broken and left hanging away from the wall. A hole in the floor made it look like one of the boards had given way when someone walked on it. After a church service Francesco was hurriedly buried along with his troubled past. He had been repeatedly accused of sodomy, a crime that was punished by burning at the stake. Four years earlier, during a trial conducted at Cenci's expense, a witness testified, "Many times I saw Messer Francesco calling the boys and leading them to the stables while I was still around. And there, in the stall and in my presence, he kissed them and undid their pants and then said to me, 'Matteo, go away.'" He was also accused of sodomy by several female servants, and defended himself not by denying the fact, but by specifying that his relations with them took place "in the ordinary way, as honest men do it, from the front." This testimony was belied by that of another servant, who gave convincing evidence of the man's outrageous behavior: "He asked me if I had any sickness, and I said no. He then said again, 'no, no, I'm afraid that you have some sickness and that I will get it. I don't want to do it like this. Turn over on your other side.' Because I didn't want to turn over, he turned me over by force and leaned me over a chair." These precedents carried some weight as mitigating factors at Beatrice's trial, but not enough.

Once buried, Francesco's case should have been closed, but things went differently. Rumors that the man had been murdered led the authorities to open a *per fama* investigation, questioning multiple suspects among the public. Once some complicated jurisdictional questions were resolved, the investigation uncovered a number of troubling circumstances. The sheets and mattress from Francesco's bed were discovered soaked in blood, whereas there was very little blood near the body, a fact that gave rise to the suspicion that he had been killed somewhere else. It was also revealed that the gap in the balcony rail was so narrow that Francesco's large body could not have fallen through it. "There is no way with a hole of that width that the body of Signor Francesco could or did pass through it. Only with great difficulty could a slender body pass through it, and Signor Francesco was fat." Even if there had been an accident, the narrow width of the gap would easily have allowed the unfortunate man to cling to the iron railing, which would then have bent toward the wall rather than in the opposite direction.

Il Catalano was arrested, stripped, and taken to the torture chamber where he was subjected to the *territio*—a technique intended to terrorize the accused just by the threat of torment. Seeing the instruments of torture lying ready was enough to convince him, and he told the whole story in all its details—how the two women lived in unjust confinement, their harsh treatment at the hands of the tyrannical Francesco, and the violence Beatrice suffered, all of which gave the impression that her father had sexually abused her. This inspired the idea of drugging Francesco's wine and then finishing him off with a club, throwing his body off the balcony to make his death look like an accident. This seed of the perfect crime turned out to be a badly botched mess. Nothing went as planned; there was not enough opium to knock Francesco out, leaving him only a little stunned, and then the murder itself took some time. "I delivered two blows to the said Signor Francesco with the aforementioned club, and thus we killed him. There was a lot of blood; it ruined the bed and soaked into the mattresses and the wool and stained and bloodied the sheets."

The inquisitors now had a confession, their best proof. The two women and their accomplices were imprisoned at Castel Sant' Angelo. Beatrice denied any crime, and both she and her brother Giacomo were convinced they would get off. Because they were of noble blood they couldn't be tortured, and their behavior in front of the judges was a mixture of ingenuousness and arrogance typical of noble defendants.

Il Catalano was tortured with Beatrice present, and that gave the ring of truth to his statements. Shortly afterward the unfortunate fellow died. Beatrice and Lucrezia continued to deny the crime, trusting that someone of importance would come to their aid. They hoped in vain, as almost no one came forward; the only exception was the unwanted help of a cleric friend who had Olimpio Calvetti murdered to avoid another confession. In a sudden and ferocious turn of events, three hired assassins cornered Olimpio in a deserted place and decapitated him. The assassination of one of the accused, who was also a witness, hardened the judges' attitude. They made the condition of the women's imprisonment harsher, and, believing that one of Calvetti's brothers was privy to information, subjected him to prolonged torture. It was Pope Clement VIII himself, however, who sealed the fate of the Cencis. In August 1599, he handed down a *motu proprio*, a personal decree in which he authorized the court to torture the two Cencis, and at the same time he found them guilty. Giacomo was subjected to the strappado "for the length of an Apostles' Creed." He confessed, but assigned all the blame to the dead Olimpio. A few days later Bernardino Cenci, another of Beatrice's brothers, and a minor, also confessed. Then it was Lucrezia's turn. As a sign of respect she was tortured without first being stripped or shorn as would normally have been the case. She also confessed, naming Beatrice and her lover Olimpio as masterminds of the crime.

Finally, on August 10, it was Beatrice's turn. The judge immediately treated her severely, admonishing her not to lie. The young woman continued to deny the accusations against her. The judge tried in his own way to help her, saying he knew about all the violence her father had committed against her. Beatrice still insisted on her version of the story. Giacomo and Bernardino were tortured again, in front of her, to force her to confess, and then she herself was hung (still dressed) from the strappado. At this point she gave in, "Hung in that way, she spoke. 'Oimé, oimé, o Holiest Mother, help me.' Then she said, 'let me down, I want to tell the truth.'"

The strappado was an almost intolerable form of torture. It consisted of tying the hands of the accused behind his back, bound with a leather strap at the wrists. A heavy rope was then attached to the strap, and the accused was pulled up and left hanging in the air for an amount of time measured by the lengths of different prayers—from the Gloria to the Apostles' Creed. It caused atrocious pain and, in the case of a clumsy or sadistic tormentor, permanent dislocations or maiming.

The crux of Beatrice's capital defense, undertaken by Prospero Farinacci, was the violence and rape her father inflicted upon her, and relied heavily on the evidence of the deceased's wickedness. Yet there was little to do, and moreover the papal *motu proprio* had already sealed her sentence—death.

At 9:30 on the morning of September 11, 1599, the brothers of the Confraternity of San Giovanni Decollato accompanied the condemned prisoners to the scaffold singing psalms. Only Bernardino was spared because of his age. He was forced, in chains, to watch the executions and was then sent to the papal galleys. Lucrezia was the first to die; hoisted up in tears, she was decapitated. Beatrice followed immediately. In an involuntary reaction to the violence of the blow, "she kicked up her right leg so hard that she almost knocked her clothes up over her shoulder." Giacomo's death was the most gruesome. He was first subjected to torture with red-hot pincers in the wagon that brought him from the prison to the scaffold. When it was his turn to be executed he was first bludgeoned on the head, then drawn and quartered.

At the end of the spectacle the immense crowd slowly dispersed. The throng was so great that, given the extreme heat, it isn't surprising that several deaths from suffocation and heatstroke were reported. The remains of the condemned were displayed for twenty-four hours, attracting pilgrims and the curious—the two women were laid out on a bier surrounded by torches, and Giacomo's quartered remains were hung on a rack. The myth around Beatrice began with her horrendous end. Rumors also started to circulate that Clement VIII had sentenced the Cenci family to death in order to confiscate their property; we know for certain that when their belongings were auctioned off a few months later the pope purchased a large part of them for his nephew.

According to some stories the two executioners, Mastro Alessandro Bracca and Mastro Peppe, met tragic ends of their own. The former died thirteen days after the execution, tormented by nightmares and remorse for having inflicted such enormous suffering, and especially for having tortured Giacomo with red-hot pincers. The latter was mortally stabbed at Porta Castello a month after Beatrice's death.

Caravaggio, accompanied by Orazio Gentileschi and his young daughter Artemisia, was certainly present in the enormous crowd that witnessed the execution of Beatrice and the others. It's quite likely that he carefully observed the behavior of the condemned, in a sort of obedience to the memory of Leonardo's advice to painters to study "the eyes of the assassins, the courage of the combatants, the actions of the actors, and the attractions of the courtesans, so as not to miss any detail in which the life in the painting itself consists," as recorded by Giovanni Paolo Lomazzo in his *Trattato dell'arte della pittura*. It was certainly no accident that both Caravaggio and Artemisia then painted the story of Judith beheading Holofernes, representing that murder with a blunt directness and seemingly excessive quantities of blood. In addition to love, both human and divine, much of what Caravaggio represented in his paintings was some sort of death or martyrdom—as he grew older, and his pain grew ever greater, these themes appeared more often. The gospels and the stories of saints and martyrs were his primary sources, but the artist also transferred the dark color of his own experience to the canvas—the black of night, the ambushes, the sudden flash of a blade, heads separated from their bodies in the uproar of a crowded piazza. In his images of Lucy, Holofernes, Goliath, and Saint John the Baptist Caravaggio painted what he had seen and experienced, and his pictures reflected all the violence of Rome.

The hidden player behind Beatrice's trial was Pope Clement VIII, Ippolito Aldobrandini. Physically he was "of average stature, his complexion between rosy and phlegmatic, [had] an appearance that was serious and noble, although he was a little bit overweight." Cautious and suspicious in temperament, he tended toward diplomacy. At that time the Curia was divided between pro-French and pro-Spanish parties; the pope refused to take a clear position between them, even as he signaled the possibility of receiving ambassadors from King Henry IV of France, formerly the leader of the French Huguenots who, after being excommunicated by Sixtus V, had begun to consider the advantages of returning to the arms of the Catholic Church.

Ippolito was quick to show emotion, relatively devout, and moved by poverty. For the purpose of this story, though, we also know that he was obsessed with sexuality, and wanted to clear the streets of Rome of prostitutes and combat nudity in art. At one point he even arranged to tour churches to assure himself that all licentious or profane images—he judged images of the Magdalene the most disturbing—were removed. When all was said and done, he was the true incarnation of the spirit of the Counter-Reformation, which had required that artistic representations be capable of reinvigorating the faith. The Council of Trent had handed down precise rules for art, requiring that it be decorous, doctrinally correct, and avoid "all that was profane, vulgar or obscene, dishonest or licentious." As early as 1564 the painter Daniele da Volterra was given the task of covering the "shameful parts" of Michelangelo's nudes in the Sistine Chapel, a commission which earned him the derisory nickname, Braghettone, after the *braghe*, or loincloths, he added to the figures. Only in Stalin's Soviet Union were there equally severe rules for art, resulting in the so-called Social Realism enforced by police, which extended first to people's consciousness, and then to works of art.

In Counter-Reformation Rome there were punishments and fines for disobedient artists, in addition to the loss of jobs and patronage. Cesare Baronio, a priest who later became cardinal, was one of the greatest advocates of this policy. He was director of the Vatican Library, was fanatically religious, and offered a theoretical basis for the type of picture we now call mediating scenes, usually martyrdoms, that were accessible to everyone through realistic figures, traditional forms, and reassuring messages, as well as faithful to Church doctrine in their content. Amongst the many martyrdoms depicted was a particular interest in early Christian virgins—Cecilia, Prudenziana, Lucy, Felicity, Perpetua, and Priscilla—a gallery of women prepared to renounce their lives but not their chastity, a sexually phobic ideology the church clung to until the twentieth century and the canonization of Maria Goretti, a girl who was murdered when she would not surrender to the demands of a rapist. It was also clear that images were more persuasive than words. Cardinal Gabriele Paleotti wrote about this, proclaiming beneficial the emotions produced by an image which everyone, including the illiterate, could understand: "Devotion grows and grips the gut, such that anyone who doesn't know devotion must be made of wood or marble."

To understand such a repressive attitude we must remember that the Church was undergoing a dramatic crisis. Northern Europe was rocked by the Reformation, the Turkish threat soon followed in the southeast corner of the continent, and only a few decades had passed since Rome had been sacked and burned by Imperial troops in 1527. In the city itself there was the constant threat that the two political factions within the Curia, the pro-French and pro-Spanish, would come to blows in the streets, weapons in hand.

In 1595 Caravaggio entered the service of Cardinal Francesco Maria del Monte, and after having lived for several years in temporary and uncomfortable lodgings, he moved into the Palazzo Madama. A few years later, in 1601, he moved to the Palazzo Mattei, the splendid residence of Cardinal Girolamo Mattei, near the Botteghe Oscure. These lodgings were far more comfortable than anything he'd previously known; the people who visited these houses included the most interesting intellectuals in Rome, especially musicians and writers, and all were ready to show off their exquisite predilections. If paintings in churches had to be orthodox and encourage piety in the faithful, in these patrician homes, whether they belonged to churchmen or laymen, pictures with daring, if not downright lascivious, subjects were freely displayed. These were generally scenes in which female nudity and bodies in close proximity were justified by calling them scenes from ancient history or mythology. This served, though, not to moderate the sensuality, but instead often to reinforce it by making the references allusive. The most licentious paintings, however, were kept in secret rooms, sometimes hidden behind draperies that the master of the house raised like a miniature theater curtain for the enjoyment of his most trusted friends.

The young painter now found himself at the center of Rome's artistic circles, populated by cardinals who were earthly princes even before they were princes of the Church. Besides Del Monte, they included Ferdinando de'Medici, Pietro Aldobrandini, and Alessandro Montalto; their palaces were the most sumptuous in town, and they had villas on the high ground of the Pincian Hill or outside the city in the Alban Hills, the most pleasant retreats from summer heat.

Caravaggio's habits didn't change along with his circumstances. He certainly enjoyed his new company, and through it found commissions as well as inspiration and figures for his paintings, but he didn't put a stop to his restless nocturnal rounds of the city. While his cardinal was with the pope in Ferrara, for example, celebrating that city's annexation to the Papal States after the death of Alfonso II d'Este, the painter was once again arrested in Piazza Navona for illegally bearing arms. His temperament didn't change, and his arrogance and conceitedness grew apace with his fame. He let himself get drawn into street brawls, offending the antagonists, and if they replied by drawing their swords he was ready to fight, or reacted with brazen gestures, like when he threw a plate of artichokes in the face of a poor waiter he had some unknown objection to. His friends, whether painters or not, were swordsmen, skillful gamers, and also quick to draw their knives; they were great companions for drinking and wenching. Caravaggio himself had carnal relations with both men and women. He never entertained a lasting relationship, and if he had some liaison that was less than ephemeral, as he did on two or three occasions, it was invariably with some young man of fine figure and shameless manners.

Despite his noisy companions, the artist's figure remains cloaked by the shadows of reservation and isolation. Caravaggio was aggressive, ready for adventure and risk, and gladly carried his sword at his side—perhaps it was the same fearful weapon to appear in his *Saint Catherine of Alexandria*. However, as the Sienese doctor and art connoisseur Giulio Mancini wrote in his *Considerazione sulla pittura*, "one cannot deny that he was extremely extravagant." We can easily decipher "extravagant" as fruit of a profound anxiety rooted in some secret inner tension, or perhaps the proud knowledge of being the most gifted of all the artists painting canvases and altarpieces in Rome at the time.

Gifted in what way? In a book like this we can only briefly touch on a topic that has already been treated at length by specialists. Caravaggio brought a realism to religious paintings that upset the canon. Poor people—we would now call them the proletariat—and in some cases even those further down the economic scale, appeared in his paintings, the same ambiguous, working-class youths Pasolini saw and wrote about in the twentieth century. A Roman boy, taken from who knows what back alleyway and involved in who knows what sort of trafficking, posed for Caravaggio's figure of Saint John the Baptist. There was nothing left of Raphael's refined beauty or Michelangelo's excellence in Caravaggio's works. Saints, soldiers, witnesses, protagonists, and even the dead didn't hide their ages—their flesh was cracked and wrinkled, bulging veins betrayed those who did heavy labor, their limbs stocky, their large feet almost always dirty, and their garb was the worn-out clothing of the poor. We understand that they are illiterate, because if they hold a book they do so with the annoyance of someone unaccustomed to such an object. The boys, nude or only partially dressed, stare fixedly at the painter (and the viewer) with an impudence never before seen, each of them with an inviting grin, winking. There are also religious pictures, but any traditional heavenly aura has vanished from them; they speak instead of the weight of the earth, the mortality of the flesh, and reek of the bad breath of vice, including those practiced as profession.

According to Helen Langdon, a biographer of the artist, this kind of painting "might be connected to the aggressive tactics of Philip Neri, to his desire to humiliate the refined elite, to push the poor to the front of religion and reassess coarse, vernacular means of expression." Who knows if this hypothesis is justified. We do know that when he was questioned about his own art in court, Caravaggio gave an almost provocative answer. Good painters, whom he called *valentuomini*, are those who "know how to do their art well, and to imitate things in nature well." This was his somewhat reductive idea of realism. Moreover, the technique he used mirrored the idea. He drew the figures directly on the canvas, perhaps with the help of a camera obscura, except when it came to plunging them into the complex play of light that only he was able to command. One landlord denounced him for the damage he caused to the ceiling in one of his rooms; it's not too difficult to imagine that the painter cut a hole so that the light would fall on his models in exactly the way he wanted. His astonishing inventions brought him fame and success, but they also attracted many critics, and not just those who were envious of him. A few of his adversaries judged him "bereft of invention and drawing, without decorum or artistry, he colored his figures by candlelight, with a plane above, without degrading them."

Often the revolutionary significance of his work escaped his patrons, as did the feeling of piety it could excite in the most humble, who in his saints and martyrs finally saw themselves. The first version of his *Saint Matthew* was refused by the priests who commissioned it because "that figure has neither the decorum nor the appearance of a saint." The painting of the *Death of the Virgin*, intended by its patrons for the church of Santa Maria della Scala in Trastevere, caused an even greater scandal. The church was connected to a monastery called the Casa Pia, a charitable organization meant to help female victims of violence who were then at risk of becoming prostitutes. The painting has none of the traditional elements associated with sacred representations; Mary is a cadaver, ashen in color, her belly swollen as if she might have drowned in the Tiber, her pose disorderly, and her feet large and bare. Far from appearing to be a Madonna, she's simply a dead woman. The apostles, bent over her, are poor old men, bald and wrought by a completely human grief. The Carmelite fathers were shocked by the image's force, and refused to accept it. Judging the composition lascivious, they were suspicious (as they said) that the model who had posed for the picture was some "filthy whore." This is the missing canvas I mentioned at the beginning of the chapter. Had it not been for those fears we could still enjoy it today in that small church in Trastevere, rather than having to travel to the Louvre, its final home after sundry vicissitudes.

It is said that this poor, dead Madonna is, along with the *Madonna di Loreto*, one of the most touching religious images created in the seventeenth century. It took the disinterested eye of a layman to truly appreciate the painting. Even if the friars weren't interested in it, dealers and connoisseurs certainly were. Rubens was called upon to appraise the picture, and brought it to the attention of the Duke of Mantua, who then bought it. He didn't really care that the artist's model for the Virgin was "some flithy whore from the Ortacci whom he loved, so scrupulous and free of devotion."

The woman who posed for the picture was in fact Maddalena Antognetti, called Lena, who had already been the model for the *Madonna di Loreto*. This is another story worth telling; it seems this girl, lover of priests and cardinals, as well as the more-or-less permanent concubine of Gaspare Albertini, was proposed to by a practicing notary. Her mother refused his proposal, and all this happened at a time when Lena was often at Caravaggio's house posing. Might there also have been an amorous relationship between the two? This was often said, but no one had any proof. It's possible—certainly Lena's comings and goings annoyed the notary, who complained to the girl's mother. Their conversation degenerated, and ended with the red-hot words of the lovesick youth, "You can have that old maid daughter of yours, who you refused to let me take as a wife and then led her to that evil painter to do as he pleased with her—good riddance." A few days later Caravaggio, armed with a hatchet, confronted the unfortunate young man in the Piazza Navona and gave him such a blow to the head that he "fell to the ground in a mess, all covered with his own blood."

A few months after the horrendous death of Beatrice Cenci and her accomplices there was another execution in Rome that was even more ferocious, cruelly motivated, and destined to raise echoes that reverberate even today; the philosopher Giordano Bruno was burned alive in the Campo de'Fiori. This horrible affair began in Venice, where the philosopher from Nola had gone after long peregrinations in London, Paris, Geneva, Frankfurt, Prague, and Zurich. He was a perennial wander, and was never really accepted by Catholics, as he was a dissident and heretical Dominican friar, nor by Calvinists or other reformers. He defined himself in his comedy *Il candelaio* as an "academic of no academy." A minor Venetian nobleman, Giovanni Mocenigo, had invited him to come to Venice to give him lessons in mnemonics. The serene city's reputation as a liberal, independent republic reassured the philosopher, especially because from Rome Pope Gregory XIV seemed to guarantee a certain degree of open-mindedness even for rebels like him. Unfortunately he was mistaken; his relationship with Mocenigo deteriorated, perhaps for trifling reasons. In May of 1592 the Venetian nobleman, defined as *delator*—informer—in the trial documents, denounced Bruno to the Inquisition. He was arrested on the night of May 24 and imprisoned at San Domenico.

The Holy Office, also known as the tribunal of the Inquisition, was a magistracy concerned with all crimes against the faith. It judged those who voiced opinions different from those of the Church doctrine, but also scientists and philosophers, as their disciplines were linked to the faith. The boundaries between them were ill-defined, as we shall see, which gave the inquisitors broad discretion. At first Bruno wasn't worried about the accusations, and dismissed them as gossip, since they were merely the dull words of Mocenigo supported by few witnesses and scarce depth. In July, at the end of seven hearings, the philosopher cut it short; he knelt and begged the pardon of the judges, confident that a light sentence would put an end to the affair.

But this wasn't to be. The Venetian tribunal was just a peripheral organ of the Holy Office, and its acts had to be sent to Rome. The Roman judges read those documents in another spirit, with a purpose that had only in part to do with the accused. Examining the acts, the Inquisition asked that Bruno be transferred to Rome to be tried again. The philosopher arrived at the end of February 1593, and was immediately jailed in the prisons of the Holy Office near Saint Peter's. He knew that the situation was now more serious, but initially continued not to worry too much, as he was counting on the mysticism of Clement VIII. It was said that the pope was sympathetic to philosophers because of his youthful friendships with Neo-Platonic philosophers in Padua. In reality Ippolito Aldobrandini, once he came to the throne of Saint Peter's, surrounded himself with advisers and confessors who persisted in repeating to him how dangerous any line of thought other than scholasticism was to the Church.

At first the tribunal seemed in no hurry to finish the inquest. The papal court was divided, Europe was rent by the Reformation, and in his handling of foreign affairs the pope had to work miracles of balance in order to avoid being swept off the stage. New evidence was gathered against Bruno, including the testimony of Fra Celeste, a Capuchin friar, and a layman from Verona named Lattanzio Arrigoni. The latter, who likely had a mental illness, had also been convicted of heresy, and had shared a cell with Bruno in Venice. The monk revealed that the accused formulated heresies in prison, bursting into obscene blasphemies. The deposition of Francesco Graziano was considered especially useful; he was a copyist from Udine who knew Latin and was thus considered an educated person capable of conversing with Bruno in a language unknown to most. According to Graziano, Bruno raised doubts about certain dogmas relevant to Christian doctrine. He added that the philosopher also practiced the occult sciences and exorcisms, denying the value of religious mass.

The months passed and the interrogations carried on—ten, fifteen, eighteen, and finally twenty-two of them—some accompanied by torture. The accused defended himself, answering the accusations: Moses was certainly a magician, but in his magic was a strong cognitive potential which it was wrong to ignore; there is certainly a multiplicity of worlds, but such a hypothesis doesn't conflict with divine omnipotence, and instead exalted it; the world in its real form was certainly created, but this didn't preclude that the material it was made from was also, like God, eternal and immutable; and finally, if this was indeed the nature of matter, wouldn't it mean that other worlds could be inhabited by intelligent creatures similar to humans? Had Adam and Eve not committed the original sin would they not also have been immortal beings?

Bruno's theory goes beyond the Copernican hypothesis of a stationary sun at the center of the universe. That theory was first formulated in the fourth century BC by Aristarchus of Samos, who was also accused of impiety. Heliocentrism didn't reappear again until 1543, in Copernicus's book *De revolutionibus orbium caelestium* (*On the Revolutions of the Heavenly Spheres*), which marked the beginning of modern astronomy. It was Bruno, however, who brought Copernicus to prominence in his masterpiece of 1584, *La cena de le ceneri* (*The Ash Wednesday Supper*), wherein he defended Copernicus and also delineated a new universe, no longer limited to our sun at the center of a system of fixed stars, but one which intuited an infinite space, with infinite worlds evolving for an infinite length of time. In his *De l'infinito universo et mondi* (*On the Infinite Universe and Worlds*), he wrote, "There exist innumerable suns and innumerable earths rotate around them." His theory anticipates by several centuries the discoveries of modern astronomers, and his theories suggested, in essence, that the universe was eternal, that the idea of God as Creator was impossible—if anything, they approached the ideas of Buddhism. Bruno had left the official sphere of Christianity, and he would pay dearly.

A few years after Bruno's martyrdom, in 1609, Galileo Galilei, an obscure professor of mathematics from Padua, came to hear about a telescope invented in Holland. He built one, pointed it at the sky, and, astonished, made many discoveries: the moon had mountains and valleys, Venus's phases were similar to the moon's, Jupiter had four satellites that orbited around it, Saturn had strange anomalies (its famous rings), the sun rotated on its own axis, and the constellations and the Milky Way were made up of an almost infinite number of stars. This news excited people, but also worried the Church. On February 25, 1616, the Inquisition, in order to "prevent disorder and damage," declared that "the idea that the sun is the immobile center of the world is an absurd proposition, philosophically false, and formally heretical for being expressly counter to Holy Scriptures." Galileo was imprisoned and tried by the Inquisition, which on June 22, 1633, ordered him, on a vote of seven to three, to abjure. Dressed in the long habit of a penitent, the scientist capitulated, asked for forgiveness on his knees, bartering his honor for his life. He remained under house arrest until his death.

Giordano Bruno, on the other hand, never bent. Months passed, and the inquisitors realized they were spinning their wheels, and the accused wasn't reacting as they had expected. Isolated before the court of an absolutist regime, Bruno had, in theory, only two ways to save himself: to abjure his ideas or to prove that he had been misunderstood, which was just another way of abjuring while saving face. In reality, he refuted the crudest accusations and defended his philosophy on the others, seeking to demonstrate that the orthodoxy he described was compatible with the official one. He equivocated, dodged, refuted, and sparred with the court, heedless of the fact that his judges had already readied the instrument that would shut him up once and for all.

At the beginning of 1599 Cardinal Roberto Bellarmino (also known as Robert Bellarmine) took decisive control of the trial. He was a Tuscan born in Montepulciano in 1542, and at the age of eighteen entered the Jesuit order, where the sharpness of his intelligence and dialectic subtlety were soon noticed. Bellarmine was more a political thinker than an expert in Holy Scripture, even though only a few months earlier he'd been named a theologian of the Papal Penitentiary and consultant to the Inquisition. His vision of the trial was synthetic and strictly political. Information and slanderous gossip didn't interest him. He intuited that the accused, with his vision of an "infinite openness and a plurality of worlds," had initiated a new era in the notion of freedom of thought, and that if he engaged in a debate about the canonical interpretation of Scripture, any number of things might begin to collapse.

The Church of Rome was a fortress under siege. The hammer blows with which another rebellious priest, Martin Luther, nailed his ninety-five theses to the church door in Wittenberg in 1517 still resounded throughout Europe. Rome was losing control of whole regions—the Scandinavian countries, which were latecomers to Catholicism, were also amongst the first to abandon it for Protestantism; England was lost, cut free with a clean blow by Henry VIII; in the German-speaking lands the protests had degenerated into open warfare; Holland and Switzerland nursed heretical sects; and even France and Poland harbored Protestant evangelists. The Counter-Reformation was necessary for the Church to regain some control over its faithful, especially in Italy. Now Bellarmine wanted to put a halt to the heresies, and give the Church back its prestige even in those areas that today would be considered intellectual fields. The chance that Giordano Bruno represented seemed tailor-made to meet these goals.

The first thing the cardinal did was to condense the almost indigestible materials of the trial into eight clear propositions to be presented to the accused. Bruno examined them and signaled that he was prepared to abjure them, but only on condition that his affirmations were defined by the Church as errors only as of that moment, not before. This was just an expedient—he wanted to admit to the court that his interpretations conflicted not with Scripture, but with the dictates of the pope, in other words, with the political necessities of the moment. Bellarmine naturally refused, and the court reaffirmed that the abjuration had to be complete and without time limits. Bruno equivocated; he tried to stay alive without betraying the heart of his beliefs. It is profoundly moving that a man imprisoned for years, without protectors or influential friends, abandoned by everyone, still put up such a resistance, gambling everything on the logical strength of his arguments.

The final session of the trial opened on September 9, 1599, and Clement VIII himself attended. The court wanted to interrogate the accused under torture again, but the pope opposed it. At the end of other controversies, Bellarmine sent the philosopher an ultimatum: either he abjure clearly and without conditions, or he would be sentenced to death. On December 21 the philosopher gave the court his definitive answer, saying that he "could not, nor did he want to, retract, that he had nothing to retract, that he had not the material of retraction, and that he did not understand what thing he needed to retract." The death sentence was handed down on February 8, 1600, in the apartments of Cardinal Madruzzo and in the presence of the inquisitors, a notary and a few spectators. The document began with these words:

> Being that you, Fra Giordano, son of the late Giovanni Bruno of Nola in the Kingdom of Naples, a priest professed in the order of St. Dominic, and being about fifty-two years old, were denounced in the Holy Office of Venice eight years ago . . .

Bruno listened to this sentence on his knees, without batting an eyelash. He was convicted of doubting the virginity of Mary, of having lived in heretical countries according to heretical customs, of having written against the pope, of sustaining the existence of innumerable worlds and eternities, of affirming the transmigration of souls, of believing magic to be licit, of identifying the Holy Spirit with the soul of the world, of declaring that the Scriptures were nothing but a dream, of believing that even demons could hope for salvation, and so on.

Only when the reading was finished did Bruno utter the tremendous words that have become the motto of every martyr for liberty: "Perhaps you pronounce this sentence against me with more fear than I have in hearing it." The judges didn't allow themselves to be moved, nor did they consider that they were writing a shameful page in human history. They were political men concerned with the immediate interests of the Church, and didn't dare to stray from them. Even Bruno's books, redundantly pronounced "heretical and erroneous and containing many heresies and errors," were destined to be "broken and burned" on a second pyre in the courtyard of Saint Peter's.

At that moment the convicted prisoner was turned over to the secular branch, embodied by Ferdinando Taverna, Governor of Rome. For the week before his execution confessors and comforters alternated visits to his cell. Had he abjured, in the end, he would not have saved his life, but could have had a less atrocious death, as he would've been hanged rather than burned alive. Rome was full of pilgrims for the Holy Year that had just begun (at the end of that Jubilee year they had seen over one million visitors), and a public burning had the added value of admonishing those who were returning to countries threatened by the Reformation. Furthermore, Henry IV, King of France and only recently readmitted into the embrace of the Holy Mother Church, had disappointed the pope by allowing Protestants freedom of worship in the Edict of Nantes, issued in 1598. Perhaps this is another reason that Bruno's execution was set in the Campo de'Fiori, practically in front of the French ambassador's residence (then in the Palazzo Orsini, at the corner of the Via Giubbonari)—the ambassador had often complained of the horror and the stench of these spectacles.

At dawn on February 17, seven religious men entered Bruno's cell exhorting him to repent. He refused, and instead continued to sustain his ideas. He was gagged, perhaps because he was cursing his persecutors. It was still dark when the grim procession set off. Bruno was accompanied by the brothers of the Confraternity of San Giovanni Decollato, who wore long hoods to hide their faces, black tunics, and carried torches. They held panels with scenes of martyrdom in front of the condemned man to comfort him. They chanted lugubrious litanies, the crowd looked on silently, and people blessed themselves as the procession passed. From the jail at Tor di Nona the prisoner traveled along the Via dei Banchi and the Via del Pellegrino before arriving at the place of his execution. There he was stripped and tied to a pole that rose out of a pile of well-dried wood. The fire quickly grew to a roaring blaze. Because of the gag the victim's agonizing screams were transformed into strange howls that were quickly suffocated by the smoke and overwhelmed by the crackling of the fire.

The burning of 1600 signaled the height of the Catholic Church's efforts to exorcise nascent modern thought. That attempt continued, albeit in slightly less cruel ways, until Pope Pius IX published his *Syllabus* of 1864, in which he refuted "modern civilization" and defined "freedom of worship and thought" as an error. When the monument to Giordano Bruno was ceremoniously set in the Campo de'Fiori in 1889, Pope Leo XIII addressed a letter of admonishment to the faithful in which the philosopher was once again defamed. The Vatican continued afterward to press for the demolition of the monument. It is to Benito Mussolini's credit that as head of government he resisted those attempts. Pius XI reacted by first having Bellarmine, the Grand Inquisitor, proclaimed a saint in 1930 and then a doctor of the Universal Church in 1931. He was to be venerated as the patron saint of cate-chists, and his epitaph read, "My sword has subdued arrogant spirits."

Two days after the execution this report appeared in the *Avviso di Roma*, a news bulletin:

> Thursday morning in Campo di Fiore the wicked Dominican friar from Nola was burned alive . . . an obstinate heretic, and having of his capriciousness formed various dogmas against our faith, and in particular against the Holy Virgin and the Saints, he wanted stub-bornly to die . . . and they say that he died a martyr and willingly, and that his soul would ascend into paradise with that smoke. But now he will see if he spoke the truth.

More recently Pope John Paul II sent his Secretary of State, Cardinal Angelo Sodano, with a message to the conference held in Naples on the four-hundredth anniversary of Giordano Bruno's martyrdom. He affirmed that this "sad episode in the history of modern Christianity invites us to reread even this event in a spirit open to the full truth of history." The cardinal noted that the philosopher's views had matured in the sixteenth century, when Christianity was divided because Luther, Calvin, and Henry VIII had taken whole nations away from Rome. He added that Bruno's "intellectual choices" remained "incom-patible with Christian doctrine." There is no doubt, he concluded, that some aspects of the procedures used in Venice and Rome to judge the friar accused of heresy and "their violent outcome at the hands of the civic authorities could not today but constitute a reason for regret for the Church." Finally a little regret, at least.

It's against this backdrop of continual violence that we need to imagine Caravaggio's life. Clement VIII died in 1605, and was suc-ceeded by Leo XI. As happened in the twentieth century with Pope John Paul I, Leo lasted on the papal throne for only a few weeks. Two vacancies at the Vatican in such rapid succession rekindled the polit-ical factions in Rome, the pro-French and pro-Spanish parties now confronted each other openly, and the city was unsettled by riots.

There was a risk of schism in the conclave of 1605, until a neutral political solution succeeded in settling the dispute and Camillo Borghese became Pope Paul V. One of his first acts was to make his nephew, the twenty-seven-year-old Scipione Borghese, a cardinal. Scipione had only a mediocre education, but he was a passionate art collector. This was good for Caravaggio, as Scipione introduced him to the pope hoping that his uncle would commission a portrait from him.

We know that at the time Caravaggio was living in a house on the Vicolo dei Santi Cecilia e Biagio (today the Vicolo del Divino Amore), not far from the Palazzo Borghese. He lived alone, with a servant named Francesco who was also registered in that parish. His house was wretched and poorly furnished with only a few belongings. The artist lived a bachelor's life, worked in solitude, and when he ate he often used the back of a canvas as a table. When he wasn't working, he went wandering around Rome "with his companions, almost all brazen people, swordsmen, and painters." Not all artists, of course, spent their evenings looking for trouble. Guido Reni, the Cavalier d'Arpino, and Annibale Carracci, for example, behaved in a wholly different manner; they knew everyone, and profitably obeyed the rules. Caravaggio, on the other hand, seemed to be incapable of behaving otherwise; he painted, went out, was involved in altercations, and fought. One day, at the end of May of 1606, he encountered a certain Ranuccio Tomassoni, an arrogant fellow who fancied himself a boss in the neighborhood. There was already bad blood between the two of them, perhaps rooted, at least in part, in politics. Caravaggio belonged to the pro-French party, and Tomassoni to a family of violent gang bosses of pro-Spanish leanings. Blades flashed, and the painter had the upper hand; perhaps he meant only to wound Tomassoni, but impulse overwhelmed him, and he killed his rival.

He was forced to flee, and with this murder on his record he began a period of exile that would last four years, first in the Castelli Romani, the hills just south of the city where he was protected by the Colonna family, then in Naples, Sicily, and Malta. He continued to paint, but his life was now unhappy indeed. All traces of eroticism vanished from his work, and instead the blackness of his own distress prevailed. In Malta he managed to join the Order of the Knights, but even this didn't soothe him, and instead he once again became involved, as he had been in Naples, in a serious incident. We know the details of this episode thanks to the work of Keith Sciberras, a Maltese scholar who traced all the records of the event in the island's state archives. Caravaggio was again involved in a scuffle, broke down the door of a house, and burst in. He was imprisoned and put in solitary confinement but managed a daring escape. An already serious matter became much more serious, given his recent nomination as a Knight of Malta. He fled the island and took refuge in Sicily, leaving behind a trail of intense ill will. What was the motive for such rancorous feelings? It's been suggested that Caravaggio had an intimate relationship with the page of an aristocratic family, committing an offence that in Malta was punishable by death.

Meanwhile, in Rome, where Tomassoni's murder had gained some notoriety, Caravaggio was condemned in absentia to a harsh punishment, perhaps even death. It took almost four years for the affair to die down, thanks in part to the efforts of Scipione Borghese. It wasn't until 1610 that Caravaggio began to put any hope in the possibility of return, and requested papal pardon. In July he boarded a felucca in Naples, carrying paintings for Cardinal Borghese on board with him. The little craft set sail, from that moment on everything becomes a veritable puzzle, and (at the risk of using a hackneyed phrase) his last days and death remain a mystery. What little we know comes from unreliable biographies. According to Giulio Mancini, "Leaving with the renewal of hope, he came to Porto Ercole where he caught a nasty fever, at the height of his glory, and somewhere between the ages of thirty-five and forty he died in poverty, without any care, and was buried in a place near there."

The painter Giovanni Baglione, who hated Caravaggio, wrote, "He set off in a felucca with only a few things to come to Rome, returning on the word of Cardinal Gonzaga that he would take up his case with Pope Paul V. When he arrived on the beach he was arrested, put in prison, and held for two days before he was released." Why was he imprisoned? Was it the result of the murder committed years before in Rome, or due instead to Maltese authorities who had followed him with an order for his arrest? Baglione mentioned only a beach—it could not be Porto Ercole, but was perhaps Palo, a small cove with a garrison just South of Civitavecchia. We learn that there was yet another version of this peculiar affair when Baglione writes that the artist, upon leaving the prison, discovered to his dismay that the felucca with all his things, including the paintings, was gone. "The felucca was no longer there and, all in a fury, like a desperate man roamed the beach under the fierce sun to see if he could spot the boat that had taken all his things out to sea."

The art connoisseur Giovan Pietro Bellori also reports, without much clarification, the crazed behavior of a man who, in the intense heat of July, in the malaria-infested Maremma, set out on foot in search of a small boat in the direction of Porto Ercole several dozen kilometers away. Every bit of this last episode in Caravaggio's history is incoherent, perhaps because of the confusion of the actual events, the fragmentary nature of the evidence that survives, or because of the strength of the legend that has developed around him, which will never fade. We don't even know if he really died from fever or rather suffered a violent death, just as his life had been violent. One of his biographers, Peter Robb, has suggested that he was murdered—killed by someone seeking revenge for the outrages committed in Malta. The only thing we know for sure is that his story will continue to be told in many different versions by any- and everyone who has sufficient ingenuity to present, while rearranging things to suit his own thesis, the few contradictory elements of the artist's life.

Of the many things said about Caravaggio, the outrageous and bitter words with which Baglione concluded his chronicle remain strong; having left prison, Caravaggio fell ill "with a nasty fever and, without any human help, a few days later died badly, just as he had lived."

V

A HOUSE ALL OF GOLD

THERE IS A PLACE IN ROME that has always inspired a distinct fascination—or better yet, has emanated a special aura. The allure of the Domus Aurea is strange because it is really just a bunch of bare walls, silent corridors, and stripped down brickwork enlivened here and there by the small remains of frescoes or mosaics. What could be the real source of the enchantment felt by visitors here, in the most sumptuous royal residence ever conceived? Perhaps it's the personality of its patron, Emperor Nero, archetype of unbridled power and determination. For me, though, the enchantment comes more from the moving traces left by the visitors, who in the sixteenth and seventeenth centuries lowered themselves through a hole in the ceiling into these subterranean rooms. At the time the space was mostly filled with dirt; crouching low and relying on the flickering light of torches (the streaks of lampblack are still visible), they examined the frescoes and copied the ornamental motifs that would become the famous grotesques of late Renaissance art: vegetal motifs mixed with small human or animal figures that were rarely realistic, almost always imaginary, and adhered to no naturalistic canon—a fantastical world in which humans, animals, and plants were fused to create lively, bizarre representations somewhere between humor and hallucination. The term grotesque comes from the Italian *grotto*, and the rooms of Nero's palace had essentially become underground grottoes, filled almost to the ceiling with dirt and debris. Their rediscovery launched a wildly popular style based on classical antiquity and the grandiose ruins of Rome, a style comparable only to the Egyptomania unleashed by Napoleon's campaigns in North Africa at the beginning of the nineteenth century.

After the disastrous fire of AD 64, Nero envisioned his new palace rising from the ashes of the devastated city. He expropriated a nearly

200-acre lot because, according to Suetonius, he wanted his palace to extend from the Palatine Hill to the Esquiline Hill. In his *Epigrams* Martial complained, "a single house now occupies the whole of the city." To get a sense of the immense spaciousness of Nero's palace, just consider that a bronze statue 35 meters tall (the equivalent of a twelve-story building) was set in the vestibule. It took a team of twenty-four elephants to move the enormously heavy sculpture, and it was for this gigantic, colossal figure that the Amphitheater of Flavius was renamed the Coliseum in the Middle Ages. The Greek sculptor Zenodorus represented the emperor nude, bearing the attributes of the sun, his right arm extended, his left bent to hold a globe. From his crown radiated seven rays (each one six meters long), representing both his absolute power and the sun, the cosmic force he wanted to be identified with. It's interesting that the ray-of-light motif has continued through the centuries, from the Colossus of Rhodes to the Statue of Liberty in New York's harbor.

The palace, Suetonius assures us, included three porticoes almost a mile long, "an enormous pool, more like a sea than a pool, surrounded by buildings made to resemble cities, and by a landscape garden consisting of ploughed fields, vineyards, pastures and woodlands—where every variety of domestic and wild animal roamed about."[1] If today we walk through it in darkness and silence, in Nero's day the residence gleamed with light because it was completely covered in gold and was studded with gems and shells set into its walls. Suetonious continues, "All the dining-rooms had ceilings of fretted ivory, the panels of which could slide back and let [out] a rain of flowers or of perfume. . . ."[2] The Domus Aurea also had splendid revetments of multicolored marbles mixed together into the polychrome compositions the ancient Romans excelled at. These stones came from Spain, the province of Numidia (present-day Algeria and Tunisia), Libya, Egypt, the Far East, Greece, Gaul, and Cappadocia. Their color and texture made each one diverse, and each had a unique hardness and beauty. These marbles continued to be popular, and centuries later Roman stonecutters gave them names that evoke a particular epoch: *portasanta*, or Holy Gate; *lumachella orientale*, named for its snail-shell pattern; *pavonazzetto*, purple with white veins, reminiscent of a peacock; *serpentino*, or serpentine; *granito degli obelischi*, or obelisk granite; *africano*, from Northern Africa; and the most precious of all, *porfido rosso*, the red porphyry reserved exclusively for the emperor.

Yet color was not the only over-the-top decorative element in this fantastic residence. Technology also played a part, and the best mechanical knowledge of the time was employed to make the circular dome of the main dining room rotate day and night, synchronized with the earth's orbit. The baths were equipped with faucets for both seawater and sulfur water. The palace's two architects, Severus and Celerus, knew that this work would either earn them eternal fame or cost them everything, including their lives. Challenged by the size of the project, and knowing the emperor's tastes, they envisioned such bizarre wonders that Tacitus remarked, "they often go against the laws of nature." The entire nearby valley, at whose center we now see the Coliseum, was flooded to make the artificial lake that Suetonius described as being almost as vast as the sea.

The palace and all its marvels barely outlasted their owner's death in AD 68. Nero only briefly enjoyed his immense home, and likely never saw it finished, nor had the time to tour all of it. His successors had most of it demolished; Domitian razed the buildings on the Palatine Hill, the artificial lake was filled with debris in preparation for erecting the Coliseum, and Hadrian demolished the vestibule on the Velian Hill to build his Temple of Venus and Rome. The pavilion on the Oppian Hill (the Domus visible today) survived until AD 104, when it was partially destroyed by a fire. When Trajan then ordered a bath complex built on that site, his architect, Apollodorus of Damascus, had the upper stories of Nero's palace torn down, and filled the lower rooms with earth. He made an immense, solid cube of it and used it as the foundation for his new buildings. Shadows replaced the light, and the gold, gems, and colored marbles were drowned under tons of earth and debris. Magnificence was substituted by ruin, and for several centuries it was forgotten—a circumstance we can thank for the partial conservation of this distinguished testimony of the past.

Visitors will be enraptured by the breathtaking paintings and mosaics, as well as the structure itself, the supreme art of its masonry, the cupolas, the arrangement of the spaces, and the play of light refracted through the *bocche di lupo*—the so-called wolves' mouths—openings in the upper part of the porticoes. A few rooms were rightly left as they were found, still filled with the dirt Trajan dumped into them. Tons and tons of earth fill our view, and in the inert mass we can make out bricks, pieces of marble, column fragments, scraps of stucco, cornices, and other ornamental debris. The aura I mentioned above also comes from this. By burying the present, Trajan unwittingly did a great service to future generations.

As for Lucius Domitius Claudius, called Nero—the tragic owner of these walls—almost all we know comes from Tacitus and Suetonius. Pliny also wrote about him, and some of that passed into Dio Cassius's *Roman History*. There is also a series of fragmentary passages, brief mentions, references, and citations disseminated here and there throughout ancient literature and in the works of the early Christian writers. Most details, however, come from those first two sources, whose histories have shaped Nero's reputation into that of the most discussed, exemplary, and loathed emperor of all time; neither of the two was kind to him. Time, of course, has layered a variety of interpretations and ideologies over the texts, and they have melded with his myth, making Nero both archetype and stereotype.

The events that brought Nero to the imperial throne would have marked anyone for life, especially since the intrigues began when the future emperor was little more than an adolescent. His mother, Agrippina Minor, was twenty-three when she gave birth to Nero on December 15, AD 37; the father was a man she didn't love, an arrogant and dissolute patrician thirty years her senior whom Tiberius had forced her to marry. His name was Domitius, but he was called Ahenobarbus because of his red beard, and named his son Lucius Domitius Ahenobarbus. Agrippina wrote in her memoirs (passed down to us in the chronicles of Pliny the Elder) that the child was born feet first, which was considered a bad omen. Suetonius, on the other hand, wrote, "Nero was born at Antium (Anzio) on 15 December AD 37, nine months after Tiberius' death. The sun was rising and its earliest rays touched the newly-born boy almost before he could be laid on the ground, as was the custom, for his father either to acknowledge or disavow."[3]

The nickname Nero came later; according to the sagacious Aulus Gellius (in his *Attic Nights*) it meant strong or courageous in the Sabine language. Later, however, it carried a different sense, suggesting by the word *nero*, or black, a tenebrous connotation affiliated with the underworld. Nero's mother, as so often happens, played a much larger role in his life than his father, who died when the boy was still young. Agrippina, daughter of the great general Germanicus and sister of Caligula, was lovely, seductive, calculating, and ambitious, and was also capable of coldly dispensing all sorts of flattery—compliments expressed in words and, no less expressively, communicated by her voluptuous body. Agrippina—more accurately Agrippina Minor or Julia Agrippina—was also the daughter of another Agrippina, called Major or the Elder. She was Germanicus's wife and denied her daughter nothing, including an incestuous relationship with her brother, whom she also shared with her other sisters.

Agrippina's husband died when their son was only three years old, and she was soon involved in a plot against Caligula, who generously spared his sister's life, and instead of killing her merely sent her into exile. The child was left in the care of an aunt who then entrusted him to two questionable tutors, a barber and a dancer. Caligula was assassinated in AD 41, and Claudius was his successor. He was Germanicus's brother, Agrippina's uncle, and was thought of as little more than a puppet both by his family and the public. In his fifties he married Messalina, a girl of barely fifteen destined for notoriety. We know that Messalina was psychologically disturbed, and was also reputed to have extravagant sexual appetites; she was bound for an early, violent death, and was killed when she was little more than twenty. Tacitus described her end: "A blow from the officer ran her through. The corpse was turned over to her mother. Claudius was still at dinner when he received the news that Messalina was dead, although it was uncertain whether by her own hand or another's. He did not bother to inquire. Asking for wine, he went on with the feast."[4]

That was in September of AD 48, and five months later, in January of AD 49, Claudius married Agrippina—it mattered little that he was her uncle, her father's brother, and therefore another incest. The empress's primary concern was Lucius Domitius, not so much because she loved her son, who was now approaching puberty, but because she had already begun calculating what objectives she could reach through him. Agrippina knew how to function in a male-dominated society, and manipulating Lucius would give her access to things that she, as a woman, was forbidden. Among her first notable moves was recalling Lucius Annaeus Seneca, the most brilliant thinker of the day, from a long and debilitating exile to become her son's tutor. At the same time she had Claudius, her husband and uncle, adopt Lucius Domitius (on February 25, AD 50); the boy's new name was Tiberius Claudius Nero Drusus Germanicus. The next step was to find Nero an appropriate wife. As soon as he turned sixteen he was married to Octavia, a twelve-year-old girl and daughter of little-mourned Messalina, whose debauchery she seemed not to have inherited.

Agrippina was just over thirty, her beauty was still intact, and her control over the emperor was remarkable. Her manipulations to prepare her son had been completed—he now had an imperial if fictitious ancestry, a wife of suitable rank, and the best tutor available. Yet there were still significant obstacles on his path to the throne, the first and foremost being that Claudius still sat upon it, and he was little more than forty and in good health. Secondly, Claudius's son Britannicus stood ahead of Nero in the line of succession. He was a shy boy, and Nero's arrival in the family had brusquely relegated him to the sideline. Agrippina had prepared for these circumstances, too, and started with Claudius, whose passion for mushrooms became his vulnerability and her opportunity. Tacitus recounted his murder:

> Later, the whole episode became known, and contemporary authors say that the poison was inserted into a choice mushroom. The full effect of the drug was not at first apparent, either through Claudius' constitutional sluggishness or through his drunkenness; and a movement of the bowels was thought to have saved him. Agrippina was desperate: but since the worst was to be feared, she brushed aside short-term disrepute and called in the Emperor's physician, Xenophon, whose complicity she had already won. He is reported to have pushed a feather lined with quick-acting poison down the Emperor's throat, while pretending to help him vomit. Xenophon had grasped the truth that major crimes are dangerous in their earlier stages, but are attended by great rewards in the end.[5]

A day later, on October 13, AD 54, seventeen-year-old Nero was acclaimed by an enthusiastic crowd and the Praetorian guards who had been complicit in the plot. Like Agrippina, many people had an interest in the succession, including Seneca, who we'll discuss later. Tacitus tells us that on his first evening as emperor a tribune came to

Nero to ask, as was the military custom, for the password to be given to the sentinels that night. He replied, *optima mater*, "the best of mothers." The hapless Britannicus was now alone in the palace. Soon he, too, would suffer his father's fate, and the instrument of death was once again poison.

Nero's great challenge, though he was little more than an adolescent, was to free himself of the two heavy burdens his mother had imposed on him: her and his tutor Seneca. At first he behaved with an almost exemplary moderation. There is a famous episode in which, when he had to confirm a death sentence, he exclaimed bitterly, "I wish I had never learned to write." Nero maintained an absolutely correct relationship with the Senate, which was always a delicate matter. His first speech there, written by Seneca, was magisterial, and in it he assured the senators he had accepted his office because the army had wanted it, but also because the authority of the Senate itself had confirmed it. He said that his youth had not been bathed in the blood of civil wars or family conflicts, and he thus nourished neither hatred nor rancor. He outlined a program for his future government that repudiated the abuses at the root of violent resentments. In his house, he added forcefully, the doors would be barred against corruption and intrigue, and the court and the state would remain two distinct entities. All told, it was an excellent debut, and he followed it up with appropriate initiatives. When some senators, eager to curry favor, proposed that gold and silver statues be erected in his honor, the young emperor refused, just as he would later dismiss the initiative to change the start of the new year from January to December, the month of his birth. At the beginning his reign was one of the best Rome had seen. Peace favored trade, the price of houses and land rose, contractors bid to win the great public works projects that were earning handsome profits, and unemployment was reduced to a minimum.

There were those who whispered in the shadows that even Caligula's beginnings had seemed promising before the emperor, transformed by his madness, deified his office and fell into all sorts of excess. These insinuations were dismissed, since Caligula hadn't enjoyed the teachings of a man as wise as Seneca. But the new emperor's apparent sanity was quickly undermined by the excesses of his mother, who had instigated a reign of terror by settling old scores and carrying out vendettas. One episode suffices to give us an idea of Agrippina's limitless arrogance. At a certain point she asked the Emperor to allow her to attend the more important sessions of the Senate. Her request was unprecedented, and she was told such a privilege was impossible, so instead the awful woman convinced Nero to convene the assembly in the library of the imperial palace so that she, hidden behind a door in the next room, could at least follow the debates and take notes on the different opinions expressed.

One of the most serious crises erupted after the assassination of poor Britannicus. Because the fact that he had been poisoned became apparent when the boy's body instantly turned pale, Nero quickly spread the rumor that he had died of one of his recurrent fits of epilepsy. He then ordered that his body be burned immediately in the Campus Martius. Seneca, who knew the truth, was charged with explaining the precipitous funeral to the Senate. The famous intellectual once again rose to the challenge, clarifying that "it was the custom of our ancestors to remove the young dead from sight as soon as possible, and not to prolong the pain of their departure with eulogies or overly elaborate funerals . . ." and so on.

Agrippina was unsettled by Nero's brutal actions. She now saw that her son was capable of making decisions on his own initiative, without her advice or help. Britannicus's murder had taken place right under her eyes, in the same room where she herself had poisoned Claudius, and the implications of the event filled her with horror. Furthermore Nero, scorning his wife, Octavia, became openly infatuated with a freedwoman named Acte who had wiled her way into his heart. "Nero became obsessed with the intrigue, with all its debauchery and secretiveness. His older friends offered no opposition; indeed they were pleased to find all his ardors satisfied by a woman of low rank. . . ."[6] And then there were his undesirable friends, violent and reckless youths, with whom the young emperor went out at night, incognito, wreaking havoc in the city's streets and taverns.

It took only a few months for the situation between mother and son to become intolerable for both. Rather than heeding his *optima mater*, the emperor was listening to his people, as was the case when he ordered by edict that the rules for exacting any tax, always secret until then, be made public; that collections neglected for more than a year could no longer be enforced; and that soldiers be granted the same exemptions as the tribunes except for items they traded. The winter of AD 54–55, before his reign began, was so harsh and rainy that Rome was at the risk of a food shortage. Nero immediately froze the price of maritime shipping and simultaneously reduced the tax on the transport of grain from overseas provinces, deciding that ships were not to be counted in the census of a merchant's worth and were thus not subject to taxation.

Shaken by his newly acquired independence, Agrippina gave her son no respite. She had organized Nero's ascent to the throne perfectly, had assassinated her husband to speed it along, and now he had ungratefully pushed her to the margins, excluding her from involvement in the most important decisions. A woman of her temperament couldn't just remain passive in the face of such a setback and the dangers it presented. At first she tried to stir up a couple of plots to have the ingrate killed, going as far as to look for a possible successor. Once she saw that these attempts all were in vain, she went in the opposite direction; fortified by the allure she exerted over men, she set out to try to seduce the emperor to whom she had given birth. At forty she was still desirable, and she was especially expert in the business of love, accustomed, wrote Tacitus, to all sorts of infamous acts:

> Agrippina was so bent on clinging to power that several times at midday, when food and wine had enflamed Nero, she displayed herself to him, primed and ready for incest. Intimates marked their sensual kisses, the embraces that were the prelude to the crime.[7]

Worried about the direction the events were taking, Seneca tasked Acte, Nero's favorite mistress, to warn him of the rumors going around, and tell him his soldiers wouldn't tolerate being led by a prince who had committed such a sacrilege. Nero got the message, and soon he couldn't even stand his mother's presence. He asked what means might be used to kill her, "veneno an ferro vel qua alia vi" [poison, a sword, or some other violence]. But things weren't so simple. Never before had a love-hate relationship been more obvious or more loaded. For the time being Nero kept his mother at a distance and refused to see her, although he continued to indulge in the lascivious fantasies she provoked. Dio Cassius tells us that even when their relationship was interrupted, the emperor often called a courtesan who resembled Agrippina, and when he made love to her he then boasted to his friends that he'd gone to bed with his mother. The desire, or perhaps necessity, of killing her arose from this dark obsession that Suetonius made explicit, "Some say that he did, in fact, commit incest with Agrippina every time they rode in the same litter—the state of his clothes when he emerged proved it."[8]

Anicetus, commander of the fleet at Misenum and an old friend of the emperor's, seems to have come up with the plan to kill Agrippina. He suggested to Nero that he invite his mother to the festival of Minerva, which was to be celebrated that year (AD 59) from March 19 to 23 at Baiae. The invitation must have been an affectionate one, because Agrippina accepted, and once they were far from Rome everything seemed easier. Embarking at Anzio, she went by boat to Baiae, where she was warmly received by her son. They dined together in a cheerful mood, and Agrippina occupied the place of honor to the emperor's left. Once they finished eating the party continued for a while with light conversation, and then Agrippina asked to be allowed to return to Bauli. Nero accompanied her to her ship, ". . . clinging to her and looking into her eyes. This may have been the final touch of hypocrisy; or perhaps this last sight of his mother as she went to her death touched even Nero's cruel heart,"[9] wrote Tacitus, and Suetonius added, "In a very happy mood he led Agrippina down to the quay and even kissed her breasts before she stepped aboard."[10]

The evening was resplendent with stars, and the sea was calm ("Noctemsideribus inlustrem et placido mari quietam"). The ship, powered by the effort of chained oarsmen, moved into the distance, rustling on the black, still water. Agrippina and her maid, Acerronia, went to the stern of the boat, where there was a luxurious couch under a baldachin. They were unaware that above the seemingly light canopy that sheltered them were several hundred pounds of lead weights. At an agreed upon signal the weights were released and fell down onto the couch. As chance would have it, though, the sides of the couch held against the weights, and the violent movement of the ship saved the intended victims, throwing them into the water. But Acerronia then did something foolish; not really understanding the tragic game she was enmeshed in, she called out for help saying that she was the Emperor's mother. She was immediately beaten to death with oars and clubs. Agrippina was more astute, and swam away silently, "until picked up by men in small boats. They brought her to the Lucrine lake, and then she was carried to her villa."[11]

The physical consequences of the attack were slight; Agrippina reported only a shoulder wound. More serious than her physical condition, however, was her situation, and the slim chances of her survival. A consummate actress, she took the most astute course. Pretending she hadn't understood what had happened, she sent a message to Nero by a freedman in which she told him that by the grace of the gods she had escaped from a serious accident, all was well, and that the emperor should not worry about his mother's health. Nero, who was obviously waiting for different news, saw through his mother's message and began to fear a vendetta—the woman might stir up sedition in the legions or manipulate the Senate against him. Uncertain what to do, he sent for Seneca and Burro, the prefect of the Praetorian guard. Seneca asked Burro if it were not time now to give the soldiers a direct order to have Agrippina killed. Burro was uneasy and equivocated, saying that his soldiers, loyal to the imperial household and the memory of Germanicus, would not dare to assassinate his daughter. He was afraid the Praetorians would refuse to obey and that the political consequences would be disastrous, so proposed a different solution to avoid that pitfall. Since Anicetus, captain of the fleet, had started the whole mess, he should finish the job. Nero was enthusiastic about this advice, which seemed to solve the problem. Seneca (although this is only a hypothesis) stood on the sidelines, happy to have a limited involvement in another murder, no matter how necessary it might be. Tacitus recounts this famous case of matricide:

> Anicetus surrounded the villa, broke down the doors, arrested any servant who crossed his path, and forced his way to the door of her bedroom. A few servants were still on guard; the rest had been frightened away by the invasion. The room was dimly lit; a single maid was in attendance. Agrippina became more and more alarmed: no-one had come from her son . . . Her maid slipped away. "You are leaving me too?" she called; and, turning, she saw behind her Anicetus, and with him a captain of a trireme, Heraculeius, and the centurion of marines, Obaritus. "If you have come to pay me a visit," she exclaimed, "you can say that I am better: but if you are planning a crime, I don't believe my son has a part in it—he never gave orders for his mother's murder!" The murderers closed around

her bed. The first blow was struck by the captain, who hit her on the head with a club. As the centurion drew his sword for the death blow she thrust out her stomach and cried, "Strike my womb!", and then she died of many wounds.[12]

I have always wondered—considering these murders, which remain quite spectacular despite their despicable motives—how much the protagonists were influenced by the spirit of the times, a personal propensity for tragic theatricality, or the examples of heroic epics passed down from archaic times. Agrippina's final words, worthy of being recorded in bronze or marble, seem designed to leave a mark on history. In Tacitus's original Latin her magnificent last words, which so clearly indicate she knew her assassins were sent by her own son, read, "Protendens uterum 'Ventrem feri' exclamavit." Having committed the crime, Anicetus finished the job by having her body cremated that very evening, with the same speed that the body of the unfortunate young Britannicus had been disposed of.

As legend has it, upon hearing the news of his mother's death Nero exclaimed, "Today the empire is truly mine." Whether he said it or not, the phrase does represent the weight of Agrippina's presence in the first five years of his reign. Seneca stayed on as the man, tutor, intellectual, and philosopher who tried to keep Nero balanced—a difficult task, since his equilibrium balanced on a veritable hairline. On the one hand he tried to do so without squelching the young prince's capriciousness, including his criminal acts, and on the other he tried to guide him toward a less ignoble goal. I have often thought, and don't frankly know if it's reasonable, that Seneca was to Nero as Machiavelli was to Cesare Borgia. Seneca knew the high moral ground; in his *On Clemency*, his *Dialogues,* and especially his *Letters to Lucilius* he defines stoic ethics and sketches a concept of philosophy based on a search for virtue and the practice of liberty in its purest sense, beginning from the inside. The philosopher was even capable of transcending his own times, and proclaimed a respect for all living creatures, charity toward the humble and unhappy, and even to slaves. Based on this generous, broad vision of the world some have suggested that Seneca was secretly a Christian, offering as proof his exchange of what are certainly apocryphal letters to Saint

Paul. While this is likely legend, it's justified in light of his *humanitas*—a humane sense that even the world of Neoplatonic thought can rarely equal.

How can we explain, then, that a man of such talent and noble sentiment also practiced usury—even if it was just what we might today call normal bank loans? Who ridiculed the recently assassinated Claudius in his *Apokolokyntosis* (a title best translated as Apotheosis of a Pumpkin-Head)? It's true that Claudius was reputed to be stupid, but he was also the man who had sentenced Seneca to seven years of exile in Corsica. Nevertheless, to mock a man who has just died is ignoble, especially in a culture that valued the precept "de mortuis nihil nisi bonum" [say nothing but good about the dead]. What about Seneca's brilliant justification to the Senate for Britannicus's hurried cremation? In this case, too, we can spot a political motive. As long as Britannicus, Claudius's legitimate son, was still alive, Nero's reign was in danger, and his death might have been considered a guarantee of the continuity of government. And what of the assistance he offered in the assassination of Agrippina? The reason here might also have been farsighted politics; Nero's mother was trying to set up a true regime of terror, and while she was alive it was more difficult for Seneca to construct the just ruler he hoped to make of Nero. Her presence caused the emperor's serious mental problems, and it was reasonable to believe that her death would allow him to regain some psychological balance.

After his mother's murder Nero spread rumors that she'd tried to have him assassinated and that, once the conspiracy had been discovered, he ordered her death. There were celebrations organized to give thanks for the danger thus avoided, and officials were slipped a bit of money to assure their loyalty. Seneca wrote the speech to report the facts to the Senate, and it was a true masterpiece of perfidy. It recounted all Agrippina's evil deeds and her unrestrained ambition, as well as that of her family. It even told the episode of the shipwreck, presenting it as an accident although, as Tacitus aptly asked, who but the vainest fool could regard that as accidental? He then referred to the attempt to assassinate Nero, which Agrippina entrusted to a freedman armed only with a sword. Tacitus asked again who could believe "that a single shipwrecked woman could dispatch an assassin through the imperial guards and fleet." Seneca took the blame, "since he had composed the dispatch which was a confession of guilt."[13]

Can such contradictions be explained? To some degree the answer probably lies in the ancient notion, already employed by Plato, that putting a philosopher, or a man inspired by one, at the highest levels of government would assure the ruler a lofty guide and a balance of power. This great opportunity offered a justification for overlooking crimes committed in his name that would otherwise have been intolerable. Seneca dreamed of a democratic monarchy in which the emperor, wisely guided, would govern in the interest of the people, a just and paternal prince to tutor the Senate. Nero's interest, on the other hand, was to have a man like Seneca he could count on to hold the evil beasts—the senators—at bay by offering the protection of his incomparable oratorical and dialectical skills, as well as his great prestige. The emperor might have imagined that in the end Seneca would guarantee him a positive balance and the overall success of his reign. Lastly, we need to remember that Nero's reign started off so well; Tacitus offered an explanation for Seneca's participation in a passage in the *Annals* that describes the crimes Agrippina was guilty of:

> A reign of terror would have set in had not Afranius Burrus and Annaeus Seneca prevented it. They were Nero's governors, and by mutual sympathy uncommon in those who share power, they established by different means an equal hold over him. Burrus did this by soldierly qualities and an austere character. Seneca by his lessons in oratory and his dignified courtesy. They helped each other to control the young prince's dangerous years of adolescence. . . .[14]

In other words, if Seneca hadn't been there things would have been even worse. The other accusations leveled against the philosopher were in some instances motivated by envy; others he took the time to refute in writing. In his *De vita beata* (*On the Happy Life*) he seems to be responding to those who chided him for the discrepancies between his life and works. He wrote, "You talk one way, you live another." Then, citing other philosophers but referring to himself, he added, "It is of virtue, not of myself, that I am speaking, and my quarrel is against all vices, more especially against my own." In the same text he answered another accusation, that a wise man might live comfortably and have money:

The philosopher shall own ample wealth, but it will have been wrested from no man, nor will it be stained with another's blood—wealth acquired without harm to any man, without base dealing, and the outlay of it will be not less honourable than was its acquisition. . . . [15]

That said, it's clear that many contradictions are mixed into the stain on Seneca's reputation, especially in the years of his early adulthood. It also seems to me that, although there are some connections between the vision Machiavelli had for Cesare Borgia and the one Seneca had for Nero, there are also fundamental differences. Seneca tried to mold his ruler, while Machiavelli limited himself to observing the deeds and political ambitions of the young Borgia. He was a scion of that infamous family, and Guicciardini wrote that the Borgia's "simulation and dissimulation were so noted in the court of Rome that a commonly known proverb arose that stated, 'The Pope never does what he says he will and [Cesare] never says what he is doing.'"

Cesare Borgia employed his profound amorality and extraordinary strength to destroy local lords and potentates one by one, including the autonomous fiefdoms and small courts of central Italy, a land perennially bloodied by factional strife. His goal was to found a great unified State with one constitution and laws that applied to everyone. This was the project that seduced Machiavelli, and there's no doubt that, had Italy been unified in the sixteenth century rather than the exhausted nineteenth century, its destiny as a nation and its place in Europe would be quite different. Judged by current criteria, a man like Borgia would certainly have been sent to the gallows. His goal, however, was grandiose, and was intended to benefit the people as much as himself, a fact clear in his ability to win the loyalty of "all those people who have begun to taste the good things coming to them."

The double dare intertwined between the philosopher and the emperor ended with a double failure. Nero's relationship with the Senate soon became unworkable. Senators either plotted against him in the shadows or prostrated themselves obsequiously, and any possibility of a real dialogue between the two institutions disappeared. Seneca slowly came to realize that his actions were in vain, and he decided, in AD 62, to retreat to a more private life. He said to his prince, "By now we've reached the limits: you, of what a prince should give his friend: I, of what a friend should accept from his sovereign."[16] What he proposed, essentially, was a friendly accommodation, but this was not enough to save him. Three years later Seneca found himself drawn into one of the most famous and complex political conspiracies of ancient times, the Pisonian Conspiracy, in which two groups, one led by the head of the Senate, the other by the head of the military, organized an attempt to overthrow Nero.

Seneca once again behaved with ingenious duplicity. He neither played a direct role in the conspiracy, nor refused Piso's invitation to join, nor did he denounce him. In taking his leave, he limited himself to wishing Piso well, "since my wellbeing depends on his." Were these few words enough to condemn him? Tacitus is probably right—Nero grabbed this opportunity to rid himself of a tutor he was beginning to find unbearable. He sent a praetorian officer to Seneca's villa on the Via Appia with the order to kill him. Tacitus's description of Seneca's death is one of his most memorable passages:

> Then, embracing his wife and relaxing his sternness a little before the terrors confronting her, he begged and prayed her to temper her grief, and not give way to it forever. Sorrow for her husband's loss could be honorably assuaged by the contemplation of a life that had been devoted to virtue. But she insisted that she had made up her mind to die, and demanded the stroke of the executioner. Seneca had no mind to deny her glory. Besides, there was his love for her, and the thought that he might be leaving the wife so cherished by him to ill-treatment. "I was trying," he said, "to show you how to make life tolerable; you prefer the glory of death, and I shall not grudge it to you to set the example. So let us show equal constancy in facing the end; yet your death will carry greater honor." After this they both severed their veins with a single stroke. But Seneca's body was old, emaciated by long abstinence, and his blood flowed slowly, so he cut the veins in his ankles and behind his knees. Exhausted by severe convulsions, and alarmed lest his agony should break his wife's spirit—and lest he himself should lose his self-control at the sight of her sufferings—he persuaded her to leave him and go into another room. His eloquence did not desert him even in his dying moments. Summoning the shorthand writers, he dictated to them at length; what he said has been published, and I shall not try to paraphrase it here.[17]

Paolina, his beloved wife, was saved from death at the last moment, and dedicated the rest of her life to her husband's memory. There were those, however, who said that she only feigned her wish to die, and that her actions were merely a comedy recited for the benefit of her dying husband—all calumnies, perhaps. Seneca, however, found that death by bleeding was too slow, and had poison brought to him, just as Socrates had. When that also proved ineffective, he asked to be carried into a steam bath, where he died of suffocation. He was sixty-nine years old.

Nero was accustomed to conspiracies. Not a season passed without the announcement of a plot to take his life, be it to protect or to trick him. Gaius Ophonius Tigellinus was the principal guarantor of the emperor's safety, and probably also crafted many of the deceptions that surrounded him. A Sicilian of humble birth, he had been exiled by Caligula because he was accused of adultery with Agrippina, Caligula's sister. He was also wealthy, and spent a couple of years away from Rome raising and training horses for the races and circuses. Recalled to the capital by Claudius, he became prefect of the Praetorians in AD 62, as well as Nero's favorite. The discovery and ferocious repression of the Pisonian Conspiracy was his political masterpiece, and became the prototype for every future action undertaken "to protect the state," and the means tyrants so frequently used to maintain their power. There were several reasons why Nero needed to rely on so terrible a man. Firstly, every man in power, no matter how great, needs some henchman to carry out his dirty work. Tigellinus's absolute loyalty to his emperor, combined with a talent for interrogation without scruples or mercy, stood him in good stead. He also shared some of Nero's vices, with lust at the forefront. As he got older and fell further into mental illness, Nero's sexual appetites became heartier and more twisted. Suetonius wrote:

> Gradually Nero's vices gained the upper hand: he no longer tried to laugh them off, or hide, or deny them, but turned quite brazen. . . . Whenever he floated down the Tiber to Ostia, or cruised past Baiae, he had a row of temporary brothels erected along the shore, where a number of noblewomen, pretending to be madams, stood waiting to solicit his custom. . . . Not satisfied with seducing free-born boys and married women, Nero raped the Vestal Virgin Rubria. . . . Having tried to turn the boy Sporus into a girl by castration, he went through a wedding ceremony with him—dowry, bridal veil and all—which the whole Court attended; then brought him home, and

treated him as a wife. He dressed Sporus in the fine clothes normally worn by an Empress and took him in his own litter not only to every Greek assize and fair, but actually through the Street of Images at Rome, kissing him amorously now and then.[18]

Poor Sporus was rechristened with a woman's name—Sabina—and it was said he could imitate a woman's sexuality in every way except the ability to reproduce. Some people observed that it would have been a blessing for humanity if Nero's father, Domitius, had also taken a wife like Sabrina. In sociological terms, today we would say that Nero was bisexual, as he could be with both men and women, in all roles. In psychological terms, however, it is clear that his was a case of serious mental illness aggravated by the irresponsible judgment his condition allowed him. Elsewhere Suetonius wrote:

> Nero practiced every kind of obscenity, and at last invented a novel game: he was released from a den dressed in the skins of the wild animals, and attacked the private parts of men and women who stood bound to stakes. After working up sufficient excitement by this means, he was dispatched—shall we say?—just as his freedman Doryphorus. Doryphorus now married him—just as he himself had married Sporus—and on the wedding night he imitated the screams and moans of a girl being deflowered.

Suetonius tended to spread gossip and maliciousness, but not even he could have invented scenes like these without some truth behind them.

In addition to sex, Nero also abused the pleasure of eating, and with it carried the Roman art of preparing food to an extreme. There is a body of eloquent works about food in Roman literature, including the ten volume cookbook—*De re coquinaria* (*On the Art of Cooking*)—by Marcus Gavius Apicius, a famous chef of sorts, and the uproariously funny novel *Satyricon* by the ultimate arbiter of elegance, Petronius.

The Roman's most important meal of the day was dinner, which started in the early afternoon (at the ninth hour, from 2:30 to 3:45 P.M. in the summer) and might last until sunset, midnight, or even (according to Petronius) until the first light of dawn. Given the scarce means for artificial lighting, Roman time was regulated according to sunlight—at least for the common citizen. A Roman got up at about 4:30

in the morning in the summer and about 7:30 in the winter, and the day was then divided into twelve hours, according to our measurements of time, between dawn and sunset. For those who could afford it (certainly not the poor or slaves), meals were consumed while reclining on a triclinium—a type of slightly inclined couch on which diners stretched out, leaning on their left arms. They also dined barefoot (a slave would already have washed their feet to remove the dust of the street), with women, be they wives or mistresses, reclining beside the men. A napkin was worn across the front of the tunic to avoid staining it. Forks were unknown, and diners used their fingers to take food from bowls placed at the center of the table or passed by servants—a custom common throughout the Mediterranean world, from Greece to Northern Africa. Spoons were available, as were toothpicks of ivory, gold, and silver. After every dish servants brought the diners cups with perfumed water to dip their fingers in. Given the extraordinary length of the meal, diners often had to relieve their bodily needs. Upon command a slave would bring a silver or bronze chamber pot for the diner's convenience. For more solid needs the necessary facilities had been prepared just outside the dining room. In one scene in his *Satyricon*, Petronius recounts how the host, Trimalchio, a rich peasant, comes back into the dining room after relieving himself:

> "You'll excuse me, friends," he began, "but I've been constipated for days and the doctors are stumped. I got a little relief from a prescription of pomegranate rind and resin in a vinegar base . . . But if any of you has any business that needs attending to, go right ahead; no reason to feel embarrassed. There's not a man been born yet with solid insides. And I don't know any anguish on earth like trying to hold it in. Jupiter himself couldn't stop it from coming . . . Well, anyone at table who wants to go has my permission, and the doctors tell us not to hold it in. Everything's ready outside—water and pots and the rest of the stuff. Take my word for it, friends, the vapors go straight to your brain. Poison your whole system. I know of some who've died from being too polite and holding it in."[19]

The Romans ate and drank a lot during these interminable banquets. Their wine was much less alcoholic than ours, and drunkenness at the table was rare. Indigestion was more frequent, and the cure was to vomit, discreetly but without leaving the table, in containers brought by slaves for that purpose. Slow service added to the length of the banquets, and the host provided entertainment between courses, be it music, fire-eaters, magicians, or female erotic dancers. But we were talking here about Nero, and I'll return to him after just two or three more observations.

One of the glories of Roman cuisine was a sauce called *garum*, which we can safely say, without hesitation, was disgusting. It was made in a big pot, or an amphora that held about 30 liters, by layering raw, fatty fish (salmon, eel, or sardines) and aromatic herbs (anise, coriander, fennel, mint, oregano, etc.). The sauce was the liquid that gathered in the bottom of the container after a few weeks. Apicius, who loved the stuff, found a way to make *garum* less offensive to the nose, treating it like the byproduct of decomposition that it really is. Distancing *garum* from nose and palate, let's instead have a look at the heights of sophistication ancient Roman cuisine could reach as described in the *Satyricon*:

> Following the dogs came servants with a tray on which tray we saw a wild sow of absolutely enormous size. Perched rakishly on the sow's head was the cap of freedom which newly freed slaves wear in token of their liberty, and from her tusks hung two baskets woven from palm leaves: one was filled with dry Egyptian dates, the other held sweet Syrian dates. Clustered around her teats were little suckling pigs made of hard pastry, gifts for the guests to take home as it turned out, but intended to show that ours was a broodsow. The slave who stepped up to carve, however, was not our old friend Carver who had cut up the capons, but a huge fellow with a big beard, a coarse hunting cape thrown over his shoulders, and his legs bound up in cross-gaiters. He whipped out his knife and gave a savage slash at the sow's flanks. Under the blow the flesh parted, the wound burst open and dozens of thrushes came whirring out! But bird-catchers with limed twigs were standing by and before long they had snared all the birds as they thrashed wildly around the room. Trimalchio ordered that a thrush be given to each guest, adding for good measure, 'Well, that old porker liked her acorns juicy all right.' Then servants stepped forward, removed the baskets hanging from the sow's nose, and divided the dry and sweet dates out equally among the guests.[20]

The second episode—one of purely licentious entertainment—describes a scene worthy of the most unrestrained eighteenth-century libertinism. To better understand, it's important to know what has just happened; the matron Philomela, a formerly skillful gold-digger turned old woman, continued her old profession by prostituting her two children, a boy and a girl. She brought both children to the house of Eumolpus, who for reasons of his own was pretending to be bedridden with an attack of gout, and left them with him:

> Eumolpus—whose frustrations had reached such a pitch that he was on the point of making me his Ganymede—lost no time and immediately invited the girl to a lesson in ritual buttock-thumping. But he had told everyone that he was gouty and cursed with a bad liver, and unless he maintained this fiction, he ran the risk of giving the whole show away. So, in order to sustain his story, he ordered the girl to sit down on his lap and test for herself at close quarters the full extent of that 'uprightness and largesse and conspicuous humanity' her mother had just commended so warmly. Then he told Corax to slip under the bed, plant his hands firmly on the floor, and stroke the cadence for him by heaving with his buttocks. Corax carried out his orders to perfection: a slow smooth stroke, every thrust so timed that it coincided exactly with the girl's expert twisting and writhing. Then, as the lesson neared its conclusion, Eumolpus shrieked to Corax to quicken the tempo. Corax promptly obeyed, humping away like mad, while Eumolpus swung there in mid-air, bouncing and swaying back and forth between the servant and the girl, for all the world like a human seesaw. The first lesson over, Eumolpus immediately began the second, much to our own amusement and also his own. Meanwhile, fearing that my long inactivity had left me out of shape, I approached the brother who was eagerly following his sister's gymnastics through a chink in the door. Sophisticated boy that he was, he made no objection, but once again the god's hostility frustrated my rising hopes . . .[21]

Even if Suetonius didn't say so explicitly, it is clear that Nero participated in scenes like this one and enjoyed the dishes described above. Amongst the women in his life, Poppea Sabina holds a special place, in part because of the dramatic beginning of their relationship. At the start of their affair Poppea was married to Rufrius Crispinus, who had, under Claudius, been prefect of the Praetorian guards. It seems that she then fell in love with the handsome Otho, who seduced her with his youth, splendor, and the aura that came from being the emperor's favorite. Poppea left her husband to marry Otho, who, convinced that sharing his wife with the emperor would advance his career, wed her and then immediately cast her into the arms of his powerful friend. The relationship took on such energy that it finally annoyed Otho, and he tried to intercede. So taken by his new love, however, Nero didn't have to think twice before he sent him as governor to Lusitania—basically the most distant spot imaginable. If we believe this version of events, Poppea was the real force behind the intrigue. According to a different version of the story she was instead forced into a game from which she couldn't escape. Whatever the lost truth might be, Poppea established herself as head of the imperial palaces, beside a man who seems to have lost his head over her. Nero divorced his wife, Octavia, for Poppea, creating a wretched succession of slander and cruel vendettas. According to Tacitus:

> [Poppea] had long been his mistress: she had ruled Nero when he was her lover, and she ruled him as his wife. She now induced one of Octavia's household to accuse Octavia of adultery with a slave. . . . Octavia's handmaidens were questioned; under torture a few made admissions that were untrue, but most of them stubbornly asserted their mistress' innocence. One even said to Tigellinus, as he stood over her, 'Her privy parts are cleaner than your face.'[22]

Poor Octavia faced the same miserable end so many of Nero's enemies had. She was exiled to a godforsaken place and then strangled by Praetorian guards after they slit the veins of her arms and legs. Her decapitated head was sent back to Rome so that Nero could verify personally that his orders had been carried out. Poppea then became the true queen of the court, the creator and curator of an unprecedented life of luxury. Augustus and Tiberius had disdained any show of magnificence, Caligula died before he could realize any part of his sumptuous dreams, Claudius's life in the palace had assumed a tone we could call bourgeois, and poor Octavia, relegated to the background and unloved by her husband, never really had a chance to make a mark on court life. It was therefore Poppea who first brought magnificence and refinement into Nero's life. He was grateful to her for that, and wrote verses about her long, blonde hair and pale, luminous skin. Women in Rome spoke of nothing but her lovely hair and the splendor of her skin, and tried to learn her secrets, went overboard with their gossip, and delighted in tales of her excesses. Pliny the Elder wrote in his *Natural History* that when the lovely and capricious empress traveled she was accompanied by four hundred donkeys so she could bathe in their milk every day—this is what gave her skin its unparalleled whiteness and freshness. Juvenal assures us that Poppea wore a mask to protect her face from any contact with impurities in the air. Most likely she used an oily and regenerative lotion that she lathered on her face and body at night and which was then removed in the morning, anticipating the popular procedures of modern beauty treatments.

Despite this evident self-adoration and the time it must have cost her, Poppea was an intelligent woman aware of the world around her. Flavius Josephus wrote in his *Antiquities of the Jews* that "she feared God," describing her as sympathetic to the Jewish world. Based on these bits of information, she developed a notorious reputation over time. It's been suggested, for example, that it was she, not Nero, who channeled popular wrath against the Christians following Rome's great fire. Others think that, given how curious and sharp she was, Poppea would more likely have been interested in Christianity, attracted by the strangeness of a religion that had transformed an obscure criminal into a God.

The many rumors and conjectures that have swirled around Poppea agree on only one point: from the moment she married Nero this fickle, sexually adventurous woman was completely faithful to the emperor. This did little, however, to stop her tragic death. Poppea died suddenly just after she turned thirty-five. Some said she was poisoned by her husband, while others claimed that Nero mortally kicked his pregnant wife in a moment of rage. It has also been speculated that she was killed by a premature childbirth that proved fatal due to the exhaustion following the many festivities she was constrained to attend. Whatever the cause of her death, Nero wanted a grandiose funeral. Her body was carried in a solemn procession to the Forum, where the Emperor himself delivered a eulogy from the same tribune that Mark Antony used to eulogize Caesar. Her corpse was embalmed rather than burned on a pyre, and according to Pliny, Arabia itself could not produce the immense quantity of perfumes that Nero, lost in a fantasy about preserving her beauty, wanted to use.

The famous fire of Rome, in AD 64—one of the chief events in the history of the city as well as in Nero's reign—remains enigmatic in many of its details. We know it happened in the middle of the summer, that it was very hot, and that Nero, who had grown fat, suffered greatly from the heat. Between one and two in the morning of July 19, a breathless messenger arrived at Anzio, where Nero was vacationing, announced that the Circus Maximus was burning, and that the flames were threatening the imperial palaces. The fire had started in a block of densely built shacks and small houses, inhabited for the most part by the Greek and Far Eastern merchants who used them as shops and residences.

Leaving immediately, with his horse at a gallop, Nero arrived in Rome in time to see the entire area transformed into a giant brazier, and his own *Domus Transitoria* (whose name referred to its portico, which connected the Palatine and Equiline hills) was also reduced to ashes. It took six days to contain the fire, and buildings in its path were demolished to prevent them from fueling the flames. Homes and shops, temples and sanctuaries—including that of Vesta where the Roman *penates* (gods of the hearth) were housed—masterpieces of Greek art, and many other ancient works were all burned. A second fire, a consequence of the first, flared up a few days later in an area that in modern Rome is defined by the triangle formed by the Piazza del Popolo, Piazza del Montecitorio, and the Villa Medici. More than 10 percent of the city went up in smoke, including all of the Forum south of the Via Sacra.

The rumor that Nero himself set the fire was to spread immediately and so widely that many authoritative voices continued to repeat it. Pliny the Elder briefly noted the event in his *Natural History*, but mentioned it as if it were fact: "Nero burned Rome." Tacitus, writing a half-century after the fact, said "We do not know if this disaster was an accident or the malicious work of the Emperor." Suetonius was even more explicit, "Nero . . . set fire to the city . . . and though a group of ex-consuls caught his attendants, armed with oakum and blazing torches, trespassing on their property, they dared not interfere."[23] Along the same lines, Dio Cassius wrote, "He wanted to execute a project that had long smoldered in him: to destroy all of Rome and the Empire while he was still alive."

Why would the emperor, unbalanced as he may have been, have engineered such an impolitic crime of such broad scope? According to Tacitus he was motivated by a desire to found a new city more beautiful than anything in existence, which would bear his name forever—Neropolis. It is true that during the reconstruction of the city the emperor suggested some urban improvements with regard to the width of streets, the alignment of buildings, their height, and some added defense against fire. Dio Cassius and Suetonius shared Tacitus's idea that in his madness the emperor actually envied Priam, King of Troy, and the sublime pleasure of witnessing the destruction of his own city and realm. All of these chroniclers, regardless of the fact that none of them were eyewitnesses, noted that while the fire raged Nero, dressed in the costume of a lyre-player and wearing a laurel crown, sang of the ruin of Troy, "comparing the present disaster to that ancient rout." They differed only in where they placed the emperor: Tacitus had him "on the stage in his palace"; Suetonius set him in the "tower of Maecenas"; and Dio Cassius put him at the "top of the Palatine Hill." Another suggestion that enjoyed wide circulation and a certain plausibility was that the fire allowed Nero to clear the site where he would build his new and magnificent golden palace. Henryk Sienkiewicz, who won the Nobel Prize for literature in 1905, offered an interesting, albeit fictitious, profile of the emperor in his famous novel *Quo Vadis?*, subtitled "a chronicle of the times of Nero." Sienkiewicz's Nero was an aesthete afflicted by the trivialities of the world, a man who knew only excesses—both of good and evil. Nero says of himself, "I know the people say I am crazy. I am not a madman, but rather a seeker. If I seem crazy it is only from boredom, from the worry of not knowing what to look for. I want to be a superman because only then will I be a great artist ... oh, how vulgar the world will be when I am no longer a part of it."

Whether or not it was Nero's doing, it is certain that the fire was seen as the work of professional arsonists, sinister figures well known in Rome at the time, as we can deduce from the severe penalties prescribed for their crime. The crudest of these laws called for the arsonist to be burned alive wearing a highly flammable tunic. In his XIII Satire, Juvenal evoked the sinister figure of this "traitor who set fires with sulfurous materials." Another example comes from the

Catiline Conspiracy, when those complicit in the plot were to signal their coup d'état by lighting a fire. But it's precisely the common occurrence of arson, and the ease with which it could be committed in a city of straight streets and wooden houses, that makes the opposite hypothesis plausible—that someone organized a vast fire in order to blame it on the emperor. In other words, even the fire could have been the result of one of the many conspiracies against Nero.

In the attempt to diffuse the popular fury he felt was building against him (we need only imagine the huge number of homeless), Nero needed to find a scapegoat. He did so by putting the blame on Christians, adherents of a new sect who were highly unpopular in Rome. In his *Annals*, Tacitus writes about this memorable moment in history in a lively passage:

> Nero looked around for a scapegoat and inflicted the most fiendish tortures on a group of persons already hated by the people for their crimes. This was the sect known as Christians. Their founder, one Christus, had been put to death by the procurator Pontius Pilate in the reign of Tiberius. This had checked the abominable superstition for a while, but it broke out again and spread, not merely through Judea, where it originated, but even to Rome itself, the great reservoir and collecting ground for every kind of depravity and filth. Those who confessed to being Christians were at once arrested, but on their testimony a great crowd of people were convicted, not so much on the charge of arson, but of hatred of the entire human race. They were put to death amid every kind of mockery. Dressed in the skins of wild beasts, they were torn to pieces by dogs, or were crucified, or burned to death: when night came, they served as human torches to provide lights. Nero threw open his gardens for this entertainment, and provided games in the Circus, mingling with the crowd in a charioteer's dress, or else standing in the car. These Christians were guilty, and well deserved their fate, but a sort of compassion for them arose, because they were being destroyed to glut the cruelty of a single man and for no public end.[24]

The coldness in Tacitus's description of the inhuman torture the Christians endured is surprising, but the brief parenthetical statement in which he suggests that the followers of that religion were "hated for their crimes," is also interesting. This is confirmed by Suetonius; even he describes them in similarly cold terms, "Christians, a type of individual dedicated to a new and evil superstition." Where did this strong antipathy for them come from? Jews and Christians were accused of hating the human race because they lived in segregated communities and didn't participate in public life or the religious ceremonies that in Rome were considered both patriotic and a civic duty. They would not put their God in the Pantheon next to the others, and insisted that theirs was the only true God. The *Pax Romana* had been enough to guarantee the coexistence of all religions, as it united countless different peoples and cults. The pretensions of the Jews and Christians undermined the whole Roman social construction, especially because the emperor incarnated a double authority, both civil and religious. Nonetheless, Christians were not openly persecuted until AD 63; after the great fire, and given their unsavory reputation, they became the ideal scapegoat for popular fury.

Nero survived the disastrous fire politically, although echoes of the event followed his reputation for centuries. Popular literature in the early years of Christianity was full of his misdeeds, and even as late as the sixth century a moralist like Boethius wrote in his *Consolation of Philosophy*, "What crimes and tragedies Nero committed, he, the abominable monster who burned the capital of the world."

The Emperor, lost now in his own madness, wrote verses, composed music, recited poetry, and wanted to be remembered as an orator and poet rather than a political leader. He married his third wife, Messalina Statilia, whose husband he'd had executed after the Pisonian Conspiracy. Yet his relationship with the castrato Sporus continued unabated. When he abandoned Rome in AD 66, as it had become unbearable for him to be there, he took Sporus, not his wife, with him. He decided to participate in the Olympic games in Greece, and departed with a huge following, leaving Aelius, a freedman, in charge of the city. In Greece he took part in every kind of poetry competition, and of course won them all. Grateful to the Greeks, he reduced their taxes drastically without considering how these holes in the budget would be balanced back in Rome. He wondered at the possibility of cutting a canal through the Isthmus of Corinth, and employed engineers and geologists to do it, ignoring the impossibility of such a feat given the technology of the time. When he returned to Rome, in March of AD 68, he brought with him the 1,808 crowns he had won in various competitions and exhibited them with jubilation at his triumphal parade. Once the festivities ended, he took possession of his new Domus Aurea, which was largely finished, although some work was yet to be done. He seemed happy, and was unperturbed by the news that the legions abroad were revolting against him—in Gaul under Vindex and in Spain under Galba. After having thwarted so many plots and rebellions, both real and imaginary, he believed he could do the same here.

But it wasn't so—the gifts of grain Rome depended on were almost canceled for lack of new provisions, and the emperor had lost touch with reality, a loss that often becomes fatal for those who govern. Nero underestimated popular discontent, and at the end of May a rebellion exploded. Galba marched on Rome from Spain, Tigellinus fled, and a year later was forced to commit suicide by order of the new emperor.

Nero might have finally understood the collapse of his reign when his officers refused his order to prepare for a new trip to Egypt. The loyal Praetorians who had followed him to Greece this time withheld their support. It was early June, Nero had just turned thirty-one after reigning for thirteen years and eight months, and for the first time he was alone. He went to bed, but his slumber was plagued by nightmares. He called out but no one came to his aid. He considered asking forgiveness of the people in such a moving way as to bring them to tears, and he wanted to abdicate and go to Egypt, where he thought he could make a living singing in theaters. He got up in the middle of the night and discovered that even the sentries had gone, "carrying off the bed linens and stealing even the box of poison." He then sought out someone to kill him, but couldn't find even that. Suetonius wrote:

> Phaon, an Imperial freedman, suggested his own suburban villa, four miles away, between the Nomentanan and the Salarian Ways. Nero jumped at the offer. He was in undershirt and slippers; but simply pulled on a faded cloak and hat, took horse and trotted off, holding a handkerchief over his face. Four servants went with him, including Sporus.[25]

The haggard group arrived at the house through subterfuge, and the former ruler of the world had to quench his thirst by drinking with hands from a puddle. Wishing to avoid the main entrance, he cut a path through the brush, tearing his cloak on the briers, and then crawled into a hole that had been dug to keep him hidden as much as possible. He lay on a pallet of straw, and after a brief rest ordered his companions to dig a grave to fit his dimensions. While they were working he exclaimed, several times and with broken-hearted conviction, "Qualis artifex pereo" [What an artist dies along with me!]. His mood changed again, he wept, and then exhorted the few men present to commit suicide, leading by example, and encouraging him to do the same. None of them obeyed, and then everything came to a head:

> By this time the cavalry who had orders to take him alive were coming up the road. Nero gasped . . . then, with the help of his scribe, Epaphroditus, he stabbed himself in the throat and was already half dead when a cavalry officer entered, pretending to have rushed to his rescue, and staunched the wound with his cloak. Nero muttered: "Too late! But, ah, what fidelity!" He died, with eyes glazed and bulging from their sockets, a sight which horrified everyone present.[26]

---

1. Suetonius, *Lives of the Caesars*, trans. Robert Graves (Baltimore: Penguin Books, 1957), 224–25.

2. Ibid., 225.

3. Ibid., 211–12.

4. Tacitus, *The Annals of Tacitus*, trans. Donald R. Dudley (New York: The New American Library, 1966), 237.

5. Ibid., 268.

6. Ibid., 275.

7. Ibid., 301–2.

8. Suetonius, *Lives of the Caesars*, 224.

9. Tacitus, *Annals*, 303.

10. Suetonius, *Lives of the Caesars*, 227.

11. Tacitus, *Annals*, 303.

12. Ibid., 305.

13. Ibid., 306.

14. Ibid., 270–71.

15. Seneca, The Moral Essays, trans. John W. Basore. The Loeb Classic Library. (London, W. Heinemann, 1928–35), vol. II.

16. Tacitus, *Annals*, 326.

17. Ibid., 363–64.

18. Suetonius, *Lives of the Caesars*, 224.

19. Petronius, *The Satyricon*, trans. William Arrowsmith (Michigan: The University of Michigan Press–Ann Arbor, 1959), 45.

20. Ibid., 37–38.
21. Ibid., 177–78.
22. Tacitus, *Annals*, 328.
23. Suetonius, *Lives of the Caesars*, 230–31.
24. Tacitus, *Annals*, 353–54.
25. Suetonius, *Lives of the Caesars*, 237.
26. Ibid., 238.

VI

THE ADVENTURE OF MOSES

OF THE MANY EARLY CHRISTIAN BASILICAS in Rome, San Pietro in Vincoli (Saint Peter in Chains) is particularly interesting for its unique mixture of history and legend. The chains the church is named after are supposedly the ones that bound Saint Peter during his imprisonment, first in Jerusalem and then in Rome. Empress Eudoxia, wife of Valentinian III, fulfilled a vow made by her parents by bringing these shackles from the Holy Land to Pope Leo the Great. When he in turn brought them near the ones in the Roman prison where Peter had been held captive, they miraculously welded themselves together. These ancient chains are still visible today in a reliquary on the high altar.

But what immediately catches the eye when first walking into the basilica are the twenty magnificent columns, ten on each side, which divide the nave into three sections. They are among the most beautiful to be seen in Rome and, I feel, the entire world. These are ancient Doric columns over six meters tall made of white marble quarried at Mount Hymettus in Greece, whose stone, to the naked eye, isn't too different from white Carrara marble. They were origi-nally cut for a Greek temple, and were then used in the city prefect's office on the nearby Esquiline Hill before being placed here. The ionic bases date to the eighteenth century. In the mid-fifth century, Valentinian III gave the set of columns to his wife as his contribution to the rebuilding of the church atop the foundations of an earlier sacred building. When I visited the basilica to prepare this chapter, one of the priests pointed out how the lower part of the columns is abraded up to a certain height, as if in the remote past humans, or perhaps animals, had been tied to them.

The two imposing beams anchored high in the right-hand wall of the central nave are just one trace of the many vicissitudes the building has endured. They're part of the truss of the original roof, which was restored in the fifteenth century by Cardinal Nikolaus Chrypffs, a scientist, theologian, and cardinal born at Cues, near Trier, known by the Italianized name of Nicolò Cusano. These enormous beams were decorated with carvings because they were in plain sight, and they bear a still-legible inscription with the date, ANNO DOMINI M ★ CCC ★ LXV. The cardinal's tomb is in the left nave, and is distinguished by a well-carved sculpture in high relief attributed to Andrea Bregno.

The church may be full of extraordinary things, but the underground chambers are even more fascinating. As part of the project begun in 1956 to replace the building's worn-down floor, the archaeologist Antonio Colini was commissioned to survey the buildings that had been covered by the basilica's construction. These excavations yielded extraordinary findings; beneath the church were houses dating from the Republican period through the third century AD, with fragments of mosaic pavements, cryptoporticus vaults, and a 34-meter-long rectangular hall ending in an apse. The remains of a villa were also uncovered, and are perhaps part of Nero's Domus Transitoria, including gardens, a portico-lined courtyard, and a fountain basin. Further excavations were carried out in the 1990s under the supervision of the engineering department of the University of Rome, La Sapienza, which is housed next door to San Pietro. The results were once again extraordinary. The church and the whole area around it were built in what had been the heart of the ancient city. The Domus Aurea and the Coliseum are just steps away, and to the west the hill steeply descends to the Suburra, which in ancient times was a densely packed working-class neighborhood.

The thick air in the spaces below San Pietro in Vincoli is just one part of a richly evocative atmosphere. The floor mosaic friezes have a sophisticated chiaroscuro modeling, and the tiny tesserae are arranged side-by-side with magisterial regularity. The walls' curvature, which breaks off toward the top, hints at the barrel vaults that were still whole when the space was a complete portico. Still visible here and there are the *bocche di lupo*—wolves' mouths, or openings—that allowed light to pass through. Now visitors need to duck in the dark to wander under the overhanging floor of the church above, but this spot once was a series of gardens and walkways inundated with sunlight, the tinkle of running water, and the rustling of tree branches. It was the Rome that scores of writers and directors imagined before the dust of history almost completely buried it. In one of the hypogea the remains of a chapel are still visible, suggesting it may once have been a mortuary chamber.

Since the moment Colini's work came to a halt, in 1959, nothing has changed, and the excavation has the air of being abandoned—new dust has settled on the ancient dust. A graffito scratched into the wall tells us a man died here in 1798. His name is no longer legible, and only the date and the word *morì* (died) remain clear, hinting at a secret death remembered only by the partial, moving graffito. A rather different memorial, of a rather different death, can be found in the venerable church above, bathed in glorious light rather than hidden down here in the dark, where Michelangelo left us one of the finest examples of both his greatness and what he termed his "tragedy." The work I refer to is his *Moses*, a huge block of stone made human—perhaps too human—by the artist's consummate skill.

The density of intertwined meanings in this statue is so great that looking at it without knowing something about it is almost like not seeing it at all. The great skill with which it was sculpted is immediately striking to anyone, but within the context of Michelangelo's life the *Moses* represents such a period of prolonged suffering that he came to call it, and the tomb it decorates, "the tragedy of my life." Let's have a look at this affair, then, as it's an indispensable premise for understanding one of the great masterpieces of human history.

In March of 1505 Pope Julius II, Giuliano della Rovere, summoned thirty-year-old Michelangelo to Rome. Julius was a warrior pope, skilled politician, and a man interested in conquest and domination. Nothing in him recalled the virtues of Christian charity or brotherly love; on the contrary, the declared objective of his papacy was the reinforcement of the Papal States. Immediately after becoming pope he led an army northward to dislodge the Baglioni family from Perugia and the Bentivoglio from Bologna in order to take their cities. He was more a Renaissance prince than a man of the church, and behaved accordingly. What did this pope ask of the artist? He wanted the Florentine sculptor, creator of the extraordinary *Pietà* and *David*, to build him the greatest tomb ever conceived. At the time the pope was sixty-two years old, and certainly wasn't young, but he remained an indomitable man, full of physical and mental energy. Why, then, would he have been so concerned about his tomb? There are several theories, but the one I find most credible is that a man like him, so avid for greatness and pomp, aimed to guarantee for himself a sort of immortality with a majestic monument.

Michelangelo's prodigious energy and the vastness of his vision were a good match, moreover, for Julius II and his desire for greatness. The two were destined to understand one another, and in this sense the pope picked the right man. "If it is to be done," the artist wrote in a letter shortly after receiving the commission, "it must be the most beautiful in the world." Just what the artist intended as "most beautiful" soon became apparent in his drawings; it wasn't going to be the average decorated wall tomb, but instead would be a tall, rectangular structure, a massive tower one could walk around and admire from all sides. It was to be something like a classical mausoleum, measuring seven by eleven meters, built on three levels: the terrestrial realm, with the famous slaves, on the bottom; the figures of Moses, Saint Paul, and two other prophets above; and the papal cenotaph at the top. There were to be a total of forty figures, all carved from marble, as well as cast bronze niches and reliefs. The interior of this dazzling monument was to house an oval room as the true tomb. It was conceived as a temple dedicated to the Della Rovere pope set within a temple dedicated to Saint Peter.

The patron was so pleased with the design that he ordered the artist to depart as soon as possible for the quarries near Carrara to find the marble best suited for the job. Receiving an initial advance of 1,000 ducats, Michelangelo headed north into Tuscany; he spent eight months in the mountains, between May and December of 1505, negotiating with quarrymen and stonecutters for the blocks of marble, then with muleteers and ship captains since the stone, once carried down to the valley, had to be transported to the docks and then travel by sea to Rome. It was then unloaded at the Ripa Grande, the city's riverbank docks, and dragged on rollers and sledges to the piazza in front of San Pietro in Vincoli. These were superb blocks, numerous enough to fill much of the square, and going to admire them became one of the most popular public diversions.

Michelangelo took up lodgings nearby and immediately started work on the tomb, and the pope, who often took a secret passageway to check the artist's progress, was most pleased. Ascanio Condivi, the artist's humble biographer, tells us that he often stayed to talk with Michelangelo, "conversing with him there about the tomb and other matters no differently than he would have done with his own brother."[1] Condivi's *Life of Michelangelo* was practically dictated to the obedient biographer by the artist himself.

We don't know the details, but it's quite likely that the statue of Moses was one of the first figures Michelangelo carved for the tomb, in part because the prophet's proud bearing and furious energy must have been very much like Julius's. Della Rovere didn't care to waste time—once he'd made a decision he wanted the project completed. He asked Bramante, leading architect of the day, to design a whole new church to replace the existing basilica, an old and venerable building commissioned by Constantine the Great in the fourth century. His vision was of a building that would be the mother church of the Christian universe, the largest and most beautiful temple ever conceived. Its dimensions were beyond all imagination, and Julius's equally immense tomb would be housed within—the surest way to guarantee that his spirit wouldn't die, even after he was dead.

What happened, instead, was that once he launched the project to rebuild Saint Peter's, the pope's enthusiasm for his tomb, so passionate at the beginning, cooled. Perhaps other, more pressing projects, distracted him, or the malice of other artists changed the pope's mind. Michelangelo believed the latter hypothesis, and years later offered an explanation in a letter: "All of the discord that grew up between Pope Julius and me was caused by the jealousy of Bramante and Raphael of Urbino. This was the reason he did not pursue his tomb while he was alive, and it ruined me." The ever-obedient Condivi was even more explicit, "[thus] the architect Bramante, who was loved by the pope, made him change his plans by quoting what common people say, that it is bad luck for anyone to build his tomb during his lifetime, and other stories."[2]

Are we to believe him? It's possible he was right, although in truth Raphael didn't arrive in Rome until several years later. Relationships between artists were never easy, and were often made worse by rivalries, envy, and jealousy, as had always happened, especially in a court setting, where a single decision-maker's mood or capriciousness may affect the commission. It's also possible that Julius II slowed work on the tomb because he'd been distracted by the more grandiose project of rebuilding the basilica, and what Michelangelo saw as malevolence on Bramante's part may only have been a political change of heart on the pope's part.

This ambiguous situation culminated in a scene famous for its high drama and mysteriousness. On April 17, 1506, the Friday following Easter, Michelangelo suddenly left, or, more accurately, fled from Rome. He was responsible for paying off the marble blocks that kept arriving, and since the pope had suspended payments to him he just didn't have the money. He repeatedly sought audience with the pope to discuss the matter, but it was to no avail, until finally, while he was waiting in an antechamber, a guard approached and ordered him out of the palace. The artist hadn't the temperament to stand such an affront, and in great fury wrote a note that read, "Holy Father, I have been thrown out of the palace this morning by Your Holiness; I therefore wish to let you know that from now, if you want me, you will need to look for me somewhere other than Rome."

The pope, informed of the incident before he even received the note, immediately sent five messengers on horseback to follow the sculptor. They didn't catch up to him until the middle of the night, however, in the town of Poggibonsi, which was in Florentine territory and outside the jurisdiction of the papacy. The confrontation was a bitter one. The messengers ordered him to obey, and Michelangelo threatened to have them killed. In the end the artist refused to allow himself to be taken back to Rome, and sent a message to the pope that, since his interest in the tomb had lessened, he considered himself freed of any further obligation. Michelangelo's absence from Rome lasted two years; the proud artist and arrogant pontiff later met in Bologna, and Michelangelo cast a gigantic bronze statue (unfortunately later destroyed) for the pope, but returned to Rome only in the late spring of 1508. He'd hoped to resume work on the tomb, but was instead greeted by a new appointment—and new letdown.

The fruit of that disappointment was an unmatched masterpiece: 300 square meters of painted surfaces filled with hundreds of figures, four years of hard work from the spring of 1508 to late October of 1512, and earnings of 3,000 scudi as recompense for unspeakable physical and emotional distress. The result of all that was the Sistine Chapel, which upon Bramante's insistence Julius II was determined to have Michelangelo decorate with frescoes. Why did the famous architect push such a project? One reliable hypothesis is that Bramante wanted to force Michelangelo into a commission and challenge utterly new to him, thus putting the sculptor's reputation at risk and hoping, secretly, that his relationship with the pope would be compromised.

Things went a bit differently. For the sculptor-turned-painter those four years were true torture, but what could've become a failure instead became one of the greatest achievements in the history of art. At first the pope asked only that the twelve apostles be painted in the chapel's lunettes and that the ceiling be painted a deep blue with a field of stars as was customary at the time. The artist took on the commission with an entirely different vision, making both divine and human history burst out across those walls. He filled the space with the figures that preceded Christ's arrival—his ancestors, as well as the prophets and sibyls who foretold his coming. He spent four years stretched out on the scaffolding boards, stooped, contorted, holding his arms out for hours on end, with his eyes so close to the wall that it affected his vision. Condivi wrote, ". . . because he had spent such a long time painting with his eyes looking up at the vault, Michelangelo then could not see much when he looked down; so that, if he had to read a letter or other detailed things, he had to hold them with his arms up over his head."[3]

Four months after the Sistine's unveiling, in February of 1513, Julius II died, creating new troubles and some serious uncertainties for the great artist. His relationship with the imperious pope had been bitter, but was also emotionally very intense for both of them. Julius had struck Michelangelo at least once with his staff, on the day when the pope had pestered the artist repeatedly with the question, "When will you finish painting this chapel?" and Michelangelo bad-temperedly replied, "When I can." For all of its difficulties, this was in any case a real rapport between two impossible men made to understand one another. Things changed under the next pontiff, as Leo X, Giovanni de'Medici, was a terrible pope who completely misjudged both how deep the feelings of the faithful were with regard to Martin Luther's insistent demands, spreading quickly across Europe, for a greater morality in the church. Luther, an Augustinian monk, had raised a very frank question—why did the pope, who was richer than Triumvir Marcus Licinius Crassus, not pay for the rebuilding of Saint Peter's from his own pocket, instead of financing it with the offerings of the poor faithful? Moreover, the Roman Curia was mired in the undignified market of indulgences, slips of paper guaranteeing the remission of sins in the next life in exchange for money in this one.

When Leo rose to the papacy he was only thirty-seven; he'd been made cardinal at the age of thirteen, and his father was the great Lorenzo de'Medici, called Lorenzo the Magnificent. His was a worldly, sensuous, lazy, and politically uncertain papacy, one in which his relatives and cronies were shamelessly favored. A man like Michelangelo wasn't much to his liking, yet he did have a little work he wanted the artist to complete—the facade of the church of San Lorenzo in Florence. The sculptor tried to avoid the commission, saying that he was busy with Julius's tomb and had just signed a new contract with the former pope's heirs. In the end, though, Michelangelo couldn't refuse the current pope. Leo was, after all, a fellow Florentine, and more importantly, the artist wanted to test himself at a new endeavor; he'd already worked in sculpture and painting, and now it was time to try architecture. His plans for the church were good, but in the end nothing came of the facade project.

Other commissions came along, not all of them successes, as well as other contracts with the executors of Julius's estate, and other troubles. There were also other popes: Leo X died in 1521 and was succeeded by Adriaan Florisz, Hadrian VI, a man of puritanical sensibilities, who shunned the ostentation and corruption of the papal court in Rome. He reigned for little more than a year before dying in September of 1523, and even though his pontificate lasted mere months, he, too, showed keen interest in Michelangelo. In this case, though, the attention was unwelcome, since he was incapable of distinguishing between the decadence of the Curia and the admonitory power of the nudes on the Sistine ceiling, confusing their uncovered members with the many examples of corruption he found in Rome. He planned to have the chapel torn down, as Vasari recounts in an episode of his *Lives of the Painters, Sculptors, and Architects*.

With the death of the Dutch pope, another Medici was elected to the Vatican throne, Giulio, the bastard son of Giuliano, who reigned as Pope Clement VII. His pontificate saw the brutal sack of Rome in 1527 at the hands of Charles V's Imperial troops, followed by the schism with the Church of England promoted by King Henry VIII. Before becoming pope, Cardinal Giulio had asked Michelangelo to design a new sacristy for the Medici church of San Lorenzo in Florence, although in reality it was a family tomb to house the remains of his ancestors, beginning with his uncle, Lorenzo the Magnificent. For the umpteenth time the artist was forced to abandon the sculptures for Julius's tomb, an obligation that had weighed on him for twenty years, in order to take up this new commission, a work that would come to rank amongst his greatest. Shortly before he died, in 1534, Clement came up with another commission for Michelangelo— he wanted a *Last Judgment* on the altar wall of the Sistine Chapel to complete its decoration.

In the meantime the artist had survived years of political tumult, wars, and sieges—events in which he was involuntarily involved— years that forced him to flee, fear for his life, and precipitously return to Florence several times, both before and after the city's ephemeral experiments in Republicanism. In July of 1531 Duke Alessandro de'Medici entered Florence as its new ruler. Condivi described him as "a fierce and vengeful young man."⁴ He also hated Michelangelo to the point of considering having him killed. He was young, just barely over twenty, when his so-called uncle, Clement VII (in reality his father), gave him the new title, making him lord of the city. With Alessandro's arrival Michelangelo no longer felt comfortable in Florence and, additionally convinced by a number of deaths in the family, he decided to return to Rome. He arrived in the Eternal City on September 23, 1534, and two days later fifty-six-year-old Pope Clement died.

At this point in the story I think it's quite clear why Michelangelo considered Julius's tomb the tragedy (though he could just as well have said nightmare) of his life. After Clement's death a new pope—and for Michelangelo a new patron—ascended to the throne. Paul III, Alessandro Farnese, came to the papacy as an old man, but he proved to be an energetic pontiff. It was left to him to convene the Council of Trent, a crucial point in Catholicism's centuries-old history. Paul III took up the idea of the *Last Judgment* for the Sistine Chapel from his predecessor, and wanted at all costs to have Michelangelo paint it, in hopes of making this immense fresco a political manifesto of papal intentions in front of Protestants and the whole world. But Buonarroti had returned to Rome obsessed by the idea that had haunted him for so long, to finish the tomb of Julius II, not least because the former pope's principal heir, his nephew Francesco Maria Della Rovere, Duke of Urbino, a warrior capable of bloody violence, publicly demanded that the unfaithful artist finally decide, after several years and delays, to finish the work he'd already been paid for.

In those same few days something happened that was as extraordinary as it was unheard of. With a dozen or so cardinals in tow, Paul III went in person to Michelangelo's house, in the area of the Macel de'Corvi, around Trajan's Forum. Once there he asked to see the preparatory drawings and cartoons for the *Last Judgment*. He was so impressed that he became even more convinced that this fresco must absolutely be executed. The artist was torn; he had Julius's tomb on his mind, as well as the recent threats of Della Rovere's bellicose nephew. The already completed statue of Moses dominated his studio. Ercole Gonzaga, Cardinal of Mantua, pointed to it and said, "This one statue is enough to do honor to the tomb of Pope Julius." When Paul III understood that the artist was reluctant to take up the *Last Judgment* largely because he was afraid of Francesco Maria Della Rovere's reaction, he said, "I will make it so that the Duke of Urbino is content with three statues from your hand, and the other three can be made by someone else." The pope was true to his word, pacified the hot-tempered duke, and assigned the artist a lifetime salary of 1,200 gold scudi to be paid, in part, by the income from the transit tolls on the Po River near Piacenza. Michelangelo returned to the Sistine Chapel in the summer of 1535 to begin the *Last Judgment*.

The plot of this chapter is the statue of Moses and its checkered destiny, but, having broached the subject of the *Last Judgment*, we can't ignore the fallout following this extraordinary work's unveiling on November 1, 1541. It aroused enthusiasm in some who saw it, but from the beginning contrary opinions prevailed. Someone said the figure of Christ was represented as too young, being beardless, and that he was thus deprived of his due majesty. The vindictive writer Pietro Aretino chimed in, noting that Michelangelo's angels and saints "on the one hand lacked any earthly grace, and on the other were deprived of any celestial bearing." What really struck those who saw it, though, was the nudity. Bernardino Ochino, a former monk, talked openly of its indecency and rebuked the pope for tolerating "so obscene and dirty a picture in the chapel where divine offices are sung." This reaction was the product of bigotry, fear of fueling the Protestant reformation, inability to recognize greatness, and sheer intellectual shortsightedness. In one of its last sessions, the Council of Trent established severe rules governing sacred representations. Wretched Pope Paul IV, Gian Pietro Carafa, successor to Paul III, called the fresco "a pit of nudity," and came very close to plastering the whole thing over. In the end, perhaps with Michelangelo's agreement, a compromise was reached that allowed loin cloths to be added to the male figures to hide their nudity (fortunately these were removed years ago). This task was initially assigned to Daniele daVolterra in 1564, the year Michelangelo died, and then to Girolamo da Fano.

Once the large *Last Judgment* was finished, the artist was bent on finally completing the tomb of Julius II, even if it meant doing so in the reduced scale agreed upon, and accepting a humble placement in the tiny church of San Pietro in Vincoli. But the tragedy—or nightmare—would continue, and once again the proposed finish was for naught. The pope wanted Michelangelo to decorate yet another chapel in his name, the Pauline Chapel. The artist's two paintings here are the *Crucifixion of Saint Peter* and the *Conversion of Saul.*

Meanwhile years passed, illness and family deaths weighed down both body and soul of the great artist, and the tomb of Julius II was yet to be completed. Not until 1545, exactly forty years after it was begun, did the so-called tragedy finally come to an end. At least five times the contract had been revised and signed; the artist had been a vigorous thirty-year-old when the adventure began, and was now an aged seventy-year-old, saddened by melancholy. Della Rovere's heirs had accused him of trying to keep the money he'd been given without completing the commission, wanting to invest the funds in real estate and make profits through usury. Contract after contract, what should have been a superb mausoleum, the most beautiful, grandiose tomb conceivable, was greatly reduced in size and the number of statues that would decorate it. It should have risen up in the middle of Saint Peter's, queen of all basilicas, and instead ended up in the corner of a much lesser church. According to the first contract there were to be forty statues, which then became twenty-eight, then twenty-two; in the contact of 1532 they dwindled to six, and the sepulcher was to have only one face, hence flanking the wall. Vasari reports, "Finally, an agreement was reached on the tomb, and it was to be finished this way: Michelangelo would no longer make the tomb free-standing and four-sided but would do only one side in whatever way he liked, and he was obliged to include six statues by his own hand. . . ."⁵

In the last compromise with the Duke of Urbino, the number of statues the artist was to carve for the tomb was reduced to three: Moses, Rachel, and Leah. The other three, a Madonna, a Prophet, and a Sibyl, were to be carved by someone else. In February of 1545 Michelangelo had both Moses and the two figures flanking him—on the left *Contemplative Life* (also Rachel, or Faith) and on the right *Active Life* (also Leah, or Charity)—moved to San Pietro in Vincoli. Four popes had maneuvered for forty years to keep the artist from finishing this work. The first was Julius himself; when he became disenchanted with the project he reduced its funding and forced Michelangelo to accept the exhausting commission for the Sistine Chapel ceiling. Leo X then made him waste years on the facade of San Lorenzo, and Clement VII later gave him the commission for the Medici family tombs and the new sacristy. Finally Paul III ordered him to finish the decoration in the Sistine Chapel by painting the *Last Judgment*—all works which contributed to the artist's glory. Nevertheless, had Julius's tomb been completed as originally planned, today it would certainly remain one of the world's wonders.

This is a rather straightforward summary of the tomb's history. So far, though, I've said nothing about Michelangelo himself, except that he had a temper. He was certainly a great artist, but what about the man? He was born into a family we would now consider part of the petite bourgeoisie. He was born on March 6, 1475, in the village of Caprese, now known as Caprese Michelangelo. His mother, Francesca, was eighteen at the time, and died fairly young, only six years later. His father, Ludovico, played no key role; he never did grasp his second child's genius, and tried to change his vocation, convinced that painting and sculpture—manual work that involved applying colors or cutting stone—were unworthy professions for the son of a man who wielded a pen and could draw up a report or keep accounts, and who had also been the *podestà*, or appointed governor, of a few small fortified settlements. He changed his mind only when he understood that by sculpting Michelangelo earned sums he'd never dreamt of. He then began instead to pester him, asking for money and then complaining that what was sent was less than he'd hoped for. Years later he remarried a woman named Lucrezia degli Ubaldini.

Michelangelo had four brothers—a merchant, a friar, an adventurer, and a mercenary soldier. Genius, however, was his alone, as was his delicate health and personality that tended toward melancholy, due perhaps to a childhood with a weak, strange father, a mother who died too young, and a stepmother he never loved. At thirteen he went to learn the artistic ropes as an apprentice in Ghirlandaio's workshop. There he assisted the painters, mixed colors, set up easels, hung cartoons, and was finally allowed, from time to time, to make a sketch that the studio master would then appropriate as his own. Lorenzo the Magnificent, poet and patron of the arts, recognized that this fifteen-year-old boy had talent, and quickly decided to bring him to live in his court. He sent for the boy's father, Ludovico, and essentially offered to adopt his son and give him a position as customs official in recompense.

What were these years like for Michelangelo? From a material comfort point of view they were as good as he could imagine; he had a room to himself, clothes worthy of his position, and the chance to sit at the most sophisticated table in Europe with people whose conversation was both brilliant and current, and whose ideas would give Europe its modern appearance. Marsilio Ficino, Angelo Poliziano, and Pico della Mirandola were guests at the Medici court, and Sandro Botticelli, Giuliano da Sangallo, Pollaiuolo, and Verrocchio all worked there. Even the streets of Florence were crowded with men who would make an impressive mark on those years, including Leonardo da Vinci, Luca della Robbia, and Niccolò Machiavelli. Then there were the churches and monuments, where the young artist could admire work by best painters of the past, from Giotto and Masaccio to Fra Angelico and Donatello. Michelangelo had neither regular schooling nor a master who trained him; just breathing the air of Florence seems to have been enough to shape him in the same vein and push him to new heights.

Those years also shaped the young artist's spirit, and, after an unpleasant incident, also changed the appearance of his face. The sculptor Pietro Torrigiano worked with Michelangelo in Lorenzo's sculpture garden, a sort of art academy; he was three years older, as well as stronger and more violent. According to Vasari he was a handsome, courageous man, with the air of a great soldier, more than that of a sculptor. Among other attributes, he was also quick to anger. The relationship between the two sculptors was bad, perhaps because Torrigiano was jealous of Michelangelo's evident superiority, perhaps because of Michelangelo's habit of teasing others even though he wasn't physically strong. Whatever the case, one day the hot-tempered Torrigiano punched him hard, breaking his nose and disfiguring his face for life. He described what happened in his own words, "It was Buonarroti's habit to banter all who were drawing there; and one day when he was annoying me, I got more angry than usual, and, clenching my fist, I gave him such a blow on the nose that I felt bone and cartilage go down like biscuit beneath my knuckles; and this mark of mine he will carry with him to the grave."[6]

While he may have been gigantic in art, Michelangelo was not a physically large man. Torrigiano's blow disfigured a face that was already unhandsome, instilling in the sensitive young Michelangelo what we would today call an inferiority complex. Torrigiano himself met a nasty end, and was forced to flee Florence to escape Lorenzo's anger. He then wandered around Europe, finally ending up imprisoned by the Spanish Inquisition, where he was left to starve to death.

Michelangelo's ambiguous sexual and romantic behavior was certainly a result of the trauma of his youth, including that punch in the face. Who knows if he really said the words Donato Giannotti, a mediocre writer and ardent republican, gave him in his *Dialogues*: "I am a man inclined to love people, perhaps more than anyone else in any time." This passionate declaration notwithstanding, Michelangelo's love life was fraught with difficulty in many ways. He definitely paid women for sex, and his relationships with men were even more complex, if we can judge from the letters he sent to Febo di Poggio and Tommaso del Cavaliere in particular. These documents, and their delicate interpretation, bring up difficult biographical problems.

Tommaso was beautiful, and Michelangelo especially admired physical beauty, be it in men or women. They met in 1532, when Tommaso was probably not yet twenty and the artist was almost sixty—

a dangerous combination indeed. There's no doubt Michelangelo loved Tommaso, who was handsome, sweet-tempered, and artistically talented. The real question regards what kind of love united them: was it carnal? Many have suggested it was, from Aretino to André Gide. Might it instead have been a spiritual love? Some believe it was, including Giovanni Papini, who wrote a wonderful biography of the artist. Michelangelo did something for the young man no one else ever had—he drew his portrait. Done in black chalk, this finished drawing appeared to be drawn by the hand of an angel. The picture showed Tommaso "with those beautiful eyes, nose, and mouth, dressed in the ancient style, beardless, and holding a portrait or a medal in his hand. All in all it was enough to frighten any lively intellect." This marvelous work has been lost, and we are left instead with several letters—four, to be exact—in which this love is apparent, perhaps even to the point of impropriety. This wasn't a love of the senses, of course, but rather the immodest and openly declared availability for love when it is total. "Your lordship," the greatest artist of his time wrote to the young man, "cannot therefore rest content with the work of anyone else, being matchless and unequalled—light of our century, paragon of the world. If, however, any one of these things which I promise and hope to perform were to please you, I should count that work much more fortunate than excellent. And if, as I've said, I would ever have the assurance of pleasing your lordship in anything, I would devote to you the present and the time to come that remains to me, and should very deeply regret that I cannot have the past over again, in order to serve you longer than with the future only, which will be short, since I'm so old."[7]

The elderly artist wrote astonishing things. He defines as "the light of our century" a boy, or little more than a boy, when he himself had made the most marvelous works of art, and he knew it. He humbled himself before a beauty that enchanted him: "Far from being a mere babe, as you say of yourself in your letter, you seem to me to have lived on earth a thousand times before. But I should deem myself unborn, or rather stillborn, and should confess myself disgraced before heaven and earth, if from your letter I had not seen and believed that your lordship would willingly accept some of my drawings. This has caused me much surprise and pleasure no less."[8]

Everyone can judge these expressions of an enraptured spirit as he sees fit. Michelangelo also wrote verses for the lovely Tommaso that open with a languorous declaration, "Oh, give me back to myself, that I may die."[9] Regardless of the nature of this love, it lasted for the rest of the artist's life. When Michelangelo died in February of 1564, the no-longer young Tommaso was among the very few people in the poor room beside his deathbed. In the meantime, he'd married and had two children. His oldest son, Emilio, became an important figure in a Florentine literary society, the Camerata de'Bardi, which invented the new genre of the melodrama.

As I mentioned earlier, the artist loved beauty in any shape, including the human form of both sexes. As a young man he dedicated lots of time and care to studying the human body, and even dissected bodies in a Florentine morgue. He pursued this study at length because he considered the mechanics of movement essential in the making of sculpture and painting. This practice included dissection, consulting anatomy books, and studying prints by other artists, including Albrecht Dürer's treatises on human proportions (which Michelangelo didn't particularly like). Condivi writes that he found Dürer's work "very weak." In his later years in Rome Michelangelo befriended Realdo Colombo, one of the most famous anatomists of the time, widely deemed "a very superior anatomist and surgeon." Colombo admired the great painter's scrupulous attention to anatomy, and one day sent him the body of a Moor, which Michelangelo used to show his biographer "rare and recondite things, perhaps never before understood." Condivi also noted that the artist's passion for analysis and scrupulous observation reached the point where the artist "would go off to the fish market, where he observed the shape and coloring of the fins of fish, the color of the eyes and every other part . . . so that by bringing it to that perfection of which he was capable, from that time he excited the admiration of the world. . . ."[10]

The results of this long, meticulous study are clearly visible in works like the famous figure of Adam who stretches his hand toward his creator; the series of slaves, sibyls, and prophets; the contorted bodies of the damned on the day of the Last Judgment; the vigor of the saved souls; the harmonious majesty of David; and the lifeless limbs of the dead Christ, held by others because his legs no longer support any weight, in the many *Pietà* he sculpted. Representations of neither the human nor the divine body had ever before been so knowledgeably faithful to its glory, neglect, asceticism, sensuality, or the mortal exhaustion of death.

Michelangelo's sublime veneration for the body is one of the reasons his art is unequaled. In the conclusion of his biography, Condivi tried to defend the artist against the charge of homosexuality, writing, "He also loved the beauty of the human body as one who knows it extremely well, and loved it in such a way as to inspire certain carnal men, who are incapable of understanding the love of beauty except as lascivious and indecent, to think and speak ill of him."[11] It was an attempt at justification that no longer carries much importance beyond strictly historic fact.

The harmony and beauty of the human body were really the only aspects of nature that interested Michelangelo. Art historians have long noted that his work almost never has an open background; there are none of the hills, trees, or bodies of water that make Italian painting so immediately recognizable. Michelangelo was an urban painter; he always lived in a city (mainly in Florence and Rome, and briefly in Bologna and Venice), and not until he was quite old did he give any sign that he appreciated the nature he'd spent so much time ignoring. In 1556, at the revered age of eighty, he was forced for the umpteenth and last time to flee from a city—in this case from Rome, which was being threatened by the army of the Viceroy of Naples, Fernando Álvarez de Toledo, Duke of Alba. Because the invaders were coming from the south, Michelangelo went north to Spoleto, where he stayed for about a month. He took advantage of this time to visit the area around the town, and hiked to the hermitage of Monteluce, one of several Franciscan sites in Umbria. He wrote to Vasari in December that it gave him great pleasure "to visit those hermitages in the mountains around Spoleto, and in such a way that I have only partly come back to Rome, since it is really true that one can only find peace in the woods."

The Michelangelo who returned to Rome was only half the man who'd left the city because a part of him remained in the woods where he'd been able to find some peace, where life was reduced to a bucolic simplicity and an uninterrupted silence, where the weighty breaths of a tired traveler resting on his walking stick might be the only noise around. This shy and solitary man plagued by melancholy, a lover of liberty who was forced to depend on commissions from the powerful in order to express himself, found in that distant autumn of 1556, in the wilds of Monteluco, the peace that neither the Papal States nor the Duchy of Florence was ever able to give him.

Let's return to the sculpture of Moses. We needn't bother to discuss its powerful perfection, since anyone can plainly see it. There is, however, another aspect of it we should investigate—the statue's meaning both for itself and the artist's life. This topic has been debated at length, and involves many different aspects of Michelangelo's art as well as his own spiritual journey. A simple biographical fact about the artist gives us an important clue: in the jubilee year of 1550 Michelangelo, who was then seventy-five, wanted to make the traditional pilgrimage to the city's Early Christian basilicas. This ritual tour was supposed to be made on foot, but Michelangelo was granted an exception by the Pope himself, allowing him to travel on horseback. This alone is enough to indicate that Michelangelo was a profoundly religious man. The next question, though, is what kind of religion; these years were crucial for the Catholic Church, which had been badly shaken by its own corruption and the reaction to the shocking behavior of the Roman Curia across Europe.

Michelangelo had a special veneration for Jesus Christ. We see this in his agonizing *Pietà*, in his letters, and in the confidences repeated by those who had spoken with him. As a boy in Florence he listened to the thundering sermons of an anti-papal and anti-Medici Dominican preacher, Girolamo Savonarola, who dreamt of a theocratic democracy and hurled invectives against the corruption of the Church. Declared a heretic, Savonarola was burned at the stake in 1498, when Michelangelo was in his early twenties. As he grew older, the artist confessed he could still hear the ring of that admonishing voice echoing inside his head. Dante and Savonarola were his chief guides, and his Catholicism was strict and ascetic—the opposite of what dominated the Vatican. In a sonnet he wrote, "Here they made helmets and swords from chalices / and by the handful sell the blood of Christ."[12] When Julius II asked him to decorate the Sistine ceiling with gold since he found it "too poor," Michelangelo replied frankly, "Those who are painted there were poor, too."

These few words directed at the pope are enough to indicate his religious fervor. Although some have suggested that Michelangelo had some sympathy for Lutheran Protestantism, this is certainly an exaggeration. It is true, however, that his circle of friends favored spiritual reform within the church, even as they conceded nothing to the Protestants. Vittoria Colonna was part of that group; she was the widow of Francesco d'Avalos, Marquis of Pescara, and had withdrawn into a semi-cloistered life at the convent of San Silvestro on the Quirinal Hill. There she gathered a court of intellectuals, of sorts—called the *spirituali*, or spirituals—and they included high churchmen, writers, poets, and artists, including Michelangelo, who gave her many gifts, including religious drawings—a *Crucifixion*, *Pietà*, and *Good Samaritan*—all now lost. Their friendship was so intense that many assumed that they were also lovers, a plausible notion that was at the same time hardly relevant, since what counted was the spiritual connections that bound them. Condivi reports that upon Vittoria's death at only fifty-six, on February 25, 1547, Michelangelo went to pay his last respects, was highly moved, and bent down to kiss her face.

Another important figure amongst the *spirituali* was Cardinal Reginald Pole, Vittoria Colonna's spiritual advisor. Pole was English but had been educated in Europe. He was a distant relative of Henry VIII, and thus a pivotal figure at a moment of real tension between the court of Saint James and the Roman Curia. The hot-tempered king protested Pole's elevation, and when Pole openly declared his position against the English schism, Henry took revenge by having the cardinal's mother decapitated and then making an attempt on his life as well, as mentioned in the first chapter of this book.

The Cardinal's prestige was so great that when he went into the conclave after Paul III's death he was one of the favored candidates to be elected to the papacy. He narrowly missed election to the papal throne, and blamed it on his own position as a strict reformer. A few years later Gian Pietro Carafa became Pope Paul IV, and a rather severe persecution of the *spirituali* ensued. Paul IV was responsible for the index of banned books issued in 1559, which went as far as condemning part of the Bible and even some of the writings of the church fathers. The pope himself personally reformed the inquisition that Paul III had announced in July 1542, giving it extraordinary power to crush any position that even slightly resembled Lutheranism. His zeal for reform reached the point of outright fanaticism, and he ordered the arrest of Cardinal Giovanni Morone, one of the church's greatest personalities and not coincidentally a friend of Colonna, Pole, and

Michelangelo. The artist had made several drawings and paintings for Morone, though none have survived. Pole's defeat in the conclave of 1549 was a blow to those who had hoped to reform and rebuild the church from the inside out.

Paul IV's reasons for such harshly repressive measures were clearly political, even if they were also driven by doctrinal concerns. He needed to parry the Protestant thrust, did so by tightening the institution's rules, and as a consequence was also forced to condemn reformist groups within the church. Lutherans believed that Catholic devotional practices were pointless, and were empty ritual, if not open superstition used by the church to control its faithful. In his short book, *Il beneficio di Cristo*, a work widely read in *spirituali* circles, Benedetto da Mantova made an argument for justification by faith, in other words that faith alone was enough to absolve sinners in the eyes of God. Without disdaining good works, ("And this faith would nevertheless be impossible without good works"), he maintains that they must flow from an intimate feeling of faith, rather than practiced to fulfill a duty or done in exchange for some reward. The pious author invited the faithful to meditate on the real benefits to be constructed from the Crucified Christ, as well as the perfection the soul can achieve by trusting entirely in Him.

The relationship between faith and good works in this justification of the Christian sinner before God was one of the fundamental questions behind the shattering of the church's unity. In some of the verses he wrote as an old man, Michelangelo hints that he had been attracted to a Lutheran theory of justification, attributing to the blood of Christ—in other words, to faith—the greatest hope humankind has for the redemption of their sins. "Although you were not miserly with your blood, / what use will be such a merciful gift from you / if heaven's not opened for us with another key?" Or, "my dear Lord, you who alone can clothe and strip / our souls, and with your blood purify and heal them / of their countless sins and human impulses...."[13]

Michelangelo took risks in writing some of the things he did, and in being seen with certain people; the circle of those who commented on Mantova's book had been identified and placed under observation by Vatican authorities, who considered them only a little less dangerous than Lutheran heretics. Indeed, championing the doctrine of justification by faith alone, reinforced by the cult of the blood of Christ, meant a conviction that the church and its hierarchy needed to be reformed in a way that would have moved it closer to the Protestant position. Michelangelo was always prudent in his politics, and was usually unwilling to take sides in public debates. The fact that he took such risks in this case suggests a strong conviction. It's nevertheless true, however, that his fame as an artist made him largely untouchable and guaranteed him privileges that would never have been granted to other artists. The most the new pope dared do to him was take away his right to the income from the tolls on the Po River that Paul III had granted him for life.

I've tried here to summarize the basic facts of a conflict that, according to some scholars, had a lot to do with the statue of Moses and its final placement. The final contract with the Della Rovere family, signed in March of 1542, established that the tomb of Julius II would be decorated with seven statues. There was to be a recumbent effigy of the pope flanked by a prophet and sibyl on the upper level, below them would be the Madonna and Child, and on the lower level would be Moses, flanked by two prisoners (or slaves). It seemed finally, after so many years, that there was a definitive design for the tomb. By July of the same year the artist was having second thoughts, and wanted to substitute the prisoners with two other figures, representations of active and contemplative life, embodied by Leah and Rachel respectively, which he'd already begun to work on.

Of the seven statues on the tomb as it now stands in San Pietro in Vincoli, Michelangelo was responsible, obviously, for Moses, the two female figures and, according to a very recent attribution, the effigy of Julius II (whose figure is very difficult to see, as it's so high up). The other figures were designed by the artist but executed, after arduous negotiations, by Domenico Fancelli and Raffaello da Montelupo.

Why did Michelangelo decide to substitute the slaves with the two female figures? The official, rather unconvincing reason he gave was that the figures of active and contemplative life went better with the rest of the composition. Some experts, however, have suggested another motive that can be found in the spiritual belief of the circle around Vittoria Colonna and Cardinal Pole. Antonio Forcellino, a Michelangelo scholar who has written on the recent restoration of the Moses sculpture, thinks that the artist wanted to substitute these figures because he was abandoning "the iconographic program, with its strong pagan associations that . . . he had defended for thirty years, in favor of one that expresses the spirituality of the *Beneficio di Cristo* with all the transgressive and subversive implications that came with that idea."

There's another document, however, that throws an interesting light on the Moses sculpture and its position. An unnamed friend of the artist told Vasari the following story: He had set up the statue of Moses, which he had largely finished when Pope Julius II was still alive, in his house, and as I found myself there looking at it, I said to him, "If the head of this figure were turned a little more this way I think it would be better." He made no response to me, but two days later, when I was again at his house, he said, "Don't you know, Moses overheard us talking the other day and in order to understand us better he turned his head." I went to see, and I found that he had turned his head . . . which was a miraculous thing; I thought so myself, thinking such a feat to be almost impossible.

This extraordinary account comes from March of 1564, shortly after the artist's death. His friend recounted the facts, but neglected to say when they occurred. Based on this story specialists like Christoph Frommel and Forcellino have suggested that the change in the position of Moses's face, and especially the substitution of Rachel and Leah for the two slaves (now in the Louvre), happened just before the final arrangement of the tomb and can thus be considered proof of the almost heretical spiritual beliefs Michelangelo held in the last part of his life.

As everyone knows, the statue has lent itself to many interpretations. In 1914 Sigmund Freud, the father of psychoanalysis, wrote a famous essay (first published anonymously) in which he wrote near the beginning:

> Another of these inscrutable and wonderful works of art is the marble statue of *Moses* by Michelangelo, in the Church of S. Pietro in Vincoli in Rome. . . . For no piece of statuary has ever made a stronger impression on me than this. How often have I mounted the steep steps from the unlovely Corso Cavour to the lonely piazza where the deserted church stands, and have essayed to support the angry scorn of the hero's glance! Sometimes I have crept cautiously out of the half-gloom of the interior as though I myself belonged to

the mob upon whom his eye is turned—the mob which can hold fast no conviction, which has neither faith nor patience, and which rejoices when it has regained its illusory idols. But why do I call this statue inscrutable?"[14]

Freud then begins a long and fascinating analysis of the figure that I can only briefly sum up here. Moses is seated, his head is turned to the left, his right leg is firmly planted on the ground and his left leg is drawn back, his foot resting only on its toes, in a dynamic pose. His left arm rests in his lap, and he holds the law tablets he's just received from God on Mount Sinai firmly with his right arm. His right hand, index finger extended, holds part of his flowing beard. The Bible says that Moses, leader of his people, had a hot temper. He came down from the mount to find that the Israelites, tired of waiting for him, had begun to worship the figure of a golden calf, and were dancing around it. Infuriated, he threw the tablets to the ground, smashing them. The Biblical Moses, however, is not Michelangelo's; Freud analyzed the positions of various parts of his body, including his beard, and concluded that the stone Moses was not a man prey to irrational sentiments like anger. On the contrary, the artist shows us a man torn between impetuousness and a firm, interior resoluteness. There is anger in his eyes, but his solemn sense of calm tells us that self control has won out. Freud concluded, "What we see before us is not the inception of a violent action but the remains of a movement that has already taken place. In his first transport of fury, Moses desired to act, to spring up and take vengeance and forget the Tables; but he has overcome the temptation, and he will now remain seated and still, in his frozen wrath, and his pain mingles with contempt. Nor will he throw away the Tables so they will break on the stones, for it is on their especial account that he has controlled his anger; it was to preserve them that he kept his passion in check."[15]

The Jungian psychologist James Hillman offers us another, more recent interpretation of this statue, suggesting that Michelangelo wanted to represent the Moses who, according to several Biblical passages, was an alchemist and magician. In his essay on this topic he cites several examples, "[t]he plagues inflicted on the Egyptians, the parting of the Red Sea, the ability to make water flow from stone and food fall from the sky, the bronze serpent which heals, to mention only some of the better known events reported in the Scriptures and elaborated in legends and *midrash.*"

Again according to Hillman, Michelangelo's Moses adapts the traits of patriarchs and magicians, including the beard, the pointing finger, the severity of the lawgiver, but also the horns of the man-animal. These horns, however, could also be the result of an error in the Latin translation of Exodus 34:29, in which the Hebrew word *karan,* or rays emanating from the face of a hero, became *keren,* or horns. Hillman concludes that the reason for them is not very important, since "those horns, whether placed there by God or by Michelangelo, restores to Moses that which he wanted to separate out and distance from himself—God and the animal, the law and instinct, duty and pleasure and Jewish monotheism and Egyptian polytheism."

Michelangelo died practically alone, and although he wasn't poor, he died like a pauper, perhaps because of avarice, or maybe just his habitual frugality. In a corner of his house at Macel de' Corvi he drew the image of Death along with a few funerary verses of commentary. He was ninety years old, and he knew the end was near. In his *Dialoghi,* Donato Giannotti gives these words to the master: "We must think about death. This thought alone lets us know ourselves ... and the effect of thinking about death is marvelous, as it destroys everything according to its nature, preserves and maintains those who think about it, and defends them from all human emotions." As he grew older, the artist frequently returned to this thought in his conversations, letters, and verses. "Whoever is born comes to die / with the passage of time, and the sun / nothing is left alive."

In early February of 1564 Michelangelo began to feel unwell, and although he tried to keep up his normal routine, his condition soon proved irreversible. Nonetheless, he was still chiseling on his last work up until a few days before he died. On a very cold and rainy day a disciple coming to visit saw him standing in the street in the foul weather, ran to him, and dragged him back home. He affectionately chided the master for his rashness, but Michelangelo answered, "What do you want from me? I am not well and I cannot find any peace anywhere." A few pupils and his servant put him back to bed. In a letter to Vasari, Daniele da Volterra wrote:

When he saw me he said, "Oh, Daniele, I am done for, and please, I beg you, do not abandon me." He had me write a letter to Lionardo, his nephew, asking him to come, and then he said to me that I should wait there in the house and not leave for any reason. I did that even though I felt more ill than well. . . . [H]is illness lasted five days, two he spent by the fire and three in bed and then he died on Friday evening. . . .

It was February 18. Daniele da Volterra, Diomede Leoni, Michelangelo's servant Antonio, and his beloved Tommaso del Cavaliere were at his bedside.

---

1. Ascanio Condivi, *The Life of Michelangelo*, trans. Alice Sedgwick Wohl, 2nd ed. (University Park, PA: The Pennsylvania State University Press, 1999), 30.

2. Ibid.

3. Ibid., 58.

4. Ibid., 69.

5. Giorgio Vasari, *The Lives of the Artists*, trans. Julia Conway Bondanella and Peter Bondanella (New York: Oxford University Press, 1991), 459.

6. Torrigiano to Benvenuto Cellini and then repeated in Cellini's autobiography. Cited in Condivi, 146, n.129.

7. E. H. Ramsden, ed., *The Letters of Michelangelo* (Stanford, CA: Stanford University Press, 1963), v.1, 193.

8. Ibid., 180, 183.

9. James S. Saslow, trans., *The Poetry of Michelangelo* (New Haven, CT: Yale University Press, 1991), 91–92.

10. Condivi, 9–10, 99.

11. Ibid., 105.

12. Saslow, 78.

13. Ibid., 483, 501.

14. Sigmund Freud, *Writings on Art and Literature* (Stanford, CA: Stanford University Press, 1997), 124–125.

15. Ibid., 141–142.

VII

FACTORY OF DREAMS

The entrance to Cinecittà, nine kilometers outside the city center along the Via Tuscolana, remains the original one, characterized (and dated) by the rounded architectural lines typical of the twenty-year Fascist period. Beyond this entrance lies a mythical place, a happy invention all the way down to its name, which literally means "cinema city" and is one of the few successful neologisms in Italian—a language that doesn't much lend itself to lexical novelty. Once upon a time you got there by the "local" tram; the last part of its route ran through open countryside, with ancient aqueducts, the bluish profile of the distant hills, and a few flocks of sheep happily grazing and providing colorful scenery. In his 1987 film *Intervista*, Federico Fellini described the brief journey and the tram's arrival at the end of the line in the middle of the countryside:

> The first time I heard that name, *Cinecittà*, I knew I'd found my home, the place I'd always wanted to be. The first time I arrived by tram—a little blue one that left from the station and then traversed kilometers of countryside—I was a little disappointed when I saw the long perimeter walls and those reddish, barrack-like buildings. They looked like some kind of hospital or hospice. Then, in the middle of a crowded scene, above all the dusty confusion, comfortably perched fifty meters up, donning a helmet, binoculars, and a silk scarf, in a veritable apotheosis of gilded clouds and sunlight, I saw the director, Alessandro Blasetti.[1]

Among the many backdrops of the movie business back then—in which special effects were made not by computer, but rather with glue, nails, papier-mâché, and daring camera angles—was that same little blue tram. When it arrived in front of the studio gate it dropped off the studio's most humble workers, mostly laborers and extras.

Their entry was closely supervised by Gaetano Pappalardo, a porter famous for his severe demeanor and, like Cerberus, seemingly endowed with six eyes. He never failed to detect the inevitable clever type trying to sneak his way in, even if only to make off with a wastepaper basket or other trifle. It was a time when even porters and watchmen radiated a certain authority that has since vanished. According to legend, on filming days the great comedian Totò arrived extremely early at Cinecittà; one morning he arrived so early that the studio gates were still locked. Seeing him pacing outside the door, the watchman hurried over, yelling, "I'm coming, Totò." The actor wasn't at all pleased, and replied, "I insist that you call me prince." Antonio de Curtis, better known as Totò on the screen, naïvely expected throughout his life that he had the right to be addressed as "Imperial Highness"; he was, after all, a descendant of the Byzantine throne and its royal emperors. Over time he added aristocratic and imperial names to his own, including Gagliardi, Griffo, Focas, and Comneno. In this case, however, it was the watchman who had the last word, as he promptly shot back, "There are lots of princes, but only one Totò." The rebuttal was satisfactory, and from then on the clever watchman was allowed to call him Totò.

There are hundreds of anecdotes about this unparalleled actor. To the waiter who had brought him coffee in his room one day he gave the large sum of a thousand lire, leaving the change as a (very generous) tip. Word of this spread quickly, and whenever Totò ordered coffee, three or four waiters raced to bring it to him. The oldest of them, however, never got there first. Totò caught on and ordered that the others give the man a 200-meter head start so that he, too, managed to earn the thousand lire—and not just once, but twice.

The Roman movie studios were a Fascist creation. In September of 1935, Cines, the old production studio on Via Veio, in the neighborhood of San Giovanni, burned down. In those same years the political importance of cinema was becoming clear, in addition to its creative and economic potential. The fire on Via Veio provided the needed impetus, and an area of about 124 acres on the Via Tuscolana was set aside for the new Città del Cinema (Cinema City). Its construction was a miracle of efficiency: the foundation stone was laid on January 26, 1936, and the whole complex was inaugurated fifteen months later, on April 28, 1937, even though not all of its departments were completed. Mussolini was able to claim with pride, "The cinema is our strongest weapon." The dictator had made radio and cinema the two most powerful propaganda tools for reaching the broadest masses, and the people responded: in 1941, 424 million cinema tickets were sold—every Italian, the elderly and children included, went to the movies at least ten times that year, on average. The importance of controlling television now is just an extension of this earlier phenomenon.

In 1937 nineteen films were produced at Cinecittà, the most famous being Mario Bonnard's *Il feroce saladino* (*The Ferocious Saladin*), staring Angelo Muscio and inspired by a revealing social phenomenon of the day—the dogged hunt for the figurines found in packages of Buitoni and Perugina products. *Saladin* marked the debut of actress Alida Valli, and a bit part of a few one-liners was given to a promising young man, Alberto Sordi, unrecognizable in his lion-skin disguise. There were forty-eight films made in 1940, and fifty-nine in 1942 despite the terrible war. In October of that year the English launched their offensive against El Alamein, which fell despite the heroic Italian resistance. That defeat was the prelude to the collapse of the entire African front. The best directors worked at Cinecittà in those years—Alessandro Blasetti, Mario Camerini, Renato Castellani, Roberto Rossellini, Mario Soldati, Luchino Visconti, and Luigi Zampa. I won't tell the whole history of Cinecittà here; all I really want to do is evoke something of its myth and to try to explain how important it was for the city of Rome to be home to one of the most important movie studios in Europe.

It can easily be said that the attraction between Rome and filmmakers was a mutual one. It was a reciprocal influence—the movie business changed the city, and vice versa. The capital empowered Italian directors to make films true to the times both in the most obvious sense (war movies in times of war, fascist films in the Fascist period) as well as in a more profound way. They were able, for example, to gather and transform on-screen certain aspects, moods, and needs, making them into stories and thereby elevating them to national characteristics. The period films of Alessandro Blasetti— *Un'avventura di Salvator Rosa* (*The Adventure of Salvator Rosa*), *La corona di ferro* (*Iron Crown*), and *La cena delle beffe* (*Dinner of Fools*)— were the silver-screen equivalents of those neo-Gothic fantasies so common at the beginning of the twentieth century and which had such an impact on literature, theater, and architecture. The following decade *commedia all'italiana,* the so-called Italian-style comedies of the 1960s, reflected the widespread sense of well-being, as well as the first symptoms of change in tradition and moral tenor that accompanied the seemingly sudden and unprecedented postwar prosperity. As for the present day, the small, intimate stories of current Italian cinema demonstrate on the one hand a refusal to compete with the immense productions of the American movie business, and on the other hand attest to the rediscovery of sentiment and the personal, private world.

After September 8, 1943, the Nazis took all the technical equipment from Cinecittà and the rest was looted by the hoards of famished people who had lost everything. Their possessions were stolen, right down to the bathroom fixtures. The large studio grounds became an encampment for troops and a shelter for evacuees. In the shattered, poverty-stricken Italy of the late 1940s and early 1950s, return to normalcy was slow. And yet the cinema, like so many other sectors of the national economy, experienced an explosion of vitality. It was as if the richness of talent and the desire to tell a story had been strengthened by the country's distress. If we can talk today of "neo-realism," films shot in the streets with actors often taken from the streets, it's due at least in part to the unavailability of the studios at Cinecittà; movies had to be made with what there was—the impoverished reality of an Italy crushed by war.

There are also many great films of that period in which Cinecittà tells its own story, and thus the making of cinema became cinema in itself. Consider Luchino Visconti's *Bellissima,* starring Anna Magnani as the nurse Maddalena Cecconi, in which the famous director Alessandro Blasetti, playing himself, seeks a young girl to cast in a film. Maddalena makes every possible sacrifice, personal and economic, to get her daughter, Maria, into the audition. Upon succeeding, she secretly goes to watch her daughter's screen test being projected, and as Maria sobs with fright on-screen the film crew mockingly looks on. In the end the girl gets the part, but, in a surprising display of dignity, Maddalena refuses the contract she'd struggled so hard to get. The movie would've been little more than a nineteenth-century throwback (it was actually made in 1951) were it not for Magnani's powerful performance and the film's foresight into the seductive power of spectacles. Television arrived three years later, and packs of girls and their mothers would come to sacrifice all their dignity just to be able to participate, no matter how marginally, in the media dream.

Even then any- and everyone went to the studios hoping to be an extra. Since everyone includes me, I can claim some personal experience with that world. I was a student then, and being an extra was one way—not unpleasant in the least, and sometimes downright exciting—to make a little extra money for vacations. Among other perks, I used the time between takes to study for exams, met a lot of pretty girls, and I saw (from a distance) the mythic American directors at work. I was a Roman legionnaire, a Nubian slave (tinted with body paint), a World War I infantryman, and a violinist in an orchestra— after a professional violinist showed us all how to hold the instrument and bow. For me the experience was mostly mere entertainment, but for others being an extra meant making ends meet and supporting a family. Fellini described the world of extras well, but other directors frequently returned to the subject, as it was so rich with color and personality. These included Ettore Scola, for example, and Dino Risi, who wrote in his book, *I miei mostri* (*My Monsters*):

> One summer I was filming a movie in Piazza Navona. Among the extras was a small man called Cardinaletti. He was a thief who specialized in climbing; he climbed into the ground floor windows he found open (that summer temperatures in Rome reached forty degrees Celsius), drugged the people sleeping inside with a narcotic spray, and robbed them. One day my camera and lenses were all stolen. Cardinaletti was a respected neighborhood boss, and cared a lot about prestige. I went to him. In a couple of hours I had my camera and lens back, and I gave him a nice tip. Two or three years later I saw him again. He no longer stole; he had married a Swiss woman with some money. He confessed to me that it was he who had robbed me. Why? He wanted me to be grateful to him.

What does Rome have to do with these personalities and scenes? If Cinecittà had been built in Turin or Milan, Italian cinema, even with the same directors, would have been completely different. The city provided a unique mixture of kindness, wiliness, and cynicism, and its citizens had a great talent, however fraudulent, for improvisation.

They possessed a detached indolence when confronting difficult situations (as long as those situations were risk-free), both skill and speed in crafts, and all the gifts the movies required, though cinema still remained a game, a pretence, an ephemeral catch: the marbles had to look eternal, even if up close they were clearly nothing but plaster and plywood; gilding that wasn't gold; and tin instead of steel; in a word, theater—illusion and deceit.

The Americans took care of redoubling our illusions and choosing Cinecittà for several Pharaonic productions set, for the most part, in ancient Rome. The war was just over, the first true general elections were held on April 18, 1948, and at the same time the great stars of Hollywood were descending on the hotels of the Via Veneto, the residences of Parioli, and the villas along the Appia Antica. They passed through Rome in multitudes throughout the fifties: Rita Hayworth and Orson Welles, Elizabeth Taylor and Richard Burton, Peter Ustinov and Ava Gardner, Robert Taylor, Deborah Kerr, Katharine Hepburn, Stewart Granger, Rock Hudson, Jennifer Jones, Audrey Hepburn, Rex Harrison, Henry Fonda, Anthony Quinn, Alan Ladd, Burt Lancaster, Charlton Heston, and Frank Sinatra. Clark Gable came, too, though he'd already seen Rome as a machine gunner on a B-17 Flying Fortress during the bombing of July 19, 1943.

Films set in ancient Rome were as old as cinema itself, and even in the era of silent films many about Rome were produced. These were short movies about the most popular figures from the distant past—Messalina, Nero, Julius Caesar, Cataline, and Mark Antony. The virtually forgotten Roman director Enrico Guazzoni (1876–1949), made a movie about the highly theatrical figure of Messalina, and his films like *Quo Vadis?* in 1912 and *Fabiola* in 1917 influenced D. W. Griffith. But the real beginning of this genre was Carmine Gallone's *Scipione l'Africano*. Publius Cornelius Scipio had been charged by the Senate to avenge the defeat of the Roman army at the battle of Cannae, and in doing so he was also to challenge the great Carthaginian general Hannibal on his own home turf, in Africa. At the end of several melodramatic adventures and the victory at Zama, the shame of Cannae was erased. The whole film, which was awarded the Mussolini Cup at the Venice Film Festival of 1937, can be read as a metaphor for the Italian military campaign in Ethiopia. Scipio talked to his army with the same rhetoric Mussolini used to address his from the balcony of the Palazzo Venezia, and the analogies between Roman conquests in Africa and those of the Fascists were numerous. The film's public success, however, was limited.

In 1948, after the war was over, Alessandro Blasetti's *Fabiola* was released and became a box-office success. Based on a novel by a cardinal and financed by the Vatican, it tells of Fabiola, a senator's daughter and convert to Christianity who meets Rhual, a young Gaul gladiator. The two fell in love, had the usual adventures, and enjoyed the usual happy ending. From that moment the so-called sword-and-sandal genre of film multiplied and began to flood the cinemas like a river overrunning its banks. These movies either succeeded or failed, were either openly derivative or displayed at best a glint of originality, and the productions were more or less opulent—dozens of films were made over the following years. It was a true foreign invasion, and with it the Americans reinvented ancient Rome in their own way just as, years later, the Italians would reinvent the Wild West in theirs.

A law (perfectly apt in those difficult times) made it impossible for the profits earned by American film producers to be exported from Italy. The only real choice, then, was to reinvest on the spot in new films. This increased both the opportunity for work and the demand for films set in ancient Rome. *Quo Vadis?* was made in 1951; it was adapted from the famous novel by Henryk Sienkiewicz (winner of the 1905 Nobel Prize in literature) and, with some slight variations, retold the story of Fabiola. This time the heroine, Lygia, was the barbarian turned Christian, and the hero, Marcus Vinicius, was the Roman pagan to be converted. Lygia is imprisoned and faces an atrocious death in the circus, but Ursus, the good slave, saves the day with his Herculean strength. This film, with its bland sensuality and happy ending, was the official beginning of a type that would soon have Charlton Heston driving a team of four horses in *Ben Hur*, Elizabeth Taylor reincarnated as Cleopatra in the film of the same name (an immense production with 26,000 costumes alone), Gordon Scott burning his hand in the role of Mucius Scaevola, Richard Harrison cutting a magnificent figure in the *Invincible Gladiator*, and Jack Palance providing the face and muscles for Revak in *The Barbarians*. Gradually the genre came to include films that parodied it (*Totò and Cleopatra*), and then slid toward *Le calde notti di Poppea* (*The Hot Nights of Poppea*) with Olinka Berova and *La peccatrice del deserto* (known in the

United States as *Desert Desperados*) with Ruth Roman—stories that involved explicitly sensual themes in both their titles and publicity. *The Egyptian* (with Edmund Purdom, Peter Ustinov, Jean Simmons, and Victor Mature) was released with the slogan, "Now in its entirety, the incest, loves, cruelty, and unrestrained pleasures of the Pharaonic Court."

Many films tried to imitate the great American productions, yet they were made without the same resources, and thus had to make a virtue of necessity. They rented used scenery and costumes, filmed during breaks in other productions, and hurried onto sets the instant after they'd been abandoned by other casts, just before bad weather had a chance to strip away the fake marble and reveal the papier-mâché and metal frames beneath them.

And what about Rome—the real Rome, the one inhabited by Romans—how did it react to this flood? From an economic point of view, the money these American productions invested made work for several thousand people including workmen, technicians, and extras. They were massive operations, and each film needed hundreds of extras. *Ben Hur*, directed by William Wyler, had a cast of four hundred people and cost fifteen million dollars (in 1958!). One hundred and twenty horses were bought in Yugoslavia for the chariot race, a scene that cost a million dollars alone to shoot. The director of the second unit was a young Italian named Sergio Leone, later famous for his spaghetti Westerns. Wyler won an Oscar, and the film swept up a total of eleven Academy Awards. Beyond their economic impact, these sword-and-sandal films created and helped diffuse an image of Rome around the globe, and contributed to its comeback as a great tourist destination.

William Wyler cast Gregory Peck and Audrey Hepburn as the stars of a delightful romance in his 1953 film *Roman Holiday*. It was just syrupy enough, and used all the capital's most famous places as a backdrop. The two lovers, aboard a Vespa, visit and admire all the sites—with Audrey as the amazed princess-in-hiding, and Peck playing the sweetly pedagogical tour guide. For years afterward the number of American tourists increased, just as it would later with the release of *La Dolce Vita*.

As obliging as the images of the capital were in *Roman Holiday*, they were also essentially false, as are most images in romantic fables. And yet Wyler was able to show Roman ruins as they really were, as true, solid stone. In other sword-and-sandal films not even this was true, rife as they were with cardboard antiquities, shiny tin breast-plates, historical events heavily counterfeited to mesh with the needs of the script, the inevitable love story, the shadow of betrayal, and the eternal villain destined to be defeated in the end after a final duel with the hero. In his book about Cinecittà Flaminio DiBiagi noted how in Delmer Daves's *Gladiators* (1954) this falsification was so over the top that it was surely an intentional irony or derisive joke. His point is illustrated by film stills that prove the director included an exact replica of Michelangelo's *David*—sculpted fourteen hundred years later—among the statues decorating the Coliseum.

The remaking of ancient Rome focused on its most popular symbol, the Coliseum. Millions of people, and not just Americans, learned to see it as the classical monument par excellence, with its ancient, weathered arches worn away by time, battered by fires, and scarred by other vicissitudes. It became the icon of the city, just as the Eiffel Tower is in Paris and the Brooklyn Bridge in New York. History, in these films, was always flexible, ready to adapt itself to any necessity of plot or cast. This included putting Nero in the imperial box at the Coliseum, regardless of the fact that during that notorious emperor's reign the lake of the Domus Aurea filled the space where the Coliseum would later stand. Vespesian did indeed begin construction of the great building, as the film shows, but not until AD 70, after Nero had been dead for two years.

For Rome the movie business represented more than just the city's reintroduction to the entire world—it also made it the "Hollywood on the Tiber," as was said back then, and even the residents of the city began to change once they were surrounded by so many actors, the carelessness of their love affairs, the accounts of their lively evenings, and sometimes colorful, drunken brawls; all of this was exactly what the city needed to satisfy its desire to start over and forget the horrors and poverty of the war and occupation. Everyone read of the drunken evenings, extraordinary dinners in Trastevere restaurants, spicy transgressions consummated in the hotels of the Via Veneto or the villas along the Via Appia Antica, exclusive parties, and instantaneous love affairs that seemed made for being photographed and detailed in illustrated magazines. The war, as well as a certain provincial attitude, had always limited gossip to small varia-

tions on the same themes, at least when it was not limited to the pitiful, impotent, and malicious politicians of the Fascist period. All of
a sudden all Rome seemed to be transformed into a movie set—
including its city squares and streets, the nearby beaches so easily
reached in a nice car, and places like Ostia and Fregene, which
seemed to give Malibu a run for its money.

This wholly pleasant, apparently easy atmosphere, and this society in which an entirely new prosperity miraculously mixed with
an old cordiality, simplicity of relationships, and sweetness of living
became contagious. Like the finale in an eighteenth-century *féerie*, a
variety of opera based on fairy tales, Rome became a place where
people willingly went to get married. Anthony Quinn and Audrey
Hepburn both chose Italian spouses; Tyrone Power, the definition of
male beauty at the time, married Linda Christian in the church of
Santa Francesca Romana in the forum, in the first truly fairy-tale
wedding after the war.

Almost without realizing it, a new and relaxed way of life had
appeared that few or no Romans had known before, and which
sometimes seemed like a movie. The little tables of the two famous
bars in the Piazza del Popolo, their clientele warmed by the first
tepid sun of spring; a rustic restaurant in Fregene with spaghetti and
telline, a shellfish caught on the beach practically in front of the diners; and cars, a sure sign of prosperity, but also an enchanted instrument of freedom, not yet the dreadful creatures of traffic jams and
pollution. This new prosperity spread like waves through Italy with
its first economic boom, and in Rome the movie industry was one
of its earliest and most important engines.

But along with development and prosperity the seeds of corruption began circulating, and even crime lost its "innocence," if it's possible to make such a statement. Early on the morning of April 11,
1953—Easter Saturday in the same year *Roman Holiday* came out—a
worker walking along the beach at Tor Vaianica found the body of
a young woman. She was later identified as Wilma Montesi, a pretty
twenty-one-year-old who had disappeared two days before after
leaving her home on Via Tagliamento 76, where she lived with her
parents. The body showed no signs of violence. Wilma, the coroner
said, had drowned. But who or what caused her to drown? An investigation was begun, and the clinical examination concluded with a

medical report that attributed her death to "fainting while bathing her feet."

Wilma was a reserved, working-class girl engaged to a *carabiniere*. It was difficult to imagine that she might've committed suicide; she'd gone to Ostia by herself and of her own free will. At least two witnesses had seen her on the train connecting the city to the beach. Her lonely journey had a plausible explanation; Wilma had eczema on one foot from a new pair of shoes, and was going to the beach to soak it in the saltwater. This also explained why the body was missing its shoes, stockings, and garter belt. It was speculated that the fainting spell may have been brought on by the fact that her period had just ended. This superficially plausible reconstruction of her death was enough to close the case, even though it continued to raise a number of doubts. To give but one example, no one could explain how her body ended up at Tor Vaianica, several kilometers away from the beach at Ostia.

The case would probably have stayed closed if the small, scandal-filled weekly tabloid *Attualità* hadn't published the rumors and suspicions that had already circulated in the editorial rooms of the newspapers. Wilma Montesi, it was whispered, didn't drown bathing her feet, but rather from a drug overdose, or a seizure during an orgy at the villa of Marquis Ugo Montagna. He'd hosted a crowded party there, and the guests included Piero Piccioni, a musician and son of the former foreign minister, Attilio Piccioni, who was at the time Vice President of the Federal Council. The unresolved death went from being an interesting court case to a huge political scandal, especially since it was known that the elder Piccioni was a candidate for secretary of the ruling Christian Democratic party.

Montagna's villa, the former royal estate of Capocotta, on the same beach where Wilma's body was found, became famous. During a debate in the Chamber of Deputies, Communist member Giancarlo Pajetta, a man of extreme temperament, turned to the Christian Democrats yelling "Capocottari!" ("Men of Capocotta!"). The secretary of the Socialist party, Pietro Nenni declared, "Capocotta will be the Caporetto of the bourgeoisie," referring to the Battle of Karfreit (Caporetto) in which Italian forces were routed.

Another young woman, Anna Maria Moneta Caglio—called the "Black Swan," and also Montagna's jilted lover—came forward to support the accusations made by *Attualità*. She confirmed that there were parties at Capocotta and that they included drug use. Caglio gave a statement to Amintore Fanfani (then Minister of Agriculture but also a candidate for party secretary) in which she repeated her accusations. What had started as rumor began to solidify into a hypothesis. Marquis Montagna and the musician Piccioni, unnerved by the girl's seizure, got rid of her, leaving her while she was perhaps still alive on the nearby beach. The scandal grew to enormous proportions. The head of the Roman police, Saverio Polito, was accused of trying to cover the case up for political reasons. Montesi's death became entwined in the power struggle within the Christian Democratic Party. In June of 1955 various people involved in the case were put on trial, and two years later, on May 27, 1957, the tribunal in Venice absolved them all, including Piccioni, Montagna, Polito, and nine other lesser defendants, of any guilt.

Even if this scandal was never entirely cleared up, one thing can be said for certain: it was the first time in the brief history of the Italian Republic that mechanisms of the State were used for political ends. Italians learned at least two rules of public life from the Montesi case. Firstly, conspiracies are rarely what they initially seem to be, and secondly, political struggles in a fragile democracy can't be stopped by any obstacle, be it judicial or constitutional—everything depends on the desire for power. Over the following years there was a lot more of poor Wilma cast up on the beach at Tor Vaianica. The Communist Party, which had tried to exploit the scandal to discredit the Christian Democrats, wasn't fully aware, at least at the beginning, that this murky affair would be used by a faction of the very same party in its own internal disputes. In any case, a year later, in 1954, Fanfani became secretary of the Christian Democratic Party.

In this period Rome was rocked by many more crimes that would forever be etched in the people's memory. Interest in these scandals seemed to go beyond a normal interest in such mysteries; instead it was as if these killings, to which the media devoted so much space, allowed people to rediscover the private dimension of violent death after the mass, anonymous deaths of the war. The murder of Maria Martirano caused almost as much of a sensation as had the death of Wilma Montesi. She was strangled by thugs hired by her husband, Giovanni Fenaroli. Here, too, the motive for the crime was never entirely clear. Maybe it was for her life insurance policy, or because of Maria's own clumsy attempt to blackmail her husband over bribes paid to him by political supporters. The Fenaroli scandal was of such interest that the courtroom where it was tried was literally besieged by curious crowds, including famous people like Vittorio De Sica and Anna Magnani. Slowly, though, a confused realization that these crimes might be a symptom of something else began to spread, and years later we saw that they had indeed been the first signs of a dark Italy in which ambition, political interests, and prosperity all played a part. From a certain point of view these murders were also cinema, in their own way. Stories based on these crimes completed the physiognomy of a country in the process of a tumultuous transformation.

The great and lasting genre of the so-called Italian comedies played on an interpretation of the spirit of those years of radical change. The French were the first to discover the usefulness of representing national defects by representing reality not as the sad awareness of neo-realism, but rather by means of comedy. One of the masters of this genre, Mario Monicelli, said in an interview:

> More than literature, painting, or theater, these comedies have changed the nature of Italians by making all their vices and taboos ridiculous. This is especially true of Southerners, with their cuckoldry, virginity, adultery, braggadocio, and Catholicism, even if it's true that the government was staunchly opposed to all that. This made the Italians more self-aware, letting them laugh at themselves and let go of excessive sentimentality, and it contributed to their evolution as a nation.

In truth, this "letting go," as Monicelli called it, went much further and then took on a life of its own. The same director said, "The fully evolved Italian moved on to become a cynic, and then a creep. Today's Italian has no principles, and has almost nothing to hold on to except the desire to get rich."

Is this judgment too harsh? There is another symbolic place—the Via Veneto—where this phenomenon can be observed. For a while in the 1950s this curving street—which joins the Piazza Barberini to Porta Pinciana, was built on the ruins of the Villa Ludovisi, and was created in the first wave of real-estate speculation in Rome a decade after it was annexed to the Kingdom of Italy—was also a popular meeting place. A group of literati and journalists occupied the small tables of the Caffè Rosati, which opened in 1911 on the upper part of the street and is now long gone. Other cafés, too, were popular— the Strega-Zeppa, Doney, and later the Café de Paris. Those who frequented the cafes of the Via Veneto also browsed in the Libreria Rossetti, one of the city's most refined bookstores. (It, too, is now gone, although there is another great bookstore, named Via Veneto just like the street, further down the street, toward Piazza Barberini.) Ennio Flaiano, already known for his novel *Tempo d'uccidere* (*A Time to Kill*), was one of the great protagonists of those evenings. Others included Gian Gaspare Napolitano, Ercole Patti, Sandro De Feo, Vincenzo Talarico, Mario Pannunzio, and Carlo Laurenzi. They stayed out late and talked about politics, what was new at the cinema, the latest book releases, and the candidates for the Strega Prize (which Flaiano won in 1947), one of the greatest literary awards in Italy. The Strega remains prestigious today despite the plethora of prizes and awards that have come along since.

Reciprocal malice wasn't unusual, and it was often condensed into a brilliant play on words. The director Lattuada, known for his jealousy and fits of rage, was nicknamed "the small Lombard vendetta"; Alberto Moravia, a slight cripple, "the bitter Gambarotto," or "Bitter Broken-leg"; and Vincenzo Cardarelli, who always wore an overcoat, even in the height of summer, "the greatest dying Italian poet." Sometimes they were even more wicked. An old critic (my discretion here is obligatory) who always had an entourage of young female students he enjoyed groping a bit was called "l'uomo con un piede nella fessa." The phrase it plays on was "the man with one foot in the grave," and the joke was the substitution of fessa (cunt) for fossa (grave). A zealous social climber who wasn't well endowed was referred to as "il carrierino dei piccoli," referring to the *Corrierino dei Piccoli*, a popular children's comic at the time, and transforming the title into "little careerist of the small-dicked." Finally, a popular Roman newspaper that was obsequious to the powerful, was the paper where "one looks at the articles and reads the photographs."

Most of these nicknames and puns were the work of Flaiano, a man of lively intellect, an excellent scriptwriter, and a great inventor of puns and jokes. When he heard that a new film by a well-known but mediocre director was coming out, he commented, "He made another film? I can't wait to miss it." Or, leaving a theater, "A terrible show, I couldn't get to sleep." Referring sarcastically to himself in the third person, he wrote in his *Diario notturno*, "He complains about the corruption of Roman life, indignantly citing a particular example. Yes, sure, it has been like this for centuries, but now it's just too much. Vice and rot. He needs to get away, but where? It makes him sad. 'Ah,' he concludes, 'if only one could retreat to the country, alone, with a kilo of cocaine, far away from this foulness.'" Flaiano also took the malicious description of a Southern Italian city and adapted it to the capital: "Rome is the only Middle Eastern city without a European quarter."

The journalist Eugenio Scalfari evoked that street and those evenings in his *La sera andavamo in via Veneto* (In the Evening We Went to Via Veneto). He describes the Caffè Rosati, which immediately after the war had supplanted another famous meeting place, the third room toward the back of the Caffè Aragno, where mildly anti-fascist artists met and on whom Mussolini kept close tabs:

> The circle of evening devotees was a tight one. The other pair, which kept the scene going along with Mario Pannunzio and Franco Libonati, was Sandro De Feo and Ercole Patti. Moravia often came as well; less frequently, Elsa Morante. Some younger guys made up the chorus: Giovanni Russo, Paolo Pavolini, Renato Giordano, and Chinchino Compagna. But at Rosati the company was broader. Between then and eleven, Brancati, Attilio Riccio, Flaiano, Pieto Accolti, Gian Gaspare Napolitano, Gorresio, Gino Visentini, and Vincenzo Talarico showed up. Around midnight Saragat made his entrance, accompanied by the less ugly of the Lupis brothers and Italo De Feo, although they sat apart from the rest. . . . After midnight, especially on warm summer evenings, the last wave came in, arriving from the Piazza del Popolo: Macari, Amerigo Bartoli, and Alfredo Mezio. Sometimes Roberto Rossellini, and sometimes Carlo Laurenzi. Paolo Stoppa, Anna Preclemer, and Eleonora Rossi Drago. . . . Pannunzio would say, "how nice it is to leave Rome in order to come back." And Flaiano, "we are a group of people undecided about everything."

That wasn't entirely true, and even Scalfari admitted it later in his book. Many of those people shared a political vision that was reflected first in the weekly magazine *Il Mondo*, then *L'Espresso,* and finally, in large part, in the daily newspaper *La Repubblica*. A liberal and progressive vision more or less united them, a vision was heedful of the secular state, which couldn't and shouldn't be identified with a single party or sole person. Key points of reference were Benedetto Croce and Gaetano Salvemini, Carlo Rosselli, Piero Gobetti, and Giovanni Amendola. From a distance John Maynard Keynes cast a benedictory shadow over them. Even today, after so many years, that political-literary society, which has since disappeared, gave the city a retrospective character. The group of artists, writers, and journalists who made the Via Veneto their club were the "liberal" Italians— people who were educated, ironic, a bit cynical, and endowed with enough secular skepticism that they couldn't fall into either of the two opposing "metaphysical" camps of Catholicism or Marxism. They were also steeped in a certain half-admitted scorn for mass phenomena, especially television.

Why did a group of artists, writers, and journalists feel the need to meet in a café? This is a typically Latin habit, shared with the Spanish and the French, and it has been studied in depth by sociologists. It comes from a series of things—a taste for conversation and jokes reinforced by common likes and dislikes, the complementary pleasure of arguing over even the smallest detail or shade of meaning, and, finally, the awareness of participating in a particular code of conduct, as well as the fact of being part of an elite. This sum of factors gave the intellectuals of Via Veneto the ability, which bordered on narcissism, to discuss their own qualities and defects with great pleasure, transforming them into excuses for jokes, aphorisms, and epigrams that could sometimes be cutting and hateful. This was the exact reproach the two "churches" of the day, Catholicism and Marxism, brought against the Roman literati—that of an exaggerated self-referentiality. They were criticized from the left in the name of the ideals of social justice, the Resistance, and neo-realism as the privileged canon for representing reality. Catholics, on the other hand, rebuked them for the secularism of their outlook, the exclusively political motives they assigned to all actions of the Church, and their disenchantment with all forms of popular religion. A half-century later, there is little or nothing that remains of that Rome. The literary society has almost entirely vanished, and gone with them are their cafés, their idealism, their utopias, and even their chatter. Only one thing, perhaps, has survived—the hostility of their adversaries or even just outsiders when confronted with men or places associated with any "radical-chic."

The Via Veneto is still home to some of the most luxurious hotels in the city (and they remain the same, although some of them changed names). One of them was the Roman home of Faruk, the deposed King of Egypt. He also spent hours seated at a small table of one of the cafés accompanied by his flame of the moment—all plump girls with flowing, raven-black hair. He was always ready to repeat his tired joke, "In a few years there will only be five monarchs left in the world—the four in a deck of cards and the Queen of England." And then there were the actors, or rather the American stars, who had a phalanx of limousines coming and going, drivers, starlets, reporters, and photographers.

In truth, though, it was the Fascists who first frequented the Via Veneto and "launched it." Galeazzo Ciano, Mussolini's son-in-law, often went to the Hotel Ambasciatori for an aperitif, and important officials were also seen there in the company of some actress or another. The dandies (called *gagà*) descended upon the Via Veneto from the nearby Piazza di Siena after the horse races, and mingled with the stars of the moment—Fosco Giachetti, Amedeo Nazzari, Alida Valli, Clara Calamai.

Federico Fellini was an astute, perceptive observer of all the activity on the Via Veneto, the conversations that took place there, and the actors who flocked to it when they arrived from the United States. The famed director was among the first to see the symbolic aspect of a street where, however coincidentally, all the signs of the country's new and often ambiguous prosperity was concentrated. Fellini began to plan his *Dolce Vita* project in the summer of 1958, and he quickly saw that the Via Veneto had to be the stage for his representation.

When the screenplay was finished (he collaborated with Ennio Flaiano, Tullio Pinelli, and Brunello Rondi on it), the director insisted that the central section of the Via Veneto be reconstructed in Studio 5 at Cinecittà—"his" studio, and the largest of the entire complex. (Much later in that same studio, on November 2, 1993, seventy thousand Romans filed past his coffin to pay their last respects). Paolo Gherardi, the set designer, reproduced the reality of the street with magnificent precision, allowing only one significant variation. He built it as if it were flat rather than with the gentle slope of the actual street. Some considered Fellini's insistence on his set a costly caprice; instead, he explained, "I shoot on a set in order to suggest a subjective reality purged of realistic but incidental and useless elements—a selective reality. Total control of the light is also important; the studio has become for me the obligatory place of my expression." For those who objected to increasing the movie's costs, he replied (lying) that it was instead a savings, and furthermore said he was willing to forego part of his percentage to offset any increased expenses.

The narrative structure of the film was rhapsodic, and lent itself to jumping from one scene to another. The main character, Marcello Rubini, was a journalist and, like Fellini, was a transplant from the region of Romagna. His job, as well as his indecision, took him to a variety of places in a perennial hunt for something new for his magazine. After some hesitation, Fellini chose Marcello Mastroianni for this role, although he thought his face "too innocent" for it. "The character," he declared in an interview, "needed to be more sinister, with a more suspicious look, like a blackmailer." To harden Marcello's rather comforting good looks, Fellini required him to make certain changes. "I had him loose ten kilos, and I did everything I could to make him more sinister—fake eyelashes, a yellowish complexion, glasses, and a black suit and tie that reeked of mourning."

The director had some experience as a journalist as he had done something of the sort (as well as working as a designer) when he first came to Rome. That the main character was a reporter made the job of writing the screenplay easier, since he could move from place to place quickly and credibly. Marcello lived with Emma, who had a possessive love for him, but he had various short-lived affairs, including one with Maddalena, a rich woman plagued by boredom who wanted the thrill of having sex with him in a prostitute's bed. One day Marcello went to see a purported miraculous appearance of the Madonna in a field near Rome; the sick and infirm had flocked there waiting for a miracle, but in reality it was a trick engineered by a couple of swindlers to make a little money. He then visited nightclubs and brothels, and attended a reception hosted by a moldy old provincial nobility. In the final sequence, in one of the many dawns in the film, the group of night owls are returning home from their revelry while the old princess is on her way to mass in the chapel, followed by her falsely pious children, their heads devotedly bowed.

The first take of the film was shot, as Tullio Kezich recalled, at 11:35 in the morning on March 16, 1959, in Theater 14 at Cinecittà. Piero Gherardi had reconstructed the inside of the dome at Saint Peter's. Anita Ekberg, dressed in black and wearing a priest's hat, appeared in the scene. The former Miss Malmö was an opulent beauty with translucent skin. Fellini Romanized her as Anitona, making her shapely figure (her measurements were 39-22-36 inches) into the emblem of the Italian boom. Given her strong inclination for alcohol, she had become a regular on the sleepless Roman night scene even before filming began.

Ekberg married the British actor Anthony Steel in Italy; theirs was a volatile relationship with frequent drunken scenes during which the two of them beat up each other. After their divorce she had various lovers, including Fiat mogul Gianni Agnelli, and then she married again, this time to the supposed German nobleman Rik Van Nutter who was, in reality, an American looking for celebrity.

There are two important meetings in the film that make a profound impression on the viewer's memory. The first is between Marcello and Sylvia (Anita Ekberg), a famous American actress visiting Rome whom Marcello accompanies until the celebrated bathing scene in the Trevi Fountain. The other is with the refined Steiner (Alain Cuny, though the role was intended for Henry Fonda), an educated man who brought artists and intellectuals together in his drawing room. Steiner seems to represent the positive pole in a disenchanted and cynical world, one without any religious or civic values, where the vulgarity of the nouveau riche coexisted with the mediocrity of a shameful middle class. His monologue is one of the movie's high points: "Sometimes at night the darkness and silence oppresses me. The peace scares me; it is perhaps what frightens me the most. I feel it like a facade behind which hell is hidden. . . ." Despite these dark omens, the later news that the character has killed himself after murdering his two young children comes as a dreadful surprise.

Fellini was not a political director; instead, he generally used autobiographical episodes behind which he might offer, on occasion, a glimpse of society. Nonetheless, some of his films became powerful and truthful portraits of contemporary Italy, including *Prova d'orchestra*

(The Orchestra Rehearsal), *Ginger and Fred,* and *La Dolce Vita*—the first strong representation of the moral decline of the new society created by national prosperity. "Seen from a distance and in hindsight," Morando Morandini wrote in his *Storia del cinema (History of Cinema)*, "*La Dolce Vita* was a watershed in the history of Italian cinema after the war. In a certain sense it signaled an end, and then the beginning of a new epoch, perhaps because it returned to the problem of neo-realism and the fact that it had been surpassed, which in those years constituted the bad conscience—and, in some cases, torment—of Italian movie critics." But why was neo-realism a problem?

The term neo-realism came into widespread use more or less at the same time as Roberto Rossellini's 1945 masterpiece *Roma città aperta (Open City)*. It is something of an exaggeration to say that it was a well-defined artistic movement. Instead, neo-realism was a way of seeing reality, an unmediated approach to collective problems. It also represented the need to have something to believe in to overcome the anxieties and deprivations of the time, something worth fighting for (the key phrase at the time was *d'impegnarsi*, something to commit to). There was often, behind the variety of things that would come to be called neo-realism, something more than an aesthetic vision—a sort of moral boost—and it was the reason those films sometimes had a moralistic tone. Whether he thought about it or intuited it, Fellini saw that that way of representing reality in terms of the profound changes then rocking Italy and the Italians, was insufficient. *La Dolce Vita* was born from that perception.

In the movie's opening scene an enormous statue of Christ with his arms outstretched flies over Rome, carried by a helicopter. It passes over the ruins of the Coliseum, skims over a group of girls sunbathing by the pool on a terrace ("Look, it's Jesus!" one of them exclaims), and then arrives at Saint Peter's. In this dizzying opening sequence Fellini foreshadows the color and temperature of this Roman epic—the classical, sybaritic facileness of the new prosperity, the sheer luxury and the superficiality of religious values. Anyone who remembers the news in those years will recognize the film's references to current events. The actress Sylvia's brutal and drunken partner (played by the former Tarzan, Lex Barker) recalls the many brawls between the prying paparazzi and actors hoping for some little scrap of improbable privacy. The striptease young Nadia performs among her friends at a villa in Fregene—celebrating her recent divorce—echoes the famous story of the Turkish dancer Aiché Nana, who was drunk and improvised a striptease at Rugantino, a night-club in Trastevere. At the same party in Fregene there is another evocative scene when an ingenuous young woman gets drunk and is ridiculed; this is certainly a reference to the Montesi case. Then there is the finale: the story in *La Dolce Vita* develops over the course of seven nights and seven dawns. The seventh dawn features Marcello, who has abandoned his dream of becoming a writer, leaving an orgy, exhausted. He finds himself on a beach, the sky a grayish color but not yet light. A gelatinous mass attracts his attention; it's a sea monster, shapeless and decayed, expelled from the sea to lie rotting on the beach. The man raises his eyes and sees, on the other side of a small canal, Paolina (Valeria Ciangottini), a young blonde he'd met by chance a few days earlier. They are two opposite symbols, corruption and purity, an all-too-transparent metaphor, but nevertheless beautifully calibrated to the narrative's flow. Marcello's exhausted face contrasts with the girl's innocent one and then hers, in turn, contrasts with the image of the decaying monster. Paolina searches in vain for something to say to him. Marcello doesn't hear the words, makes a resigned gesture, and leaves with his dreary companions. Paolina smiles.

The film debuted in February of 1960. Filming took five months, and at the end of it Fellini had fifty-six hours of film to edit down to 167 minutes. The scandal it caused was immediate. In the most conservative Catholic circles there was talk of pornography, blasphemy, and the threat of excommunication not just for the film's makers, but also for anyone who went to see it. At the end of the premiere in Milan the director was punched and spat upon. The extreme right called for his arrest, and organized noisy demonstrations against the movie, practically guaranteeing its immediate success. The box office receipts exceeded all expectations, and praise from critics around the world was unanimous. *La Dolce Vita* won the Palme d'Or at the Cannes Film Festival, and it was nominated for an Oscar; it was not Fellini who won, however, but Piero Gherardi, for his set designs and costumes. The film's success was both artistic and moral. For almost a decade the work was considered a symbol—the turtleneck sweaters worn by some of the characters became the popular "dolce vita" sweaters, photographers of current events have ever since been called paparazzi, and the Via Veneto and Trevi Fountain were transformed into postcards that were purchased and mailed home by hoards of tourists.

What matters most to us at the end of this story is that once the film appeared Rome became the unenviable emblem of the emerging new Italy. The relationship between the director and the city was so intense that it's easy to forget that Fellini was not born there, that he came from Rimini and arrived in Rome for the first time by train (like the protagonist at the end of another film of his, *I Vitelloni*) in January of 1939. He was nineteen and had a suitcase full of short stories and vignettes which he would manage to sell to *Marc'Aurelio*, a biweekly and mildly satirical humor magazine responsible for some very popular characters. Aldo Fabrizi, a great (and large-girthed) Roman, who was also a wonderful comedic and dramatic actor, introduced Fellini to Rome. Fabrizi took him on such a bewitching tour that the city—from the historical center to Mussolini's planned suburb, EUR, and from the present of *La Dolce Vita* to the distant past of *Satyricon*—became the almost imperative backdrop for so many of Fellini's films. There is one place where Fellini's memory is publicly applauded, although quite discreetly. The doorway at Via Margutta 110a is marked with a simple sign, a tribute from the street's antique dealers, with the names of Fellini and his wife, Giulietta.

Fellini was neither the first nor the last director to use the magnificent Trevi Fountain in a movie. A *Fontaine de Trevi* had already appeared in a catalogue of the work of the Lumière Brothers in 1896, but its role in *Roman Holiday* is the most popular one. It was one of the places the enchanted Audrey Hepburn discovered on her tour of the marvels of Rome. The grandiose fountain marks a terminus of the Acqua Vergine (the restored Roman aqueduct called the Aqua Virgo in antiquity), the work of city planner Nicola Selvi, finished by Giuseppe Pannini. Fellini's scene, however, is the one etched in the collective conscious, for obvious reasons. The statuesque beauty of Anita Ekberg as she emerges from the fountain's water recalls the earthly Venus. Ettore Scola's 1974 film, *C'eravamo tanto amati* (*We All Loved Each Other So Much*), pays tribute to Fellini, reconstructing the famous scene of the bath in the fountain with the real protagonists playing themselves. Nino Manfredi, an orderly in a hospital, meets an old flame, Stefania Sandrelli, by accident as he passes in front of the fountain in an ambulance. She is trying to meet Fellini in order to get a part in *La Dolce Vita*. *C'eravamo tanti amati* is one of Scola's more successful films (its screenplay was written by two masters, Age and Scarpelli). It centers on a sad re-examination of the first years after the war, the hopes and energy that accompanied that period (including the cinema's neo-realism), and the later wrecking of those hopes. The characters and episodes in Scola's film identify and describe the end of the progressive decline of morality. Fellini's *La Dolce Vita* described the beginning of that same process.

Cinecittà is a place often cited in movies. Dino Risi mentioned it, for example, in his 1960 film, *Un amore a Roma* (*Love in Rome*), taken from Ercole Patti's story of the same name. The lead character visits the movie studio, and his wandering becomes an opportunity to show various aspects of the production complex. We even see Vittorio De Sica playing a director—that is, himself—who is trying desperately to coax a performance out of an actress. An even more appropriate citation comes in another, more successful film by Risi, *Una vita difficile* (*A Difficult Life*), made in 1961. The main character, Silvio Magnozzi (played by Alberto Sordi) is a former partisan who tries at the end of the war to return to civilian life. He's quite discontent, and entertains literary ambitions; he goes to Cinecittà to offer a script to the great Blasetti, who appears as himself in the movie. Silvio's petulant insistence annoys the director, who's about to begin filming a scene and manages to escape from him by raising the dolly on which the scene is being prepared. Here, too, as in *Bellissima*, the two faces of the movie business are revealed—the fascination, appeal, and the lure of big earnings and then the harshness, the pathetic side, and the precariousness and humiliation. Magnozzi's attempt to approach Blasetti is a failure, and the unfortunate man takes advantage of a chance encounter with an old friend, working as an extra, to eat his bag lunch.

The relationship between Rome, Cinecittà, and the movies—their entanglement, consonance, and in some cases complicity—was extraordinary right from the start. This is perhaps because Rome has no other industry (aside from the construction industry), or perhaps because of the city's theatrical character, or the temperament of its inhabitants—indolent and sly, but also capable of sudden bursts of creativity. Be that as it may, the cinema and Rome were destined to meet and like one another. There isn't a single neighborhood in the city that hasn't at one time or another been a movie set, whether in the center or in the outskirts, and this includes it monuments and markets, churches and prisons, the central train station and the more distant suburbs. In 1988 the experimental filmmaker Peter Greenaway directed *The Belly of an Architect,* a movie set in appropriate places around the city, including the Mausoleum of Augustus, Saint Peter's, the forum, Piazza Navona, and especially the Monument to Vittorio Emmanuele on the Piazza Venezia. His is perhaps the only film in which that mastodon of a monument, so lovely but so hard to photograph, is at the heart of a story.

The studios on the Via Tuscolana have weathered many other seasons. One example is the spaghetti Westerns invented by Sergio Leone, who ended his career with *C'era una volta il West* (*Once Upon a Time in the West*) and *C'era una volta in America* (*Once Upon a Time in America*), both filmed almost entirely at Cinecittà. Leone was taken to the studios for the first time at age thirteen by his father, Roberto Roberti, a director who had been blacklisted by the Fascists. During the 1920s Roberti managed only once to find a backer to finance one of his films, discovering later that he was a provocateur and agent of the political police.

These fake Westerns (though they were sometimes more realistic than their American counterparts) were a sort of impetuous genre that, perhaps from the force of its own energy, burned out rapidly. Of the forty-eight films made at Cinecittà in 1968, seventeen were Westerns. Outdoor sequences were shot in the south of Spain or, more familiarly, in the National Park of the southern Italian region of Abruzzo. Actors and directors were given new, Americanized names— Bob Robertson (Sergio Leone), Dan Savio (Ennio Morricone), Montgomery Wood (Giuliano Gemma), John Welles (Gian Maria Volonté), and so on.

With the recent decline of the movie industry, the studios at Cinecittà have been used more steadily to film commercials and host big television spectacles, including reality shows. Keeping such an important production center economically viable is enough to explain these changes, yet some regret remains at having witnessed the decline of one of the places that so thoroughly reflected Rome—one where the city constructed, and sometimes rediscovered, its identity.

Fellini tried to narrate the city in his film *Roma*, shot in 1970 and 1971. Even though it is not one of his best works, the movie is something of a redemption of the director's vision of the spectacle perpetually played out on the capital's streets. At the beginning the film is almost a documentary, and then it becomes a story in which the artist relives the charms and irritations of Rome, its past, and its ominous future. The film ends with a sinister circling of motorcyclists in the Piazza del Quirinale. First, however, Fellini revisits his passionate love for a city in which everything is eternally mixed—magnificent gardens and horrible apartment blocks, large, open spaces and small, overcrowded neighborhoods, gypsies who sleep on the steps of the Temple of Castor and Pollux, and humble shops next to the proud palaces of princes. In *Roma*, Fellini recounts his arrival at Termini, the city's central station, the brothels, the Fascist officials, the theatrical curtain raisers, and the courtyards of the apartment blocks in which voices and songs on the radio passed from one window to the next— the same memories that Ettore Scola shared in his memorable film *Una giornata particolare* (*A Special Day*).

Fifteen years separate Rossellini's 1945 masterpiece, *Open City*, from Fellini's 1960 masterpiece, *La Dolce Vita*. Two different techniques and two different visions, the tragic atmosphere of the occupation against the cheerfulness of an often suspicious affluence that threatens to swallow up everything, including memory. There are scenes filmed in the streets versus those carefully reconstructed on studio stages; is this reality versus fiction? Perhaps it's simpler to say that they're two different ways of capturing the same immutable landscape—Rome in its passage from one adventure to another, in the theatricality of its life, and in the eternally changing color of its light.

1. Federico Fellini, *Intervista* (New York: Castle Hill Productions, Inc., 1992), film. The quote paraphrased here is from the Italian; Castle Hill Productions, Inc. distributed a version with English subtitles in the United States.

VIII

TOWERS OF FEAR

THE APPROACH TO THE CHURCH of the Santi Quattro Coronati (Four Crowned Saints) ascends from below, along the Via dei Querceti. As soon as you turn left at the corner of the Via dei Santi Quattro a gigantic fortress appears; powerful, ancient walls rise before you, inspiring the immediate impression that you're standing before something truly exceptional—and that's precisely what this out-of-the-way, little-known corner of Rome, the church of the Santi Quattro, is. According to one legend the four saints were legionaries (with the names of Severus, Severianus, Carpoforus, and Vittorinus) who were martyred because they refused to worship the statue of a false god. Yet another legend says they were four Dalmatian artists killed by Diocletian because they refused to sculpt that same statue. Their remains, whoever they may have been, are buried in a crypt of the church. What really counts is the building itself, a fundamental testament of the distant past, laden with messages and news, much like a time capsule.

The church was first built in the fourth century, and was constructed on the foundations of a pre-existing Roman building, as was typical of that era. The earlier structure must have been usually impressive, given the size of the surviving vaulted apse, which is enormous when compared to the rest of the building. The original church was much larger, as can easily be seen by the partially walled-in columns between the nave and side aisles. After Robert of Guiscard's Norman troops sacked the city in 1084 Santi Quattro Coronati was rebuilt, and today all that remains of the first church is its apse. There is a semicircular crypt under the high altar, and the reliquaries of the martyred saints so venerated by the pilgrims were placed at its center. From the left aisle of the church a door opens (after ringing a bell) onto a beautifully decorated cloister with a twelfth-century fountain at its center for ritual ablutions, a portico of paired colonnettes, and capitals decorated with aquatic foliage. Recent excavations revealed an underground passage that connects this fortified basilica with the cathedral church of Saint John Lateran. This tunnel was an escape route for popes who would have found a secure refuge at Santi Quattro Coronati if they needed it. All of the many magnificent columns here, with both smooth and fluted shafts, obviously came from older temples and other Roman buildings. There are two courtyards in front of the church, and the second was originally part of the first basilica. The impressive tower dates to the ninth century, and served the purpose of both observation platform and defensive keep.

This brief description provides a basic idea of the church complex and its buildings, but much more can be said about their frescoes, decorations, and furnishings. The most striking aspect of Santi Quattro Coronati is the atmosphere of the place as a whole and the evident strength of its venerable walls, which would survive even if they were reduced to bare stone. Two convents are housed within: the first belongs to an order called the Little Sisters of the Lamb, and the other to cloistered Augustinian nuns. Father Paul Lawlor, an Irish Dominican and archaeologist of the church of San Clemente with whom I visited the complex, brought these details to my attention.

On the left side of the portico of the first courtyard there is a heavy iron grate over a small window next to a *ruota*—a sort of spinning table or lazy Susan where unwanted newborns were left to be cared for by the nuns. At the sound of a bell the fleeting shadow of a female figure appeared in the half-light. In exchange for a Euro she gave us the key to the door leading to the Oratory of Saint Sylvester, an extraordinary place for two reasons. Its first treasure is the series of frescoes, executed by Byzantine masters in the thirteenth century, representing the *Constitutum Constantini*—the famous donation in which Emperor Constantine ceded his supremacy over Rome, Italy, and the whole of the West to the Pope. Innocent IV commissioned these frescoes at the same time he was struggling with Emperor Frederick II. Today we'd deem them propaganda, and I'll explain later on exactly why.

There is a scene of the Last Judgment above the entrance door showing Christ enthroned between the Madonna and Saint John the Baptist. Two angels hover above Christ—one sounds the trumpet

calling all souls to judgment, and the other rolls up the starry firma-
ment as confirmation that everything, including time, has come to
an end. This is one of the few surviving examples of this evocative
medieval iconography inspired by the Book of the Apocalypse;
Giotto's frescoes in the Scrovegni Chapel in Padua are another
important example. There are shell-shaped openings at the top of the
walls that allowed the cloistered nuns to carry out the holy offices
without being seen.

Upon leaving this complex we go back down the hill along the
Via dei Santi Quattro toward the Via di San Giovanni in Laterano.
At the corner of the Via dei Querceti is an ancient aedicule, almost
reduced to mere ruins, whose history through the centuries has been
documented by the archaeologist Rodolfo Lanciani. It is tied to the
legend of Pope Joan, but we'll come back to her later on; just a few
meters beyond this niche we come to the Basilica of San Clemente.
Of all the Roman churches and basilicas, this one, at least from a historical point of view, is the most amazing. The sheer fact that it consists of at least three buildings, constructed one atop the other over
the course of several centuries, is enough to get a sense of its singu-
larity. The first structures on the site were built in Roman times,
before the great fire of Nero's reign in 64 AD. In the second century
a private house, or domus, was built here, and had a Mithreum in its
courtyard. The ancient subterranean temple is still there today, and
was constructed according to a standard plan, with a pair of facing
benches for the faithful and the altar with an image of the sacrificial
bull bending its head low to the ground. Mithraic beliefs were tied to
the cosmos and the seasons, and its rituals were celebrated in caverns.
The hypogeum here is an artificial cave with stucco stars and eleven
openings on the ceiling—the smaller ones represent the principal
constellations, and the four larger ones the seasons.

A basilica was built over the house and Mithreum in the fourth
century, and later damaged during the devastating Norman sack of
the city in 1084. The partially destroyed buildings were filled in to then
serve as the foundations of a new basilica. This brief outline of the
site's history is necessary in order to truly "see," through the inter-
vening layers, the original spaces. Visitors are also immediately struck
by the sound of rushing water beneath the floor of the church's low-
est level; it's a small branch of the stream that runs down the side of

the Lateran Hill toward the Coliseum. Father Lawlor's excavations have unearthed evidence of a Roman conduit, and it seems likely that it was part of the hydraulic system that fed the lake in the gardens of the Domus Aurea.

The right wall of the lower church has a very important fresco cycle that dates back to about 1080. It tells the curious story of Sissinius, who one day discovered that his wife, Theodora, of whom he was very jealous, had gone to a place where Christians secretly gathered. He was filled with such ire that he became both deaf and blind. Some time later Clement, one of the Christians, met and healed him. The experience did little to mollify Sissinius, who ordered his servants to bind the holy man and take him away. The servants, however, as if driven out of their senses, bound and carried off a column rather than Clement. What's particularly interesting here is that in painting this scene the artists added little cartoonlike bubbles with explanatory texts; these passages are among the first written examples of the transition from Latin to Italian, in a language we now call the vulgate.

In one of the main scenes Sissinius gives orders, and the servants hurriedly get to work under their master's shouted commands, "Falite dereto colo palo, Carvoncelle, Gosmari, Albertel traite. Fili dele pute traite" ("Forward with that lever, Carvoncello, Gosmari, Albertel—pull, pull, you sons-of-bitches!"). There is an inscription at the center of the scene that sums up the moral of the story, "Duritiam cordis vestries saxa traere meruisti" ("For your cruelty you deserved to drag stones").

These sacred buildings I've concisely described take us back to the high Middle Ages, a period that unfolded around the year 1000, give or take a century. This was one of the densest, most tragic, and decisive periods in the city's history. It was a major period of transition, as the last traces of ancient Rome's glory disappeared. Rome became a holy city, and as such it became a pilgrimage destination as well, but it also remained in a constant state of civic unrest stoked by the bloody rivalries between the baronial families that held the city in a tight vise of violence. Let's enter this medieval city, have a look around, and try to understand what it meant to spend a lifetime, often running some risk, in such a place.

"I really believe that one must admire with great enthusiasm the entire panorama of a city in which so many towers rise that they seem like stalks of grain, and there are so many palaces and buildings that no one has been able ever to count them. . . . After admiring this infinite beauty for a long time, I realized in my heart, thanks to God, that I wanted to describe these magnificent works of men in this book." These moving words were written, in Latin originally, by someone who signed himself "Magister Gregorius." According to scholars he was most likely a learned Englishman who visited Rome at the end of the twelfth or beginning of the thirteenth century. He was so struck by what he saw that he wrote a short book about the surviving wonders of ancient Rome, describing "de mirabilibus quae Rome quondam fuerunt vel adhuc sunt," or "the marvels that were once upon a time in Rome and still exist today."

One of the first wonders—or rather the absolute first wonder—that struck the visitor was the panorama. Most pilgrims who came to Rome traveled by way of the Via Francigena. After a last stop at Sutri before they entered the city, they found themselves at the top of Monte Mario, which was then called the Mons Gaudii, or Mountain of Joy, because of the profound emotion provoked upon first glimpsing the city. The splendid view also meant that the long, arduous, often dangerous journey had come to an end.

Until the year 1000 guidebooks, or what might pass for early written guides, limited themselves to describing the principal monuments and how to reach them. One of the most famous, the *Einsiedeln Itinerary*, dates to about the ninth century and is named after the Swiss monastery where it is preserved. This type of guidebook developed into something more elaborate, and beginning in the twelfth century scholars note the appearance of a large number of descriptive texts generally referred to as *Mirabilia urbis Romae* (The Marvels of the City of Rome). They include the *Graphia aurea urbis Romae* and also the *Liber pontificalis*, which offer us valuable information about the lives of the early popes and thus the history of the city as well.

The principal purpose of Master Gregorius's short book was to look at the surviving monuments of classical Rome, and he did so almost with the eye of a humanist, considering them regardless of any symbolic or religious value they might have. He almost completely ignores Christian Rome, mentioning only one basilica, and including that merely as a point of reference. When he refers to the

Church as a community of the faithful, it was to criticize those who were responsible for ruining the marvels of antiquity because they encouraged, or at least tolerated, the rampant despoiling: "This all-marble palace [of Augustus] offered abundant and precious materials to build the churches of Rome. Since so little remains, there is little to say." Master Gregorius accused the papacy, including famous popes like Gregory the Great, of leading the destruction of temples and statues, stating that in its desire to stamp out the pagan religion it also destroyed a civilization.

He accuses the people of Rome, judging them guilty of scraping every trace of gold from the statues and stripping every ancient monument of anything that had any value, either in itself or as reusable building material. Yet in spite of all the ruins, despoiling, and carelessness, the Rome that Master Greogorius related remained a city of marvelous monuments. He often wrote things such as, "Par tibi, Roma, nihil, cum sis prope tota ruina" ("There is nothing comparable to you, Rome, even though you are [reduced to] an almost total ruin"); or, "Roma quanta fuit, ipsa ruina docet" (The selfsame ruins attest how great Rome once was").

Gregorius's book contains a wealth of information, but also has some amusing misunderstandings; one has to do with the bronze statue of a seated boy intent on pulling a thorn from his foot (today it is in the Capitoline Museum). Placed on an elevated spot, such as on top of a column, the statue's height created a sort of curious misinterpretation. The boy's testicles, visible between his legs, were confused for his glans, creating the impression of a member quite out of proportion with the rest of the figure. Gregorius's chapter about this statue is called "De ridiculoso simulacro Priapi"—"On the ridiculous simulacrum of Priapus"—and the text states, "There is another ridiculous bronze statue, which is said to be a Priapus. His head is lowered as if he is trying to pull a thorn he has just stepped on from his foot, and he looks like he is suffering from some painful wound. If you look up at it from below to try to understand what is happening, you will see a sexual organ of extraordinary size."

Another statue noted in his book, said to have exercised a "magical seduction" on the viewer, was a Venus identical to the Capitoline Venus, if not the famous sculpture itself. Master Gregorius described it like this: "This image is made of Parian marble with such marvelous skill that it seems a living creature rather than a statue, similar to a woman who is blushing because of her nudity. Her face seems suffused with a red tone. Whoever sees it has the real impression that the statue's face, white as snow, actually flows with blood. For its marvelous face, as well as some magical seductive power it had, I was compelled to come back thrice to look at it." (This Venus is now housed in the Capitoline Museum.)

Leaving Gregorius's very "English" discoveries and preoccupations, let's return to the view of Rome I mentioned earlier, the one where "so many towers rise that they seem like stalks of grain." In the first centuries of the second millennium, Rome offered the visitor a panorama of towers not unlike what we see today, for example, in the famous town of San Gimignano. Many of Rome's towers remain, although they have since been remodeled, restored, or reconceived, and their presence on the city's horizon is camouflaged.

The two most impressive towers are the Torre dei Conti and the nearby Torre delle Milizie. The Torre dei Conti stands at the intersection of the Via dei Fori Imperiali and the Via Cavour, and was built as part of a fortified precinct in 1200. What's now left of it, including an enormous basement, gives a good sense of its original dimensions. The Torre delle Milizie, on the Largo Magnanapoli, is also massive and was purchased at the beginning of the fourteenth century by Pope Boniface VIII who fortified it to protect himself from attacks by the Colonna family, his enemy. In the mid-fourteenth century an earthquake caused the ground to shift and the tower to lean slightly, an effect still visible today. Many towers were eventually subsumed into later buildings, and the tower in the Piazza Tor Sanguigna is one example. It was built by the family of the same name, rivals of the Orsini family, and was part of a fortress. The tower was later enclosed in another building. One of the loveliest towers is the Torre dei Frangipane, also called Torre della Scimmia, or Tower of the Monkey, which is also now encased in a more recent building. A lamp burns at its top, in front of the image of a Madonna, and according to ancient legend the lamp was lit as a votive offering for the safety of a young girl who had been dragged up the tower by a monkey. The Piazza Margana, itself one of the smallest and most fascinating squares in the city, boasts the Torre dei Margani, a lovely example of a fortified medieval residence. Its portal was made with marble fragments from the late Imperial period, and it is one of many medieval houses in which classical building materials were reused. Another Margani tower, in the Piazza di San Pietro in Vincoli, underwent a similar transformation, and was turned into the bell tower for the church of San Francesco di Paola.

I could go on, as there's no shortage of towers, but the real attraction of these towers poses a question: why were so many built in the period around the year 1000? The answer is in the title of this chapter—fear. Towers were a type of building, sometimes used for military purposes, but most often intended as residences, dictated by the critical and continually dangerous conditions that prevailed in Rome. Whoever could, whoever wanted to exercise some authority, whoever wanted visibility and prestige, or whoever feared an attack built a fortified residence, the tower of which was most useful for observation and defense. Even the Coliseum was used as the fortified perimeter of a castle built within its walls. The same was true of the Tomb of Cecilia Metella on the Via Appia. The counts of Tusculum built a fortress next to it in the eleventh century and used the ruins of the tomb as its tower. But why was there so much fear? What terrible things made medieval Rome such a dangerous place?

The era we now call medieval lasted some ten centuries, from the collapse of the Western Roman Empire in 476 to the discovery of America in 1492. Even if historians have taken a more nuanced view of this period for some time now, many people continue to imagine it as a savage time—dark years of deep shadow, crime, and bloody love affairs. We still often think of it as a wild and barbaric period, one which, significantly, existed in complete ignorance and indifference to the splendor of classical antiquity. The fact that Jacopone da Todi, Dante, Petrarch, and Boccaccio all lived in the Middle Ages counts for little, as does the fact that the remarkable system of Scholastic philosophy, championed by Saint Thomas Aquinas, was also a product of this era. The idea of a dark age between the two shining lights of antiquity and the Renaissance is a persistent one. This notion was especially strong in the Romantic period, when it was sustained in popular literature, lyric opera, genre paintings, and by the strength of contemporary legend.

Jacob Burckhardt, the Swiss historian who wrote *The Civilization of the Renaissance in Italy* in 1860, accepted this idea of the Middle

Ages. He turned the Renaissance into a separate culture, one that finally recognized the value of the individual. The same idea of a period of dark decadence permeates the German historian Ferdinand Gregorovius's monumental *History of the City of Rome in the Middle Ages*. Written between 1859 and 1872, its vision of the Middle Ages was reinforced by a liberal ideology that exaggerated the instances (remarkable enough in and of themselves) of popes who were unworthy of office. Gregorovius saw the papacy as a completely political institution, product of a Latin idea much like the idea of empire, and removed from any religiosity. The Italian author Giosuè Carducci adopted this same notion, including its antipapal position, and helped reinforce it. Not until 1919, with the Dutch writer Johan Huizinga's book *Autumn of the Middle Ages*, did a more nuanced view of the period begin to take hold.

That said, if there were anywhere in the world where such a dark vision of the Middle Ages seems justified by the facts, that place was Rome. For centuries the former *caput mundi* continued to decline, and the relics of its extraordinary past were left to decay or be pillaged. For two or three centuries the throne of Saint Peter's was held by popes from Roman families in perpetual struggle with one another for power. Their only concern was the quest for authority, and the towers, these "stalks of grain," rose up to defend the temporary victors, and were also arrogant symbols of recently acquired power. They were the result of fear and the desire to hold on to past conquests. Behind every arrow-slit was a weapon ready to strike at anyone who approached with hostile intentions.

During the millennium Rome's Aurelian walls, originally built in the third century, were strengthened to make them a more effective defense. Nonetheless, they weren't enough to protect the city in 1084 from the Norman onslaught, one of the most devastating invasions in Rome's history. The Leonine walls around the Vatican and Saint Peter's were built in the ninth century. (The famous elevated passageway from the papal palace to the fortress of Castel Sant'Angelo was added four centuries later.)

The city's situation was one of complete decay. Abandoned and exposed to the travails of time and the elements, the imperial buildings collapsed. At the same time the Tiber continuously flooded the central area around the river bend. When the waters receded, they left behind an insalubrious muck that worsened health conditions in the city. Only a few streets and passageways were able to maintain any semblance of stability and decorum, and they were used for Rome's most important ceremonies, solemnities, and processions. Furthermore, an ailing economy and the almost total absence of an entrepreneurial class meant that the most common activity was the exploitation of the city's classical patrimony. Over periods of months and years swarms of workmen pried loose marble facades, smashed statues into bits and pieces, and melted down bronzes to make valuable new raw materials. Among these ruins there were occasional bubbling cauldrons in which the most admired fragments of ancient marble sculpture were reduced to simple lime. Everyone stole—the Romans did so to survive, and foreign visitors to bring home souvenirs—many souvenirs, cartloads of souvenirs. Even Charlemagne, who came to Rome to receive his imperial crown from Leo III on Christmas Day in 800, left with a caravan of carts packed with statues, bronzes, columns, and art objects. He wanted his royal residence at Aachen to look as much as possible like a new Rome. A thousand years later Napoleon did the same thing, but extended his plundering to all of Italy.

Life in this despoiled city was resilient. Parts of Rome teemed with a sort of instinctive vitality stronger than any misfortune. The Suburra, the old plebian neighborhood that stretched from the Coliseum to the slopes of the Esquiline Hill, was packed with people. The same is true of the areas near the Theatre of Marcellus, now the quarter around Piazza Campitelli and the Via delle Botteghe Oscure. The Isola Tiberina—also called the Isola di San Bartolomeo—was also densely populated. Five bridges spanned the river—the northernmost was the Ponte Nomentano (which crossed the Aniene, not the Tiber), then the fortified Ponte Milvio, the Ponte Sant'Angelo, and the two bridges on the Isola Tiberina. The remains of the Pons Aemilia stood downriver; built in the second century, and the Romans called it the Ponte Rotto, the Broken Bridge, and this curious fragment can still be seen today, stranded in the middle of the river. In a city where no one worried about anything but himself and the present day, the construction of new bridges was never discussed. The languishing economy, moreover, made them unnecessary.

How did the Romans survive? One might ask, too, what vision of reality existed among these malnourished people who lived in deplorable hygienic conditions, were afflicted by diseases that almost no one knew how to cure, and believed in a religion shot through with superstition and a strong inclination toward idolatry. I use the term "vision of reality" because such circumstances favored the kind of talk in which magic, illusion, credulity, and stupor were all mixed together. Piero Camporesi, one of the great twentieth-century scholars of popular mythology, used documents and firsthand accounts to aim at a reconstruction of the conditions in which many of these people lived. In his book *Bread of Dreams*, he described immoderate excesses at the table, and even consumption of food that could provoke hallucinations:

> The cuisine of the imaginary, dream-inducing diet, sacrilegious gastronomy (cannibalistic, vampirical and dung-eating), human ointments and plasters, profane oils and sacred unctions, "mummy" fragments and cranial dust, medicinal powers *de sanguinibus*, breads filled with seeds and powders bestowing oblivion, expansive and euphoria-producing herbs, narcotic cakes, stimulating roots and aphrodisiacal flours, aromas and effluvia of devil-chasing plants and antidotes for melancholy (*balneum diaboli*), and "seasoned" and "fostered" spells created by a network of dreams, hallucinations and permanent visions. By altering measures, relations, proportions and backgrounds, they made "three fingers seem like six, boys armed men, and men giants . . . everything much bigger than usual and the whole world turned upside down."[1]

This delirious world made miraculous and inexplicable events seem plausible—and not just among the most backward segments of peasant society. Camporesi continued, "the people of the town and city . . . lived immersed in a world of expectation, in a suspended and bewitched condition, where portent, miracle and the unusual belonged to the realm of the possible and the everyday: the saint and the witch (in her own way a saint of a different type) reflected the two ambiguous faces, the face side and reverse of the same neurotic tendency toward the separation from reality, the voyage into the imaginary and the leap into the fantastic."[2] In such a society the boundaries between reality and unreality, possible and impossible, sacred and profane, abstract and concrete, holy and damned, purity and filthiness, indecency and sublimity became even less certain. In compensation, the city swarmed with churches; there were more than three hundred of them, many of which either adapted extant ancient temples or were built on their remains.

Many areas of the ancient city that had been built up with dense construction reverted to arable land. Even Garibaldi's troops, the famous *bersaglieri* who entered Rome in 1870, found vast plots of open land within the walls that had been transformed into gardens and vineyards or had simply been abandoned. (This prepared the way for the boom of building speculation right after unification that gobbled up every open space as quickly as possible.)

The majority of the population lived in miserable conditions. Because the influx of pilgrims and *romei,* or people going to Rome, was so great, money changing, often combined with pawn brokering, was one of the most common jobs in the city. The Church forbade Christians from loaning money with interest, and thus it was almost always the Jews who performed this service. The most skilled of them even helped finance papal undertakings. Then there were the craftsmen, whose presence is still evident in the names of some of the medieval streets—the Via dei Chiavari (locksmiths), Via dei Librai (booksellers), Via dei Giubbonari (coat tailors), Via dei Coronari (rosary makers), Via dei Pettinari (barbers), and Via dei Banchi (both Vecchi and Nuovi, banks or moneychangers, old and new). Then there were the *tabernarii,* the innkeepers, who were indispensable in a city frequented by foreigners. They served wine accompanied by simple food, and even in the early twentieth century it was not unusual to see shop signs that advertised "Vino con cucina," wine with food.

Houses were constructed with the spoils of older buildings, health was precarious, and hygienic services were nonexistent. Many of the old water pipes (once the pride of Rome) and sewers of the ancient city were either broken or diverted, causing every sort of health and safety consequences you can imagine. Most buildings were only two stories, and it was not unusual to use some preexisting Roman construction used as a foundation. And yet there were also magnificent and luxurious houses, their interior furnishings were those of the imperial era simply removed from their original location—columns, portals, windows, candelabra, mosaics, and marble

mbs of the English poet John Keats (*above, left*) and Italian Communist Party founder
tonio Gramsci (*below*) in the English Cemetery near Porta San Paolo, one of Rome's
ost romantic spots.

Aerial view (*left*) and detail (*opposite, bottom*) of the Baths of Caracalla. The sheer scale of the ruins suggests the grandeur of the original building complex.

Two views of the tomb of Cecilia Metella. In the photograph at bottom the medieval Caetani Castle can be seen next to the tomb.

The Porta Latina and adjacent temple of San Giovanni in Oleo.
A view of the third-century Aurelian walls.

Fascist leader Ettore Muti, posing with his typical audacious stance.

An exterior view of Porta San Sebastiano, one of the most grandiose portals in the city walls, seen from the ancient Appian Way.

Two views of the interior of Muti's residence inside the Porta San Sebastiano, designed by the famed architect Luigi Moretti.

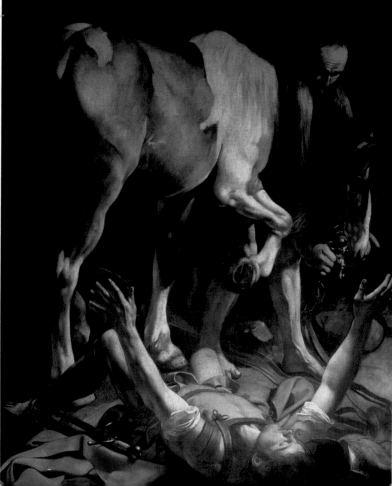

Some of Caravaggio's works visible (with the exception of one) in Roman churches. On the facing page, a detail of the *Martyrdom of Saint Matthew* (*above*) in San Luigi dei Francesi and the *Conversion of Saint Paul* (*below*) in Santa Maria del Popolo.

This page: The *Crucifixion of Saint Peter* (*above, left*) in Santa Maria del Popolo and the *Madonna di Loreto* (also called *Madonna of the Pilgrims*, *above, right*) in Sant'Agostino.

On the right, a detail of the *Death of the Virgin*. Rejected by the priests who commissioned it for Santa Maria della Scala in Trastevere, it is now at the Louvre.

The archaeological excavations in the Largo di Torre Argentina (*above, left*); at their far end is the site of the Curia of Pompey, where Julius Caesar was killed in AD 44.

The Roman Forum (*above, right*), which also included the Domus Publica, Caesar's last residence.

Vincenzo Camuccini's *Death of Julius Caesar* (*left*), at the Capodimonte Museum in Naples.

The Theater of Marcellus; note the wall extensions in the archways, which have since been removed, and the poor state of conservation.

Two views of daily life in the early twentieth century: a sandal maker at work, and a woman hanging laundry out to dry between the ruins of ancient buildings.

On the facing page, the tomb of Julius II in San Pietro in Vincoli, with Michelangelo's powerful statue of Moses (*detail at right*).

The central nave of the same church, built with magnificent columns taken from an ancient Roman basilica.

The first take (*above*) of the propagandistic Fascist film *Scipione l'Africano*, directed by Carmine Gallone.

Anita Ekberg, symbol of the *Dolce Vita*, exits an airplane at Ciampino airport in 1959.

On the facing page, the entrance of the Cinecittà film studios, often used by Federico Fellini, and one of the film sets inside, with Benito Mussolini looking on.

Three of the many medieval towers built throughout the city—typical examples of architectural defenses.

The imposing foundation and walls, partially demolished, of the Torre dei Conti (*left*).

The Torre delle Milizie (*below*), near Trajan's Forum; its slight tilt is the result of an earthquake that occurred sometime during the past few centuries.

On the facing page, the so-called Torre della Scimmia (Tower of the Monkey).

The courtyard of the Chiesa dei Santi Quattro Coronati, one of the most evocative medieval corners in Rome. In one of the church's chapels is a fresco illustrating the apocryphal donation of Constantine.

The altar of San Clemente, an extraordinary example of an Early Christian basilica built over three vertical levels dating back to distinct time periods.

Rome, March 23, 1944: men lined up by officials of the Nazi occupation following a partisan attack in Via Rasella.

The bodies of Nazi mass murder victims found in the area of the Fosse Ardeatine after the city's liberation.

The monument and inscription commemorating the barbaric Nazi massacre.

QUI FUMMO TRUCIDATI
ME DI UN SACRIFICIO ORRENDO
DAL NOSTRO SACRIFICIO
SORGA UNA PATRIA MIGLIORE
DURATURA PACE FRA I POPOLI

DIS CLAMAVI
DOMINE......

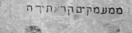
ממעמקים קראתיך ה

Two rooms of the Borgia apartments in the Vatican.

The Sala dei Santi (Room of the Saints), with frescos by Pinturicchio (*above*). At right, a detail of young Lucrezia Borgia portrayed as Saint Catherine of Alexandria debating with the church leaders.

On the facing page (*above*), the so-called Sala del Credo (Room of the Creed).

Pope Alexander VI, Rodrigo Borgia, was an able politician but rather questionable religious leader. Pinturicchio portrayed him (*opposite, bottom left*) kneeling in the Sala dei Misteri della Fede (Room of the Mysteries of the Faith).

Two views, at right and below, of the Vittoriano, or Altare della Patria (Altar of the Fatherland). Initially conceived to honor King Vittorio Emmanuele II, its meaning was later enriched after World War I, when the Tomb of the Unknown Soldier was added.

The Vittoriano is the monument that best condenses and expresses the lay religiosity of the newly created Italian nation according to mid-nineteenth-century canons.

Below, on the facing page, a Fascist celebration for the Unknown Soldier following the march on Rome in 1922.

Five glimpses of bourgeois Rome, which began to grow only after the city was annexed to the Kingdom of Italy as its capital on September 20, 1870.

On the facing page, bottom, a group photograph of a middle-class family, circa 1915. This happens to be the Augias family; the third from the left, dressed as a sailor, is the author's father.

In the early nineteen-
twenties Gino Coppedè
designed a small neighborhood encompassing a
few city blocks along Via
Tagliamento. The buildings
are characterized by an
exuberant, eclectic style,
and are marked by an
accentuated imaginative
appearance.

The exterior of the so-called Villa Vascello, site of violent clashes during the French attack on the Roman Republic in 1849.

In the walls around the Janiculum Hill near Largo Berchet are two inscriptions right next to each other: one, in Latin, commemorates the quick restoration of the walls following the French attack, and the other, in Italian, honors the patriots who sacrificed their lives defending the Roman Republic.

The temple built by Bramante in the church cloister of San Pietro in Montorio.

Marquis Camillo Casati and his wife, Anna (*top*), protagonists of one of the most turbid murders of the early postwar years.

Massimo Minorenti, Anna Casati's lover (*above*).

FINALMENTE ESCLUSIVA MONDIALE 212 PAGINE
150 FOTO IN NERO E A COLORI

IL DIARIO DELLA MARCHESA

ANNA CASATI FALLARINO

LA DONNA DAI DUE VOLTI

LA NOBILE

L'ESIBIZIONISTA

E' UN DOCUMENTO ESPLOSIVO

A view of the Jewish ghetto at the beginning of the twentieth century; the narrowness of the buildings favored outdoor life on the streets. Ancient Roman marbles were used as marketplace tables for showing off goods, including food (and fish in particular).

Two dramatic scenes of Nazi round-ups in the ghetto of Rome. Of the 2,091 Jews deported to concentration camps only 73 men and 23 women returned.

A butcher shop in Via del Portico d'Ottavia. The doorway lintels are from an ancient Roman shop.

Above, right, an evocative view of the Portico d'Ottavia with the church of Sant' Angelo in Pescheria in the background.

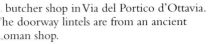

Ancient and modern worlds are closely mixed throughout the streets of the ghetto.

The EUR neighborhood is one of the chief urban designs of the Fascist period. One of the bas-reliefs sculpted by Publio Morbiducci (*left*); Giorgio Quaroni's mural *The Foundation of Rome* (*top*); three of the enormous bronze portraits of Mussolini and Vittorio Emmanuele III in the Palazzo degli Uffici (*above*), whose impressive facade is visible below.

LA TERZA ROMA SI DILATERA SOPRA ALTRI COLLI LVNGO LE RIVE DEL FIVME SACRO SINO ALLE SPIAGGE

intarsia. There were also jewels, gems, precious cloths, rugs, tableware, and glassware. The privileged people who enjoyed this splendor were abbots and prelates, magistrates and members of families competing to control the ultimate source of power—the papacy.

As is always the case, the value of land varied over time and depended on location. We know that until the year 1000 the areas around the Lateran neighborhood, close to the papal residence, were especially desirable. When the papacy moved across town to Saint Peter's, the Vatican and surrounding areas rose in value. The streets around what is now the Piazza Santi Apostoli and the Column of Trajan, at the bottom of the Quirinal Hill, have always been considered elegant. It was no accident that Michelangelo chose to live in that area, on a street called Macel de' Corvi; his house may have been modest, but he certainly had a good address.

Why did the popes move their seat from Saint John Lateran to the Vatican? There were important and complicated questions behind the move, including the centuries-old debate over which of the two ancient basilicas was built first. In 1569 Pius V issued a bull that put an end to the controversy of which came first, giving primacy to the Lateran, seat of the bishop of Rome. Polemics aside, the transfer to Saint Peter's was motivated by the simple fact that the area around the Vatican was easier to defend, especially after the construction of the Leonine walls at the end of the ninth century. In a city torn by internal conflicts and threatened from the outside, security became an essential issue. The Vatican complex, with the addition of the Borgo and Hadrian's Mausoleum (Castel Sant'Angelo) offered an existing configuration that could be transformed into a fortified citadel. In the end the decision of where to place the papacy was based on the same emotion that led to the building of the towers—fear. The climate was such that Pope Gregory XI agreed to return to Rome in 1378, ending the exile of the papacy in Avignon, only when ownership of Hadrian's Mausoleum was given in perpetuity to the papacy.

The basilica of Saint John Lateran has so few traces of the original building complex left that it's not easy to remember the various dates of each part. The first structural nucleus was commissioned by Emperor Constantine in the fourth century. The Lateran Palace, so skillfully added along the church's right side, dates to the end of the sixteenth century. Sixtus V had the crumbling old buildings of the

Patriarchìo (the papal residence) torn down, and commissioned Domenico Fontana to design a new palace—only a few steps away lies a street named for the architect. For many centuries both basilicas, Saint John and Saint Peter's, played important roles in the inaugural ceremonies for new popes. The election itself took place in the former, and the coronation in the latter. This double location required a procession, moving across the city twice as it traveled to and from Saint Peter's. In *Roma dal cielo*, one of his many well-researched books on the city's history, Cesare D'Onofrio reconstructed the itinerary of these papal processions. Walking the same streets today is still a meaningful experience for anyone who wants to really understand the ancient layout of the city, so it's by traveling these streets that we'll rediscover ancient Rome.

When a new pope was named, the bishops who elected him went to call the pope-designate, who then had to pretend he didn't want the high office and was supposed to hide from his electors. Once the ritual of refusal was complete, the newly elected pope made a solemn entrance into the Lateran, where he sat in the *stercoraria*. Around him were churchmen intoning a psalm to remind him that God had elevated him to his new office, raising him up from the dust and filth of the human condition. He then went to the second floor of the Patriarchìo, where he was again seated, this time in a marble chair with a hole at the center of the seat. The pope sat in the almost unseemly, semi-reclining position used by women during childbirth, with a basin placed in front of the chair to facilitate the symbolic birth. At that moment the pope represented, and indeed incarnated, *Ecclesia Mater*, Mother Church. To cement the significance of this moment, a *sella obstetrica*, or gynecological chair, was used. Over time, this ritual assumed a completely different meaning tied to strange and legendary circumstances I will return to later.

The newly elected pope blessed the crowd from the Benediction Loggia, which looked out over the basilica's main entrance and faced the obelisk (the oldest and the tallest in Rome). The people were excited, and raucously packed around the equestrian monument of Constantine, anxious to follow the procession, not least for the practical benefits they might earn. I mention the equestrian monument of Constantine because that was the identification of the statue we now know is really Marcus Aurelius, visible today in the Capitoline

Museum. Bernini later made a statue of Constantine (now in the Vatican Palace), but that only came five centuries later. So why was the Marcus Aurelius at Saint John Lateran rather than the Capitoline, where we are accustomed to seeing it?

The future emperor Marcus Aurelius was born in a patrician house surrounded by gardens that once stood where the hospital of San Giovanni is today, with its sixteenth-century facade. For centuries the great bronze equestrian statue of the emperor stood in those gardens, protected by their high walls. It was later moved to the middle, more or less, of the Campus Lateranensis, the open yard in front of the Lateran basilica. The figure was erroneously identified as Constantine, the emperor who first tolerated Christianity, a misidentification that ultimately helped save it from destruction. Constantine had lived for a few years in the residence at the Lateran, so it wasn't unlikely that his statue might be found in the area. To add some color to our sense of his personality, note that after his victory over Maxentius in the famous battle at the Milvian Bridge, in October of 312, Constantine quickly had a triumphal arch built (it still stands next to the Coliseum), sped along by the snatching of sculptures and friezes from other monuments. He was a politician of great stature and equally great contradictions. The historian Santo Mazzarino wrote that he was the most revolutionary politician in European history. He handled the novelty of Christianity, which had fused with the pagan cult of *sol invictus* (the invincible sun) and some elements of Mithraism, with remarkable wisdom. He convened the Council of Nicea in 325 and dealt harshly with the Arian heresy, yet the emperor himself was not baptized until just before he died in 337. He'd never much liked Rome, and as soon as he had the chance he moved East to found his own capital, Constantinople, at the junction between the Bosphorus and the Sea of Marmara.

Constantine was the son of Helena, a resourceful woman who'd started out as a *stabularia* (a stable girl) and worked her way up to concubine of the Emperor Constantius, who was called Chlorus, or Pale One, because of his greenish complexion. Helena was repudiated when she was only thirty-six, but she continued to exercise an enormous influence over her adolescent son. When she was about seventy, she converted to Christianity and went on a pilgrimage to the Holy Land. According to legend, she brought back several pieces of Christ's cross and founded the church of Santa Croce in Gerusalemme in Rome to house these relics.

But let's get back to the papal court. Once the new pope had received the crowd's acclaim he left the basilica and proceeded along what is now the Via San Giovanni in Laterano—the Romans called it the *stradone*, or big street—toward the Coliseum. The final section of the street was blocked by the Ludus Magnus, ruins of the old gladiators' barracks, and a detour had to be made around it. Thus the procession turned onto the Via dei Querceti, and then almost immediately onto the Via dei Santi Quattro Coronati. I mentioned earlier that the thirteenth-century frescoes in this church were intended to confirm the supremacy of religious authority over civil powers, and you'll now see how.

About four centuries after Constantine's death a document called the *Constitutum Constantini* (which can be translated, rather freely, as the Imperial Constitution) began to circulate in European courts. The text of the document confirmed that the first Christian emperor had given the Lateran basilica, the city of Rome, and the whole of the Western Empire to Pope Sylvester and his successors. The impetus for the Emperor's spectacular gift was his miraculous recovery from leprosy. When he first showed evidence of the disease, evil priests had prescribed a bath in the blood of innocent children. His mind still clouded by paganism, the Emperor was preparing to commit this sacrilege when the sight of the weeping mothers moved him to mercy. The following night two holy figures came to him in a dream. They directed him to the pious bishop, Sylvester, who was living in a hermitage on Mount Soracte and would show him the true cure. After a judicial inquiry in which the emperor recognized his holy visitors in portraits of the apostles Peter and Paul, Sylvester immersed him three times in water in the Lateran baptistery. At the end of this purification ritual the foul symptoms of his disease had disappeared, and the miracle was followed by prayers of thanksgiving and general rejoicing.

In the introduction to the document, which is also known as the Donation of Constantine, the Emperor recognized the supremacy of the Apostle Peter: "You are Peter (*Petrus*), and on this rock (*petrus*) I will found my church," Matthew 16:18). This is the basis for later papal claims to imperial status. "And, to the extent of our earthly imperial power, we decree that his holy Roman church shall be honoured with veneration; and that, more than our empire and earthly throne, the most sacred seat of Saint Peter shall be gloriously exalted; we giving to it the imperial power, and dignity of glory, and vigour and honour."[3] Having established the supremacy of the Roman pope over all earthly rulers, Constantine then gave him and his successors in perpetuity the Lateran Palace, the city of Rome, the province of Italia and the western regions of the empire. In the past canon lawyers have suggested that the pope, as universal monarch, was Lord of the earth and thus had the right to assign portions of his territory to one terrestrial state or another.

In reality this document was a skilled forgery fabricated by the Vatican chancery. It served, though, as the judicial basis for the claim of papal supremacy during the long struggles between the pope and emperor. The implications of this forgery lasted for centuries, conditioning the political situation of Rome and even Italy (the famous "Italian question"). It also lent the weight of tradition, if not authenticity, to the temporal power of the Church, the traces of which even survived in the 1948 constitution of the Italian Republic.

Ariosto, Machiavelli, and Guicciardini all viewed the papacy as the chief cause of great woes, and blamed many of Italy's troubles on the papacy's political power. Dante and Petrarch, on the other hand, praised the "Roman-ness" of the papacy, although the former launched this harsh invective against Constantine's donation in Canto XIX of the *Inferno*:

> 'Ah, Constantine, to what evil you gave birth,
> Not by your conversion, but by the dowry
> that the first rich Father had from you!'[4]

In more recent times the writer Alessandro Manzoni, a distinguished exponent of liberal Catholicism, was enthusiastic when the Piedmont army occupied the Papal States in 1860. His daughter, Vittoria, vividly remembered her father's reaction; "When the news came in September of the expedition in Romagna, father was beside himself with happiness. He cried, laughed and clapped his hands yelling, 'long live Garibaldi!'. . . . Father was convinced that the loss of its temporal power was providential for the Church. Once freed of all earthly concerns, it might better govern its spiritual domain." Manzoni and others, like the Catholic philosopher Antonio Rosmini, turned out to be right. At the beginning of the twenty-first century a defender of the "doctrine of faith" like Cardinal Ratzinger, now Pope Benedict XVI, also admitted the enormous advantage to the church in the loss of its territorial power. It demonstrates the vitality of Catholicism that, in places far from the environment of the Roman Curia, and without any hint of temporality, the Church built its authority on spirituality and the relief it brought to the poorest people.

The frescoes in Santi Quattro Coronati illustrate this story, from Constantine's illness to his final donation. Much like the stained-glass windows of other great cathedrals, this decoration of figures was intended to explain, even to those who couldn't read, the history and remote tradition on which the papacy based its "imperial" legitimacy. It is only a shame that they illustrate one of the most sensational forgeries in the history of the West, on par with the famous anti-Semitic *Protocols of the Elders of Zion* published in early-twentieth-century Russia.

The Via dei Santi Quattro has yet another surprise in store, because it was here, at the corner of the Via dei Querceti, that another famous and heavily symbolic event took place. According to legend, in the early ninth century an attractive and intelligent young man arrived in Rome. His ecclesiastical career was brilliant, and took him all the way to the papacy upon his election as Pope John VIII. This young man held the office for more than two years, until a sensational incident occurred. One day while riding the papal mule along the Via dei Santi Quattro on his way to Saint Peter's, the Pope, surrounded by a boisterous crowd, fell to the ground from the saddle and, to the amazement of the crowd, gave birth to a child. Thus the legend of Pope Joan was born. No one knows whether it is true or if it refers to some fertility ritual, or perhaps to the influence women had in the early Church. Yet the consequences—again, according to rumor—were important. From then on the ritual of the *sella obstetrica* assumed a completely different significance from what I described earlier. After the newly elected pope had been seated in it, a priest approached and felt beneath the opening in the seat to ascertain the sex of the pope-elect. Having verified that he was a man, he announced to those waiting anxiously, "Habet testes!" (He has testes.) For some time after the Via dei Querceti was also known as the Vicus papissae, or the Street of the Lady Pope.

The festive procession that marked the installation of the new pope then circled the Coliseum and proceeded up the hill, on streets that no longer exist, and back down toward the Torre dei Conti, crossing the evocative Via del Colosseo. The tower was named for the family of the Counts of Segni, who saw one of their kinsmen, Lotario dei Conti, elected Pope Innocent III in 1198. The procession would then have continued along what is today the Via Tor de' Conti, skirting the Suburra neighborhood along the Via Baccina, and passing under the Arco del Grillo, next to the tower of the same name. It then made the arduous ascent up the steep slope of the Quirinal Hill arriving, at the top, at the Torre delle Milizie, which is still one of the city's most impressive towers. Followed by a jubilant crowd, the papal procession then descended the Via della Pilotta to the basilica of the Santi Apostoli, where it paused for a break. When it resumed, it briefly followed the Via Lata (now the Via del Corso), passing several small streets and then turning onto the Via dei Coronari, which followed the winding course of an old Roman street. Finally it came to the Ponte Sant'Angelo and the impressive fortress of Castel Sant'Angelo. Beyond the labyrinth of the Borgo neighborhood the basilica of Saint Peter's was visible. This was quite a long route, and crossed the whole city from southeast to northwest.

The pope took a different route back to the Lateran, allowing as many people as possible to participate in events of his inauguration. Before the procession departed again, coins were thrown to the crowd in the courtyard of Saint Peter's. We can only imagine how eagerly awaited this was, and then how hard fought the struggle for the coins must have been. The tumult surrounding the transition from one pope to the next wasn't limited to fighting for tossed coins. Gaspare Pontani noted in his *Diario romano* that, as soon as the news of the death of Sixtus IV (Francesco Della Rovere) spread through the city, "Rome fell into an uproar." Groups of hotheads congregated at the palace of one of the pope's nephews and sacked it, "leaving not a single door or window intact." Others hurried to a farm belonging to another family member where "they stole a hundred cows and all the goats, as well as many pigs, donkeys, geese, and lots of round cheeses from Parma." When Paul IV (Gian Pietro Carafa) died in 1559, the Romans "ran to the prisons and broke down their doors, freeing everyone inside." As soon as news of the death of Sixtus V

(Felice Peretti) spread in 1590, the Jews who had money-changing stalls in Piazza Navona packed up and fled, for fear of being sacked. It was a long time before this "most wicked of customs" came to an end.

Let's return to the papal procession; once it had crossed the Ponte Sant'Angelo again, it continued along the Via del Banco di Santo Spirito and then the Via dei Banchi Nuovi. The pope received the homage of the city's Jewish community in the Piazza dell'Orologio. Rome's chief rabbi gave him a Bible and, in Hebrew, urged him to venerate it as the word of God according to the laws of Moses. The pope agreed, but also condemned the Jewish interpretation of the scriptures, since the messiah had already come in the person of Jesus Christ. Sometimes the Roman people demonstrated against the Jews, shouting insults at them and making hostile gestures. For the most part, that behavior was the result of a hatred for Jews systematically encouraged by the Church, which considered them guilty of deicide. Saint John Chrysostom was one of the first to suggest that it is the duty of Christians to hate Jews because even God hated them. Saint Augustine taught that the Jewish people cannot disappear, but survive and suffer as evidence of their guilt. Even the great philosopher Saint Thomas Aquinas claimed that, because of their crimes, the Jews would be held in eternal servitude. It took the vision of Pope John XXIII to cancel the curse of the *perfidies judaeis* (the idea of the treacherous Jews), which had for centuries afflicted a whole people.

Coins were again thrown to the crowd at the Piazza dell'Orologio, and again at the site of what is now Palazzo Braschi. From there the procession continued along the Via della Botteghe Oscure (*ad Apothecas Obscuras*, named for the sooty workshops where ancient marbles were burned to obtain lime), skirting the edge of the Theatre of Balbo, a monument whose history is interesting enough to merit a brief digression.

Lucius Cornelius Balbo distinguished himself in several battles, siding first with Caesar and then Augustus. As is always the case with unscrupulous politicians, he grew immensely rich. In 14 BC, with war booty from Africa, he decided to build a theatre in one of the most desirable parts of the city, the plain between the Capitoline and the Tiber. His theater, the third largest in Rome after the theaters of Pompey and Marcellus, was richly decorated and, including the backstage area, occupied a large portico-lined spot. During the medieval period its perimeter walls were used as foundations for new constructions. An exedra on its eastern side was used in the seventh century as a dumping site for household garbage (amphorae, pottery, and broken or unused things) and as a workshop which produced what we would today call luxury items. It's an archaeological treasure trove, and many casting rejects, unusable molds, jewelry seconds, fibulae, and small bottles have been unearthed there.

The site where the remains of the Crypta Balbi lie is perhaps the best and most moving place to observe how Rome was rebuilt upon its own bones—slowly changing from a city of emperors to one of popes. Examples abound: the floor in a sixteenth-century shop was laid directly over Roman pavement; and the original ancient portico became the foundation for a palace in the high Middle Ages. The Crypta Balbi makes clear to modern visitors that, despite the barbarian invasions, the ancient city persisted all the way up to the end of the seventh century. Foodstuffs, raw materials, and oil continued to arrive here from all over the Mediterranean world—from as far as Palestine and Byzantium—much as it had during the imperial period. The city's real decline only began some decades later.

But let's return once again to the papal procession; coins were tossed for a fourth time to the crowd at the church of San Marco, located in the maze of alleyways that crisscrossed one another at the foot of the Capitoline Hill before the Fascists gutted the area. Traversing what is now the Piazza Venezia, the tumultuous procession then passed through the arch of Septimius Severus and into the fantastical landscape of the Roman Forum. The new pope and his noisy entourage followed along the ancient Via Sacra, passing the Arch of Titus, the Meta Sudans (a fountain constructed by Titus and demolished during the Fascist period), and the Arch of Constantine. It crossed the Via Labicana and came, finally, to the intersection now at the Piazza San Clemente, named for the second church mentioned at the beginning of the chapter.

The procession paused in front of the church to allow the pope to change conveyances. We know this from a document published by Jacob Burckhardt who, referring to Pope Innocent VIII in 1488, recounts this episode in his *Civilization of the Renaissance in Italy*: "Once he arrived at the church of San Clemente, the pope dismounted from his horse and left the baldachin behind. He got into a sedan chair in which he would be carried to the door of the Lateran Palace. He made the change because the people at the Lateran would try to take the horse and baldachin, which they claimed was their right. In doing so they would set off such a furious scuffle that the pope himself would be put in danger."

Such was the greed of the people who followed the procession, noisily demanding a reward. They were encouraged by their own extreme misery, as well as widespread fanatical rants; their brand of religion wasn't too different from paganism. The crowd, however, represented only the vociferous and popular fringe of Roman spiritual life—other issues and passions were at work at the center of the church in Rome. The powerful, driven by their own interests and ambitions, were also motivated by a struggle for dominance and the accumulation of wealth. Supremacy, once acquired, sometimes legitimated the use of violence. For centuries certain Roman families had sought and obtained power by fighting amongst themselves, siding sometimes with the pope and sometimes with the emperor, depending on how they judged their interests. They might unite against the papacy, only to immediately break that alliance and resume their endless fighting. These men were blinded by their own ambitions, and deaf to any inkling of mercy. They lacked even the vaguest sense of religion or, it seems to me, any human feeling. Members of these families committed murder, assault, and theft, obeying only the ruthless brutality of their own plans.

The chronicles of the period are full of names like the Crescenzi, the Counts of Tusculum, and the Frangipane. The truncated remains of a Crescenzi house still stand at the corner of the Via Petroselli and the Via del Foro Olitorio, a rare example of domestic architecture from the period just after 1000. The house makes extensive use of salvaged Roman building materials, and it was located here to guard the ford across the Tiber. The fortified residence of the Pierleoni was built on the ruins of the Theater of Marcellus; it then passed to the Savelli, and is known today, after many alterations, as the Palazzo Orsini. The fortress, also built on the strong foundations of the theatre, was meant to control the river crossing at the Isola Tiberina. Another contemporary fortress was built at the end of the Ponte Fabricio, also called the Bridge of the Four Heads and, in the Middle Ages, the Pons Judaeorum because of its proximity to the Jewish ghetto. The Torre Caetani is all that is left now of that construction, and it, too, stands strategically near the river.

The arrogant and unscrupulous Crescenzi family was able, at the end of the tenth century, to put one of their own on the papal throne with the name of John XIII, and he succeeded in solidifying the family's fortune. Holding the papacy was a key move in the game of wealth accrual for oneself and one's family, since it permitted the appropriation of the goods and property of less fortunate rivals. When John XIII died, Emperor Otto I "favored" the election of a pope loyal to him and therefore supported Benedict VI, the Roman-born son of a German called Hildebrand. A member of the Crescenzi family, not yet satisfied with the riches he'd accumulated thus far, imprisoned Benedict in Castel Sant'Angelo and put Cardinal Francone on the throne of Saint Peter as the antipope Boniface VII. Boniface's papacy was brutally ferocious, and his own contemporaries even called him the Monster. One of his first acts was to have his predecessor, Benedict VI, strangled in the prison at Castel Sant'Angelo. When the troops of Otto II approached Rome, Boniface fled to Constantinople, taking the church treasury with him. In the meantime, the Crescenzi family again manipulated the papal election, seeing that the son of a favored priest became John XV. When he too died, Otto III, son and successor of Otto II, put one of his own relatives, Bruno of Carinthia, on the papal throne as Gregory V, the first German pope. This choice did not please the Crescenzi, and as soon as Otto had departed they dethroned him by fomenting a popular revolt, and then replaced him with another antipope, Giovanni Filagato, Bishop of Piacenza, who came to the throne as John XVI. To insure his election Crescenzio Nomentano asked the Byzantine Emperor Basil II for assistance. Basil was an efficient solider and extremely cruel man (one need only know that after his victory over the Bulgarians at the Battle of Kleidion he had fourteen thousand prisoners blinded in retaliation). Otto III was not pleased by this move and swooped down on Rome. The authors of the coup sought to flee, but John XVI was caught at Torre Astura, near present-day Nettuno, mutilated, blinded, and dragged back to Rome, where he was pilloried and finally killed. Crescenzio Nomentano, supposedly betrayed by his own wife, was decapitated in Castel Sant'Angelo.

I have no historical pretensions, so will stop here with examples, as the ones given so far provide an adequate sketch of the atrocious demeanor of those centuries, as well as the frightful decadence of the Church. Torn apart by the greed of families vying to dominate it, it rapidly become an outlet and instrument of savagery, corruption, and simony.

One last curious and macabre episode to illustrate the abyss into which the Church had fallen is the lugubrious story of Pope Formosus, who reigned from 891 to 896. When the attempt to reunite the Holy Roman Empire collapsed at the end of the ninth century, Guido, Duke of Spoleto, was annoyed at the partitioning of his territory. He convinced Pope Stephen V, a noble Roman, to crown him emperor, even though, as Gregorovius pointed out, his crown was merely of papier-mâché. A few months later, in 891, Formosus, Bishop of Porto, became pope. He reconfirmed Guido's coronation as emperor and extended it by heredity to his son, Lamberto. At the same time, however, he complained to Arnulf of Carinthia, King of the Germans, that the pressure exerted by Guido was intolerable. Arnulf rushed to help the pope, and was acclaimed emperor in every city he passed through. Upon Guido's death his son claimed the crown for himself and called on the people of Rome to help him. The anti-German revolt spread, and the pope had to take refuge in Castel Sant'Angelo. The city was in chaos, and riots and bloody battles broke out between rival factions. A few weeks later Formosus died, perhaps after having been poisoned. He was succeeded by Boniface VI, the priest who set the record for the shortest pontificate, as it lasted a mere twelve days. Lamberto and his mother, the terrible Duchess Agiltrude, manipulated events so that the Roman bishop of Anagni, their man, was elected Pope Stephen VI. They then insisted that the dead Formosus be tried for treason.

According to Gregorovius, "The corpse of the Pope, taken from the grave where it had lain for eight months, and clad in pontifical vestments, was placed upon a throne in the council chambers. The advocate of Pope Stephen arose, and, turning to the ghastly mummy, beside which a trembling deacon stood as counsel, brought forward the accusations; and the living Pope, in his insane fury, asked the dead: 'Why hast thou in thy ambition usurped the Apostolic seat, thou who wast previously only Bishop of Portus?' The counsel of

Formosus, if terror allowed him to speak, advanced no defense. The dead was judged and convicted; the Synod signed the act of his deposition, pronounced sentence of the condemnation upon him, and decreed that all the clergy ordained by Formosus should be ordained anew. The Papal vestments were torn from the mummy; the three fingers of the right hand, with which the Latins bestowed the benediction, were cut off; with barbarous shrieks the dead man was dragged from the hall through the streets, and amid the rush of the yelling rabble was thrown into the Tiber."⁵ This happened in February of 897, and a year later Pope Theodore II gave the remains of poor Formosus a decent burial in the basilica of Saint Peter.

It would take a politically strong pope, one conscious of his office as well as gifted with broad vision and great energy, for this undignified situation to change. Such a pope finally arrived on the scene in 1073, when Hildebrand of Savona was elected to the papacy as Gregory VII. Gregorovius wrote, "[m]arvelous was the strength with which he won the freedom of the church, and founded the dominion of the hierarchy."⁶

His pontificate, from 1073 to 1085, would leave a profound mark on the Church regardless of the fact that it coincided with the investiture controversy and the period famed for major papal schisms. The *Dictatus* that said that the pope is the universal bishop—with the power to judge anyone without being subject to anyone else's judgment and able, as a result, to depose the emperor—was penned by his hand. Gregory VII also harshly increased the punishments for simony and marriage of priests. When in 1075 Emperor Henry IV (the previous emperor had been the pope's mortal enemy) appointed several bishops and abbots, Gregory rebuked him for having violated both divine and canonical law. A furious struggle ensued, in which the emperor declared that the pope was deposed, and the pontiff, with the support of many German princes, excommunicated the emperor. Henry was forced to humiliate himself, famously going as a penitent to Canossa, where Gregory was a guest of the Countess Matilda. He obtained a pardon, but the emperor was not placated; his desire for revenge was only sharpened by the humiliation he'd suffered. As soon as the political situation allowed it, he returned to the position from which he had the right to appoint church officials as he saw fit, and Gregory excommunicated him a second time. Henry then nominated an antipope, Clement III, and occupied Rome.

The incursion of Imperial troops into Rome forced Gregory to barricade himself inside Castel Sant'Angelo. The Romans begged him to recognize the imperial title granted to Henry IV, but in vain— the pope didn't budge. The most he would concede to the emperor, he said, was to lower his crown on a rope to him from the castle's terrace. Henry obviously refused, and on Easter Sunday of 1084 was crowned emperor by Clement III. The city was almost entirely in his hands, with the exception of Castel Sant'Angelo and the Isola Tiberina, residence of the Pierleoni family. Fearing complete defeat, Gregory VII sent word to the Duke of Normandy, Robert Guiscard, who was then campaigning in the south of Italy, requesting assistance.

Guiscard's troops arrived in Rome at the Porta Asinaria (now the Porta San Giovanni), which had been barricaded by the people, necessitating negotiation for his entry. The omnipresent Frangipane family found a compromise, and the gates were opened. The duke had 30,000 troops, including Calabrians keen to plunder all they could, as well as battle-hardened Saracens from Sicily, and they spread out through the city sowing destruction and violence as they went. The pope was freed and brought to the Lateran while the city was left prey to ruthless devastation. Before he abandoned the city, on May 21 in the terrible year of 1084, Henry demolished the towers of the Campidoglio and the Leonine walls, and destroyed the Septizonium, the part of the Palatine that faced the Circus Maximus. Gregorovius wrote, "The unhappy city, however, which was surrendered to his soldiers for plunder, became the scene of more than Vandal horrors. . . . The city fought valiantly but in vain; the despair of the people was stifled in blood and flames . . ."[7]

The fire swallowed up the densely populated area between the Lateran and the Coliseum, including the streets through which we followed the papal procession. Nor were the Coliseum, the triumphal arches, or the remains of the Circus Maximus spared. Contemporary chroniclers agree, even without factoring in the stealing and violence committed by individuals, that the catastrophe devastated the vast majority of the city; the streets were strewn with debris, statues were smashed, arches violently broken apart, and for days there were lines of unfortunate Romans sold into slavery by the

Normans. Rome hadn't suffered such a disaster for centuries, and it was the first time it had been destroyed by an enemy since Totila had dismantled the city walls. Several decades later the still-visible ruins of the city moved Bishop Hildebert of Tours to tears, and he recorded the experience in his collection of poetry.

When discussing the invasions of Rome scholars inevitably point to May of 1527, when the Imperial troops of Charles V entered the city and committed every sort of violence and plundering. It was without doubt an atrocious event, especially in terms of lives lost. Nonetheless, considering the broader point of view of the ancient city and what survived of the imperial capital's greatness, May of 1084 was immeasurably worse. In 1527 the new Rome, tied to the splendor of the Vatican and the magnificence of the Renaissance artists, had already been born and was flourishing. In the abysmal darkness of 1084, on the other hand, all that existed were the faintest traces of a glorious past. There was nothing but the relatively new temples of Christianity and a few wealthy residences amongst a sea of hovels and ruins. The Norman occupation of Rome inflicted the worst outrage the city had ever suffered. When the Lutheran reform began to spread through Europe, five centuries after Guiscard's devastation, the Protestants still remembered those horrible facts, summarizing them in the brutal judgment that Gregory I had saved Rome from the Longobards and Gregory VII allowed its destruction by the Normans.

The exercise of power knows no mercy and focuses only on results. Gregory VII, political pope par excellence, chose to put his own salvation and that of his throne before that of the city. The Romans of the time never forgave him, and the pope, once the sack was finished, was forced to leave Rome with Guiscard. He died a year later, at the age of sixty in Salerno, reading some verses from the Psalms to excuse his culpability: "Dilexi justitiam et odivi iniquitatem, propterea morior in exilio." (I loved justice and hated iniquity, and thus I die in exile.) His reform of the church, however, survived almost to the present day. A final, brief passage from Gregorovius's *History* puts the strength of that papacy and the tragedy of 1084 into perspective:

The sack of Rome remains a dark stain on Gregory's history, as also on that of Guiscard. It was Nemesis that compelled the pope, however hesitantly and reluctantly, to gaze upon the flames of Rome. Was not Gregory VII in the burning city (and it burned on his account) as terrible a man of destiny as Napoleon calmly riding over bloody fields of battle? Leo the Great, who preserved the sacred city from Attila and obtained alleviation for her fate from the anger of Genseric, forms a glorious contrast to Gregory, not one of whose contemporaries has recorded that he made any attempt to save Rome from the sack, or ever shed a tear of compassion for her fall.[8]

1. Piero Camporesi, *Bread of Dreams. Food and Fantasy in Early Modern Europe*, trans. David Gentilcore (Chicago: University of Chicago Press, 1989), 20.
2. Ibid., 21.
3. Ernest F. Henderson, *Select Historical Documents of the Middle Ages* (London: George Bell, 1910), 319–329.
4. Dante Alighieri, *Inferno*, trans. Robert and Jean Hollander (New York: Doubleday, 2000), 321, lines 115–17.
5. Ferdinand Gregorovius, *History of the City of Rome in the Middle Ages*, trans. Mrs. G. W. Hamilton (London: George Bell, 1900), v.3, 225–26.
6. Ibid., 257.
7. Ibid., 246.
8. Ibid., 247–48.

IX

"IST AM 24.3.1944 GESTORBEN"

Via Rasella, Via Tasso, and the Fosse Ardeatine—these three places are enveloped by the tragic memories of the most atrocious period Rome endured during the mid-twentieth century. The 268 days between September 8, 1943, and June 4, 1944, when the city was occupied by Nazi troops, were characterized by a mixture of episodes—as usually occurs at such difficult moments in history—of heroism and villainy, resignation and rage, rebellious outbursts, acts of war, and collaboration with the oppressor.

The cruelest part of this short story begins in the Via Rasella, a brief uphill street that connects the Via del Traforo to the Via delle Quattro Fontane. It's a strange name, seemingly derived from a corruption of Rosella, the name of a family that owned property in the area. Not many people remember, but Via Rasella was the site of one of the harshest confrontations between Resistance fighters and the German troops that occupied the city. It happened on March 23, 1944—a Thursday.

This street was part of the route the Eleventh Company of the Third Battalion of the SS Regiment Bozen took each day as it returned from training at a firing range at Tor di Quinto. Many of its soldiers came from the South Tyrol, or Alpenvorland, as it's known in German. Every afternoon at two o'clock, marching loudly across the ancient cobblestones with their steel-heeled boots, 156 men in battle dress were escorted by armored cars equipped with machine guns as they made their way along the Via Rasella defiantly singing a happy tune, 'Hupf, mein Mädel (Turn, My Darling).

The SS, whose berets were adorned with a skull, were the most feared police force in occupied Europe. The Bozen Third Battalion was scheduled to go on active duty the next day, March 24. The regularity of its movements suggested to a Group of Partisan Action

(GAP), whose members belonged to the Communist Party, that it might be a good target to attack. In its final form, this siege consisted of eighteen kilos of TNT loaded into a street sweeper's cart. The fuse was to be lit exactly forty-five seconds before the column of German soldiers passed, and immediately after the explosion other partisans would attack the enemy with machine guns and hand grenades. The operation's key man was medical student Rosario Bentivegna, who would light the fuse with his pipe; his girlfriend (and future wife) Carla Capponi would wait for him at the top of the hill with a rain-coat to cover his street sweeper's uniform.

Every afternoon at exactly two o'clock the column of SS soldiers made a left turn off the Via del Traforo and began marching up Via Rasella—every afternoon, that is, except March 23. That particular Thursday was special: the Fascists were celebrating their party's twenty-fifth anniversary following its 1919 founding in Milan's Piazza San Sepolcro. Furthermore, rumors had circulated in the Nazi com-mand that there might be some substantial resistance operations afoot. As a result the SS troops were kept longer at the firing range that afternoon. For the GAP members lying in wait, time passed intolerably slowly; they wandered around pretending to look at ad posters or read a newspaper. If they loitered for too long, though, they would raise suspicions and potentially provoke a fatal search, as they were all armed. In the meantime, a half hour passed, then forty-five minutes—the clock struck three, then quarter after three, and there was still no sign of the SS. Some were tempted to postpone or entirely abandon the attack, but even calling it off wouldn't be so easy. The garbage cart was heavy, so it would be nearly impossible to take it back to its hiding place, and leaving it unattended was unthinkable. Franco Calamandrei, who was to give the signal, was lying in wait at the corner of the Via Boccaccio; exactly ninety paces separated him from the garbage cart packed with explosives. Carlo Salinari, a literary critic, was waiting at the end of the street, where he would be the first to spot the SS column as it left the Piazza di Spagna. Once an hour and a half had passed the risk was becoming too great. The men exchanged ever more worried glances, and post-ponement seemed the most reasonable solution.

Just seconds before the order to abandon was issued, a deep and rhythmic rumbling of footsteps could be heard in the distance.

Via Rasella is a narrow street, lined with relatively tall buildings and not much sunlight. It was a little after three thirty, and the shadows were already lengthening when the first line of the battalion turned to climb the street. The signals were given according to the codes agreed upon earlier. Bentivenga held the bowl of his pipe to the end of the fuse, then moved away as calmly as he could toward his girl-friend. The powerful bomb exploded at three forty-five with a roar that could be heard throughout the city center, and the others then attacked with volleys of machine gun fire and four hand grenades, one of which never detonated. Some armed civilians and police offi-cers went to the scene of the firing. There were twenty-six SS dead and sixty wounded, some critically. A young Roman civilian, Pietro Zuccheretti, was also killed in the blast.

The German reaction was almost immediate. General Kurt Mälzer, the local commandant, arrived at the scene within minutes of the explosion, drunk (as usual). Mälzer and SS Colonel Eugen Dollmann had a violent argument right there in the street, in front of many witnesses. The general wanted to blow up the entire block, while Dollmann counseled an icy restraint. Compromising, they decided to search and seize apartments in the area, often kicking in their doors; inhabitants and anyone else found with them were lined up along the fence of the nearby Palazzo Barberini, hands on their heads, men separated from women and children. The confusion was indescribable, and the neighborhood filled with the echoed cries, shouted orders, and curses. The roundup was carried out with the brutal violence so common throughout Europe in those years, in this case made even heavier by the brashness of the attack, its bloody out-come, and the occupying forces' desire for revenge.

During the months of occupation Gestapo headquarters were set in a rather ordinary building at Via Tasso 145. Like the Via Rasella, but in a different area, Via Tasso was a short, sloping street in the neighborhood around the basilica of Saint John Lateran. The small apartment building, which belonged to the noble Ruspoli family, had been rented to the German embassy's cultural office, but after the armistice of September 8 it was converted into a prison. The windows were entirely walled up, except for miniscule openings, and the doors of rooms to be used as cells were armored such that they received no light or ventilation. Other rooms were designated for the interrogation and torture of prisoners. The building next door (at Via Tasso 155, a twin of number 145) was outfitted with residences for active officers and non-commissioned officers, storage and warehousing facilities, as well as some offices, including that of Lieutenant Colonel Herbert Kappler, commander of the army's security services. Kappler, a native of Stuttgart, was thirty-seven at the time and considered Italy his second home—he loved Italian art and collected Etruscan vases. He also organized the arrest and mass deportation of Roman Jews, as we'll see in a few chapters.

Cell number seven in the prison of Via Tasso had a certain reputation; one of its walls bordered the southern wing of the building where the Nazis brought their lovers and sometimes organized group orgies. It's hard to imagine a more sinister mixture than the screams of people being tortured combined with the noise and laughter of such amusements. The worst, however, was cell number three, narrow as a coffin and used for solitary confinement. Air Force General Sabato Martelli Castaldi, one of many others, was confined there for sixty-six days. Despite his harsh imprisonment he managed to send a note to his wife, in which he gave this description of his confinement:

> I think about the night they gave me twenty-four lashes on the bottom of my feet. I was also beaten and punched in other vulnerable areas. I did not give them the satisfaction of uttering a single complaint, and only at the last stroke did I reply by blowing them a raspberry, at which the thugs were taken aback like three real nitwits. That tongue-out taunt was true poetry! Via Tasso trembled, and the flogger dropped his whip. What a laugh! It nevertheless cost me a belated flurry of punches. What bothers me most is the lack of air. I eat very little, otherwise I would be sick and lose the lucidity of mind and spirit so essential here at all times.

General Martelli Castaldi ended up dead at the Fosse Ardeatine. Others were more fortunate, and managed to survive by following the unpredictable rules of the situation. Lieutenant Colonel Arrigo Paladini recounts in his book, *Via Tasso*, how his imprisonment ended after he'd endured unimaginable torture:

> When the door opened I was ready, at least as ready as a wreck of a man can be when he cannot stand and is only barely able to lean up against the wall. I left behind the isolation cell where I had

been imprisoned for an entire month and in inhuman conditions, without air, with nothing to sleep on and often without any light. . . . I looked at the men who surrounded me . . . illuminated by the lamplight, their faces seemed like cadavers to me, many terribly swollen. . . . The pain in my legs and body almost drove me crazy, and I had to curl up on the floor. I couldn't move my jaws, and one of my eyes was so swollen I couldn't see out of it . . . it was five in the morning on the 4 [of June, 1944, the day the Allies entered Rome], I tried to stretch out on the floor but the booming of cannons was too near to be able to endure putting my head on the floor. It seemed like the building shook to its foundations. Yet, because of the exhaustion and pain with which they destroyed me, I fell asleep, or at least lost consciousness. I awoke with a jolt. Outside someone was yelling, and the door flew open. Some of my cellmates dragged me up the stairs . . . suddenly I found myself in a sea of blue and I breathed in the morning air. I glimpsed several Germans who were shuffling along looking disoriented, their faces white as chalk. Then I fainted.[1]

From a literary point of view, one of the most intense accounts comes from the writer Guglielmo Petroni in his book *Il mondo è una prigione* (*The World Is a Prison*). His reconstruction of the moment he left his cell in Via Tasso is beautiful, calm, and haunting:

I paused for a moment outside the prison door, waiting for that breath that expands through your chest when you come back to life, when you see the sky and people again after having almost lost them forever. . . . I realized that I violently regretted the hours when my life might have ended at any moment. I regretted the hunger, the darkness, and the uncertainty that, this time, I was finally leaving behind me.[2]

Today the building in Via Tasso houses normal apartments, with the exception of two floors occupied by the Museum of the Liberation of Rome. In those days, though, the mere name—*Via Tasso*—had a sinister sound. We knew prisoners there were being savagely tortured with the usual ruthless instruments of the inquisitor, with electric cables attached to the genitals, suffocation pushing the very limits of endurance, brutal twisting of arms and legs, teeth and fingernails ripped out, and savage blows that broke bones and caused internal lesions.

My father was a member of the Resistance, and he fought in Colonel Giuseppe Montezemolo's band. I was sent for safety's sake to a Catholic boarding school (Santa Maria), whose back wall bordered part of the infamous building on Via Tasso. Even after so many years, I can still clearly remember the screams that sometimes broke the stillness of the night and penetrated all the way inside our dormitory. One day something happened, and at the time I understood little or nothing of the episode. While we were at recess in one of the courtyards close to the high wall of the prison, out of the corner of my eye I caught a glimpse of a rapid, furtive movement, as if someone were moving quickly and trying not to be seen. Something or someone, little more than a shadow, slipped away amongst the black robes of the priests and the lay "prefects" who watched over us and disappeared quickly down a hallway. I asked the prefect of my class—not because I suspected anything, but because I was curious—what had happened. He curtly replied, "Nothing, nothing," and made a vague gesture with his hands. Only months later, well after the liberation, did I learn that a prisoner had managed to escape from the Gestapo prison, miraculously jumping the wall. The priests had hidden him among their group, and then allowed him to run away through one of the building's side entrances.

This distant episode can be added to the vast and contradictory listing of the Catholic Church's behavior in that period. Many endangered resistance fighters, heads of anti-Fascist groups, and future leaders of the Italian Republic were hidden in convents and religious institutions, and the upper echelon of Vatican officials certainly knew this was happening. Anti-Fascists of any political stripe—Christian Democrats, Communists, Socialists, and Liberals—found long-term sanctuary in the extraterritorial Vatican City.

At the end of May 1944, ten days before the Allies arrived in Rome, the sixty-nine-year-old Pope Pius XII (Eugenio Pacelli) granted a secret audience to Karl Wolff, the SS's supreme commander in Italy. Some have suggested that there was an agreement at the end of the meeting that arranged the release of several prisoners held by the Gestapo in exchange for an assurance that after the war the Church would help Nazi officials, even those guilty of war crimes, to flee to South America by procuring for them passports, money, and ocean passages. No proof of such an agreement has ever been found, yet it is, in fact, precisely what happened.

Throughout the occupation Pius XII's primary concern was that the transfer of power from the Nazis to the Allies happen without violence, avoiding any rebellion that might in some way benefit the communists, who were the heart of the armed resistance to the Nazis. On Christmas Eve of 1943, six months before the liberation, the pope specifically urged Romans "to remain calm and refrain from any rash act that would do nothing but provoke even greater misfortunes." He'd taken the same position two months earlier when the Nazis searched the ghetto looking for Jews.

The third place that recalls the terrible memories of the occupation is the also the saddest—the sanctuary of the Fosse Ardeatine, on the Via Ardeatina between the catacombs of Domitilla and San Calisto. The area was originally a quarry for *pozzolana*, a type of volcanic tufa in use since ancient Roman times to make mortar and plaster, first mined at Pozzuoli, from which its name derives. This site provided large amounts of the materials used in the 1930s to build the new neighborhoods planned by the Fascists. The mining activity left a labyrinth of tunnels that extended several dozen meters into the side of the hill. Today it looks nothing like it did then, and considered architecturally, from a monumental point of view, the sanctuary opened there in 1949 is one of the most successful projects of contemporary Rome. The bronze gateway is by Mirko Basaldella, the marble sculpture of three tortured prisoners is by Francesco Coccia, and an enormous tomb slab blocks all but a sliver of light from the interior. Visitors feel nearly crushed, weighed down by the strong emotional effect of the semi-underground crypt, designed by Giuseppe Perugini, Nello Aprile, and Mario Fiorentino, where 335 tombs are grouped.

After the attack of Via Rasella, the Nazis decided to punish Rome, making an example of it. Far-fetched ideas were considered, including dynamiting entire neighborhoods, deporting the whole of the city's male population between the ages of eighteen and forty-five, and murdering thirty Italians for each German killed in the attack. In the end, after tense consultations between Rome, the German Quartermaster General in Verona, Himmler (head of the SS), and Hitler (at the "Eagle's Nest" in Berchtesgaden), it was decided to execute ten Italians for every German killed. The Ardeatine quarry was chosen as the place to kill the hostages, and Colonel Kappler was charged with drawing up a list of *Todeskandidaten*, the "candidates" to be killed. He spent most of the night between March 23 and 24 on this task, and his criteria were to include men who had already been tried and condemned to death, those who hadn't yet been tried but were very likely to be condemned, and any Jews who had been stopped or detained. Kappler's first list had ninety-four names, but thirty-two Germans had died in the attack, so he was still far from the number needed. After additional work, his second list included men who weren't guilty of anything and over whom he had no judicial authority; this got him up to 270 names. At that point, exhausted, he ordered his Fascist collaborators to give him the fifty names he lacked. At dawn on March 24 two men—Pietro Koch, a sadistic torturer who ran a sort of private prison in a pensione at Via Principe Amadeo 2, and Pietro Caruso, the police chief of Rome, a man of modest intelligence and a long-term Fascist—presented themselves in Kappler's office in Via Tasso.

Trembling, Caruso didn't dare refuse the charge, but he hoped at least to share the responsibility. It just so happened that Guido Buffarini-Guidi, Minister of the Interior of the Republic of Salò, was also in Rome to celebrate the twenty-fifth anniversary of the founding of the Fascist party. Upon leaving Via Tasso, Caruso hurried to the Excelsior Hotel on Via Veneto and asked to meet with Buffarini-Guidi. It was eight o'clock in the morning, and "His Excellency" was still asleep. After insisting rather vehemently he was finally allowed to wake him, and the sleepy minister received the police chief in his pajamas. Caruso related the problem, the request for the names of fifty men to be shot, and then said, "I rely on you, Your Excellency." There were several things Buffarini-Guidi might have done—he could've spoken to Mussolini and asked him to intervene with Hitler, or directly contacted Wolff, with whom he had a good rapport, and at least ask for a delay. Instead all he could say was, "What can I do? You must give them a list. Otherwise who knows what might happen. Yes, yes, give it to them," or so Caruso said when he testified at his own trial after the war. He said that last phrase, "give it to them," was an order. He was convicted and sentenced to death.

The entire third wing of Rome's infamous Regina Coeli prison was reserved for political prisoners. Most of the last *Todeskandidaten* were found there. Kappler continued to pressure the two Italians, as the twenty-four-hour period Hitler had given for his orders to be carried out was rapidly coming to a close. At noon Kappler went to meet with General Mälzer in his office on the Corso d'Italia and assured him that the list was being finalized. It took hours to decide who would actually carry out the executions, as one man after the other tried to dodge the assignment. Major Hellmuth Dobbrick, commander of the battalion that had sustained the attack, was the first one mentioned; Mälzer told him that, because his company was attacked, the honor of avenging the crime fell to him. The Major refused, offering a series of excuses that ran from religious reasons to the fact that his men were superstitious and many would refuse this macabre duty. Kappler reported Dobbrick two days later for insubordination. When a second officer refused the job, Mälzer turned to Kappler, ordering, "Well, now it's your turn."

The Colonel assembled his men and told them that within a few hours 320 people would have to be executed, and that it had to be done quickly and kept secret to avoid a possible insurrection. He had twelve officers, sixty non-commissioned officers, and one soldier— seventy-four people in all, including himself. At his trial after the war, Kappler described how he'd handled the job, "I tried to be conscious of how much time I had. I divided my men into small squadrons which were to alternate. I ordered each man to shoot only once, specifying that the bullet should enter the victim's brain through his cerebellum. This way no shots were wasted, and death was instantaneous." Captain Erich Priebke was charged with checking off the names of the men to be executed as they passed in front of him and then to make sure they were all dead.

In the meantime another hospitalized soldier from the Bozen Battalion died from his wounds—320 hostages were no longer enough. That very morning Capitan Kurt Schultz and his men had managed to round up another ten Jews who were being transported to the Regina Coeli prison. Their names were immediately added to the list, thereby rebalancing the macabre accounting.

At two o'clock that Friday afternoon the first load of hostages arrived at the quarry. The prisoners' hands were tied behind their backs, and they were transported—with frightful appropriateness— in trucks that usually made butcher shop deliveries. Tied together in pairs, the first men were pushed into the tunnels. SS troops, leaning against the walls, held torches to provide some light inside the quarry. The first group included the priest Don Pietro Pappagallo, who with exceptional strength managed to free himself from the ropes and, raising his arms, blessed his fellow captives. The executioners didn't dare interrupt this small gesture of pity (Don Pappagallo was also Rossellini's inspiration for the priest in his film *Open City*). Five men were dragged to the end of the tunnel and forced to kneel against the wall while their executioners moved up behind them, pistols readied. In that dark, dank place, filled with the acrid stench of mold and dimly illuminated by the smoky fire of the torches, Captain Schulz gave the order to fire and the first five victims fell. A shepherd tending his flock atop the hill hid behind some bushes when the trucks began to arrive, and later testified that he heard the first shots at 3:30.

The massacre continued uninterrupted throughout the afternoon in an orgy of shots and screams, the smell of smoke, blood, and excrement, and executioners who ultimately needed to get drunk in order to continue the wretched task. The precision and speed Kappler had envisioned didn't turn out as planned: laid side-by-side the cadavers blocked the tunnels, so new arrivals had to climb over the bodies to be executed themselves, and once the soldiers were drunk they no longer shot with much precision. When the tunnels were reopened after the city's liberation, it was discovered that some prisoners had only been wounded by the initial shots, and had crawled several meters before dying. A few unfortunate men were found with their fingernails dirty and broken after trying to dig out toward the light. Thirty-nine had been shot with so many bullets that they were decapitated; others were found with their skulls shattered by a blunt object, perhaps the butt of a rifle used to quell any rebellion.

Some men were so broken by torture that they had to be dragged by their arms to the place they were to be killed. The heroic colonel Giuseppe Montezemolo came off the truck staggering, his face devastated by the beating he'd received. Pilo Albertelli, a writer, philosophy teacher, and member of the Partito d'Azione (the leftist Action Party), was so severely tortured by Koch's men that he arrived at the quarry nearly dead. (Although he was almost killed by his tormentors, Albertelli never revealed a thing about his comrades. When

Police Chief Caruso was told of his obstinate silence he suggested torturing his wife in front of him to convince him to talk.) Lieutenant Maurizio Giglio, who had transmitted messages to the Allies from a secret radio, had to be dragged from his cell because he couldn't stand up on his own.

In their rush the executioners ended up killing more than the sufficiently tragic total of 330 men; by day's end 335 had been executed, five more than required. The dead included policemen and peddlers, workers and waiters, doctors and officers, *carabinieri* and bureaucrats, railroad workers and musicians, students and printers, professors and peasants. Seventy were Jewish. The oldest was a seventy-four-year-old merchant named Mosè Di Consiglio, who was killed along with five members of his family; the youngest was fourteen, and many were between eighteen and twenty. In one of the victim's pockets a letter to his parents was found, miraculously preserved amid the surrounding putrefaction. It read, "If it is our fate not to see each other again, remember that you had a son who willingly gave his life for his country, looking his executioners in the eye."

During Captain Priebke's trial held in June of 1996 in Rome, the presiding judge asked Karl Hass, a former major in the SS, why the extra men were assassinated. He replied that, as Priebke was checking off the list, he noticed that some of the names weren't on it. He realized that—one, two, three . . . up to the total of five times—someone had made a mistake in choosing the prisoners. Finally, when everyone else had been killed, those five unfortunate souls were still tied up in a corner, and the soldiers didn't know what to do with them. Kappler asked, "What should I do with the five guys who've seen everything?" The witness didn't tell the court who had replied, "Kill them too."

In reality there were 336, rather than 335, dead. The last victim was a seventy-four-year-old woman from Gaeta, Fedele Rasa, who lived in a nearby refugee camp called Villaggio Breda. She'd gone, as she did every day, to gather chicory in the fields around the quarry. A German sentry had yelled at her to halt where she stood, but Fedele was a little deaf, and didn't hear him. He fired, fatally wounding her. This episode was discovered by Cesare da Simone as he examined the emergency room records at the former Littorio Hospital (now called San Camillo). In the days following the massacre many of the victims' relatives, although certainly not poor Fedele's, received terse messages noting, with Teutonic precision, that Mr. So-and-So had died on March 24, 1944—"Ist am 24.3.1944 gestorben."

Beyond its sheer cruelty, the phrase "Kill them too" has a historical importance. At eight o'clock that Friday evening, after four and a half hours of uninterrupted killing carried out by exhausted executioners drunk on cognac and blood, savage Colonel Kappler remained worried that the operation was still secret. "They saw everything." Nothing could leak out before the official communiqué. Once the massacre was finished, German engineers blew up the cave entrances with dynamite (the craters made by these explosions are still visible). When the stench of decay began to spread over the next few days, they dumped two truckloads of garbage to stifle the stench in front of what had been the quarry's entrance.

The secret was rigorously guarded for the entire twenty-eight hours between three forty-five on the afternoon of March 23, the time of the attack on Via Rasella, and eight o'clock on the evening of the 24th, when the massacre at the Fosse Ardeatine was finished. The many debates through the years about the fact that the men who carried out the original attack never turned themselves in to save the hostages all ignore this one key element. They wouldn't have been able to even if they'd wanted, because literally no one said anything. There were no radio appeals, no street demonstrations; the only information came from the Stefani Press Agency, directed by Luigi Barzini. The news was distributed to papers and press offices at about eleven o'clock on Friday night, but wasn't printed until the next day, Saturday, March 25. Because of the citywide curfew, newspapers were printed in the morning and didn't reach newsstands until about noon. The official communiqué read:

> On the afternoon of March 23, 1944, criminal elements executed an attack, bombing a column of German police traveling up Via Rasella. As a result of this ambush thirty-two members of the German police were killed, and many more were wounded. This vile ambush was carried out by Communists and Badogliani [followers of Field Marshall Pietro Badoglio, Mussolini's successor appointed by the king]. An investigation is still underway to determine to what extent this criminal incident can be attributed to Anglo-American encouragement. The German command decided to quash the activity of these scurrilous bandits. No one can sabotage the newly

reaffirmed Italo-German cooperation with such impunity. The German command therefore ordered that for every German assassinated ten Communists and Badogliani would be shot. This order has already been carried out.

The communiqué was signed "Stefani." EIAR (the Italian state radio) didn't report news of the bulletin until the afternoon. *L'Osservatore Romano*, the Vatican newspaper, also came out in the afternoon, and its front-page headline read, "A communiqué from Stefani about the events of Via Rasella." Based on information from the German command, it made the following comment:

> Faced with these facts every honest soul must be profoundly saddened in the name of humanity and Christian sentiment. Thirty-two victims on one side, 320 people sacrificed on the other for the guilty who have escaped arrest.

With barely apparent balance the Vatican newspaper—in reality hostile to "the guilty who have escaped arrest"—validated the notion that the real blame for the slaughter at the Ardeatine quarry lay with the "criminals" who didn't turn themselves in to the German authorities after the attack. The debate over this point lasted for some time. According to Alessandro Portelli, author of an excellent book on the subject titled *L'ordine è già stato eseguito* (*This Order Has Already Been Carried Out*), this was "the only event in which the position of the far right coincided with the common, moderate view." It was probably this, Portelli asserts, that was the real, lasting success of the Nazi reprisal. The daily paper *Il Messaggero*, directed by Bruno Spampanato, was more awkward in its obsequiousness, and described the massacre as an instance of "exemplary German justice."

Mussolini himself was kept in the dark about the reprisal. If we're to believe the memoirs of his wife Rachele, when he was informed about the massacre he exclaimed, "I was not in time to stop it, only to protest," and then, "the Germans believe they can treat the Italians like they treated the Poles, but this serves only to create new enemies." Here he's just another poor guy, reduced now to the rank of vassal.

In time two widely held beliefs about the nature of the attack and the reprisal emerged, and both were easily exploited for political ends. The first suggested that the men of the Third Battalion of the Bozen regiment were old, innocuous non-combatants. In reality they were SS soldiers between the ages of twenty-five and forty-one, well armed, and were scheduled the following day to begin taking repressive measures against the Roman resistance. The second claimed that there were posters throughout Rome that urged the attackers to turn themselves in, proclaiming that their evil nature was guilty of sending 335 innocent men to their deaths. No one can say whether the partisans would've turned themselves in had they had been invited to. It's certain, however, that the members of the GAP first learned of the massacre from the newspapers on March 25. The decision issued by the Corte di Cassazione (the Italian Constitutional Court) in February of 1999 finally put an end to the polemics around the attack itself, at least in the judicial sense, by conferring the status of Institution of the Republic on the resistance movement, and thus recognized the partisans' attack as a legitimate act of war. Freed Italy had declared war on Germany on October 13, 1943, and after landing at Anzio the Allies' radio broadcasts urged the resistance forces "to fight with every means possible and with full strength . . . we must sabotage the enemy . . . striking any- and everywhere it shows up."

Was Pope Pius XII aware of the imminent reprisal? Two surrounding events are fairly clear: at the end of the afternoon on the day of the attack itself, SS Colonel Dollmann came to the Vatican to meet with Abbot Pancrazio Pfeiffer, a Bavarian acting as liaison between the Holy See and the occupation forces. Dollmann warned him in advance that the Nazi reprisal would be bloody, and begged that he pass that information on to the pope. According to historian Robert Katz, and based on documents from the OSS (the American intelligence service, precursor to the CIA), Dollmann was an Allied informant at the end of the war.[3] The second event happened on Friday the 24 at quarter past midnight—five hours before the killing began, and almost ten hours before it was over. Engineer Ferrero, a city government official, informed the Vatican Secretary of State that for every German killed in the Via Rasella attack ten Italians would be executed. What Ferrero didn't say (and perhaps didn't know) was that these executions would take place within twenty-four hours. Neither Dollmann's nor Ferrero's information produced any effect in the Holy See.

As the days passed the massacre and the spot where it took place became a frequent topic of discussion, quickly gaining an aura of legend. The quarry, devastated by the explosion rigged by the German engineers, became a popular pilgrimage destination. The garbage spread by the Nazis was covered with flowers, notes, and relics. Only after the liberation, however, was the event's truth painfully verified. In early July, less than a month after the Americans arrived, a commission chaired by Attilio Ascarelli, instructor of medical law at the University of Rome, La Sapienza, began its difficult work. The group had to dig down, remove a lot of earth, and slowly venture into the tunnels—all in terrible conditions. Ascarelli wrote:

> As the visitor went into the lugubrious tunnels a sense of cold permeated him, and he was overwhelmed by the contaminated stench that was hard to withstand, a stench that caused nausea and vomiting. No one who has gone even once to that sad place of martyrdom can come away without an unforgettable sense of horror, a sense of compassion for the victims and execration for the killers. . . . The members of the commission were terrified.

Their terrible work lasted for six months of almost unbearable discomfort. The commission was able to identify 322 of the 335 victims, in almost every case because of personal objects found on the bodies. Identification by family members was excluded, either because it was impossible, or because it was something that simply couldn't be asked of the victims' loved ones. Ascarelli, who was Jewish, was also uncle of two victims.

> There was little left of the bodies to see, but the grease from the cadavers had permeated the earth and *pozzolana* that amalgamated the bodies, a foot emerging here, a pair of shoes there, a whole or crushed skull, here a limb, there a piece of clothing. Insects swarmed over the few miserable remains, a myriad of larvae fed on the mangled flesh, and lots of large rats ran around, pouring out from among the unburied, unattended remains and crushed skulls.

Herbert Kappler was captured by the English and turned over to Italian authorities in 1947, and in 1948 he was tried by military tribunal in Rome. His defense relied on two points: first of all, he was only obeying the orders of his superiors; second, the attack of Via

Rasella was an illegal act, and therefore the reprisal was justified. The court established the illegitimacy of the reprisal noting, as a point of law, that ten of the victims weren't under German jurisdiction, and five were killed in error. Kappler was sentenced to life in prison and sent to the military prison at Gaeta. He was later transferred to the Celio Hospital in Rome because of bad health, and on August 15, 1977, assisted by his wife, he managed to escape—she carried him out in a trunk. He died a year later in Stuttgart.

Erich Priebke was distinguished by his knack for the brutal torture of prisoners at the Via Tasso prison. Arrigo Paladini, an OSS agent, wrote, "I remember perfectly Captain Priebke's interrogation methods. He hit me on the chest and testicles with the brass knuckles he used on prisoners." Priebke was capable of even worse, and told Paladini that his father had been shot because of his refusal to talk. "In reality this was untrue, since my father died in a concentration camp some months earlier, but I didn't know that at the time." The shock was so great that even years after the liberation Paladini often awoke at night, screaming.

After the war Priebke managed to flee to South America using the so-called Rat Line, a secret organization run by high Vatican officials. The former captain admitted this when he was captured in 1994. "I want to thank the Catholic Church for its help," he said to the Buenos Aires newspaper *Clarin*. In fact, the Vatican had given Priebke a Red Cross passport, and thousands of other Nazis used the Rat Line to flee to South America. Priebke was tried in Rome and condemned to life in prison. Given his age, most of his sentence was commuted to house arrest in the comfort of a Roman friend's home.

Caruso, the cowardly police chief, and the sadistic Pietro Koch were tried and shot by the Italians at the end of the war. The director of the Regina Coeli prison, Donato Carretta, an innocent man who'd tried to help his prisoners, was lynched by a mob in an inhuman explosion of violence.

In addition to Don Pappagallo, another priest inspired Rossellini's cinematic masterpiece—Don Giuseppe Morosini, a prisoner at Via Tasso who was shot at Forte Bravetta in early April 1944, a few days after the massacre at the Fosse Ardeatine. *Open City* combined these two heroic priests into a single character played by Aldo Fabrizi.

Was there a resistance in Rome comparable to the movement so active in Northern Italy? Undoubtedly there were dozens of attacks. German soldiers, Fascists, and important officials were hit and in some cases killed, even in the city center. The first instance of armed resistance came in the hours and days following the armistice signed on September 8, 1943. There was a bloody battle at the Porta San Paolo against overwhelming German forces, as well as smaller, scattered encounters provoked by isolated detachments of the Italian army, usually commanded by young officers. They fought and died in accordance with their duty and fealty to their oath—no one asked them, and no one thanked them. Today there is a plaque near the Porta San Paolo, and others around the city, to remind us of the sacrifice made by all, whether military or civilian, who resisted.

During the nine months of occupation military garrisons, warehouses, trucks, garages, telephone switchboards, the headquarters of the German military tribunal in Via Veneto, and rail convoys were also attacked. As a child I witnessed one of those attacks when a military supply train en route through Ostiense Station was blown up not far from the Piazza Zama. It burned for some time among deafening bursts of exploding munitions, and no one tried to extinguish the fire that, if I remember correctly, burned for a couple of days.

The Germans never responded, either before or after the attack on Via Rasella, with as ferocious a reprisal, although there was certainly no shortage of police roundups, petty crime, women raped before being killed, and other executions. The most serious reprisal after the slaughter at the Fosse Ardeatine was the sweep through the working-class neighborhood of Quadraro. A number of resistance groups were active in the southern and southeastern parts of the city, some politicized (from the CLN, or Committee of National Liberation, to the independents of the so-called Bandiera rossa, or Red Flag), some simply motivated by a hatred for the Nazis (like the band of the so-called Gobbo del Quarticciolo, or Hunchback of the Quarticciolo neighborhood). In one of the many exchanges of gunfire, three Germans were killed. On April 17 Kappler had the entire neighborhood surrounded and then searched house by house. All able-bodied men, around two thousand in total, were arrested. Of these, seven hundred men and boys between fifteen and fifty-five were sent to forced labor camps in Germany. Less than half of them returned.

There were also mass executions. Seventy-two people were shot at Forte Bravetta, and ten at Pietralata. In the last such massacre, fourteen men, including the trade unionist Bruno Buozzi, were shot on June 4 at La Storta, along the Via Cassia, just as the Germans were retreating and the Americans entered Rome. Ten women were also shot at Ponte di Ferro after staging an assault on the local bakeries; hunger was one of the constant elements of the occupation, and was the source of an indefinable rage and unrest that almost never had any political or patriotic motivation. It nevertheless kept many of the poorer neighborhoods, especially peripheral areas, in a state of open rebellion.

Personal memories of mine are closely tied to that period. Because my father and his companions were all fugitives in hiding, I often went with my mother to gather chicory in the fields along the Roman walls, just like the poor woman shot outside the Fosse Ardeatine. I became rather good at it, and could spot the plants from a few steps away. A farmer from the countryside around Rome, a former collaborator of my father's, sent us the fantastic gift of a bottle of oil. Boiled chicory flavored with some oil and lemon seemed like an exquisite dinner.

Bread was also always a problem, although many made it at home when they could find a little flour. Numerous attacks on bakeries occurred, and in some cases, when the women also had political motives, they became anti-Fascist demonstrations. On March 25, 1944, daily bread rations were reduced from 150 to 100 grams per person; the idea was to punish the entire population for the attacks. The famous Roman *rosetta*—a rosette role made with chickpea flour, chopped leaves, rye, and bran—often inspired a suspicion that sawdust was mixed into the dough, and sometimes your teeth did actually hit hard slivers. "Vegetina" was a popular homemade product; it was a type of fine flour that was made into a focaccia that looked, at first, like chocolate. It tasted terrible, and many said that that flour was really ground sorghum, the plant brooms were made of.

When we began to hear the sound of artillery, especially at night, we understood that the Allies were coming our way. Looking south, we could see the profile of the Alban Hills in the light of the intermittent flashes of artillery fire. On the evening of June 3, feigning a great calm even though the retreat was already underway and many office archives were being burned, some high-ranking Nazis went to the opera to hear the famous tenor and Nazi sympathizer Beniamino Gigli perform in Verdi's *Un Ballo in Maschera*. Twenty-four hours later the streets swarmed with people crazed with joy. In the afternoon the city's electricity was cut, and Rome was absolutely dark, but even this couldn't dampen the happiness so visible on everyone's faces. One small event can give you some idea of the almost dreamlike atmosphere of the true liberation in those days: an American soldier gave me a chocolate bar from a box in his jeep—the first real chocolate I ever tasted. Nibbling on it as I headed home, an old man stopped me and asked in a hesitant voice if he might have a piece. Without delay I held the candy out to him and, taking out a pocketknife, the man cut a piece, thanking me, more than with words, with an unforgettable brilliance in his eyes.

After landing at Anzio in January, the Allies took six months to break through the Gustav Line. They did so at a slightly accelerated pace in the final phase, after they fought past the fortification at Monte Cassino in March, at the cost of the complete (and militarily pointless) destruction of the historic abbey. In the face of obstinate German resistance, the commander-in-chief of the Fifth Army, General Mark Clark, grew increasingly impatient. He wanted to be sure to enter Rome before all the space in American newspapers was filled with news of the invasion of Normandy, an operation that would open a new continental front. The Americans entered Rome on June 4, 1944, and the invasion of France came at dawn on June 6. For an entire day, but one day only, the general had the attention he wanted.

Despite the more-or-less self-serving equivocations, political motivations, and justifications of the parties involved, it remains difficult to understand what real reasons inspired a reprisal against the Italians that was unequaled in all of occupied Europe. I'm not talking only about the Fosse Ardeatine; there were armed confrontations everywhere between Nazi troops and partisan groups, battles and skirmishes in which it wasn't always easy to distinguish between the regular German army and the SS given that, as the historian Gerhard Schreiber wrote in *Vendetta Tedesca* (German Vengeance), "even the highest officers in the Wehrmacht didn't hesitate in executing illegal orders." Exactly where did this hatred, which cost more than 60,000

Italian lives, come from? According to reliable (although necessarily approximate) estimates, 6,800 of them were soldiers executed by orders that were often contrary to all international laws, 45,000 were resistance fighters killed in battle, and 9,180 were civilians executed in reprisals or during the *Bandenbekämpfung*, the struggle to eradicate gangs. If the massacre at the Fosse Ardeatine is the most serious one to have been carried out in a city, SS detachments commanded by Major Walter Reder moved through the countryside like furies, killing 576 defenseless civilians in Sant'Anna di Stazzema, in Tuscany, and 1,830 in Marzabotto, in Emilia. The latter was a reprisal for partisan attacks, but even this pretext didn't exist at Sant'Anna di Stazzema—it was simply an act of "pure criminality studied in its smallest details" according to Marco de Paolis, military prosecutor at La Spezia.

Why so much savagery? Maybe the Italians were finally paying for the original esteem and near-psychological subjugation that Hitler felt for Mussolini. His disillusion began with the campaign in Greece, a stupid attempt in which the Germans had to rescue the Italians to avoid disaster, and then continued to grow along with the number of defeats in Africa and Russia. Incapable of seeing his own error and folly, Hitler made Italy the scapegoat for the unhappy progress of the war. Schreiber notes that it was a real "racial degrading of his Fascist ally." Hitler makes this clear in his *Political Testament*, "I think that, at least in one way, this war made one thing unequivocally clear, and that is the unstoppable decline of the Latin peoples . . . their effective impotence is exacerbated by a ridiculous arrogance. This weakness, be it in the Italians, our allies, or the French, our enemies, was equally inauspicious for us." It was so inauspicious that he wished his Italian ally "had been kept far from the battlefield." This resentment and contempt for the military capabilities of his Fascist ally was the cause of this inhuman savagery. Certainly the "betrayal" of September 8, which caused Field Marshall Albert Kesselring, commander-in-chief of German troops in Italy, to say, "there can be no leniency shown to the traitors," also carried great weight. This tangle of emotion and resentment couldn't escape even the simplest soldier, and no one was exempt when it came to the merciless killings done without regard for culpability, sex, or age: *Weiber, Kinder, alles mögliche* (women, children, everything).

One of the reasons for the hostility the Germans felt toward their Fascist allies was their perception that the Italians treated the Jews too leniently. Joseph Goebbels, Nazi minister of Culture and one of the principal architects of the campaign against the Jews, noted in his diary on December 13, 1942, "The Italians are very mild in their treatment of the Jews. They protect the Jews both in Tunisia and occupied France. They do not allow them to be called up for forced labor, nor do they force them to wear the Star of David."

Eight years after the war Field Marshall Kesselring still regretted that there hadn't been more bombing campaigns against the civilian population. He approved or personally directed the major acts of repression, including those directed at innocent people. In his first service order, as commander-in-chief in Italy, he announced, "I will protect every commander who exceeds usual limits in the severity of methods used against the partisans." Once the war was over he said he deserved a monument from the Italians. Professor Pietro Calamandrei, rector of the University of Florence and founder of the journal *Il Ponte*, responded by composing a testament to his ignominy, now engraved in a large marble plaque in the town of Cuneo. I can't well judge what effect these rhetoric-filled words, dictated by the vivid pain and indignation of the time, might have today; I read them as a boy, and for me their meaning has never changed. I transcribe them here as they were written back then, in memoriam:

YOU WILL HAVE, COMRADE KESSELRING,
THE MONUMENT YOU EXPECT FROM US ITALIANS
BUT WHAT STONE WE USE TO CONSTRUCT IT
IS UP TO US TO DECIDE
NOT WITH STONES BLACKENED BY THE SMOKE OF
INNOCENT VILLAGES
TORN APART BY YOUR DESTRUCTION
NOT WITH THE EARTH OF THE CEMETERIES
WHERE OUR YOUNG COMPANIONS
REST IN SERENITY
NOT WITH THE PURE SNOW OF THE MOUNTAINS
WHICH DEFIED YOU FOR TWO WINTERS
NOT WITH THE SPRINGTIME OF THESE VALLEYS
THAT SAW YOU RETREATING

BUT ONLY WITH THE SILENCE OF THE TORTURED
HARDER THAN ANY STONE
ONLY WITH THE ROCK OF THE OATH
SWORN BY FREE MEN WHO GATHER VOLUNTARILY
FOR THE SAKE OF DIGNITY, NOT HATRED
RESOLUTE TO REDEEM THE WORLD'S SHAME AND TERROR
IF EVER YOU RETURN TO THESE STREETS
YOU WILL FIND US IN OUR PLACES
THE LIVING AND THE DEAD WITH THE SAME COMMITMENT
A PEOPLE STANDING TOGETHER AROUND A MONUMENT
NOW AND FOREVER CALLED
RESISTANCE.

---

1. Although no English translation of *Via Tasso* exists, an essay by Paladini is included in Stanislao G. Pugliese's anthology *Italian Fascism and Anti-Fascism* (Manchester: Manchester University Press, 2001).
2. Guglielmo Petroni, *The World Is a Prison*, trans. John Shepley (Evanston: Marlboro Press, 1999).
3. Robert Katz, *The Battle for Rome: The Germans, the Allies, the Partisans, and the Pope, September 1943–June 1944* (New York: Simon and Schuster, 2004).

X

THE MOST BEAUTIFUL
LADY OF ROME

MANY PLACES THROUGHOUT ROME are associated, albeit often erroneously, with the detested Borgia family. After more than five centuries recollections of the family's wicked deeds are vivid as ever, and the grain of truth at the heart of each memory is stoked by frightening rumors and legends. On the left side of the Via Cavour, 200 meters uphill from Via degli Annibaldi, there is a menacing palace, partially covered by vines, with a small balcony on the facade. Known as the "palazzetto dei Borgia," or little palace of the Borgia, the oldest part of the building has since been incorporated into the former convent of San Francesco di Paola, next to the church of the same name. An arched, sixteenth-century window opens onto the little balcony and has a rather romantic air—it's not hard to imagine a Juliet or a Lucretia (to keep to our current subject) standing there. A steep staircase leads up from the street to a shadowy passageway, which is dark even in the middle of the summer and is the perfect place to stage an ambush or assassination. Halfway up this alley, on the right side, is a heavily reinforced doorway with a pointed arch. According to legend, Rodrigo Borgia's second-born son, Don Juan, Duke of Gandia, exited through this door and vanished into thin air, almost certainly murdered by his brother Cesare, the future "Valentino." The facade facing the Via Cavour resembles an ancient fortress and has a romantic air, but there is no evidence that any Borgia ever lived within its walls. According to another popular myth, the modest palace was linked to the Borgia family because it belonged to Vannozza Cattanei, the widely recognized mistress of Pope Alexander VI (Rodrigo Borgia).

Another, older legend regarding this mysterious alleyway may have reinforced its sinister fame. It was said to be the notorious *vicus sceleratus*, the site of an appalling, bloody crime committed early in Rome's history. Servius Tullius, sixth King of Rome, had two daughters, both named Tullia. Tullia senior was married to Arunte and soon became the lover of Lucius, her brother-in-law (who was married to her sister, Tullia junior). Lucius became the seventh and last king of Rome under the name Tarquinius the Proud. Tullia senior, a veritable Lady Macbeth before her time, organized a conspiracy in which her cuckolded husband, Arunte, her sister, and even her father, the king, were assassinated. When the king fell, rather than mourn, the horrid woman did no less than jump into her carriage and run over his corpse, crushing it under the wheels—a gruesome event recorded in a famous engraving by Bartolomeo Pinelli. All this happened in the sixth century BC, and if ever a street were worthy of the name *sceleratus*—cursed—it's certainly this one, site of such a brutal parricide.

The other, more significant place associated with the Borgia family is the second floor of the Vatican palace, beneath the rooms decorated by Raphael. This was the apartment of Pope Alexander VI, who lived here in a series of private rooms called the "stanze segrete." Alexander's successor, Julius II, also lived here before moving upstairs, tired of seeing the image of the "boor of evil and unfortunate memory," as he called his predecessor, in the decorative frescoes by Pinturrichio (and his assistants Pier Matteo d'Amelia, Antonio da Viterbo, called Il Pastura, and Tiberio d'Assisi). These ill-famed rooms recall a turbulent period whose key players included Alexander and his two mistresses, Vannozza Cattanei and Giulia Farnese; his children Cesare, Lucretia, Juan, and Jofré; and a vast circle of courtiers, mercenaries, and hired assassins.

The sequence of spaces in this apartment begins with a reception hall called the Room of the Sibyls, and proceeds to rooms dedicated to the Prophets, the Creed, the Liberal Arts, the Saints, and the Mysteries of the Faith. The first are in what is known as the Borgia Tower, and those rooms, along with all the following ones, are associated with turbid memories marked by evidence of terrible events. Lucretia's husband, Alphonse of Aragon, was assassinated in the Room of the Sibyls, as was one of her lovers, a young man named Perotto. Here the Borgia also prepared the murderous poisons used to get rid of their enemies. Pinturicchio painted the protagonists of these excesses and crimes. Pope Alexander VI appears kneeling, in a pious pose, in the Room of the Mysteries of the Faith. His lover, Vannozza, might be the Virgin Annunciate, and Giulia Farnese, the very young lover of the old pope, may have been the model for the Madonna and Child painted above the door in the Room of the Saints. Although this identification is hypothetical, it seems likely—Giulia was the pope's favorite, and he commissioned the work. It isn't unreasonable to think that the painter, whether on his own or at Alexander's request, would have recorded her likeness here. The young Lucretia Borgia also appears, depicted as Saint Catherine of Alexandria intent on debating with the Doctors of the Church (at the beginning of the fifteenth century Masolino painted the same scene in the basilica of San Clemente). Cesare can be found close by, dressed in Turkish-style garb and standing with his sister Lucretia. Although he included members of the Borgia family in his frescoes at the pope's request, Pinturicchio retained his own pictorial style. His typical, heavy reliance on antique motifs—grotesques, hieroglyphs, and references to astrology and Egyptian myths—are present in several rooms, beginning with the Room of the Sibyls, and a variety of pagan themes are represented in the Room of the Saints. The latter also included the image of a bull, Alexander VI's heraldic emblem and the predominant decorative element throughout the apartment. (Today some of these rooms house a collection of modern religious art established by Pope Paul VI in 1973.)

More than in any of the places associated with them, the Borgia live on in the memories of their actions, and the actions attributed to them, passed down to us in popular stories. Their legend is enhanced by the extraordinary combination of two complementary, opposite figures: a man, Alexander VI, who was strong and dominating; and a woman in which the fascination of a femme fatale was combined with the innocence of a girl forced by circumstance to abandon all virtue. This woman was none other than Alexander's daughter, Lucretia, and any Borgia story must start with her.

"Lucretia Borgia is the most unfortunate woman in modern history. Is this because she was guilty of the most hideous crimes, or is it simply because she has been unjustly condemned by the world to bear its curse?"[1] This question, posed by Ferdinand Gregorovius at the beginning of the book he dedicated to her, is still unresolved, and seems destined to stay that way. Over a century has passed since these words were written, and our sources of information about Lucretia have changed very little. There's no definitive answer because the documents we do have only allude to events and behaviors; they are vague, and at times downright cryptic. Even when they appear less veiled, we can't really know how much jealousy, political rivalry, and conflicting interests may have influenced what they say. Based on this documentation, Victor Hugo represented Lucretia as an immoral monster, and the story he wrote about her spread that reputation throughout Europe. Other biographers, like Geneviève Chastenet, have seen her instead as a near heroine, a victim of circumstance and the terrible family to which she belonged. Alexandre Dumas, on the other hand, offered this grim, vivid portrait of her in his book *The Borgias*:

> In these matters the sister was quite worthy of her brother. Lucretia was wanton in imagination, godless by nature, ambitious and designing: she had a craving for pleasure, admiration, honours, money, jewels, gorgeous stuffs, and magnificent mansions. A true Spaniard beneath her golden tresses, a courtesan beneath her frank looks, she carried the head of a Raphael Madonna, and concealed the heart of a Messalina.[2]

But let's stick to the facts as much as possible. Lucretia was born in Subiaco on April 18, 1480, to Vannozza Cattanei (she's mentioned in a notarial document as Vanotia de Captaneis), lover of Cardinal Rodrigo Borgia, the future Pope Alexander VI. Her father chose her lovely name to recall an earlier Lucretia, the supremely chaste patroness of ancient Rome. When she was still very young, the first Lucretia was raped by Sestus, son of Tarquinius the Proud, King of the Etruscans. After telling her family about the outrage she'd suffered, the unhappy young woman took her own life right in front of them; her suicide became the first domino to fall in a series of incidents that led to the end of the monarchy. This was clearly a demanding name for the daughter of a man like Rodrigo, driven by such enormous ambitions.

Rodrigo was born on January 1, 1432, in the town of Játiva, near Valencia, in Spain (the family's name was originally Borja). He was forty-eight when Lucretia was born, and had already fathered a number of children by several women. Vannozza had given him Cesare in 1475—the first of their children together, who later became the model for Machiavelli's prince—and Juan in 1476. Lucretia followed, and Jofré was born in 1481. At the age of seventeen Rodrigo was summoned to Rome by his uncle, Cardinal Alfonso Borgia, and he came of age in the secret-filled air of the Vatican. He rose quickly in the church hierarchy, and at twenty-four his uncle, who had since become Pope Calixtus III, made him a cardinal. He was courageous, astute, and a skilled negotiator. He lacked any sense of morality, aside from the feigned morality used to increase his power, and manipulated conclaves and the election of several popes until he himself rose to the papal throne.

Rodrigo Borgia was the incarnation of the stereotypical sixteenth-century man, perhaps even more so than his first-born son Cesare.[3] His constitution was vigorous; he wasn't really handsome, but had an appealing personality and intelligence, and was endowed with such sexual appetite that the Bishop of Modena called him, not unjustifiably, "the most carnal of men." He pursued an ecclesiastical career, becoming a cardinal and then pope (in 1492, the same year that the Americas were discovered), because that was the circle he grew up in. With the same luck and bravura he could easily have been a great war captain, or one of the many local potentates who populated the small and quarrelsome peninsula, so full of wonders and ferocity. Rome was at its center—if not politically, at least symbolically—and the Vatican was just another of its many courts, the seat of a non-dynastic monarchy ruled, like any other secular state, by an autocrat—in this case, the pope. The Papal States were one of the most important in all Italy, and bordered the Republic of Venice to the North, and the Kingdom of Naples to the South.

Rome, however, had become a miserable place, deprived of any memory of its own past, and littered with ever more diffuse signs of its moral spinelessness. Its spiritual life had been weakened, and the papal court itself contributed to the general moral laxity. Religion was reduced to mere pomp and circumstance, meant primarily to intimidate other princes and keep the masses at bay. Priests and cardinals kept one or more concubines "to the greater glory of God," as the historian Stefano Infessura wrote, while the papal master of ceremonies, Johannes Burchard, noted that female convents were "almost all of them brothels," and that little or nothing distinguished religious women from prostitutes, a situation which, as we shall see, had important consequences for Lucretia's life.

In his biography of Lucretia, Gregorovius wrote that she "was indeed born at a terrible time in the world's history; the papacy was stripped of all holiness, religion was altogether material, and immorality was boundless. The bitterest family feuds raged in the city, in the Ponte, Parione and Regola quarters, where kinsmen incited by murder daily met in deadly combat."[4]

And yet, amid all the chaos and bloody tumult, one can also catch the first glimpses of what would soon become the Renaissance. Guicciardini noticed, and wrote in his *History of Italy*, that "It was obvious that ever since the Roman Empire, more than a thousand years ago, weakened mainly by the corruption of ancient customs, began to decline from that peak which it had achieved as a result of marvelous skill and fortune, Italy had never enjoyed such prosperity, or known so favorable a situation as that in which it found itself so securely at rest in the year of our Christian salvation, 1490, and the years immediately before and after."[5]

The whole papal court, including seventeen-year-old Lucretia, was present when the young Michelangelo's *Pietà* was unveiled. According to Gregorovius, the extraordinary sculpture "appeared in that time of dark morality as a pure flame of sacrifice, ignited by a large, serious spirit, in the profaned sanctuary of the Church." Even as crimes and misdeeds were being committed in the Vatican, Alexander summoned some of the greatest geniuses of the time to the papal court: Bramante painted the Borgia court-of-arms in the basilica of Saint John Lateran; Copernicus was given the astronomy chair at La Sapienza, the University of Rome; Leonardo da Vinci, perhaps the greatest intellect of the period, served the cruel Cesare as a fortress-building engineer; Pinturicchio and Perugino frescoed the papal apartments, and the former portrayed the pope adoring a Virgin who resembled Giulia Farnese, his teenage lover. The atmosphere of the time shifted from sublime to corrupt between one minute and the next.

There is a portrait by Girolamo da Carpi of Lucretia's presumed mother, Vannozza, in the Galleria Borghese. The cardinal's lover was a woman of warm, languid beauty, blonde like her daughter, with full lips and a straight nose. She is said to have started out as a courtesan before becoming Borgia's favorite. According to Gregorovius, "Vannozza doubtless was of great beauty and ardent passions; for if not, how could she have inflamed a Rodrigo Borgia? Her intellect too, although uncultivated, must have been vigorous; for if not, how could she have maintained her relations with the cardinal?"[6] She certainly had some qualities, since she was able to hold the attention of a man as powerful and restless as Rodrigo for fifteen years. To cover up their relationship and give their children some sort of legitimacy (they were officially Rodrigo's niece and nephews), the pope twice arranged for her to marry complaisant men, who would play the role of putative husband and discreetly disappear when her lover came around. Vannozza also had a son with one of these husbands, Giorgio de Croce, or at least attributed the child to him.

But for Lucretia's upbringing Rodrigo chose another woman, Adriana de Mila. She was a somewhat ambiguous figure, and played a substantial role, effectively becoming the girl's real mother. Adriana was the daughter of Don Pedro, Rodrigo's cousin and the nephew of Calixtus III, making her Lucretia's cousin, too. The cardinal placed great importance on blood ties, and wanted his beloved daughter to be raised within the family. Adriana had married Ludovico Orsini, Lord of Bassanello, and bore one son, Orso (or Orsino). She was perhaps on even more intimate terms with Rodrigo than Vannozza; he confided in her, and she dispensed advice to him in her fine house at Monte Giordano, near the Ponte Sant'Angelo. The girl's childhood was spent between this house and the convent of San Sisto, at the start of the Via Appia, which the pope called a "religious and very decent place."

Lucretia was beautiful, as is confirmed by several people, including many of the papal court ambassadors. "Her face," they wrote, "is rather long, the nose well cut, hair golden, eyes of no special colour. Her mouth is rather large, the teeth brilliantly white, her neck is slender and fair, the bust admirably proportioned. She is always gay and smiling."[7] We also know that she was of average height, and slender. She was afflicted with frequent and severe headaches, as well as a recurrent pain in her sides that would worsen with age. Medical historians have suggested the latter was symptomatic of a form of tuberculosis. She also had the same receding chin as her father, visible in several profiles and medals, which was but a minor defect. She was pretty, and like every girl soon became aware of it. She had a superficial education, learned to play a few musical instruments, and loved to dance, as it allowed her to show off her gracefulness. Her father—like the Tetrarch Herod with Salomé—stared at her, enchanted, as she danced.

Her public debut was in December of 1487, when she was seven. The marriage of Maddalena de'Medici, Lorenzo the Magnificent's daughter, and Franceschetto Cybo, son of Pope Innocent VIII (Giovanni Battista Cybo) was celebrated with extraordinary pomp on December 17. The bride was fourteen, her husband was forty. Rodrigo was master of ceremonies for the day; at the time he was vice-chancellor of the Vatican, and was more than pleased to receive the wedding procession at his magnificent palace, and thereby have a chance to show off his delightful young daughter.

Franceschetto was a debauched night owl who chased after prostitutes and was mired in gambling debts he shamelessly repaid with indulgences. Maddalena was, on the other hand, a delicate child who had been educated by the eminent humanist Poliziano. A friendship developed between Maddalena and Lucretia; it's easy to imagine it as an almost childlike friendship, despite the fact that the young Florentine was, two years after her marriage, already a mother.

The most important friendship to accompany Lucretia over many years was yet another. In 1488 Adriana de Mila arranged a marriage between her one-eyed son, Orsino, and the fourteen-year-old Giulia Farnese, who was six years older than Lucretia. Even though she was just an adolescent, Giulia was so pretty, and gave off such sensuality, that the Romans called her "Giulia la Bella"—the beautiful Giulia—and, more derisively, when she became Rodrigo Borgia's lover, "the Bride of Christ." It is curious, and perhaps intentional, that there are no clearly identified portraits of her. We can only imagine her beauty. Many claim she is portrayed in one of the several images of women with a unicorn painted in the Renaissance, and others see her in the pretty, kneeling figure in Raphael's *Transfiguration*. Still others have identified her in the figure of Justice reclining at the feet of Paul III in his tomb in Saint Peter's or, as I have already noted, in Pinturicchio's *Madonna and Child*. These are all only hypotheses. We know, however, that Giulia had dark eyes ("niger oculus") and beautiful black hair. Other sources report that she shone with grace and mirth ("gratia" and "allegrezza"), thus uniting good looks with a jovial and pleasant personality. Court ladies said later that she ordered black silk sheets for her bed so as to better contrast with her pearly complexion and reinvigorate the aging pope's passion. Her rosy cheeks hinted at her ardor.

When Rodrigo saw her he was immediately smitten. She was fifteen and he fifty-eight, but he was also the most powerful cardinal in Rome. No one could even consider refusing him, and, indeed, Giulia didn't resist; in only a few months' time everyone in Rome knew. When Borgia was elected to the papal throne, Burchard wrote openly that the girl had become the pope's concubine. Giulia, Adriana, and Lucretia had taken up residence in a new home at Santa Maria in Portico, near Saint Peter's (the building was demolished in the middle of the seventeenth century to make way for Bernini's colonnades). The proximity of her residence allowed the cardinal, and then the pope, to pay discreet visits to his young lover. Those three women made a strange and dark combination. Adriana, Giulia's mother-in-law, and Lucretia, the cardinal's daughter, both witnessed and hid Rodrigo's carnal relationship with the girl. The three women lived in comfort and enjoyed it, if we can believe the wonderful domestic scene painted by Lorenzo Pucci—a man of the papal court destined to be a powerful cardinal. He wrote to his brother, Giannozzo, "Madonna Giulia has grown somewhat stouter and is a most beautiful creature. She let her hair down before me and had it dressed; it reached down to her feet; never have I seen anything like it; she has the most beautiful hair. She wore a headdress of fine linen, and over it a sort of hair net, light as air, with gold threads woven in it. In truth it shone like the sun! I would have given a great deal if you could have been present to have informed yourself concerning that which you have often wanted to know."[8]

Up until then the Farnese had been a modest seignorial family from Northern Lazio. "The Farnese," Gregorovius wrote, "became prominent in Etruria as a small dynasty of robber barons . . ."[9] Giulia would change the family's fortune. The pope compensated his young lover for her favors by making her twenty-five-year-old brother, Alessandro Farnese, a cardinal. He later became Pope Paul III.

An exchange of letters between Giulia and Rodrigo gives us some understanding of the complex psychological nature of their relationship. She wrote, "Being away from Your Holiness, and depending on you for all my well-being and happiness, I can take no satisfaction in any pleasures because where you are, my treasure, so is my heart." Rodrigo replied, "we thus understand your perfection, of which truly we have never been in doubt. And we wish that, like us, you recognize this clearly . . . and that no other woman is loved."[10]

The adoration in Rodrigo's words is typical of an old man who's lost his head for a girl so much younger than him, but there is also a worried jealousy. He was afraid that Orsino, who was, after all, Giulia's legitimate husband, and had so discreetly retreated to his holdings at Bassanello to prepare his militia, might re-enter her life—and that's exactly what happened. At one point Rodrigo got the impression she'd recently seen her husband, or had some such intention. The pope's jealousy exploded in an incredible letter:

> Ungrateful and perfidious Julia . . . can we totally persuade ourselves that you should use such ingratitude and perfidy towards us, having so many times sworn and pledged your faith to be at our command and service and not to concile yourself with Ursino? That now you want to do the contrary and go to Bassanello with express peril to your life. I would not believe that you would for any other reason, if not to plunge again into that water of Bassanello . . . [a euphemism for resuming marital relations with Orsino, which on a previous occasion resulted in the birth of their daughter, Laura].[11]

At the end of the letter, angered to the point of becoming grotesque, the cardinal forbids Giulia from going to her husband's estate:

> Under pain of excommunication and eternal damnation I command you not to depart . . . nor even to go to Bassanello for things that concern our state.

A prince of the Church, in rudimentary Latin and ungrammatical Italian, threatens his lover with excommunication, fearing that she might be pregnant with her legitimate husband's child.

When all this happened Giulia was about twenty years old, and Lucretia was thirteen or fourteen. Rodrigo had already arranged and then annulled two engagements for his daughter, decisions inevitably made to suit his own pleasure and political calculations. The first happened when she was eleven, although the marriage contract stated that the marriage would only be celebrated and consummated two and a half years later. According to Gregorovius, "About her [Lucretia] saw vice shamelessly displayed or cloaked in sacerdotal robes; she was conscious of the ambition and avarice which hesitated at no crime; she beheld a religion more pagan than paganism itself, and a church service in which the sacred actors—with whose conduct behind the scenes she was perfectly familiar—were the priests, the cardinals, her brother Cesare, and her own father. All this Lucretia beheld . . ."[12]

Finally the wedding day arrived. The man her father chose for her, with political ends in mind, was Giovanni Sforza, a young man of twenty-six who was already a widower—his first wife, Maddalena Gonzaga, had died in childbirth. The wedding contract was signed on February 2, 1493; Lucretia was thirteen and brought a dowry of 31,000 ducats and another 10,000 in clothing and jewels. The wedding was celebrated in June, and it was as sumptuous as befitted the daughter of a pope. The bride wore a violet dress with gold and pearl trim, fitted as far as the waist, broad and flowing below. A gilt cord supported and enhanced her tender young bust, and her train was carried by a young African slave girl. Giulia Farnese, her friend and "stepmother" of sorts (she'd already given the pope a daughter, Laura), led the procession of 150 Roman ladies. The pope, dressed in white and seated on the papal throne, awaited the procession surrounded by a dozen cardinals in scarlet vestments. Cesare Borgia, his oldest son, stood on his father's left side; he was an archbishop at the time, and later his father would make him a cardinal.

The party that evening was sumptuous as all the rest. The Ambassador of Ferrara, in a report to his sovereign, wrote of the seemingly endless gifts, including, "[Cardinal Ascanio's] present, which consisted of a complete drinking service of silver washed with gold, worth about a thousand ducats. Cardinal Monreale gave two rings, a sapphire and a diamond—very beautiful—and worth three thousands ducats; the protonotary Cesarini gave a bowl and a cup worth eight hundred ducats; the Duke of Gandia a vessel worth seventy ducats . . ."[13] The night passed, the punctilious ambassador concluded, with dance, song, and a licentious comedy suggestive of the imminent consummation everyone was waiting for. The wedding bonbons, sugar-coated almonds, were distributed in hundreds of cups and then tossed by the handfuls into the ladies' generous décolleté for the men's added pleasure of then fishing them back out.

Only around dawn was Lucretia—who must have been exhausted (she was only thirteen!)—finally accompanied to her nuptial chamber, where a much-discussed event took place. The young bride waited for her groom next to the nuptial bed with her father and Cardinal Ascanio Sforza in attendance. Was this just a short and discreet farewell visit, or was it proof of an incestuous relationship between Alexander and his beloved daughter, a rapport that would explain the pope's morbid curiosity? Johannes Burchard wrote, "They say many other things which I will not write down; perhaps they are true, and if they are, I find them unbelievable." These are ambiguous words that clarify nothing, but it's nonetheless a hint that only increases the mystery.

Geneviève Chastenet researched the episode and concluded that, in being present at the moment when the couple undressed and got in bed, Alexander was simply respecting a royal custom. She cites an event two years earlier, at the wedding of Alfonso d'Este and Anna Sforza: "The couple was put to bed and . . . everyone gathered round them, joking about it. Madama Anna, the bride, kept her good humor; yet to both of them it seemed strange to see the bed surrounded by so many people saying things in jest, as was custom."

Custom or not, use or abuse, the fact remains that the wedding night didn't quite go as planned. Perhaps it was the child-bride's reluctance or Giovanni's scruples—he was twice her age—or maybe it was the sheer exhaustion at the end of an exciting yet debilitating day. The pope summoned the young man, who'd taken refuge from an outbreak of plague in his dominion at Pesaro, back to Rome, writing, "We stipulate that beginning on the 10 or 15 of this October, when the air will be cooler and healthier, that you come to us in order to fully consummate your marriage to your wife."

This awkward union lasted about four years, and then the pope's plans changed. In 1497 Alexander decided it would be advantageous to form an alliance with Spain and the Kingdom of Naples. Lucretia once again became an instrument in his plan, but she first had to be freed from her current marriage; such liberation was easily in the pope's power, so he began planning. His son Cesare was more impatient, and proposed they just kill poor Giovanni and dump his body in the Tiber, as was often done back then. The chronicler Pietro Marzetti recounts in his *Memorie di Pesaro* that one evening, while Lucretia was in her room with Jacomino, her husband's servant, her brother Cesare was announced: "On her command the chamberlain concealed himself behind a screen. Cesare talked freely with his sister, and among other things said that the order had been given to kill Sforza. When he had departed, Lucretia said to Jacomino: 'Did you hear what was said? Go and tell him.'" The servant obeyed immediately, and Giovanni "threw himself on a Turkish horse and rode in twenty-four hours to Pesaro, where the beast dropped dead."[14]

In the end the pope's approach prevailed over Cesare's bloodier plan. The marriage, which had grown to involve at least a little affection, as the above incident suggests, was annulled on the grounds that it had not been consummated. The pope told his daughter the news himself, returning her to the official status of virgin. She confirmed this in writing with a document that declared she'd had no "carnal relations or coitus, and was ready to submit herself to a gynecological examination." The experience must nevertheless have been painful for her, not only for the delusion it caused, but also the shame and violence her family subjected her to, followed by the traumatic end of something that had perhaps come to resemble love.

This tragicomedy was drawing to a close when something else happened—this time it was a decidedly dramatic event. Don Juan, Duke of Gandia and second of the two Borgia brothers, was mysteriously assassinated one night as he rode home alone. He had just left a dinner his mother Vannozza had given in a vineyard she owned near San Pietro in Vincoli. It was commonly said, and never denied, that Cesare had murdered his own brother out of jealousy for the affection his father showed the younger son. Perhaps there was an even darker motive, since Juan had insisted that Lucretia return to the convent of San Sisto a Caracalla, where she had spent time as a child, thus removing her from Cesare's influence. Alexander was dismayed by the news of his son's barbarous death, stabbed to death in a dark street and thrown into the river at the exact point where a large drain dumped sewage into the water.

As the process of annulling her marriage to Giovanni proceeded, Lucretia entertained the twenty-two-year-old Pedro Caldes, called

Perotto, one of the pope's chamberlains, at the convent. Their meetings must have become quite affectionate because one day Lucretia
found herself pregnant—a rather embarrassing condition that con-
trasted with her official virginal status. The situation was complicated
even more by the fact that Giovanni Sforza, reluctant to play the role
of impotent husband, wrote to his uncle, Ludovico il Moro, Duke of
Milan, assuring him that ". . . he had known her an infinite number
of times. But the Pope had taken her away from him only in order to
have her to himself."[15] Giovanni was among the first to suggest, and
the rumor was soon widespread, that Alexander and his daughter had
had carnal relations.

When Lucretia appeared before the ecclesiastical tribunal in
December 1497 to confirm her condition of *virgo intacta*, or intact
virgin, the ritual gynecological exam was omitted to avoid the
embarrassment of verifying her advanced pregnancy. Things went a
bit worse for the unfortunate Perotto. Walking down a corridor at
the Vatican one day, he encountered Cesare Borgia by chance. The
moment he saw Cesare, Perotto knew from the look in his eye what
was about to happen, and fled at breakneck speed, pursued by the
other, who'd pulled out his dagger. This race ended in the papal audience chamber, where the terrified servant threw himself at the feet
of the pope himself, begging for protection. It wasn't enough. Cesare
hurled himself on Perotto, stabbing him with such force that the blood
flew into the pope's face, staining his white tunic a deep red. The stab
wounds, however, didn't finish off the poor wretch. He was carried,
dying, to the dungeons at the Castel Sant'Angelo, and his body was
found in the Tiber a few days later. A few months later eighteen-
year-old Lucretia gave birth to a son, given the generic name of *Infans
Romanus*, who was immediately taken from her. Was he Perotto's son?
Popular rumors suggested instead that he was the product of an
incestuous relationship between the pope and his daughter, and it
took several years before Lucretia was able to assure the child's legitimacy and guarantee him an income.

Alexander VI participated in the horrors that surrounded him
with the shrewd coldness of a political man interested only in his own
goals. He loved his son Juan, and another son, Cesare, had assassinated
him. He loved the young Perotto, who was perhaps also one of his
lovers, and Cesare slit his throat right before his own eyes. Lucretia

remained in the papal court, as did Cesare, whose intelligence and cruelty the pope learned to appreciate. Alexander's own plans also remained, and he nourished them with opportune actions.

At that point his attention was focused on a scion of the Neapolitan dynasty, Alonso or Alfonso (the illegitimate son of King Alfonso II) who, as his son-in-law, would consolidate the alliance between the papacy and the Aragon dynasty in Naples. Alexander's project played out in two phases: the first was a marriage between Lucretia and Alfonso; and the second was a marriage between Carlotta, a daughter of King Federigo of Naples, and Cesare, who'd been officially returned to status of layman to allow such a union. The plan was meant to create a sort of embryonic Kingdom of Italy under the aegis of the Borgia. Cesare was fascinated by the project, and Machiavelli was amongst the few to understand its strategic importance. Everything went up in smoke, however, because Federigo didn't want such a disturbing man in his family, and because Carlotta insisted she had no desire to be "la cardinala," the lady cardinal. Cesare was highly offended by this double refusal.

Things went better for Lucretia; when she finally met seventeen-year-old Don Alfonso she was, according to all accounts, smitten. She had a dowry of 40,000 ducats, and he was made Duke of Bisceglie. A little while later, the Mantuan ambassador to the Holy See wrote to his sovereign, "Seduced by his attentions and his handsomeness, Madonna Lucretia has a real passion for her husband."

On August 13, 1498, Cesare renounced his rank of cardinal and hurried to leave for France, where Louis XII had promised him the Duchy of Valence (the Valentinois, part of the dauphin's lands), as well as the hand of a French princess. King Louis had his own good reasons for such generosity. He intended to marry Anne of Bretagne, but he needed first to free himself from his wife, Jeanne, and only the pope could annul that union. (Not everyone had British King Henry VIII's impulsive temperament. When he decided to marry Anne Boleyn he severed both his ties to his wife, Catherine of Aragon, and all ties to Rome with a single stroke.) Whether out of love or fear, Alexander VI could no longer refuse his son anything, and therefore gave him a papal bull authorizing the King of France to marry his new flame.

On November 1, 1499, Lucretia gave birth to a son named Rodrigo, after his grandfather. His baptism was celebrated with great pomp in the Sistine Chapel (the chapel Sixtus IV had constructed in the Vatican palace wasn't yet decorated with Michelangelo's frescoes). It seems Lucretia had finally achieved relative happiness. Among other gains, she'd extended her own land holdings, since her father had given her property confiscated from the rebellious Caetani family—including the areas of Sermoneta, Ninfa, Norma, Cisterna, and San Felice Circeo. Jacopo Caetani protested this confiscation from prison so vociferously that the pope felt constrained to silence him with poison.

Stabbing, beating, and drowning were the normal means of assassination in those days; poison was a more refined, subtle, and bloodless variation on the theme. The most common poisons were generally a slight improvement on those already used by ancient Romans and the Arabs. From plants they obtained the toxic vapor of laurel leaves—which Pythia of Delphi inhaled in minute quantities before pronouncing her oracles—and nepenthe, a mixture of several plants, primarily henbane and mandrake. The latter was also known from its use in mythological tales. Jason used it to drug the dragon guarding the Golden Fleece, and it freed Ulysses from the spell of the sorceress Circe. A tincture of poisonous mushrooms was also highly valued, including the *Amanita phalloides*, which Agrippina used to kill Emperor Claudius. Infusions from almonds and cherry pits were first used in the medieval period, and contained amygdalin, a substance that mixed with gastric juices in the stomach to produce a fatal hydrocyanic acid. There were also animal poisons, including menstrual blood (said to provoke dementia), snake venom, and leopard bile, which acted a lot like viper venom. Horse and donkey sweat caused putrefaction of the bowels. Back then, much as now, the king of poisons was arsenic, which had the advantage of looking like flour or sugar and caused no flavor change in the foods it was mixed with. It resulted in seemingly natural symptoms, especially if administered in small doses over time, and could also be sprinkled on clothing or sheets to be absorbed through the skin. It's no coincidence that arsenic is the preferred poison in many mystery novels, and in the 1960s the United States Secret Service even considered using it to assassinate Fidel Castro.

King Federigo didn't want his daughter to marry Cesare Borgia for fear that he might then be deposed from the throne. Cesare wasn't one to give up easily, and he vowed to conquer the kingdom through the help of King Louis of France, who was now his protector. The year 1499 was nearly over, and a jubilee year was to begin the following January. Rome would be filled with pilgrims from all over Europe (including the German monk Martin Luther, who was horrified with what was happening at the Vatican). The city prepared for the usual chaos, throngs at holy sites, ambushes, petty thefts, and predictable murders that came with such an event. According to Marin Sanudo, who wrote an endless diary of the jubilee, "each day the bodies of murder victims are found, four or five a night, including bishops."

In the meantime Cesare Borgia, as lieutenant of the King of France and vicar of the Catholic Church, had conquered various small principalities in the nearby Romagna region. When he returned to Rome he was ostentatiously welcomed, and apparently warmly embraced, by his father. Given his ambitions in the Kingdom of Naples, his brother-in-law Alfonso became something of a hindrance. Gregorovius wrote, "[I]n his opinion his sister's marriage to a Neapolitan prince had become as useless as had been her union with Sforza of Pesaro; moreover, it interfered with the plans of Cesare, who had a matrimonial alliance in mind for his sister which would be more advantageous to himself. As her marriage with the Duke of Biselli [Bisceglie] had not been childless, and, consequently, could not be set aside, he determined upon a radical separation of the couple. July 15, 1500, about eleven o'clock, Alfonso was on his way from his palace to the Vatican to see his consort; near the steps leading to Saint Peter's a number of masked men fell upon him with daggers. Severely wounded in the head, arms and thigh, the prince succeeded in reaching the pope's chamber. At the sight of her spouse covered with blood, Lucretia sank to the floor in a swoon."[16]

Who organized the attack? The Venetian ambassador wrote, "It is not known who wounded the duke, but it is said that it was the same person who killed the Duke of Gandia and threw him into the Tiber."[17] The poet Vincenzo Calmata was even more explicit when he wrote to the Duchess of Urbino, "Who may have ordered this thing to be done, everyone thinks to be the Duke Valentino [Cesare]."[18] Pope Alexander VI guessed better than anyone else who was responsible for the crime, and ordered that Alfonso be cared for at the Vatican, granting him a guard of sixteen men. For a few days the youth hovered between life and death, but then his strong constitution won and he began to recover, nursed by Lucretia and her most loyal ladies-in-waiting. One day Cesare told his sister he intended to visit the wounded man, a meeting Lucretia consented to, stipulating that the Venetian Ambassador and pope himself were also to attend. It was a tense ordeal, as one can imagine, between a would-be assassin and his victim. There were some bitter jokes and whispered sentences on both sides.

In the late afternoon of August 18, thirty-three days after his first attempt, Cesare tried again. Accompanied by several thugs led by Micheletto Corella, he entered Alfonso's room and chased everyone else out. Lucretia understood what was happening, and ran to her father for help. Micheletto jumped on the convalescing youth and strangled him with a rope under Cesare's cold gaze. When Lucretia returned with her father's men, they prevented her from seeing her husband's body, telling her only that the unfortunate man, weakened by his wounds, had slipped and died of a hemorrhage. With imperturbable precision, Burchard noted in his diary, "On the 18 of this month of August, the illustrious Alfonso of Aragon, Duke of Bisceglie, who on the evening of July 15 was gravely wounded and then carried to the tower where he was guarded with maximum care, as he seemed unwilling to die of his wounds, was strangled in his own bed."

For Lucretia this was a terrible blow. Several days on end she lay in bed, delirious with fever, and in an attempt to revive her the pope ordered that her small son Rodrigo, only a few months old, be brought to her each day. Alexander feared that if he lost Lucretia his future plans would be hampered. The child's presence gave her some relief, even though she (a young woman of barely twenty) continued to languish. Visitors noted that her beauty began to show traces of the strain, so Alexander sent her, accompanied by a small band of courtiers, to the castle of Nepi, a retreat he'd given her as a present. The passage of time took care of the rest. Gregorovius noted, "Her father recalled her to Rome before Christmas and received her again into his favor as soon as her brother left the city. Only a few months had passed when Lucretia's soul was again filled with visions of a brilliant future, before which the vague form of the unfortunate Alfonso sank into oblivion."[19]

Perhaps the pope's new scheme to marry her off accelerated the poor woman's recovery. Summarily informed of the plan, Lucretia, who was now a mature woman, showed a certain complacency when faced with yet another marriage to a man she didn't know. This time it was Alfonso d'Este, heir to the Duchy of Ferrara, reputed to be a determined man. As such, he could offer Lucretia a good defense against her father, not to mention her brother's ferocity. The new court she seemed destined for was also far from Rome, the city's intrigues, and the blood her family so easily shed.

If we accept the idea that Lucretia was really just a victim of her circumstances, we can easily imagine that this new marriage might've offered a way to cut the ties linking her to the horrors of her father's papal court. But was this really the case? It's hard to shed light on the deep shadows surrounding her life. There's certainly no lack of evidence of the immoral monstrosity Hugo attributed to her. On the other hand, Gregorovius, who's more reliable on this subject, wrote, "Had she not been the daughter of Alexander VI or the sister of Cesare Borgia, she would have attracted little attention in her own time, and been lost in the multitude as just one more seductive and much courted woman. In the hands of her father and brother she became an instrument and victim of political calculations she had no strength to resist."

Lucretia could only behave according to the way she'd been raised. Her education was that of a princess, and the examples around her—beginning with her father who, when she was a mere child, came to her house to bed her friend Giulia—must have given her a rather approximate moral compass. It's worth noting, however, that this wasn't so different from any other sixteenth-century court; there wasn't a single prince, duke, or lord—and not just in Italy—who didn't have a palace full of legitimate and illegitimate children, and who didn't have his choice of a favorite from among the court's women, be they maidens or married. This was the canon of behavior, a standard considered perfectly normal. Even today adultery, concubines, bigamy, and births outside sanctioned union are common. In the past, for families of rank, this was the norm, especially since marriages were arranged to suit inheritances or dynastic concerns. "Love" (whatever that might mean) was a luxury allowed, on occasion, to the humblest classes. All others—noblemen and rulers—had other concerns, focused on wealth, possessions, and power, so falling into in one bed as opposed to another, as long as the right guarantees were offered, was, all told, a secondary concern.

So it was all a question of guarantees, and Duke Ercole d'Este certainly requested abundant guarantees in return for permission of a marriage between Alfonso and Lucretia. He first needed to overcome the resistance to it in his own family, as his daughter, Isabella d'Este, Marquise of Mantua, and sister-in-law, Elisabetta Gonzaga, Duchess of Urbino, had declared themselves wholly opposed to the union. Lucretia's history weighed heavily in their judgment—her long line of husbands, lovers, abortions, and widowhoods were just too much, even for the elastic morals of that period. Toward the end of November 1501 an anonymous letter began to circulate, a true indictment of the Borgia family, carrying unsavory words about Alexander VI, his son Cesare, and (indirectly) Lucretia as well. According to some historians Emperor Maximilian of Austria, who feared an alliance between the Borgia and Este families, penned the letter. It's true that the missive seemed to be addressed to "Magnificent Lord Silvio Savelli, in care of the Most Serene King of the Romans," that is, in care of Maximilian, who held the title of Holy Roman Emperor. Among its many accusations, the letter affirmed that:

> Now everything for the pope is an object of venal exchange—dignities, honors, the making and dissolving of marriages, divorces, and the repudiation of brides. . . . In Rome and the papal residences there is no crime or wickedness that is not publicly committed; assassinations, robbery, rape, and incest do not complete the list of how many there are . . . Such is the foulness of sons and daughters, there are so many prostitutes and crowds of pimps that the palace of St. Peter has become a meeting place; in any brothel or house of ill repute they live more modestly. On the first of November, the solemn festival of All Saints, fifty municipal prostitutes were invited guests at the palace to give an odious and wicked spectacle, and such that there would be no lack of even more scandalous events, a few days later there was the spectacle of a mare in heat which, with the pope and his children watching, was set upon so arduously by stallions that she was driven into a paroxysm of fury.

This went on for many pages, and when it ended there was no signature, only a place: "Written at Taranto, at the royal encampment, on the 15 of November, 1501," suggesting that it was sent from the camp of Consalvo of Cordoba, which was in Taranto at the time and engaged in a siege against the son of King Federigo of Naples.

The episodes of fifty prostitutes and the mare in heat referred to in the letter are confirmed in another source. Johannes Burchard wrote that one night, at one of the usual parties the pope gave:

> [T]here took place in the apartments of the Duke Valentino in the Apostolic Palace, a supper, participated in by fifty honest prostitutes of those who were called courtesans. After supper they danced with the servants and others who were there, first clothed, then naked. After supper the lighted candelabra, which had been on the table, were placed on the floor, and chestnuts thrown among them which the prostitutes had to pick up as they crawled between the candles. The Pope, the Duke, and Lucretia, his sister, were present looking on. At the end they displayed prizes, silk mantles, boots, caps, and other objects which were promised to whomever should have made love to those prostitutes the greatest number of times, and they were then publicly enjoyed in the same room.[20]

It's hard to imagine anything closer to the definition of an orgy. And these scenes, worthy of a decadent Roman emperor, took place in holy palaces. A few days later Burchard refers to the other episode, of two mares brought to the palace:

> Four stallions were then freed from their reins and harness and let out of the palace stables. They immediately ran to the mares, over whom they proceeded to fight furiously and noisily among themselves, biting and kicking in their attempts to mount them and seriously wounding them with their hoofs. The Pope and Madonna Lucretia, laughing and with evident satisfaction, watched all that was happening from a window above the palace gate.[21]

Rumors of this circulated throughout Italy, and Duke Ercole found them slightly disturbing. He continued to delay, although it's unclear if this was on account of his family's opposition to the marriage or, more probably, in hopes that a long wait would increase the bride's dowry. In the middle of December 1501, his emissaries in Rome were able to assure him that:

> The portion will consist of three hundred thousand ducats, not counting the presents which Madonna will receive from time to

time. First a hundred thousand ducats are to be paid in money in instalments [*sic*] in Ferrara. Then there will be silverware to the value of three thousand ducats; jewels, fine linen, costly trappings for horses and mules, together worth another hundred thousand. In his wardrobe she has a trimmed dress worth more than fifteen thousand ducats, and two hundred costly shifts, some of which are worth a hundred ducats apiece; the sleeves alone of some of them cost thirty ducats each, being trimmed with gold fringe. . . . It is said that more gold has been prepared and sold here in Naples in six months than has been used heretofore in two years. . . . The number of horses and persons the Pope will place at his daughter's disposal will amount to a thousand.[22]

Faced with such figures Ercole d'Este, known for his greed, decided he could overlook his future daughter-in-law's bad reputation; at the same time a political alliance with the pope seemed more convenient than any of the alternatives. On December 9, 1501, the guard of honor, led by his son, Cardinal Ippolito d'Este, left Ferrara for Rome to escort the bride. It took fourteen days on horseback, in the cold of winter, to reach Saint Peter's city, but the reception was splendid—perhaps the most magnificent Alexander had ever arranged, excepting his own coronation. In the basements of the Vatican, bankers from Ferrara counted the dowry, ducat by ducat, verifying not only the amount, but also the weight of the coins. It's quite possible that the gold coins were "shaved," or scraped lightly to remove some of the gold, which could then be sold on the side. The dowry was then locked in sealed chests and sat in storage until it could be shipped to Ferrara.

As all this happened, the impression Ippolito and Ercole's other envoys had of Lucretia radically changed. One batch of messages delivered to the duke brought the good news that his future daughter-in-law was a woman who "had much grace in everything, with modesty, beauty, and honesty." They continued, "we are impressed by her goodness, decency, modesty, and discretion," and "there are excellent reasons to be satisfied by this illustrious lady, perfect in manner and habit," and so on. Great dowry, great bride—what more could he want?

The wedding had already been celebrated four months earlier by proxy, but the pope wanted the rites repeated in an appropriately regal fashion. Lucretia arrived at Saint Peter's on December 30, by torchlight, at the center of an impressive procession ending with a hundred pages dressed in gold livery. Another of Ercole's sons, Don Ferrante, put his finger on the wedding ring, and then Ippolito, very elegant in his scarlet cardinal's robes, gave her a box of jewels valued at more than 70,000 ducats, at least according to the quick calculations of Antonio Pallavicini, Cardinal of Santa Prassede.

The festivities continued the following day, and included a bull-fight in Saint Peter's Square. The matador was none other than Cesare himself, and after some bold maneuvers, to the spectators' great delight and amid enthusiastic cries, he killed two bulls.

On January 6, 1502, Lucretia, not yet twenty-two, left Rome for the last time and headed to a new city and new life. We'll leave her at this point, with an emotional seventy-year-old pope waving her one last good-bye from the loggia above. A light snow fell in the grey winter air as a phalanx of Roman knights escorted her along the Via Flaminia as far as the Milvian Bridge. They stopped there, and the impressive wedding procession headed for Ferrara continued, vanishing into the snowy white.

For anyone curious about the fate of such characters, I'll add that Lucretia passed her most glorious (and perhaps happiest) years in Ferrara, where in 1505, upon the death of her father-in-law, she became duchess. Her husband may have loved her, and in any case the union was blessed, as they say, by the birth of several children, some of whom survived. Lucretia became a patroness of the arts and artists.

The famous poet Pietro Bembo dedicated adoring verses to her, signs of a love that was perhaps carnal as well as spiritual. A lock of her hair was found amongst his papers, a token laden with affectionate allusions. Once she passed thirty she retired more often to a convent, even though her husband, Alfonso, had charged her with administering the city in his absence. Lucretia died at only thirty-nine on June 24, 1519, after giving birth to yet another child, a still-born girl. Two days earlier she had written a moving letter to Pope Leo X asking for his blessing:

> Most Holy Father . . . with every reverence of spirit I kiss the holy feet of Your Beatitude. . . . Having suffered greatly for more than two

months because of a difficult pregnancy; as it has pleased God on the 14 of this month at dawn I had a daughter: and I hoped that, having given birth, illness must also be alleviated: but the contrary happened: so I must yield to nature: Our most clement Creator has given me so many gifts, that I recognize the end of my life and feel that within a few hours I shall be out of it . . . as a Christian although a sinner, it came to me to beseech your Beatitude that through your benignity you might deign to give from the spiritual Treasury some suffrage with your holy benediction to my soul . . . In Ferrara, the 22 day of June, 1519, at the fourteenth hour. The humble servant of your Beatitude, Lucretia da Este.[23]

Her father, Alexander VI, had died in 1503, not long after his beloved daughter left Rome. Her brother Cesare died in 1507 at the age of thirty-two, and his end befitted the life he'd led as a clever and sinister adventurer. Abandoned by the King of France, and seeing his dream of a Kingdom of Romagna vanish before his very eyes, he entered the service of his brother-in-law, Juan d'Albret, King of Navarre, who sent him to fight Louis of Beaumont outside of Viana, near Pamplona. Cesare was drawn into (or perhaps voluntarily threw himself into) a trap during a furious nocturnal assault, pushed by the sheer sadness that, amid his other excesses, had characterized his life. Isolated from his soldiers, he took on several of the enemy alone. He was first wounded, then unsaddled, and finally pierced by a pike, stripped of his fancy armor, and thrown into a ditch—the nude cadaver of a man Machiavelli had seen as the possible unifier of the Italian peninsula.

Notice of her brother's death reached Lucretia while she was busy with affairs of state in Ferrara. She replied with scant words of ostentatious resignation, or perhaps mere ambiguity: "The more I try to please God, the more he tries me. Thanks be to God, I am content with what pleases him."

---

1. Ferdinand Gregorovius, *Lucretia Borgia*, trans. John L. Garner (New York: D. Appleton, 1903), xvii.

2. Alexandre Dumas, *The Borgias* (Project Gutenburg e-book, released August 15, 2006: http://www.gutenberg.org/catalog/world/readfile?fk_files=97831&pageno=1)

3. Although Rodrigo Borgia had several illegitimate children before the family he began with Vannozza, the terms first-born, second-born, etc., here refer to the children she bore him.

4. Gregorovius, 1903, 14.

5. Francesco Giucciardini, *History of Italy*, trans. Sidney Alexander (Princeton: Princeton University Press, 1969), 3–4.

6. Gregorovius, 1903, 11.

7. Ibid., 69-70.

8. Sarah Bradford, *Lucrezia Borgia. Life, Love and Death in Renaissance Italy* (New York: Viking Press, 2004), 35.

9. Gregorovius, 1903, 36.

10. Bradford, 2004, 41–42.

11. Ibid., 46.

12. Gregorovius, 1903, 95-96.

13. Ibid., 60-61.

14. Ibid., 104.

15. Bradford, 2004, 59.

16. Gregorovius, 1903, 147–48.

17. Ibid., 148.

18. Bradford, 2004, 90.

19. Gregorovius, 1903, 158.

20. Bradford, 2004, 120–121.

21. Ibid., 122.

22. Gregorovius, 1902, 207–8.

23. Bradford, 2004, 365.

XI

THE RISE OF THE BOURGEOISIE

THE MOST CONTROVERSIAL MONUMENT in Rome is undoubtedly the Vittoriano, also known as the Altar of the Nation, in the Piazza Venezia. This mountain of dazzling white marble, an immense theatrical set, is loaded with symbolism that, to many people, is as incomprehensible as numerous other aspects of state, history (even recent history), and collective memory. Right from the start its saga was filled with some fairly unclear aspects, and it's only grown more complicated as another meaning was laid over the original, creating a mixture of events and echoes of disparate nature and intensity.

To begin with, its name alludes not to victory, but to a specific Victor—King Vittorio Emanuele II—portrayed as the proud, stern, bellicose man in the equestrian statue perched atop an enormous pedestal at the center of the entire scene. He died of pneumonia in 1878, before his sixtieth birthday, and the monument was originally designed in his honor. The statue is so big that sixteen workers held a banquet inside the horse's belly a few days before the monument's inauguration. A famous photograph shows them with broad smiles as they raise their glasses toward the lens in a toast. The situation soon changed, and a decade or so later the "great king" was forced to share his monument with a second important figure, the Unknown Soldier. The latter's presence, especially after the fall of the monarchy in 1946, was destined to overshadow that of the king.

The Vittoriano was dedicated in an opening ceremony on June 4, 1911, a rainy morning despite the swiftly approaching summer. Later on the sun came out, as did the royal family, accompanied by ministers of state and other high officials, who smoothly ascended the staircase to the stage on the monument's lower terrace. The ladies flaunted the season's latest millinery fashions, the little princes and princesses were dressed in sailor suits, and a few parasols were opened for shade. The dignitaries were flanked by wings of trade unionists, war veterans, soldiers, marching bands with bright brass instruments glinting in the sun, and a big crowd.

In keeping with a deeply rooted national tradition, not even this solemn occasion could occur without the requisite public debate: socialists expressed reservations about the monument's appropriateness; republicans scheduled a separate demonstration that same afternoon at the statue of Garibaldi on the Janiculum Hill, which thousands of people attended; and Freemasons distributed bitterly anticlerical pamphlets pointing out that the new monument rose up "in sight of the ever-vigilant and expectant Vatican," a sort of lay counterpart to the unsettling cupola of Saint Peter's.

One of the most significant speeches at the monument's inauguration was delivered by Rome's mayor, Ernesto Nathan, who was also an anticlerical Freemason, follower of Mazzini, and a progressive. Nathan was born in London and didn't become an Italian citizen until he was about forty years old. Elected mayor of the capital—one of the best the city has ever had—he was an advocate of public housing and educating all, including the city's poorest. That morning, among other things, he proclaimed, "This impressive mass rising atop the Capitoline Hill as the Altar of the Nation is not just a monument to the king, but symbolizes the dawn of the Third Italy! And while the equestrian monument of Marcus Aurelius, emperor-protector of legal rights, stands on the Capitoline Hill, that of the Gentleman King, protector of the national faith, takes up the throne in the one we have just unveiled."

Once inaugurated, the Vittoriano became the crux of a memorable year, which opened with fiftieth-anniversary celebrations of the Kingdom of Italy and closed with the war in Libya (to the notes of the song "Tripoli, bel suol d'amore"). Among the public-works projects undertaken for the national jubilee were the new Palace of Justice and the bridge connecting the Villa Borghese to the Pincian Hill, which still soars high above the Viale del Muro Torto. Large exhibitions were organized, including the international fine arts show at the Valle Giulia. Preparation for this exhibition involved the construction of a number of foreign academies, as well as the large building that later became the Galleria nazionale di arte moderna (the National Gallery of Modern Art, popularly known by it's initials, "GNAM," which also means "yum"). Two new bridges were built across the Tiber in 1911, the Ponte Flaminio (an audacious plan for that era, built of a single span of reinforced concrete) and the Ponte Vittorio Emanuele, which connected the old city with the newer residential neighborhoods across the river, as well as a lovely archaeological park. The extraordinary Naiad Fountain was installed to complete the Piazza dell'Esedra, the Castel Sant'Angelo and the Baths of Diocletian were restored, and the vast area between the Vigna Cartoni and the slopes of Monte Mario was cleared to host an exhibition in honor of the kingdom's fiftieth anniversary and prepare for future development of the Mazzini neighborhood. Putting all questions of style and taste aside, no other urban administration could have done more to prepare the city for such an international event, even if, admittedly, the major flooding of the Tiber in 1870 had convinced the government to start building the huge embankments that now contain the capricious river.

In addition to the numerous people in attendance, another presence hovered in the air around the Vittoriano that morning— the immaterial yet palpable, downright intrusive spirit of Giosuè Carducci. This bard of "La Terza Italia"—the Third Italy, mentioned in Nathan's speech, that emerged after unification—and a national poet if ever there was one, was a republican (although he wasn't hostile to the monarchy), anticlerical activist, and Freemason. The monument resembled him, and he resembled the era so visible in the monument. The idea of liberty Carducci so often extolled in his poetry is the same one that appears in Delacroix's famous painting *Liberty Leading the People*—exciting, bloody, and surrounded by smoke and commotion. Badly dressed but heroic soldiers advance over the barricades along with an old rifleman and a fearless twelve-year-old Gavroche, much like the little Lombard lookout in Edmondo De Amicis's famed novel *Cuore*. Scattered throughout the scene are weapons and flags shredded by enemy assaults. This ragtag group is led by the young, beautiful, and courageous figure of Liberty; breast bared, she holds the tricolor (of France, in this case) high above the blood and mud.

Te giova il grido che le turbe assorda
E a l'armi incalza a l'armi i cuor cessanti,
Te le civili su la ferrea corda
Ire sonanti:

E sol tra i casi de la pugna orrendi
E flutti d'aste e fulminose spade
Nel vasto sangue popolar discendi,
O libertade.

(For you, the cry that deafens turbulent crowds / And spurs weakened hearts to battle, / For you, the people's fury echoes on the iron cord. / Solely in the horrific times of brandished fists / And waving flags and fulminous swords, / Into the vast blood of the people you descend, / O Liberty.)[1]

The same spirit inspired Carducci's *Ode to Satan*, which caused furious debate when it was published:

To thee my verses,
Unbridled and daring,
Shall mount, O Satan,
King of the banquet.

Away with thy sprinkling,
O Priest, and thy droning,
For never shall Satan,
O Priest, stand behind thee.[2]

Once again a few verses manage to provoke anti-Romantic polemics; reason, progress, the imminent future, and the positive spirit of the times rise up against the surrounding smoke, be it the smoke of ecclesiastical incense or of the more pernicious, muddled, Manzoniesque metaphors:

Hail, O Satan,
O Rebellion,
O you avenging force
Of human reason![3]

Carducci writes of an Italy that no longer exists, if ever it had. His pulsing visions of civic ardor and the flames of fantasy are so plainly dated that they either touch a sentimental nerve or make us chuckle. The Vittoriano expresses the same pathos, and its marble brings back the same spirit.

"At this particular point in its history," the Socialist daily *Avanti* wrote in March of 1911, "the Italian bourgeoisie feels the need to step forward to receive the admiration of other national bourgeoisies, as well as its own." You can think whatever you want about the monument—over the years it has, in fact, been compared to a wedding cake or a spectacular typewriter. The fact remains that, at the beginning of the twentieth century, it embodied the image European nations believed they needed to project. Because it suited the prevailing taste of the times and encompassed the spirit of the period, the enormous Palace of Justice in Brussels resembles it, as does Walhalla, the German hall of fame in Regensburg, the Altes Museum in Berlin, the Opera Garnier in Paris, the arch of the State Palace in Saint Petersburg, and so many of the monumental buildings along Vienna's ring road. And, had they not been destroyed in World War II bombardments, many of Berlin's buildings would still look a lot like it. There's no question that, upon its completion in 1911, the Vittoriano was an opportunity for the small and in many ways old-fashioned Kingdom of Italy to show other nations that, despite its many contradictions, it aimed to join the continental "concert."

The monument's construction began in 1885, consumed millions of lire, and caused a number of scandals. Its architect, Giovanni Sacconi, was born near Ascoli Piceno in 1854 (he died in 1905, before his magnum opus was finished). He decided to clad the monument in white Botticino marble to create a candid contrast with the warm Roman Travertine. This stone was quarried in Rezzato, near Brescia, and the Honorable Giuseppe Zanardelli, a member of parliament from the same region, had a lot to do with that choice. A mountain of marble blocks began to descend on Rome from Brescia, and they were refined, squared, and stored near the train station in Trastevere before being sent along to the building site.

Even photographs fail to capture the extent of the massive gouge dug into the side of the Capitoline Hill to create the monument's foundations. Numerous Roman ruins were uncovered during the excavations; some were saved, others were incorporated into the Vittoriano's foundations. One of the strangest finds was the fossilized skeleton of a prehistoric elephant embedded in a stratum of clay. A few of the bones were transferred to the university's geological collection, the rest stayed where they had been found.

Large-scale demolitions preceded the excavations, and included the wonderful Tower of Paul III (a few photographs of it remain), as well as the bridge connecting it to the Palazzetto Venezia. The Ara Coeli convent was also largely destroyed—a perfectly executed amputation, but no less painful a loss. Traces of this are still evident in the lower terrace of the Vittoriano, where there is a walkway that marks, so to speak, the boundary between the new construction and the old; an impressive scar, not entirely sutured, is visible between the two buildings.

Some twenty years later, in 1931 and the following years, Mussolini ordered further demolitions in the area as he prepared for the tenth anniversary of the Fascist march on Rome. The whole area between the Coliseum and the Vittoriano, and part of the neighborhood on the Velian Hill, were completely razed to create the Via dei Fori Imperiali. Apartments, stores, and craftsmen's workshops all succumbed to the wrecking ball, and the dense fabric of modest houses gave way to a broad arterial destined to become the stage for grandiose military parades.

The idea of honoring an Unknown Soldier as representative of all soldiers killed in war was proposed by Colonel Giulio Douhet, and began a tradition adopted in many other countries. In August of 1921, parliament approved a law that allowed "the remains of an unknown soldier" to be interred in the Vittoriano. For once there was little debate, and the vote was unanimous. This decision kicked off a glorious and macabre tradition steeped in nationalist rhetoric and despair. The Great War had ended a few years before, and a commission made up of officers, non-commissioned officers, and regular soldiers visited several war cemeteries around the country to exhume the remains of war dead. They rejected any remains that could be identified by dog tags or even a regimental insignia, and then chose six unidentified bodies to be placed in matching coffins. On October 28, 1921, Maria Bergamas, mother of a missing soldier from Trieste, chose one of the coffins by throwing her black veil over it. That was the one taken to Rome, and the other five were to be buried in the cathedral of Aquileia. During the rites Maria, accompanied by four soldiers whose service was honored with the gold medal for valor, held a white flower in her hands, which she was then to set on the coffin chosen earlier. She made a mistake, and either equivocated or was overwhelmed by emotion. Instead of tossing the flower on the coffin, she draped it with her *mater dolorosa* black veil, symbol of the mourning mother. The spontaneous gesture was perfect, though, because it unconsciously underscored the depth of an inconsolable grief.

The train transporting the coffin was manned by engineers, all decorated with medals for their wartime valor, and as it crossed Italy the tracks were lined by a nearly uninterrupted line of people, many kneeling as it passed, most with tears in their eyes. Women made up the majority of the front row—filled with sorrow, mourning, in great pain—and took close part in one of the most heartfelt collective commemorations in the country's history. The rail convoy consisted of sixteen wagons, all of which became increasingly covered by wreaths and flowers. The car with the coffin was decorated with an inscription from Dante, "His shade returns that was departed," and the date, MCMXV–MCMXVIII. A solemn funeral was held upon the arrival in Rome, and then, on the morning of November 4, the coffin was taken to the monument and buried there. A banner on the front of the basilica of Santa Maria degli Angeli read, "His name unknown / his spirit shines, wherever Italy is / with a weeping yet proud voice / innumerable mothers say, / "he is my son." November 4 was then declared a national holiday.

Today the Vittoriano belongs largely to him, that poor rural infantryman who came from who knows what part of Italy, dead without wanting or knowing it, blinded by the darkness of the earth. But the monument also houses several interesting museums, including a naval museum and one dedicated to the Risorgimento. The latter is a treasure trove of objects and memorabilia of the nation's unification: Nino Blixio's pistol; the boot Garibaldi was wearing when it was pierced by a bullet at Aspromonte, as well as the bullet extracted from his wound; photos of the Mille, Garibaldi's thousand troops; busts; swords; glorious flags; diaries; and the memories of an epic period we're all descendants of, even if the many feelings surrounding our common past sometimes seem to tarnish it.

At one point there was a plan to demolish the Vittoriano, and proposals were submitted to use it in a variety of different ways, or just to let it grow over with plants, transforming it into a sort of marble forest. I think it's fine as it is—actually, I find it quite beautiful. Regardless of what you might think about it, it nevertheless remains a testament of sorts to the ambitions of a newborn Italy; it's a picture of what the kingdom wanted to be when it "grew up." It's a gigantic snapshot of the germinating national spirit, a dedication to future memory in which, unfortunately, it's not always easy to recognize ourselves.

Not everyone has a good impression of what Rome was in the early twentieth century; the transformations wrought by the arrival of the "Italians" and the city's designation as new national capital were enormous. The small breach Captain Alessandro La Marmora's cannonade made in the walls of Rome, about 100 meters west of the Porta Pia, was in itself more symbolic than militarily significant, yet that small opening in the walls let fresh air enter the ancient city for the first time in ages. That cannonball ended centuries of isolation in Rome, and in only a few years—almost a matter of months—life was so transformed that it was actually traumatic for many of Rome's citizens.

Everything changed: the population suddenly began to grow; the city's urban fabric expanded, covering what had until recently been vineyards, pastures, and light forest with houses and streets; incomes rose, and customs changed; finally, even the language changed, as did pastimes, work and leisure schedules, and even the types of crime.

In the first two years after the walls were breached at Porta Pia the city's population grew by 10 percent, and over the following years its rate of growth steadily increased. Within thirty years (according to the 1901 census) the number of Roman citizens had increased by 150 percent, surpassing half a million inhabitants. Fewer than half (46 percent) were born in Rome, and the new arrivals pouring in through the breach included officials, office workers, merchants, professionals, politicians, journalists, and a fair number of speculators who'd made a lucky guess at all the business that could be done—much of it with public funds. The plebian masses were changing as well, or at least were about to change. One journalist wrote, "Today's rabble is not what it was one hundred years ago, or even half a century ago. Time changes everything, an incessant wave of civilization is penetrating everywhere, and not even the priests could halt it at the gates of Rome."

But the greatest change, lagging a good century or so behind other capital cities, was that even Rome began to have a middle class. Under papal dominion the city's population consisted of nobles, priests, and the poor. With the arrival of the *Piemontesi* (the Piedmont troops, Garibaldi, and Cavour) and modern public administration, an intermediate class was created, which would soon become the engine of further changes affecting everything from lifestyle to politics, publishing, and the performing arts.

In a well-mannered chronicle from that period I found a profile of a "middle-class" interior: "The maid, in her large white apron, was intent on ironing Grandfather's starched collars with a charcoal iron; gold buttons attached the collar to a shirt and regularly slipped out of his hand. The buttons made me think of my father, who wandered through the house, moustache curlers immobilizing his lips . . . while my mother was seated in a dressing gown before her vanity, brushing out her long braids." This domestic scene is already imbued with the atmosphere of Turin, or maybe Paris, or some city more continental than Rome, at any rate.

One of the bourgeoisie's main ambitions was a *buon partito*, a "good catch" for marrying off their daughters. For a long time the plate glass windows of the Ronzi & Singer café, at the corner of the Corso and the Piazza Colonna, was called the "Campo Vaccino"—the name originally given to the cattle market that occupied part of the Roman Forum—because of the ostentatious display Roman matrons made of their marriageable daughters there. Foreign wives were also in vogue, "Russian girls, pale, plaintive, and passionate, came, as did English ones, who were tall, educated, rich or poor, and sometimes just extravagant, some looking for a husband and taking advantage of the craze that now reaches all the way down to the *travetti*, the bureaucratic class, to marry any kind of foreign woman, as a millionaire should." The *travetti*, based on the French term for the mass of public-sector employees, had already defined, for better or worse, one of Rome's chief characteristics. One fierce critic observed, "*Travettismo* really means a crowd of beggars in ministerial get-up."

Naturally the birth of the modern city came at a certain price. The heftiest and most painful, due to its spectacular nature, was the criminal destruction of Villa Boncompagni Ludovisi. It now takes great effort to imagine the area of the Via Veneto, and the surrounding streets running from the Porta Pinciana to just beyond Palazzo Margherita (now the American Embassy), all covered by a centuries-old park decorated with statues and temples of such majesty and beauty that they inspired Henry James to remark on their beauty. The area was divided into lots by the owners, setting an atrocious precedent that would certainly have been followed by the Borghese princes, if it weren't for the lucky addition of a few legal stipulations to their deed just in time to stop them.

In the preface I mentioned the book *Dame al Macao* by Alberto Arduini, a refined antiquarian with a shop on the Via Frattina that later moved to the Piazza di Spagna, next door to the Keats-Shelley House. The writer Ennio Flaiano maliciously described him as "the only Roman mentioned in Gide's *Journal*," referring to the French author's notorious homosexuality. The Rome described by Arduini was more likely a desire than reality, yet it was a city that had the character and visionary imprint Arduini described, though it only existed in literature. We need to go back thirty years, from 1911 to 1881, to the moment one particular eighteen-year-old lad first set foot in Rome. His last name would have been Rapagnetta, had his father not permanently assumed the name of the relatives who had adopted him— D'Annunzio. Recalling his arrival, the young Gabriele described the Rome of those feverish years:

> It was a time when the busy occupations of demolisher and builder were most turbidly fervent. Along with clouds of dust a sort of building craze swept through the city, with sudden whirlwinds. . . . It was everywhere, like a veritable contagion of vulgarity. In the incessant clashes of business, the almost ferocious furies of appetite and emotion, and the exclusive, disorganized practice of "useful activity," all aesthetic sense and all respect for the past were utterly deposed.

Rome attracted the young poet, or, to use one of his terms, it bewitched him. D'Annunzio looked around as he left his modest lodging at Via Borgognona 12, and everything looked lovely to him, worthy of being retold in writing. He enrolled at the university, in the department of literature, which had been his original reason for coming to the capital, but he spent a lot more time at salons and newspaper editorial offices than in class. A few weeks after he arrived the fashionable periodical *Cronaca bizantina* published one of his sonnets.

Rome's residences and houses, the city's outskirts—all of it attracted him. Above all, women fascinated him, awaking within him a highly sensual temperament. In February of 1883 he met Maria Hardouin di Gallese, fell in love with her, and three months later, after an evening walk through the Villa Borghese, they made love. The poet rushed to tell all in a short poem, *Il peccato di maggio* (*May's Sin*):

> Or così fu; pe'l bosco andando. Era sottile
> la mia compagna e bionda. Su la nuca infantile
> due ciocche . . .

(So it went, wandering through the forest. My companion / was slim and blond. On the youthful nape of her neck / were two fine tresses . . .)

The two strolled together, arms entwined, tender, and aware—it's easy to assume something was about to happen. Something, indeed:

> . . . La testa
> in dietro a l'improvviso abbandonò. Le chiome
> effuse le composero un serto ov'ella, come
> per morire, si stese. Un irrigidimento
> quasi un gelo di morte, l'occupò. Lo spavento
> m'invase . . .
> Ma fu morte
> breve. Tornò la vita ne l'onda del piacere.
> Chino a lei su la bocca io tutto, come a bere
> da un calice, fremendo di conquista, sentivo
> le punte del suo petto insorgere, al lascivo
> tentar de le mie dita, quali carnosi fiori . . .

(. . . head / tilted back, suddenly in full abandon, her loose locks / composed a wreath where she, as if / about to die, lay down. A rigidity, / a near deathly freeze, overcame her. Fright / filled my veins . . . / But such death / was brief. Life returned in a wave of pleasure. / I bent above her mouth as if to drink / from a chalice, shivering at such conquest, I felt / the tips of her breast rise at the lascivious / searching of my fingertips, carnal flowers . . .)[4]

And so on. More than a poem, this is running commentary fit for radio broadcast. But because, at heart, it describes the intimacy of two "poor lovers" consummated behind the cover of a bush on a lawn of the Villa Borghese, we see just how gifted the young writer was at imagining and transforming. A well-timed wedding followed. In his own way, Gabriele loved his wife. His own way meant transforming the marriage into a relationship of convenience, separated from both his artistic pursuits and his numerous ties to other women.

If we choose to view D'Annunzio as a turn-of-the-century chronicler, we easily see how quickly the lives of certain Roman classes became modern, uninhibited, and even licentious. Here's his description of a woman undressing, a study in feminine sensuality:

> She begins with slow, languid, sometimes hesitant gestures, stopping from time to time as if to listen for something. She removes her fine silk stockings
> . . . and then unties the ribbon at her shoulder, which holds the last bit of clothing, her softest, most precious blouse. . . . The snow of this blouse flows across her breast, follows the arch of her loins, stops for a moment at her hips, and then falls at once to her feet, like a spray of sea foam. . . .

The poet gave the nascent bourgeoisie in Rome (and the whole country) the primary material with which to construct their erotic fantasies. In describing certain situations he also contributed to creating them; this happened when he transferred these visions into his narrative masterpiece, *Il piacere*, initially published in 1889 and later published in English as *The Child of Pleasure*. His disturbing female protagonist, Elena Muti, was based on two models: the Neapolitan journalist Olga Ossiani, who signed works with the pseudonym Febea and was his first lover after he wed; and Elvira Natalia Fraternali, a woman one year his senior, with whom he had a relationship of almost total and unlimited sensual harmony. Elvira—who he called Barbara or Barbarella, and took the last name Leoni after a brief and unhappy marriage—was the one woman who, of his many lovers, best knew how to satisfy his predilections. Their amorous trysts occurred on an almost daily basis between April and June 1887, and took place in two studios of his friends, one in Via San Nicola da Tolentino, the other in Via de' Prefetti. This passionate affair lasted for five years. Here is an excerpt from one of the hundreds of letters he wrote her:

> When I think back to the kisses I gave you all over your body— on your small, perky breast; on your belly, perfect as the statue of a

virgin; on the rose as warm, alive, and soft on my lips as your mouth; on your thigh, soft as velvet, with the taste of succulent fruit; on your knees, which you tried in vain to deny me, laughing and writhing; in the fold of your knees, so delicate, soft, and childlike; on your golden back, scattered with golden beads, marked by a furrow where my tongue runs quick and wet in sweet caress; on your loins, and your marvelously beautiful thighs; on your neck, and your hair, and on your long, palpitating eyelashes; on your throat—when I think of the wave of joy that flowed through my veins when I so much as looked at you, nude, I shiver, burn, and tremble. . . .

What a difference from the rustic, brutal couplings of common-ers written about only a few decades earlier in Belli's work. Those primitive actions were replaced by the delights of seduction, the coarse clothes of common folk changed for the rustling of fine fab-rics, perfumes, and suggestive penumbra. D'Annunzio initiated a cult of sensuality that continued through the course of time, often adapt-ing to custom, and more often anticipating it.

Pietro Pancrazi, after thorough research, outlined the kind of life and events D'Annunzio described, "The receptions, auctions, foxhunts, streets, shops, concerts, fencing schools, the silvery shine of the courts, and the feathers that decorated the large hats of 'Tiberine ladies' [Roman women] all made up the choir of its [Rome's] grand ballet."

There are "interior" scenes that correspond to "exterior" ones, equally indicative of the era. In his essay "D'Annunzio arredatore," Mario Praz discovered that these interiors and their furnishings painted a picture of strongly contrasting colors—Chinese vases, pseudo-Renaissance bronzes, musical instruments, ivories, arms, bits of Baroque altars, busts, sarcophagi, coats-of-arms, velvets, metal bra-ziers, carpets, animal skins, African weapons, consoles, screens, fans, and palms.[5] D'Annunzio created rooms and furnishings that con-tributed to forming the taste of much of the Italian middle class for decades to follow, but he also painted wonderful verbal pictures of the enchanted Rome he saw, or imagined, around him. Here are two instances from The Child of Pleasure, one sunny, the other rainy:

On this May morning Rome shone resplendent under the caressing sun. Here a fountain lit up with its silvery laughter a little piazzetta still plunged in shadow; there the open gates of a palace disclosed a vista of courtyard with a background of portico and statues; from the baroque architecture of a brick church hung the decorations for the month of May. Under the bridge, the Tiber gleamed and glistened as it hurried away between the gray-green houses towards the island of San Bartolomeo. After a short ascent, the whole city spread out before them, immense, imperial, radiant, bristling with spires and columns and obelisks, crowned with cupolas and rotundas, clean cut out of the blue like a citadel.[6]

. . .

It was raining. Andrea went to the window and stood for some time looking out upon his beloved Rome. The piazza of the Trinità dei Monti was solitary and deserted, left to the guardianship of its obelisk. . . . And as he gazed, one sentiment dominated all the others in his heart; the sudden and lively reawakening of his old love for Rome—fairest Rome. . . . On the distant heights the gray deepened gradually to amethyst. . . . Under this rich autumnal light everything took on a sumptuous air. Divine Rome![7]

D'Annunzio didn't ignore the fact that the oases of refined comfort his characters inhabited were surrounded by a sea of degradation and misery. The suburbs, crowded with the city's newest immigrants, and the Roman countryside were still those Belli described with such dark realism. D'Annunzio's aestheticism prevented him from really absorbing those aspects of life (except where they could be used to express disdain), but he did record them with a chronicler's precision. In the following scene Elena and Andrea, the two protagonists of *The Child of Pleasure*, go to an inn for a glass of water during a horseback ride in the Roman countryside:

The people of the inn showed not the faintest sign of surprise at the entry of the two strangers. Two or three men shivering with ague, morose and jaundiced, were crouching round a square brazier. A red-haired bullock-driver was snoring in a corner, his empty pipe still between his teeth. . . . The woman of the inn, corpulent to obesity, carried in her arms a child which she rocked heavily to and fro.

While Elena drank the water out of a rude earthenware mug, the woman, with wails and plaints, drew her attention to the wretched infant.

"Look—signora mia—look at it!"

The poor little creature was wasted to a skeleton. . . .[8]

One of the driving forces behind the new life animating Rome was Queen Margherita, wife (and cousin) of King Umberto I. For a quarter century Margherita was the true engine of Rome's worldliness, and she was certainly the regal figure more suited to the role than any other the Kingdom of Italy ever had; she was the first queen in a city that, for centuries on end, had been ruled by bachelor kings. Margherita opened new hospitals, gave highly frequented receptions, offered patronage to writers and poets, and when her carriage drove up the Corso it met with large applause. Despite her conservative ideas she performed a priceless service of branding and public relations, as we would say today, for the kingdom, the Sabauda Dynasty, and the city of Rome itself.

Following her example and driven by complex national events, life in Rome was enlivened by an attempt to conform to other European capitals. New neighborhoods rose up, and the sea of buildings made for an ever-increasing population including a few eccentricities that are also stylistically interesting. The self-taught architect Armando Brasini built a curious castle of sorts, at Via Flaminia 489, from materials salvaged from buildings demolished in the historic center. It is a complex of towers, pinnacles, spires, and buttresses, but comes closer to something from a fairy tale than anything truly medieval. Eugène Viollet-le-Duc had done something similar in France about ten years earlier, using his restoration projects to reinvent a canon of Gothic architecture.

Gino Coppedè did much the same thing when he built a whole neighborhood in the early 1920s. He constructed about forty small apartment buildings and houses in a rectangular area of over seven acres along the Via Tagliamento. In a city where building patterns were often disorderly, the Coppedè neighborhood was distinguished by its sense of unity and the rationality of its urban design. Coppedè took the so-called eclectic style that flourished at the turn of the century to its extreme. His designs borrowed genially from any and everything, giving the results a fantastical quality: pinnacles, spires, balconies, small towers, hobnailed doors, and heavily embossed street lamps. Two key buildings on the Piazza Mincio, the so-called Ambassadors' Palaces, were joined by a huge arch decorated with a mask, giving the piazza a theatrical backdrop. The Frog Fountain is at the piazza's center, and is a reworking of the theme of the famous Turtle Fountain in the Piazza Mattei; local lore claimed this was the meeting place of witches. The Palazzo del Ragno was named after the spider motif in the mosaic decoration framing its doorways. The spider was seen as a silent and indefatigable weaver, and was hence a symbol of industriousness repeated in architectural decoration. The Villino delle Fate, or House of the Fairies, was enlivened with frescoes that recall a sort of mythical Renaissance Florence more imaginary than real. It's not difficult to see the models the architect was drawing on in each of the buildings—medieval castles, Swiss chalets, Victorian mansions—creating a sort of eclectic architectural folly that has gained an evocative patina over the last century.

Equestrian sports were imported from England, and the upper bourgeoisie and so-called white nobility—the new aristocracy created by the Kingdom of Italy, as opposed to the so-called black nobility created by the popes—began to attend races at the track of Capannelle, Tor di Quinto, and the Villa Gloria. The lugubrious, deserted countryside was suddenly enlivened by the passing thunder of foxhunts. Clubs for chess and hunting opened in town, and exclusive salons appeared. Rome, now populated by huge numbers of foreigners, had two courts, one belonging to the pope, the other to the Savoia. It also had two diplomatic corps, and for a few decades the Roman nobility was split between two allegiances that many felt were irreconcilable—the throne and the altar. In January of 1875 Pope Pius IX (Giovanni Mastai Ferretti), now prisoner of his own reactionary positions, exhorted the nobility "to abstain from public activities," recommending them to "stay in your houses and attend to your domestic responsibilities." Most of the aristocrats loyal to him—the Aldobrandini, Altieri, Barberini, Borghese, Chigi, Corsini, Lancellotti, Massimo, Orsini, Patrizi, Rospigliosi, Salviati, Soderini, and Theodoli families—did just that. Others, however, came to terms with the new regime, and included the Boncompagni, Ludovisi, Cesarini Sforza, Colonna, Doria, Odescalchi, and Santafiora families.

These problems were lessened, though they didn't entirely disappear, when the pope died, which remarkably happened just a few weeks after the death of Vittorio Emanuele II. The king, who'd been excommunicated after the fall of Rome, died at the Quirinal Palace on January 9, 1878, and even after his death he was attacked by the most extremist Catholic newspapers. When the pope died, on February 7, the atmosphere was so tense that Cardinal Manning, Archbishop of Westminster, feared the worst, and suggested the conclave be held in Malta. Rumors about reprisals the Freemasons were planning for when the pope's corpse went on public display ran rampant throughout Rome, but nothing happened. Nevertheless, the fear was real enough that the maintenance of public order was entrusted to a battalion of infantrymen. Many people wanted to pay their last respects to the pope, each in his or her own way. The police official Giuseppe Manfroni wrote in his memoirs that, while the faithful waited patiently in line to pay homage to the dead pontiff, "court ladies, secretary generals, other ministry officials, senators, and deputies with their families," as well as members of the papal nobility, entered the basilica by a side door.

The religious "black" nobility's estrangement from the new state soon vanished. Sooner or later everyone understood that the pope, deprived of his power, could only promise them the distant blessings of heaven, while the new regime offered more immediate and promising business opportunities, especially when it sold former agricultural land, valued at its weight in gold, for real estate development.

In this same period the demand for spectacle and entertainment also increased. Because not everyone could be received at court or in noble palaces, several public venues for entertainment opened, a novelty the city had never had before. The first *café-chantant*, or music hall, opened in the early 1880s, and with it came many *kellerine* and *sciantose* (Roman corruptions of the German *Kellnerin* and French *chanteuse*, respectively), the women who sang in the new clubs. For a little while café-concerts, with musical entertainment provided solely by an orchestra, competed with the *café-chantant*. As a note on the concerts dated 1893 reports, "songs in Roman dialect are all the rage. At the Cornelio, now impeccably adapted for the orchestra of the wonderful maestro Alberto Cavanna, there is, and always will be, loud applause from the refined public." Queen Margherita, the beloved of all Italians, had both a theater and a Neapolitan pizza named after her. There was even a music hall named for Umberto I; the rest of the variety halls resorted to the usual exotic names—Alhambra, Trianon, Olympia, Eden, Kursaal, and Alcazar.

The peculiarity of the *café-chantant* was that theater seating was replaced by small tables in an interior decorated with velvet and mirrors and beneath a ceiling populated with amorous stucco allegories. Thus, while the variety artist or chanteuse was performing on stage, the hall was filled with the constant bustling of waiters and animated conversations. This atmosphere encouraged exchanges between the audience and the stage, the public and the artists. These were lively places, popular providers of a mild eroticism that was just enough to satisfy the peaceful middle class's modest hunger for transgression and bad behavior, and seem to have come straight out of a Maupassant story. Because they were so popular these cafés also had relentless critics. In the *Almanacco Italiano* of 1899 we read that "the *café-chantant* has caused immense damage to the theatre. It has corrupted taste and spoiled the very character of the theatres themselves." (This is more or less the same accusation now aimed at television with respect to the movie industry.)

The dynamic entrepreneur Domenico Costanzi opened the new opera house in November 1880, in the city's so-called De Merode neighborhood. It had twenty-two hundred seats, the most advanced staging technology of the time, splendid lights, and broad foyers. It opened on the evening of the 27th with a performance of Rossini's *Semiramide*. The public admitted that there was no comparison with the older Roman theaters (Tor di Nona, Argentina, and Valle), and complained only about the fact that "Il Costanzi," as the opera house came to be called, was built all the way at the top of the Via Nazionale, far away from everything.

Cultural life also improved. La Sapienza, the historic University of Rome, was expanded, the musical academy of Santa Cecilia and the Accademia dei Lincei were restored, and a science laboratory destined for a glorious future opened on the Via Panisperna. Innovative art shows opened at the new Palazzo delle Esposizioni, an enormous exhibition hall on the Via Nazionale, and archaeological excavations and the creation of parks intensified.

Let's be clear, though—deep down Rome remained the same old skeptical and uncultured city it's always been and always will be. Rumors about speculators manipulating public works projects spread, and veritable scandals erupted. All told, however, the Third Rome of Umberto I and city politician Giovanni Giolitti was culturally more lively and better suited to its times than papal Rome ever had been, and more adapted than Fascist Rome or the post–World War II city of the Christian Democrats would be.

There's just one last aspect of this period I'd like to mention—its major court trials. Crime and judicial news is always a powerful way to see the reality hidden beneath the official veneer. The birth of a new Rome, accompanied by an overwhelming shift in behavior, a rapid increase in population, and the beginning of numerous public and private building projects, couldn't help but leave a significant mark in the legal record books.

The most outrageous scandal at the end of the nineteenth century was, without a doubt, the one at the Banca Romana. Its president, Bernardo Tanlongo, was nominated senator on the eve of the announcement of sensational charges against him. It had come to light that the bank, which was among the few authorized to print paper money, had put into circulation a double series of bills with the same serial numbers. This was the most conspicuous part of a vast web of fraud. It was clear, when the affair was completely unraveled, that the banks highest officials, as well as other bankers, politicians, and journalists were all involved.

On January 21, 1893, the *Corriere della Sera* described Bernardo Tanlongo, star of the scandal, as having "never been a ladies man, he never gambles, he is the antithesis of elegance, and his frugality closely resembles avarice." Tanlongo, called "Sor Bernà" by his close friends, was seventy-three years old, always dressed in worn-out clothes, and had grown up in the Rome of the "pope-kings," where he learned every type of trickery. The citywide scheming intensified in the feverish building boom following unification in 1870. In Garibaldi's Rome Tanlongo acted as a spy for the French, and when the political winds shifted, he sought favor with both the Jesuits and the Freemasons. He leant the bank's money with shrewd wisdom, taking special care of his own interests, and secretly adjusted the bank's books. When it became clear that accounting tricks were no longer enough to hide its stunning deficit of 28 million lire, he began to sign double banknotes with the complicity of the bank's treasurer and his own son.

The real "insurance" he was counting on, though, was the information kept in his own files. When the *Corriere della Sera* interviewed him on the eve of his arrest, Tanlongo spoke clearly; "if they want to hold me responsible for crimes I didn't commit, I will be forced to create a scandal." Parliamentary members Francesco Crispi and Giovanni Giolitti, who nurtured a mutual hatred, understood the message and began a race to see who would be the first to blame the other for having known about the mess and covering it up. Tanlongo, not surprisingly, was acquitted at the end of July 1894, providing further proof that only simpletons, chicken thieves, and those foolish enough to have neglected preparing a defense for their crimes ended up in jail. This scandal still resonates in the history of fiscal crime, as it anticipated our own corrupt "modernity."

Great interest was also stirred up by several trials for individual, semi-private crimes, generally of a sexual nature. One good example is the political-marital scandal that led to the murder of Raffaele Sonzogno, publisher of *La Capitale* newspaper. The trial for the murder of "Countess Lara," the pseudonym aesthete Eva Cattermole Mancini used to sign her "D'Annunziesque" poety, was also closely followed. Daughter of an Englishman and a Russian woman, Lara wrote a column called "il Salotto della signora" ("The Lady's Salon") in the tabloid *La Tribuna Illustrata*. She was best known, however, for her highly active and tempestuous love life. Married at a young age, she separated from her husband when he killed one of her lovers in a duel. She quickly replaced him with numerous other lovers, and in the end one of them killed her.

The notorious "Fadda Trial" excited public curiosity and was also of great interest to journalists. It even caught Giosuè Carducci's attention, and he wrote an off-the-cuff essay about it included in his collection *Giambi ed epodi* (Iambics and Epodes). The indignant poet wrote, "The deliberations of the trial held in Rome from September 20 to October 21, 1879, for the assassination of Captain Fadda, committed by Riding Master Cardinali at the instigation and with the assistance of Raffaella Saraceni, the captain's wife and the riding master's lover, had, among the enormous crowd that attended it, a large number of matrons and maidens from the best families of Roman society." Scandalized by this excessive and morbid interest, Carducci shot off fiery verses condemning the hypocrisy of the many women present in the courtroom.

This was Rome in the years between the *bersaglieri*'s entry into the city at the Porta Pia in 1870 and the inauguration of the monument to Vittorio Emanuele II in 1911. In this period the old city finally entered the modern era, although it held on to many peculiar traits, including some major defects in the collective behavior of its inhabitants. Reading the newspapers reveals a situation no better or worse than that of any other great European city, though there was an extra sense of anxiety, as if the city wanted to make up quickly for lost time while the rest of the world rushed toward the future.

Looking at these people and events with a comfortably distanced hindsight, we can clearly see, in their nascent state, many of the characteristics that still distinguish the city. In those forty years Rome shed its skin; the city, along with the whole country, gained a secular ruling class, political representation, and the middle class that had been absent for centuries, which brought with it real productive activities. All these small, laborious moments of grandeur and remarkable misfortune made Rome what it is today.

---

1. Giosuè Carducci, *Opere di G. Carducci VI, Juvenilia e Levia gravia* (Bologna: Zanichelli, 1891). No English translation of this volume has yet been published.

2. Giosuè Carducci, *Poems*, trans. Frank Sewall (New York: Dodd, Mead & Co., 1892), 58.

3. Giosuè Carducci, *Poems*, trans. David H. Higgins (Warminster: Aris & Phillips Ltd., 1994), 35.

4. Gabriele D'Annunzio, *Il peccato di maggio*; this poem hasn't been published in English translation, but is discussed in the Italian edition of Salvatore Quasimodo's *Poesie e discorsi sulla poesia*, edited with an introduction by Gilberto Finzi (Milan: Mondadori, 1971), 256–57.

5. Mario Praz, "D'Annunzio arredatore," in *La botte e il violino*, 1964, no. 1, 79–90. Although this essay hasn't been published in English, see Praz's excellent book *An Illustrated History of Furnishing from the Renaissance to the Twentieth Century*, trans. William Weaver (New York: Braziller, 1964).

6. Gabriele D'Annunzio, *The Child of Pleasure*, trans. Georgina Harding (Boston: The Page Company, 1914), 86–87.

7. Ibid, 175, 178.

8. Ibid, 63.

XII

"FRATELLI D'ITALIA"

THROUGHOUT THE CITY there are still some traces of the battles fought to defend the Roman Republic, a brief but glorious adventure that lasted for five months. From February 9 to July 3, 1849, this small republic gave concrete form to the dreams and aspirations of a generation of Italian patriots who flocked to Rome from all regions of the peninsula. The streets on the Janiculum Hill, site of the republic's fiercest defense, are named in memory of its heroes and the men who gave their lives to the cause: Dandolo, Sterbini, Bassi, Induno, Armellini, Saffi, Dell'Ongaro, Casini, Daverio, Mameli and others.

Going up the Via Garibaldi, rounding its steep hairpin turns, we come to San Pietro in Montorio. This church is packed with artistic masterpieces, and it's also where Beatrice Cenci is buried, near the high altar but with no stone to mark her grave. Bramante's *Tempietto*, commissioned by Ferdinand and Isabella of Spain at the very end of the fifteenth century, is in the church's courtyard, the spot traditionally thought to be the site of Saint Peter's crucifixion. This is, of course, myth, and is likely attributable to the grand panorama visible here; before he was executed, the apostle saw Rome for one last time thanks to the hill's spectacular view of the city. The name Montorio is a contraction of "monte d'oro"—golden hill—a popular appellation derived from the rich light it reflects at sundown.

On the left side of the church a cannonball is lodged partway up the wall, one last touching reminder of the furious bombardment that finally broke through the defensive lines manned by supporters of the Roman Republic. A little farther up the hill, near the memorial to the men who sacrificed themselves to the republic's cause with the valiant cry now inscribed on the monument, "O Roma o morte"—Rome or Death!—the Republican battery was set up for the city's defense. An ossuary in the memorial contains the ashes of

Goffredo Mameli, among many others. Mameli was wounded in battle at the Villa Vascello, and at first it seemed only a bad leg wound, but gangrene soon set in, and even amputating the limb couldn't save him. As they marched out of Rome, his fellow soldiers passed in front of the Pellegrini Hospital, where the poet lay dying in agony, singing "Fratelli d'Italia" ("Brothers of Italy"). He had written the words to that hymn, and it became the national anthem of the Italian Republic in 1946, with music composed by Michele Novaro. Mameli was only twenty-two when he died.

Another curious reminder of those troubled months is visible in the wall surrounding the Villa Sciarra, on Largo Berchet. It carries two stone plaques side-by-side: the one on the left is in Italian, dated 1871, and memorializes the sacrifice of the patriots who defended the Roman Republic; the other is in Latin, dated 1850, and celebrates the rapid restoration of the walls to erase all traces of that brief experiment, as well as the help French troops provided in taking back the city.

Remnants of the Villa Vascello's former protective walls stand just meters outside the Porta San Pancrazio, before the Via Aurelia Antica forks off from the more modern section of the Aurelia. This spot became legendary as one of the last bulwarks of the resistance to the French. So little is now left that it takes a vivid imagination to see it as it was then, amid broadly sweeping fields, herb gardens, vineyards, and formal gardens. Here and there a magnificent villa rose up from the landscape, and the Vascello was just one of them. The grounds of the Villa Doria Pamphili begin just outside the Porta San Pancrazio and rise toward the so-called Arch of the Four Winds. This green oasis is now a cheerful place, filled with children, couples, and joggers, but in the past it was soaked—and not just rhetorically—with blood. The arch was designed by Andrea Busiri Vici in 1856, and built where the Villa Corsini had been, until it was destroyed by French artillery fire during the battle. The attackers took the building almost immediately, and used its elevated site to position their heavy siege canons. The finale of the furious battle for the city was fought between the Vascello and Corsini villas. The Republicans had barricaded themselves in the Villa Vascello and along Urban VIII's walls, which were hammered by artillery fire, opening at least eight breaches in the walls around the Villa Sciarra through which French soldiers quickly stormed. Nevertheless, it took another month, and many more deaths on both sides, before Rome surrendered.

The promenade atop the Janiculum, shaded by large plane trees, also recalls these epic events, and the avenue is lined with busts of the many volunteers who fought for unification and Rome. A majestic equestrian statue of Giuseppe Garibaldi, cast by Emilio Galdieri in 1895, stands at the center of the piazza at the promenade's end. A monument to Garibaldi's wife, Anita, was commissioned from Mario Rutelli and added to the piazza in 1932. A nineteenth-century cannon located in the small square beneath the piazza is fired every day at noon after the signal to do so is received from the Capitoline Hill. This tradition began in 1904 and has continued, uninterrupted, ever since.

The Roman Republic's sheer heroism and tragedy make its story worth telling, but it's even more fascinating when viewed as a sort of harbinger, at least in hindsight, of so many later events. The errors committed back then—fueled by foolish ambition, emotional outbursts, misunderstandings, passion, zeal, idealism, feuds, unlimited generosity, utopianism, visions, and divisions—are clear to us now. In the Republic's few months of life—in the acts and laws it promulgated, and the behavior of its leaders—we can see a lot of what would later characterize, after 1946, another republic—present-day Italy.

The brief history of the Roman Republic starts a few years before its official founding, on June 16, 1846, when Monsignor Giovanni Maria Mastai Ferretti, Bishop of Imola, was elected Pope Pius IX. His appointment was met with widespread joy, the pealing of bells, sidewalk celebrations, and congratulations from courts throughout Europe. When his predecessor, Gregory XVI (Bartolomeo Cappellari), died on June 1, 1846, two thousand papal subjects languished in prison, and the Papal States suffered from widespread social backwardness, a result of the desire of those in power to preserve their privileges, paid for by the poverty of the lower classes. Even Metternich's conservative government in Austria made it known during the conclave that it was time to elect a pope with slightly broader views, and Pius IX represented a reasonable compromise.

An attractive, jovial fifty-four-year-old with a bright wit, Pius IX was weak in theology and even weaker in political justice, but he was an excellent violinist. At first he seemed to want to keep his promise of reform, and a month after his election he declared an amnesty for political prisoners. Surrounded by young prelates who seemed open-minded, he permitted some freedom of the press, and allowed the city of Rome its own constitution. On April 17, 1848, he ordered the gates of the Jewish Ghetto torn down and declared the equality of Jews—a good decision, but one that calls for some clarification. The Jews were first emancipated in 1798, when the driving principles of the French Revolution surfaced in Rome, but freedom for the Jews proved ephemeral, and the restrictions that had governed their lives in the past were reinstated shortly afterward. The measures taken in 1848 were equally short-lived, and when Pius IX returned from exile in Gaeta, in the spring of 1850, the Roman Ghetto was re-established. According to Giorgio Bouchard, the trauma the pope suffered during his forced stay in Gaeta was so extreme that, when Rome was restored to him, he undertook a plan to roll back his reforms, including new provisions against the Jews. It took the arrival of the *piemontesi* in 1870, and their dream of unification, for the Jewish community to finally be liberated.

The new pope was popular for the first few months of his pontificate. Among other things, he sponsored a public works program that reduced unemployment and, as a consequence, reduced the high crime rate. Italians began to cheer for him, "Viva Pio IX"—"long live Pius IX"—and even Giuseppe Mazzini encouraged him, from London, to take a leading role in the movement to unify Italy. The severe and intransigent Mazzini could do so without fearing his policy would be confused with the "neo-Guelphism" of Vincenzo Gioberti. But regardless of its sincerity, Mazzini's enthusiasm was misplaced, and if it was meant to encourage the pope toward reform, it failed.

In 1848 all of Europe was shaken by revolutionary fervor. In the region of Piedmont, Prince Charles Albert was constrained to allow a constitution in early March, and by the end of the same month he was forced to declare war on Austria. Rome was alive with trepidation—what would the pope do? Would he take to the battlefield to fight the "barbarians?" Pius IX wasn't so inclined, however, and in a famous speech he declared that, as representative of a peaceful God, he couldn't take sides in any war between nations. His troops were already on the march toward the northern border of the Papal States when they were recalled.

Events, however, transpired of their own accord. In September the pope named Pellegrino Rossi his prime minister. Rossi was a talented man, a naturalized French citizen, and professor of political economy; he was sent to Rome as an ambassador, and there he was made a count in reward for his diplomatic abilities. He accepted the position, but had a precarious path ahead; he had to restore the authority and reputation of the papal regime, and at the same time create a less backward administration and institute essential economic reforms. If anyone could pull off such a feat, it would've been Rossi, but he unfortunately never got the chance. Just two months after his nomination he was stabbed to death by a group of opponents as he was climbing the stairs of the Papal Chancery to open a session of Parliament. Among his assassins, perhaps, was Luigi Brunetti, son of Angelo Brunetti, a prosperous wine carter, liberal reformer, and well-known political figure better known as Ciceruacchio—little Cicero. (It's interesting to note that in the monument dedicated to Angelo on the Lungotevere Ripetta the sculptor, Ettore Ximenes, represented him as he faced an Austrian firing squad, his son Lorenzo at his side; his other son, Luigi, was not included. The sculptor was criticized for this omission, but it makes sense if you consider that Luigi was deeply shadowed by his crime.)

Pius IX barricaded himself in the Quirinal Palace after Rossi's assassination, and the crowd laid siege to it, setting into motion a chaotic revolt that had no real political scope. The people called on the pope to declare war on Austria, abolish entrenched privileges, allow an Italian constitution, and institute social reforms. They protested, and the Swiss Guard opened fire. After initially dispersing, the rebels regrouped. The crowd included a number of soldiers and members of the civic militia, its actions quickly escalated from chanting to fighting, and several attempts were made to occupy the pope's residence. The papal secretary was killed during one of them, and Pius IX decided to abandon the city. He fled on the evening of November 24, dressed as a simple priest, with the assistance of Karl von Spaur, the Bavarian ambassador to Rome. Posing as a family tutor, he escaped south to Gaeta, in the Kingdom of the Two Sicilies, and therefore outside of papal and Roman jurisdiction.

Monsignor Emanuele Muzzarelli presided over the new government in Rome, and Giuseppe Galletti became Minister of the Interior.

Muzzarelli was a liberal priest, but now found himself faced with terrible economic problems. The public coffers were literally empty, with no funds even for the day-to-day operation of the city. Interest-bearing loans were forbidden because of their potential resemblance to the sin of usury; this gives you some idea of the Papal States' administrative backwardness, as the obvious result was a thriving black market of loans made with exorbitant interest rates.

Muzzarelli reacted as anyone would have—including poor Rossi, had he been given the chance—and steered a middling course, issuing treasury bonds to meet immediate financial needs while promising reforms, some of which he knew could never be instituted. In short, he attempted to govern, but it wasn't easy, especially because the pope, still smarting from the trauma of the rebellion and his flight, declared from Gaeta that all acts of the new government were null and void. Rome answered that, in fleeing the city, he'd created a new situation that instead nullified his own power. On December 26, the government approved the convocation of a constitutional convention, and two days later parliament was dissolved, with new elections called for January 21, 1849, the first elections to include direct and universal (at least male) suffrage.

Facing this rapid turn of events, the pope committed another of his many political errors, and nominated a governing commission (essentially a government in exile in Gaeta), to be headed by Cardinal Castracane. Furthermore, he forbade "good Christians" from participating in the elections, an action he defined as sacrilegious, and threatened any who voted with excommunication. Many moderates didn't vote, and the result was—with an extraordinary turnout of 50 percent of the electorate, and in some places as much as 70 percent—an elected assembly dominated by extremists. This just about brings us to the end of our quick pre-history of the Roman Republic. The new assembly was inaugurated on February 5, 1849; on February 9, from atop the Capitoline Hill, it proclaimed (with 120 votes in favor, 10 opposed, and 12 abstentions) the *decreto fondamentale*—the so-called Fundamental Decree—which read, "The papacy has forfeited *de facto* and *de jure* the temporal government of the Roman State. The government of the Roman State will be a pure democracy, and will take the glorious name of the Roman Republic." The flag they chose was the Italian tricolor. This happened on February 9, 1849, and the new state would last only five months.

Following great emotion, many tears of joy, and the exhilaration regarding their glorious future, those who supported the new state were soon faced with the problem of governing it. The assembly chose a triumvirate to head the government. The public's lack of confidence was such that merchants refused to accept both the coupons and banknotes printed by the treasury, so in practice coins became the only viable tender. The government tried to fix the situation by passing several urgent (i.e., desperate) measures. On February 21 the assembly voted to confiscate all church property—real estate, bank accounts, and valuable ecclesiastical furnishings worth a total of about 120 million *scudi*. This measure was not only insufficient, but also caused a great stir. The government then decreed forced loans, obliging anyone with an income greater than 2,000 *scudi* to hand a percentage of it "temporarily" over to the state, in sums ranging from one-fifth to two-thirds of their total income. Finally, it decreed the forced circulation of banknotes, with severe penalties for those who refused them.

The republic got off to a bad—very bad—start, giving rise to a new institutional system that required popular consensus, in a city where for many centuries the masses had been kept far from any sort of participation in public life other than processions, gifts tossed to the crowd, and holy rituals. Yet its beginning was even worse when you consider the fact that Pius IX made continuous appeals from Gaeta to the Catholic nations of Europe to help him re-establish his temporal domain. Acting as Secretary of State, Cardinal Antonelli sent a message to the chanceries of Spain, France, Austria, and the Kingdom of the Two Sicilies saying that, among other things, "The affairs of the Papal States have fallen victim to a devastating conflagration set by a party of rebels from every social class. Under the specious pretexts of nationalism and independence it has stopped at nothing to achieve full realization of its evil intentions. The so-called *decreto fondamentale* is a document brimming with the darkest of felonies and the most abominable impieties." It concludes, "[The pope] turns again to the same powers, especially the Catholic ones, that have already demonstrated their decisiveness with great generosity of spirit . . . in the certainty that they will, with all promptness, offer moral support so that he may be restored to his seat." The cardinal spoke of "moral support," but he was in fact alluding to armed intervention, and that's precisely how his message was understood.

In the meantime the Roman Republic was clinging to life despite the myriad problems it faced and the many disagreements that sprung up between its supporters. The vital economic reforms proved difficult to enact, as the expropriation of church property fueled an anticlerical current, while the humbler classes, who'd hoped for an immediate improvement in their situation, were disillusioned. At the same time military spending had to be increased to fend off the attack everyone thought imminent. In the meantime Charles Albert was again defeated by the Austrians, this time in Novara, in March of 1849. His first loss had happened in Custoza, in July of 1848, and it was now clear that the republic couldn't count on him for much help.

Some have suggested, and I agree, that it was precisely this desperate situation that gave the short-lived Roman Republic its glory, and not the Romantic notion that favors the weak when they are threatened or bullied. The glory came instead from the legal principles on which the republic was founded. In less dramatic circumstances, perhaps, a constitution as advanced as the Republic's might never have been written.

The governing triumvirate of Giuseppe Mazzini, Carlo Armellini, and Aurelio Saffi was formed in March. They immediately began to discuss the contents of the constitution, and it was soon clear that Mazzini in particular wanted to attach extraordinary and almost utopian political ideals to this experiment, which even he believed would be brief. This explains both the urgent practical measures the government passed and the very advanced—for its time almost inconceivable—ideas enshrined in the new constitution. In April the triumvirate decided to use impounded church property to house the very poor, and in this way the republic tried to encourage the participation of citizens who'd been marginalized in the past, and not only in terms of housing, by the papal administration. It also tried to reduce unemployment, the underlying cause of the city's widespread criminality. Mazzini was the real engine of reform; in a less forgetful nation he would still be venerated, much like Lincoln in the United

States or, on a different level, Montesquieu in France. But fate seems to stipulate that only truly great countries are able to keep the memory of their founding fathers alive.

In Mazzini's ideology, the republic was "founded first and foremost on the principles of love, greater civilization, and fraternal progress for everyone, and on the moral, intellectual, and economic betterment of all its citizens." His patriotic axiom was that revolution must be "by the people and for the people." He thought a "Third Rome"—after Imperial Rome, which had united the whole of the ancient world, and Papal Rome, which united it under Christianity—would guide people toward universal fraternity by means of the liberty and independence of its citizens. Aware that this experiment was destined to be short-lived, Mazzini wanted the written constitution to preserve the strict political morality that had inspired it. The Roman Republic was the first European state to proclaim, in Article 7 of its constitution, that "civil and political rights do not depend on the exercise of religious belief," and it was the first to eliminate the death penalty. Indeed, it enacted everything described in articles 2 through 21 of the declaration of human rights as approved by the French National Assembly in 1789. As the most advanced founding charter in Europe, it declared, among other things, "A democratic regime has as its rule equality, liberty, and fraternity. It does not recognize any noble titles or privileges conferred by birth or class" (article 2). "Municipalities all have the same rights. Their independence is only limited by state laws promulgated for the greater good" (article 5). "The head of the Catholic Church will receive from the Republic all guarantees necessary for the independent exercise of his spiritual authority" (article 8). Regarding the rights and duties of its citizens: "The death penalty or forfeiture of property is outlawed"; "the home is sacred, and entering it is forbidden except in ways and circumstances described in the law"; "the expression of ideas is to be free"; "education is to be free"; "the confidentiality of letters is inviolable"; "free association, without arms or the intent to commit a crime, is guaranteed"; "no one can be forced to forfeit property without a public hearing and just compensation"; and so on. No one had ever formulated such advanced laws before. Those who have some familiarity with the constitution of the Italian Republic, approved in

1948, will recognize that some of its principles were taken wholesale from this first document, written a hundred years earlier.

In Gaeta, in the meantime, Pius IX was preparing for a possible return to the throne by appealing both to European powers and the clergy. Addressing the diplomatic corps in February, he said:

> Hasty papal subjects, as always led by the same dangerous and deadly faction of human society, have fallen into the deepest abyss of misery. We, as temporal prince, and even more so as Head and Pontiff of the Catholic Religion, hear the pleas and supplications of the vast majority of the aforementioned subjects, who ask that the chains oppressing them be untied. We demand at the same time that the sacred right of the Holy See to temporal dominion be maintained.

In a speech to the College of Cardinals given the following April, he further admonished:

> Who is there who does not know that the city of Rome, principal seat of the Catholic Church, has now become—alas!—a forest full of wild beasts, overflowing with men of all nations, be they apostate, heretical, or masters, as they say, of Communism or Socialism, and animals with a terrible hatred of Catholic truths. These men, whether in speech, writing, or whatever other way they practice, have made every effort to teach and disseminate pestilential errors of every kind, and to corrupt everyone's hearts and souls, so that in Rome itself, if it were possible, the sanctity of the Catholic religion would fail.

Camillo Benso, Count of Cavour, tried several times, always in vain, to emphasize that the pope's own spiritual interests should compel him to abandon his anachronistic pretensions to temporal power. Cavour, who would later become prime minister, returned frequently to this theme, arguing, reassuring, and inviting reflection. In March of 1861, for example, when the Roman Republic was already a distant memory, he declared to the chamber of deputies, "All those weapons with which both Italian and foreign civil powers have armed themselves will be useless when the papacy is restricted to spiritual power. And the pope's authority, far from being diminished, will grow stronger in the sphere that is its rightful competence." His exhortations were alternated with reassurances, "By whatever manner Italy wins the Eternal City—and it *will* get there, whether with an agreement or not—as soon as it has declared the temporal power of the Church forfeited, it will proclaim the principle of separation of church and state, and will immediately implement the principle of the freedom of the Church on the broadest bases."

For Pius IX, who claimed his spiritual power could not be separated from his temporal authority, these guarantees weren't enough. The motto Cavour thought so reassuring—"A free Church in a free State"—frightened the pope as much as popular insurrection. Let's try to follow Pius along his tormented journey: on December 8, 1854, he declared the dogma of the Immaculate Conception, a decision that caused great perplexity, and not just in the Protestant world. The pope knew he was embracing popular religious feeling demonstrated, for example, by the "visions" of the shepherdess Bernadette Soubirous at Lourdes only a little while afterward. Ten years later, on the exact anniversary of that proclamation, Pius released his encyclical titled *Quanta cura*. The notorious *Sillabo* was attached to it, in which he condemned progress, liberalism, modern civilization, and liberty, including the freedom of thought, in no uncertain terms. According to Pius, everything on the following list should be considered a grave error: divorce; the abolition of the papacy's temporal authority; the belief that Catholicism is not the only State religion; the idea of the separation of Church and State; tolerance for the public exercise of other religions; the open display of any opinion or thought that does not conform with clerical directives; and the idea that the pope should conform to modern society. These errors were defined as "the greatest evil"—and then there was socialism. The pope saw the dangers of a free society, and was almost obsessed with them. He also understood that modernity was accompanied by religious indifference. In one of his encyclicals he issued a sorrowful lament:

> But who does not see and clearly perceive that human society, when set loose from the bonds of religion and true justice, can have, in truth, no other end than the purpose of obtaining and amassing wealth, and that (society under such circumstances) follows no other law in its actions, except the unchastened desire of ministering to its own pleasure and interests?[1]

Today we can see how prophetic these words were. Greed and moral relativism are now characteristics of contemporary society in the West, dominated by money and a frenetic consumerism. Having identified a possible evil, Pius IX offered the wrong cure by advocating a return to an already impossible absolutism. His position was summed up in the proclamation of papal infallibility at the first Vatican Council, held in 1870. That meeting was manipulated so that the bishops who favored dogma prevailed, while those who opposed it were subjected to pressure and even threats. The dissident theologian Hans Küng has recently written that the first Vatican Council was "more like a totalitarian party's congress than an open assembly of free Christians." Many of the bishops who opposed the document left Rome before the final vote. The approved text affirmed, among other things, that "the dogma and principles defined by the pope are in themselves unquestionable (*irreformabiles esse ex sese*) and do not express the consensus of the Church." In July of 1870 Twenty German Catholic historians left the Church. A few days later the Franco-Prussian War broke out and the council was suspended, never to be recalled.

Yet Pius IX's passionate beliefs would have an effect on posterity. His successor, Leo XIII (Vincenzo Gioacchino Pecci), in the 1888 encyclical *Libertas* (*On the Nature of Human Liberty*), returned to the issue of the fundamental rights of the individual, affirming that, "from what has been said it follows that it is quite unlawful to demand, to defend, or to grant unconditional freedom of thought, of speech, or writing, or of worship, as if these were so many rights given by nature to man."[2] To be completely fair, however, I should add that this pope also wrote the famous encyclical on capital and labor, *Rerum Novarum*, which earned him the nickname "the workers' pope."

This mistrust of the individual's rights as defined by the French Revolution continued after Leo's pontificate. One of his successors, Pius XI (Achille Ratti), tranquilly declared—and this was well into the twentieth century—that "if there is a totalitarian regime, totalitarian in fact and by right, that regime is the Church. Because men are creatures of the good Lord, men belong entirely to the Church. . . . And the Church is the only representative of the ideas, thoughts, and rights of God." Even John Paul II (Karol Wojtyla), so vigorous a defender of peace, reaffirmed in his encyclical *Evangelium Vitae*, that "democracy, contradicting its own principles, effectively moves towards a form of totalitarianism" when it approves ethical positions opposed to the teachings of the church. John Paul repeated this idea frequently, and it's revealing about who has ultimate authority and sovereignty when it comes to personal rights.

Let's return to the Roman Republic. On April 25, with Neapolitan troops moving north, the French forces commanded by General Oudinot disembarked at Civitavecchia and prepared to march to Rome along the Via Aurelia, convinced the Romans would surrender without a fight. The triumvirate wrote a pathetic but noble letter (now preserved among the mementos in the Capitoline Archives) to the French commander:

> Au nom de Dieu, au nom de la France et de l'Italie, Général, suspendez votre marche. Évitez une guerre entre frères. Que l'histoire ne dise pas: la république française a fait, sans cause, sa prémière guerre contre la république italienne! Vous avez été, évidemment, trompé sur l'état de notre pays; ayez le courage de le dire à votre Gouvernement et attendez-en de nouvelles instructions, Nous sommes decides de répousser la force par la force. Et ce n'est pas sur nous que rétombera la responsabilité de ce grand Malheur.

(In the name of God, in the names of France and Italy, General, stop your march. Avoid a war between brothers. Do not allow history to say: the Republic of France, for no reason, waged its first war against the Italian Republic! You have evidently been misinformed about the conditions of our country; have the courage to report this to your government and then wait for new instructions. We are determined to meet force with force. The responsibility for this enormous disaster will certainly not rest with us.)

These words obviously had no effect. Two days later the first French attack rained down on the Janiculum, the southernmost hill in a modest ridge that begins at Monte Mario and continues along the high ground of the Vatican. This ridge faces the Tiber River and the historic city center, and it offers both an extraordinary panorama of Rome and a strategically important military position. Most travelers and pilgrims who visited Rome approached along its path, as did the "barbarians" who came to attack the ancient imperial capital. In the medieval period the Via Francigena, which roughly corresponds to the present-day Via Cassia, was the most well-traveled road to Rome. It was inconvenient, though, because it arrived at the Milvian Bridge, where the river's fluctuating levels made it difficult to cross. Therefore travelers often preferred to continue along the crest of the hills, following the Via Trionfale, an entrance route into Rome later described by so many nineteenth-century travelers on the Grand Tour. It originally had the added advantage of easy access to the ford at the Isola Tiberina and the Ponte Sublicio, which at the time were the only places the river could easily be crossed.

The French vanguard attacked on April 30. They expected only token resistance, and were surprised by the determination of the Italian forces. In a single day of fighting the attackers lost five hundred men to death or serious wounds. Volunteers from many parts of the peninsula had come to Rome, including large numbers from the northern regions of Lombardy, Piedmont, the Veneto, and Romagna. This battle, which involved fierce hand-to-hand combat, was fought on the grounds of the Villa Doria Pamphili and along the Via Aurelia. Facing a stiffer resistance than they had expected, the attackers retreated, chased by the volunteers until they agreed to a ceasefire.

One of the novelties of that brief but cruel war was the use of photography to document the combatants. For the first time, albeit when the skirmishes were largely over, someone thought of documenting the outcome of the conflict by photographing the battlefield and "posing" the French soldiers. Through these photographs we get a firsthand view of the rubble that the Corsini, Savorelli, and Vascello villas were reduced to, and can see soldiers preparing a meal next to a cannon, showing off their equipment or doing guard duty.

As the French attacked, two more columns of troops—one Austrian, the other, as noted above, from the Kingdom of Naples—were heading toward Rome. The Austrians faced staunch resistance in the city of Ancona, which slowed their progress, and the Neapolitans were defeated by Garibaldi at Velletri. The plan to encircle Rome seemed, for the moment anyway, to have been foiled; but everyone in Rome knew that the ceasefire would be brief.

People have always wondered why, after his first defeat, General Oudinot continued to attack the most highly fortified position on the Janiculum, when he might've chosen a less dangerous approach. In reality, there were other attempts; the French assembled a provisory bridge of boats in the Magliana area, just south of the Janiculum along the Tiber, and attacked the Milvian Bridge, upstream of Monte Mario, where they were able to break through despite some stiff resistance from defenders, who then retreated to barricade themselves in the Parioli neighborhood. Once they reached the Porta del Popolo, however, the French stopped. Oudinot concentrated the bulk of his thirty thousand men in the area between the Porta Portese and the Janiculum, in what is now the Monteverde neighborhood. This strategy was likely the result of the general's fear that if he entered the city too early he'd run up against barricades and be forced to conduct combat by slowly proceeding from one street to the next amid dangerous nests of snipers. The head of the "barricades commission" was a young Lombard named Enrico Cernuschi, who'd been battle-tested in the "Cinque Giornate," the famous five-day battle of Milan in March of 1848, and would, ironically, participate in defending Paris during the Battle of the Commune. (In Paris there's a street and a museum of Asian art, begun with Cernuschi's collection, named for him.) Despite all difficulties, once the French took the Janiculum it allowed them to dominate the city from above, safe from any guerrilla attacks.

On May 19 a ceasefire was declared, officially issued to evacuate French citizens living in Rome, but effectively issued to allow for the arrival of reinforcements. Viscount Ferdinand de Lesseps, the man in charge of French diplomatic affairs in Rome, who also later designed the digging of the Suez Canal, signed the ceasefire, but Oudinot violated the agreement and ordered an attack on the night of June 2–3. His excuse was that the ceasefire only applied within the city walls, not the surrounding area. This surprise tactic worked, and the French gained the high ground at the Villa Corsini. This gave their artillery optimum positioning during the worst days of the siege, and when Garibaldi (who had just been promoted to the rank of Brigadier General) attempted to retake the position he lost nine hundred men, including both the dead and wounded, in a single day. This overwhelming number gives you some idea of the sheer ferocity of these battles; Rome was under siege, re-supply was difficult, the discomforts and risks were great, and many wounded were brought down from the outposts on the Janiculum Hill.

At the political triumvirate's side was a staff of women that worked to oversee the city's hospitals. It consisted of three exceptional women, Margaret Fuller Ossoli, Enrichetta Pisacane, and Princess Cristina di Belgiojoso. According to Balzac, Cristina was Stendhal's inspiration for

Sanseverina in the *Charterhouse of Parma*. She was beautiful, seductive, sensual, and well aware of the desire she aroused in men; many considered her a quasi-courtesan. She had married, separated, and had innumerable lovers, including Liszt and Musset.

Italian attempts to mount a counterattack continued for days, but all proved bloody and unsuccessful. Taking in the situation, Garibaldi created a second defensive line along the city's Aurelian walls, which helped him resist the enemy for several weeks. In the meantime, batteries of French artillery continued to hammer the walls, opening wide breaches. The Italians were forced to retreat, and the French were able, from the new positions captured, to shower the city itself in shellfire. A few monuments were damaged, and several shells fell in Piazza Santa Maria in Trastevere, causing some civilian casualties. When the walls around the Porta Portese were finally surrendered it became clear that the end was near.

The famous patriot and sergeant Giacomo Venezian from Trieste was killed in the Italian counterattacks, and men like Capitan Gorini, Giovanni Cadolini (who was little more than a boy), and the painter Giacomo Induno were all wounded. One of the most moving deaths was that of Luciano Manara, who was wounded while attempting a desperate resistance at the Villa Spada. Emilio Dandolo recorded a devastating account of his last hours, writing, "He begged me to take his body, with his brother's, back to Lombardy to be buried. Noticing I was crying, he asked, 'Are you sorry I'm dying?' Seeing that I could not answer, stifled by my sobs, he added softly, but with the most pious resignation, 'I'm sorry, too.'" His fellow *bersaglieri* carried the hero's remains through the streets of Rome to the church of San Lorenzo in Lucina, where Father Ugo Bassi presided over his funeral, calling him "one of the strongest sons the Fatherland has lost."

The artillery shelling had become so violent that Oudinot was sent a letter of protest through consular channels. "This means of attack," it read, "not only puts the lives and property of neutral and peaceful citizens at risk, but also those of innocent women and children." It begged the general to refrain from "another bombardment to avoid the destruction of the 'City of Monuments,' considered to be under the moral protection of all the world's civilized nations." In Paris the left demonstrated against this expedition and in support of the tiny Republic, but the demonstrations didn't move the government, and Oudinot was focused on quickly finishing his task—the artillery shells continued to fall.

Political support in France for this military expedition came only after some hesitation, as the following months soon made clear. In October of 1849, after the ordeal had been fully concluded, there was a debate in which both Foreign Minister Alexis de Tocqueville and Victor Hugo took positions strongly critical of the government. Both men were dismayed, albeit in slightly different ways, by the renewed papal repressions and because the restored papacy wanted to return to the *ancien régime* and forget everything that had been conceded in the 1848 constitution. Hugo, who'd initially favored military intervention, said that Rome had never had any legislation in the true sense of the term, but only "an accumulation and chaos of feudal and monastic laws," held together for the most part by a "clear hatred for progress." When the French deputies, including the liberals, approved the expedition, they never expected an outcome like this. "The National Assembly," the great writer added, "voted for the Roman expedition given the issues of humanity and liberty the Prime Minister described to them; it voted to balance the Battle of Novara, to put France's sword where Austria's saber fell . . . to avoid it being said that France was absent when both humanity and its own interests called to it, and to defend, in a word, Rome and the people of the Roman Republic against Austria."

Louis-Napoléon, nephew of Napoleon Bonaparte, was president of the French Republic; in a coup d'état in 1852 he proclaimed himself Emperor of France with the name Napoléon III. Hugo called him "Napoléon le Petit," a mocking reference to the greatness of his uncle. As had so many others, the young Louis-Napoléon had dabbled in revolutionary activities. In Italy he'd been an adherent of the Carboneria movement, a secret political group, and as a twenty-year-old he'd participated in revolutionary movements in Romagna. As he approached his most important position, this mediocre man felt he needed the support of the Catholic Church, and this was the chief reason he decided to intervene in Italy in 1849. Hugo, however, alluded to another, equally important reason—his fear of Austria taking all the credit for saving the temporal power of the papacy. Louis-Napoléon feared the pope might undermine French interests across the peninsula. Thus France, which had wanted to impose a

Republic in Rome at the end of the eighteenth century, fifty years later resorted to forceful means to suppress a second, spontaneously risen republic. Such are the adventures and contradictions of politics.

The French also played a part in the third and final episode of this affair. After his defeat at Sédan in 1870, during the Franco-Prussian war, Napoléon III was forced to withdraw the garrisons that had protected Rome since 1849; the same conflict had also caused the interruption of the first Vatican Council. This was the moment Cavour was waiting for, and on September 20, a clear, autumnal day, the *bersaglieri* of General Cadorna entered the city of Rome.

This is how the paper *La Gazzetta*, published on the afternoon of that fateful day, reported the news: "From Rome, September 20. This morning Italian troops, under the command of General Cadorna, opened fire at 5:30 on the walls of Rome between the Porta Pia and the Porta Salaria. At the same instant the Angioletti Division attacked the Porta San Giovanni and the Blixio Division the Porta San Pancrazio. At ten o'clock in the morning our troops, after a lively but brief resistance, entered the city. Papal soldiers stopped firing, and flew white flags from all the pope's batteries. A negotiator was sent to General Cadorna's headquarters." The next day a brief communiqué issued by the War Ministry listed the loses at "21 dead, 117 wounded, and 9,300 prisoners." Other sources put the dead at thirty-two Italians and twenty papal soldiers. A few days later, on October 2, the territory of the Papal States was annexed to the Kingdom of Italy by plebiscite.

But all this happened several years after the period we've been talking about; back in 1849 the Roman Republic resisted in any way it could. The villas where the defenders had barricaded themselves were now reduced to piles of rubble, the city walls were breached, and the hardships and dangers of the siege had worn out the city's inhabitants. Mazzini, with visionary strength, wanted to call the people to arms, grab their bayonets, and retake the lost positions. Garibaldi, equally visionary, dissuaded him; in this case he was able to see the situation more realistically than Mazzini, with more military experience, and also saw that the soldiers' morale was already resigned to defeat. Yet there were still several episodes of incredible valor at the Villa Vascello that are worth remembering.

On June 26, preceded by intense shelling, the French Zouaves tried to take the building, but were repelled by a small group of men.

On June 27 the Villa Savorelli, just inside the Porta San Pancrazio, was abandoned. On the 29th, the feast day of Rome's patron saints Peter and Paul was celebrated quietly, but that evening the dome of Saint Peter's was illuminated to show the enemy the great serenity with which the siege was being met. After a violent thunderstorm that same night, three columns of French soldiers began to enter the city. Garibaldi, outflanked on the front lines between the Villa Savorelli and the Porta San Pancrazio, ordered those positions to be abandoned.

The next day Mazzini proposed three possible courses of action to the assembly on the Capitoline Hill—capitulation, the continued defense of the city with street barricades, or a total withdrawal of troops in an attempt to incite the provinces to rebel. The assembly decided to summon Garibaldi to hear his opinion. The general appeared covered in gunpowder and blood, and was given a standing ovation. Speaking slowly, he seemed moved; he admitted that any further resistance was useless, and announced he would leave the city with any volunteers who wanted to follow him, "Wherever we are, Rome will be, and the Fatherland, condensed within us, will live on."

That afternoon the city sent a delegation to General Oudinot to negotiate its surrender. The conditions imposed, however, were so harsh that they were refused, and the triumvirate deliberated, letting the French occupy the city unconditionally. An armistice was signed on June 30, calling for the French to enter Rome three days later. Garibaldi assembled his troops in Saint Peter's Square, and said to the huge crowd waiting there to salute him, "I am leaving Rome. Those who want to continue the war against the foreigners, come with me. From those who follow me I expect love, the strength of the Fatherland, and proof of daring hearts. I cannot promise pay, nor leisurely breaks. You'll have bread and water when we find them. Once we pass through the gates of Rome, a step backward is a step toward death."

At about eight o'clock that evening, having gathered up some four thousand men with eight hundred horses and one cannon, the strange army of *Garibaldini*, Lombard *bersaglieri*, students, revenue officers, and papal dragoons who'd joined the Italian volunteers set off. On July 3, around noon, squadrons of French infantrymen descended from the Janiculum to occupy Trastevere, the Castel Sant'Angelo, the Pincian Hill, and the Piazza del Popolo. At about four o'clock, in front of an immense crowd, General Giuseppe Galletti, president of the assembly, solemnly proclaimed the founding of the Roman Republic from a balcony on the Capitoline Hill and read its constitution aloud. On the evening of the 4th a battalion of Alpine soldiers occupied the Capitoline and invited the assembly to leave. The deputies signed a joint letter of protest which read, "In the name of God and the people of the Roman States who freely elected us as their representatives, in the name of Article 5 of the French Constitution, the Roman Assembly protests in front of Italy, France, and the whole of the civilized world the violent invasion of the French army into its seat, which occurred today, July 4, 1848, at seven o'clock in the evening." It was the Republic's last gasp. From a legal point of view, the constitution was dead just a few hours after it had been born.

In the face of a few hostile acts committed in the city, General Oudinot had a manifesto circulated throughout Rome. It began with these words:

> People of Rome! The army sent here by the French Republic has as its goal the restoration of order so desired by this city's population. A few partisans and misled people forced us to assault your walls. We are now in control of the city. We will perform of our own accord. Among the kindness we have met, a true demonstration of the real feelings of the Roman people, there are also some hostile noises that force us to immediately repress them. Take heart, those of you who are well meaning, the true friends of liberty. Know, you enemies of order and society, that if ever aggressive actions provoked by foreign factions are renewed, they will be severely punished.

The history of the Roman Republic ends here, but some of you may be wondering what happened to that strange group Garibaldi led out of Rome. The men headed northeast toward Tivoli, looped around, and continued on to Terni, Todi, Orvieto, Città della Pieve, Cetona, and Arezzo. It was a long peregrination, without any apparent destination. At the group's approach several towns (Arezzo and Orvieto, for example) closed their gates and refused to allow them entry. The ranks became progressively thinner, and at the end of the long march the four thousand men who had begun were reduced to few more than a hundred. Garibaldi's wife, Anita, was pregnant and ill, and traveling on horseback had fatally compromised her health.

On the evening of July 31, Garibaldi left San Marino and, after marching all night and through the entire next day, reached Cesenatico, where he disarmed the Austrian garrison. With his few remaining men he embarked on thirteen local fishing boats, called *bragozzi*, at dawn on August 2 and set sail for Venice. His attempt at escape wasn't successful, and the fragile fleet was surprised by the Austrian Navy at Punta di Goro. Five boats surrendered, while the other eight, including Garibaldi's, managed to escape. The next day the remnants of the rag-tag army went ashore between Migliavacca and Volano and dispersed into small groups.

Anita was now so sick she had to be carried. She died on the evening of August 4, and Garibaldi couldn't even take the time to bury her because of the men trailing him close behind. Dressed as a peasant, he left.

---

1. *Quanta Cura*, Encyclical of Pope Pius IX Condemning Current Errors, December 8, 1864. (http://www.saint-mike.org/papal-library/PiusIX/Encyclicals/Quanta_Cura.html)

2. *Libertas*, Encyclical of Pope Leo XIII, June 20, 1888. (http://www.vatican.va/holy_father/leo_xiii/encyclicals/documents/hf_l-xiii_enc_20061888_libertas_en.html)

XIII

MURDER ON VIA PUCCINI

IN ROME EVEN A NEIGHBORHOOD as new as Parioli cannot escape the weight and memory of history. This quarter was originally a large area of tufa hills along the Via Flaminia, noted since antiquity for its many caves and inhabited primarily by sorcerers and soothsayers. Roman matrons ventured there by night, accompanied by torch-bearing maids who lighted the way, to ask for horoscopes, love potions, and concoctions that would guarantee fecundity—or its opposite, with mixtures that would get rid of an unwanted pregnancy. Throughout the hillsides, which were covered with dense vegetation just as they still are, magicians lit fires to boil their pungent brews, much like Macbeth's witches. After pocketing their fees they handed over their magic potions and left the poor women, who were exhausted from sleeplessness and the whippings they'd apparently endured, believed to make the rites more effective.

On another hill, just behind Parioli, there is a garden named Villa Glori, also called Park of Remembrance because of an event that took place there during the Risorgimento. The park was designed in the early 1920s by the architect Raffaelle De Vico, who wanted to create a pleasant place to stroll among stands of pine, oak, horse chestnut, and olive trees. The hill beneath Villa Glori is, like nearby Parioli, made of tufa, and is equally dotted with deep caverns, some of which date back to the prehistoric period. Most of these caves are now filled in, and among them is a partially excavated hypogeum, most likely a tomb from the imperial era.

On October 20, 1867, a company of seventy *Garibaldini* led by the brothers Enrico and Giovanni Cairoli disembarked at the foot of the hill. These brave men had come down the Tiber by boat from Terni, and brought arms to reinforce the patriots planning a revolt against the papal government. The insurrection never came together, though, and most of the population sat idly by as papal troops easily subdued the many small, disorganized revolutionary groups. The pope's army fired on the band from Terni as they disembarked, causing a slaughter. Enrico was killed, and Giovanni died a few months later of the wounds received there.

In 1886 the poet Cesare Pascarella (1858–1940) wrote twenty-five sonnets, published in a volume titled *Villa Gloria,* about the beautiful yet tragic mission ended at the foot of that hill. He dedicated the verses to Benedetto Cairoli, brother of the two fallen leaders and an important figure of the historical left, who between 1878 and 1882 served three terms as prime minister. Giosuè Carducci, a fellow poet known to exaggerate at times, said that in Pascarella's work "never has poetry in any Italian dialect reached such heights." Even without Carducci's enthusiasm, Pascarella's narrative power admittedly rings clear in the first sonnet of *Villa Gloria*:

> A Terni, dove fu l'appuntamento,
> Righetto ce schierò in una pianura,
> E lì ce disse: «Er vostro sentimento
> Lo conosco e nun c'è da avè pavura;
> però, dice, compagni! Ve rammento
> che st'impresa de noi nun è sicura,
> e Roma la vedremo p'un momento
> pe' cascà morti giù sott'a le mura.
> Per questo, prima de pija' er fucile,
> si quarcuno de voi nun se la sente,
> lo dica e sòrta fora da le file».
> Dice: «Nun c'è nessuno che la pianta?».
> E siccome nessuno disse gnente,
> dopo pranzo partissimo in settanta.

(In Terni, where the meeting was set / Righetto lined us up on a plain / And there he said, "I know how you're feelin'" / And there's no need to fear; / "But," he says, "Friends! I remind you / That this scheme of ours ain't so safe / And we'll see Rome for just a sec / Only to fall down dead at the city walls. / "So, before taking up your rifles, / If any o' you wants out, / Just say so and step aside." / He says, "No one's quittin'?" / And 'cause nobody said nothin', after lunch the seventy of us set out.)[1]

From an administrative point of view Villa Glori is in the Parioli neighborhood (if we were in Paris we'd be talking about *arrondissements*), while the Viale Parioli and Via dei Monti Parioli are in the Pinciano neighborhood—it's just one of Rome's place name anomalies. The Pinciano neighborhood includes Villa Borghese, the zoo (now called a "bio-park"), and Villa Balestra, so it's an area with large, open, verdant expanses. It includes the National Gallery of Modern Art, the Etruscan Museum at Valle Giulia, the Galleria Borghese, and the San Valentino and Sant' Ermete catacombs. I could include Renzo Piano's new auditorium on this list, but then I'd be straying outside the Pinciano and back into Parioli.

In the early twentieth century this neighborhood was dotted with houses and small apartment buildings surrounded by lush gardens. It quickly became a desirable place to live, which in turn led to rampant real-estate speculation, a construction boom, and the inevitable pressures that a postwar city government couldn't well resist. This gave the neighborhood its somewhat hybrid character. There was dense development of apartment houses—some as tall as nine stories—along the Via Archimede, for example, especially in the section toward the Piazza Euclide. Other small enclaves, on the other hand, like the Via Rubens, Via Sassoferrato, and Via Dolci, have managed to preserve something of the area's original character, with beautiful gardens lining the streets.

The Parioli neighborhood has a number of examples, even among the more recent buildings, of good architecture. The best include Clemente Busiri Vici's building, erected in 1928 at Via Paisiello 28. Nearby, at number 38, is a building designed by Mario Fiorentino and Wolfgang Frankl in 1949; it's more interesting than successful, and consists of four floors built in a 1950s style over a turn-of-the-century base. A lovely building called "il Girasole" (the Sunflower), by the masterful architect Luigi Moretti, stands at Viale Bruno Buozzi 64, and was also built in 1949. Federico Gori's pretty villa at the corner of the Via dei Monti Parioli and Via Ammannati is called "Casa del Maresciallo" (the Marshall's House), and was built in 1957. Proceeding along the Via Rubens we climb a hill along the Salita dei Parioli. Around the first curve we pass a single-family house nestled against the hillside, designed by the Monaco-Luccichenti architectural firm in 1952. It's a lovely, solitary place, ideal for a romantic evening stroll. The Piazza Euclide opens at the foot of the hill, next to the Villa Glori, in a fairly chaotic space, but the unique church (dedicated to the Sacred and Immaculate Heart of Mary) that graces the piazza is worth stopping to look at. It was designed by the eccentric architect Armando Brasini in 1923, but for a variety of reasons wasn't built for another thirty years. The result is a sort of insolent, out-dated monumentality, exacerbated by the fact that its planned dome was never built, due to a budget shortage or some other reason. The cupola's imposing base has a fairly benign covering, which accentuates the mismatch of proportions of the building's different parts.

If we leave this part of the neighborhood and head back toward the other side of the Pinciano we come across a short street called the Via Puccini. It connects the Corso d'Italia and Via Pinciana, a street whose name (just like the neighborhood name), refers to the *gens Pinciana*, the ancient family that owned the hill. The Via Puccini is flanked by solid upper-class buildings built in the early twentieth century, elegant residences not unlike those of Paris's sixteenth arrondissement or the nicest neighborhoods of Brussels. On the west end of the street the buildings overlook the tall pine trees of Villa Borghese. As far as Roman residential neighborhoods go, this is the best the city has to offer, and is also where one of the bloodiest crimes of the postwar period occurred. This shocking multiple murder characterized the period, and is worth recounting because of its numerous repercussions, many of which remain relevant today.

The first call to the police station rang at ten o'clock on a Sunday evening, August 30, 1970. Strangely, the day had been almost autumnal, a rarity for that time of year. The caller reported a murder in the Pinciano neighborhood, at Via Puccini 9, a building of upper-class bourgeoisie apartments. Valerio Gianfrancesco, head of the station's homicide division, was first to arrive at the crime scene, in the elegant home of Marquis Casati Stampa di Soncino, a two-story, terraced penthouse with a view of Villa Borghese. He later spoke of what had happened in an interview with Ezio Pasero, a journalist with the *Messaggero* newspaper: "As soon as the alarm came to the station, we rushed to that splendid penthouse, with no idea of what had caused the problem, obviously. Instead I thought—judging from the names, the neighborhood, and the luxuriousness of the residence—

that it must have been an attempted robbery, or maybe even a kid-napping gone wrong. I was the first to go into the den and see the horrible scene. A woman was heaped in an armchair with an incred-ulous expression still on her face, the marquis was on the floor next to a rifle, and a young man was balled up behind a small overturned table." All three were dead.

Who were the three leading actors of this tragedy? The woman was Anna Fallarino, whose married title was Marquise Casati Stampa di Soncino. The man next to the shotgun was her husband, Marquis Camillo, who friends referred to as Camillino. The third victim, the young man the policeman mentioned, was Massimo Minorenti, a twenty-five-year-old university dropout who some described as a Fascist thug, and others as a simple "activist" in the (neo-Fascist) movement. Given the scene of the crime, its motive seemed imme-diately apparent—a murder inspired by jealousy. She was a beautiful forty-one-year-old woman; he was the husband of noble counte-nance, thin, and almost bald; and the lad in his twenties was clearly the "other man." In reality, as became clear over time, this both was and wasn't the motive. The story behind the crime was much more intricate, and the emotions that both united and divided these three people were much more complex.

Of all the violent crimes committed in Rome after the war, the one in Via Puccini is perhaps the most memorable because of the circumstances that surrounded it, the twisted personalities of the husband and wife, and the intrigues that emerged in the days after the murder. It truly was, for once, a situation worthy of the overused label "turbid." It's also memorable because of the thorny issues that arose in trying to settle the marquis' large estate after the crime.

The facts themselves are difficult to forget, at least in their broad outlines, since for months afterward newspapers printed lurid photo-graphs (and I'm referring to the publishable ones, a fraction of the total), revealed new details, unearthed new witnesses, and offered new theories about Marquis Camillo's rage after living with Anna for eleven years. Was it a sudden fury? No one can really know, but he definitely suffered brief outbreaks of temper—outbreaks that quickly ended, but were nevertheless very violent.

The murders of Via Puccini are interesting because of the history behind them, and because the protagonists' lives are emblematic of the city and its mores after the hardships of war had passed and an economic boom enabled even people lower down on the economic ladder to enjoy some financial well-being. A comfortable life suddenly seemed within the reach of anyone with sufficient ability, luck, or unscrupulousness to have a grab at it—and sometimes simply having a little beauty was enough.

Anna Fallarino had bet on just that—beauty. Her eyes were lovely, as were the regular features of her face and her shapely figure. She was a little heavy from the waist down, but those were the days of curvaceous women, so even that was an asset. She was born on March 19, 1929, in Amorosi, where the last name Fallarino was common. Amorosi was a town in Campania, in the province of Benevento. As the German army retreated from southern Italy at the end of World War II it passed through Amorosi, and Anna, an adolescent at the time, was touched by the war. Her family came from the lower middle class; her father was a clerical worker, and his marriage wasn't the happiest of unions. At the age of sixteen, when the war had just ended, she moved to Rome, a big city where a pretty girl had lots of opportunities, could make a good future for herself, and find a good catch. She went to live with her uncle Mario, a public security officer, at Via Milano 43, apartment 5. The Via Milano was a cross street of the Via Nazionale, just steps from the Palazzo delle Esposizioni, halfway between the Piazza Venezia and the Piazza Esedra (also called the Piazza della Repubblica) with the Naiad fountain at the center, decorated with four beautiful, shapely women—women a bit like Anna.

As chance would have it, a young man named Remo, son of a butcher specializing in wild game, lived in the building across from Anna's, in apartment 4. Remo had the modest ambitions allowed him by his social condition and the times. Anyone who lived through those times knew what Rome was then—a city still immersed in its past and dazed by war, regardless of the liberation that arrived in early June of 1944. The capital, like the rest of Italy, functioned in an economy of poverty, with clothes turned inside out rather than washed, long lines at the public fountains for a flask of fresh water, and the rare automobile, an indisputable sign of wealth. That was the Rome Dino Risi portrayed in his film *Poveri ma belli*. Many young people, however, recognized themselves and their lives in Luciano Emmer's *Domenica d'agosto*, a film in which nothing happened and a sense of events developed only as they happened. "Vacation" meant taking the electric train to the beaches at Ostia with a bag full of *panini* (not yet called by the English term sandwiches) filled with omelets or chicory.

Moving from one neighborhood to another was rare. There were Romans born in the Fascist-built suburbs who'd never set foot in the city center. And the center—the dense network of streets crossed by the ribbon of the Via del Corso, still devoid of cars—preserved its nineteenth-century air. Italo Calvino's description in his book *Città invisibili* (*Invisible Cities*) also described Rome in those years: "The city, however, does not tell its past, but contains it like the lines of a hand, written in the corners of the streets, the gratings of the windows, the banisters of the steps, the antennae of the lightning rods, the pole of the flags, every segment marked in turn with scratches, indentations, scrolls."[2] The capital was like this, too, its past indented, scratched, and motionless in the hundreds of small marks on its surfaces.

In the early 1950s, when Anna walked arm-in-arm with her Remo on Sunday afternoons to admire the windows of the elegant shops on the Via Condotti, Rome still had the air of another era. The atmosphere was transparent, the light on certain clear winter days had the brightness of porcelain, and the monumentality of it all seemed more intense in the deserted streets, where passing automobiles were still a rarity. Anna and Remo may have gone dancing in the courtyard of a block of flats in the suburbs, in the Garbatella or Tuscolano neighborhoods, or on a floating pier along the banks of the Tiber where the dance floor had a straw roof and was decorated with pieces of colored paper or light bulbs painted red and blue to give it a more festive feeling. In these proto-*discoteche*, young tenors with weak voices, accompanied by two or three instruments, sang songs about anemic young women who dreamed of love, or femme fatales cloaked in exoticism, with lyrics like, "Down in Copacabana / woman is queen / woman is sovereign." Potent images of cinemato- graphic sensuality projected this fantasy onto the silver screen, much like Rita Hayworth in *Gilda,* who swayed to the strains of *Amado Mio.*

The sentimental education of girls like Anna was generally imparted in weekly magazines with comic-strip soap-opera stories titled *Grand Hotel* or *Zazà.* These enchanted stories' heroines were invariably a common girl, a secretary or salesgirl, who met her soul mate—a lawyer or, better yet, a journalist, or even an airplane pilot.

The stories always offered the glimpse of a bright future, which was as much as anyone could ask. A few years earlier a song had described that future in detail: "una casettina in periferia, una mogliettina giovane e carina, tale e quale come te . . . senza esagerare, sarei certo di trovare tutta la felicità" ("a little house in the suburbs, a little wife, young and cute, just like you . . . I'm not exaggerating, I'd surely find true happiness").

The stories in those weeklies also delivered strong moral messages. In them a reckless girl often fell into the clutches of a scoundrel: first she was seduced, her feeble and unconvincing refusals notwithstanding, then she was abandoned as soon as she became pregnant. No one talked about contraception then, and abortions were performed by back-street abortionists, or abroad, for those who could afford to go. Bishops equated civil marriage with being a concubine, and divorce was only available to the rich, masked by the name "annulment by the Sacra Rota." Anna Fallarino knew both of these very different worlds—first the one, where she looked from the outside in, and (later on) the one full of privileges.

Upon hearing of the tragedy at Via Puccini Anna's former fiancé Remo said, "We went steady for three years. We were supposed to get married, but in the end it never happened. I can't believe she ended like this. The newspapers talk about orgies, perversions, and the strange things she did with the marquis. I remember her as she was then, a down-to-earth girl who could take care of herself. I can only remember her that way, and I want to say so to everybody who's talking about her now like some fallen woman. Anna never would have turned into that if nobody had led her so astray."

The girl followed a pretty normal path; she found work as a salesgirl in a clothing shop where she hung various garments from the balcony hoping to convince clients to buy them, and the most satisfied would give her a little tip. She could have been satisfied, the "little house in the suburbs" was within her reach. Anna, however, only had one thought in her mind—how to really make the most of her own beauty. The women who won the Miss Italy contests had nothing on Anna. When she saw them parading in the news reels before the main feature at the cinema, in those pretty white bathing suits that clung to their bodies, the cups filled by firm breasts and wearing high heels that made their legs look so long, Anna knew she wouldn't be out of place in their midst. She thought she deserved the winner's bouquet as much—or more—than they did, along with the popping flashbulbs, the tiara, and the chaste congratulatory hugs of some handsome undersecretary. She only needed to figure out how to get there, since that world led to the movies, to the best beaches, to motorboats docked at Piazza San Marco in Venice, and brightly colored cocktails on the terraces of luxury hotels, where the air was filled with the sound of ice tinkling in crystal goblets.

With a bit of hard work—because she certainly had far to go—she found occasional work as a runway model, and learned how to carry herself stiffly, walking with one foot set carefully in front of the other while hardly moving her thighs, which were already generous, and needed little to make her stand out. And she finally made it to the movies; in 1949 Mario Mattoli, who was directing his umpteenth film with the famed comedian Totò, titled *Tototarzan*, gave her a bit part. It wasn't much, but she saw it as her debut. The film also starred Giovanna Ralli, Sophia Loren (who was Sophia Lazzari at the time, which was a step ahead of where she started, as Sophia Scicolone), and a young Tino Buazzelli. Anna appeared for a few seconds on screen next to Totò. Her cinematic career began and ended with this movie, although it's possible she might've garnered some attention had she been a bit more persistent. Her Mediterranean good looks and ample proportions corresponded to the popular taste of the times, after years of hunger and sadness during the war, for sumptuously full-figured women.

Anna didn't stick with it because in 1950, the same year *Tototarzan* was released, she found something better. She was just twenty when she met Giovanni Drommi, a twenty-eight-year-old engineer and industrialist, scion of a well-heeled Roman family. His nickname was Peppino, he frequented the most fashionable salons in town, and led the sort of life Anna had only dreamt of. When she went out with Remo she had to be home by nine o'clock at the latest. Speaking later about their relationship, Remo made it clear that he'd never had the chance to lay as much as a finger on her, and that for some reason it was her parents who pressured them to break up. When she started going out with Peppino, Anna was more or less in the same position. They started to talk about marriage almost immediately, and she sent him cards that said, "I pray that the Virgin lets us marry soon." And so it went. They were married in a church, complete with white dress, confetti, rice, applause, tears, and all the rest. Peppino Drommi was a longtime friend of Marquis Camillo, but Anna didn't yet know that, and ignored the weight their friendship would soon have on her own life.

This first marriage lasted ten years. They had no children, but their life was more comfortable than anything anyone in the Fallarino family had ever known. When Anna told her parents about the things she did, the clothes she bought, the places she'd seen, they could hardly believe their ears. This change corresponded to the more general transformation then underway in Rome and Italy; Anna Fallarino was living a personal version of the boom the country as a whole was experiencing in those same years. Italy—almost unbeknownst to its people, and still rife with contradiction—was undergoing the transformation from a patriarchal, essentially agrarian society to an industrial power of the first order. This change had more than economic consequences; it also affected the country's customs, including its sexual mores, and it's important to keep that in mind as we examine the events that were about to overtake Anna Fallarino Drommi.

The life, background, culture, and behavioral models of Camillo Casati Stampa di Soncino were entirely different. He grew up in a family with an ancient lineage. In 1848, during the "Cinque Giornate" Battle of Milan, Gabrio Casati headed the provisional government, and later he would be Minister of Education, enacting a school reform that lasted until 1923. Gabrio's sister, Teresa, married Federico Confalonieri, an exponent of Lombard liberalism who was sentenced to death by the Austrians and imprisoned at Spielberg (the infamous prison where the political revolutionary Silvio Pellico was also held). He was later pardoned, largely through the efforts of his wife. Looking a little deeper we find that Camillo's ancestors also include the Nun of Monza made famous in Manzoni's novel *I promessi sposi* (*The Betrothed*).

Another of Camillo's ancestors—his namesake—married Luisa Amman in the early twentieth century. She was originally an Austrian woman of overpowering personality. The futurist writer Filippo Tommaso Marinetti called her "the greatest futurist in the world," Jean Cocteau dubbed her "the lovely serpent of earthly paradise," and Gabriele D'Annunzio said, "She is the only woman who ever astonished me." Beautiful, tall, green-eyed, eccentric, and passionate, Luisa Casati mingled with the most important European artists and literati of the 1920s and 1930s, including D'Annunzio, Cocteau, Marinetti, Man Ray, and Cecil Beaton. She was their muse, friend, and occasional lover. She adored black clothes, which is precisely how the futurist painter Giovanni Boldini dressed her in a fiery portrait. She said black set off her pale complexion, enhancing her beauty with a turbid languidness. For a long time she refused the ardent advances of D'Annunzio, the national poet, while accepting others much less "worthy" than him. Finally, though, she gave in, and their relationship lasted about ten years. Luisa was one of the women who warmed the poet's later years. When she died, in 1957, she was completely broke, having squandered her fortune with immoderate spending and sumptuous parties. One soirée, held in Venice's Piazza San Marco, is memorable because she'd rented the entire square from the city government.

Little or nothing remained to our Camillo, who was born in 1927, of his family's radiant past. Perhaps he inherited an awareness of the name that, without any other qualities, managed to transform itself into an unjustifiable arrogance. His wife Anna said of him, "Camillo began his personal war with servants as a child; it seems he had the habit of kicking them in the shins." After the tragedy his impeccable butler, Felice, reported, "The marquis was a man full of contradictions. We domestics remember him as exemplary, a fine, mannerly gentleman. . . . For example, sometimes he found it unbecoming to speak directly to the staff, and when he addressed us it was through a third person, even if we were only a step away from him. Once he even behaved this way with my wife, Oliviera, who was the marquise's personal maid. She took it rather badly. He summoned her for a rebuke, and then had her stand, frozen still, in front of him. He called the marquise, and then only spoke to Oliviera." Turning to his wife, Camillo said, "Oliviera needs to know she made a mistake. I do not want that mistake repeated." Anna repeated this to the dismayed domestic, "You've made a mistake! The marquis wants it never to be repeated." The poor woman fled in tears. Another time the marquis struck a servant, drawing blood, because he'd awakened him too early. The consequences of this rocky relationship with his domestic staff also played a part on the evening of the tragedy.

Camillo was friendly with Rome's *nobiltà nera*, the "black" nobility faithful to the pope (as opposed to the *nobiltà bianca*, the "white" nobility faithful to the Savoy rulers). He'd studied in a Swiss boarding school, and passed the days pursuing his two great passions—hunting and crossword puzzles. He practiced the latter everywhere he went. He had several homes: the Roman apartment on Via Puccini; a vacation house on the island of Zannone, in the national park of Circeo; a luxurious apartment in Milan; and estates in Velate Milanese, Cinisello Balsamo, Muggiò, Nova Milanese, Trezzano sul Naviglio, Gaggiano, and Bareggio. At Cusago his vast estate included a viscount's castle, and he also had a seventeenth-century villa in Arcore, in the Brianza area north of Milan, which included a collection of fifteenth- and sixteenth-century paintings and a library of over ten thousand volumes. The marquis' normal routine was relieved by the occasional extravagance. One of his servants recalled, "When he was staying at the Palazzo Soncino in Milan, the marquis would go out with a bag full of hardboiled eggs to a café on the Piazza Santa Beltrade. He stayed there all day, chatting with the regular customers as he ate his eggs and drank champagne. . . . In the evening he came home, but not before leaving a 100,000 lire tip at the bar."

This idle affability would alternate with sudden outbursts of absolute fury. The butler Felice revealed that Camillo once had to back his car out of the courtyard of the building on Via Puccini. Another car was a bit in the way, but it didn't block his exit. The marquis lost his patience, and in a terrible burst of anger repeatedly ran his Rover 3000 smack into the other car. He would move forward a few meters, throw the car into reverse, and ram it into the offending obstacle. "He gritted his teeth, it was frightening. He did it over and over and over, until he saw the other car reduced to a heap of scrap metal." The next day he paid the bill for the damage without saying a word.

It is not my intention here to tell Marquis Camillo's life story—I only want to point out a few things that help us better understand the tragedy that brought his life, as well as that of two other people, to a quick end. In 1950, the first Holy Jubilee Year after the war, in more or less the same month that Anna married her engineer, Camillo married Letizia Izzo, a Neapolitan dancer. They had a daughter, Annamaria, the following year; she was nineteen at the time of the tragedy in 1970, and this, too, has some importance, because at the time people were officially considered minors until the age of twenty-one.

In 1958 something happened in Cannes, it seems, that first set Peppino and Camillo in competition in Anna's eyes. They were staying in a luxurious hotel in the city, right on the Côte d'Azur, and there was a party. Those soirées had the air, more than they would today, of a truly grand event, giving attendees a sense of having exclusive privileges. Porfirio Rubirosa was among the guests, and although his name seems like something straight out of fiction, it actually belonged to one of the most famous, luckiest lady-killers of the 1950s. Anna was elegant and lovely; Rubirosa wasn't the only man to notice her. Unlike the others, though, he wasn't content just to look. He approached her and began a conversation with the inane and pleasant fluidity that only years of experience and great self-confidence permit. As he spoke he put one of his hands familiarly on her bare back. This was a gesture of a bit too much confidence, and caused a rather heated reaction, but to really understand why this happened, we need to know a little more about the event's central character.

Porfirio, a Dominican, wasn't very tall, but was good-looking. Above all, he was famously well endowed where it counts, and reputed for his exceptional endurance. Americans rather brutally referred to it as "the Rolls Royce of genitalia"; Latin Americans were a tad more subtle, calling him "el rey de todos los playboys del mundo" ("king of all the world's playboys"). The name Porfirio came from an eighteenth-century comic opera, a funny name for a man born in 1909. With nothing better to do, he began an ordinary military career in the Dominican Republic, which at the time was ruled by the ferocious dictator Rafael Trujillo. One day the dictator sent the witty captain to the airport to pick up his seventeen-year-old daughter, Flor de Oro (Golden Flower, another name that perfectly fit the situation), who was returning home from high school in France. A few weeks later the two were married. Their union didn't last long, but years later Flor de Oro confided to a friend that it took her a week to recover from her wedding night, so ardent was her bridegroom's enthusiasm.

Rubirosa had everything the most hedonistic man could want— palaces, race cars, money, and horses. He also had dozens of the most beautiful women in the world, each ready to do anything for him because, as one Latin American newspaper put it, he "exudaba una sensación de romance y aventura" ("exuded a feeling of romance and adventure"). These women included Eva Perón, Zsa-Zsa Gabor, Jayne Mansfield, Veronica Lake, Ava Gardner, Marilyn Monroe, Susan Hayward, Danielle Darrieux, and Dolores Del Rio. Among his several marriages were the 1947 union with Doris Duke, heiress of an enormous American tobacco fortune, and later Barbara Hutton, granddaughter of Frank Winfield Woolworth, another of the world's richest women. As a wedding present she gave him a B-25 bomber refitted for civilian use. One of Porfirio's favorite sayings was appropriate to the role he played, "Most men are eager to make money; I'm eager to spend it."

But much of all this was theater. In truth Rubirosa knew he was play-acting through years in which everyone just wanted to forget the war, a time ripe for his antics. Taki Theodoracopulos, the famous journalist and bon vivant, wrote, "When he got drunk 'Rubi' would pick up a guitar and sing 'Soy solo un chulo'" which means, essentially, "I'm nothing but a poor devil." His last marriage was more successful than the others, at least in terms of how long it lasted. When he was just shy of fifty Porfirio married Odile Rodin, who was only seventeen and had just begun an acting career. They were married in October of 1956, and despite the thirty-year age difference they got along well. Porfirio died in Paris in 1965 in a manner appropriate to the way he had lived. After partying all night to celebrate the victory of his polo team in the French Cup he got in his beautiful Ferrari and bade his friends a cheerful farewell. It was seven thirty in the morning, and shortly afterward his car slammed into a tree in the Bois de Boulogne.

It's not hard to understand Peppino Drommi's concern when he saw Porfirio's hand resting on his wife's bare back—not even Odile's presence reassured him. Yet the gesture seemed to bother Marquis Camillo even more. Peppino approached the "king of all playboys" and asked him to remove his hand. Porfirio smiled indulgently at him and went on talking to Anna as if nothing had happened. Camillo, meanwhile, succumbed to one of his fits of rage, and sprang to his feet. Peppino threw the first punch, and Rubirosa (who was also an amateur boxer) quickly reacted. Camillo hurled himself at his face. It was just like a brawl in the movies. Tables were overturned, glasses shattered, a lot of people screamed, beautiful women were frightened, and there was also a hint of amusement in the air.

Some say the first sparks between Anna and Camillo were ignited by this famous brawl fought in her honor in that grand hotel on the Côte d'Azur, which may well be true. In any case, a few months after this episode Camillo requested an annulment of his marriage to Izzo. It became a costly undertaking; the former marquise wanted an enormous sum, as well as a place in the family tomb in order to secure her role before the ecclesiastical court. Apparently she told him, "I was born among the poor, but I want to end up buried among the rich," words worthy of an epitaph. In the end she got her place in the Casati Chapel in Muggiò. Peppino Drommi also recited the necessary lines to get an annulment, and sometime later was remarried to Patrizia de Blanck, a former host on the popular television show *Il Musichiere*. Anna and Camillo were married in a civil ceremony in Switzerland in April of 1959, and again, in a church, on June 21, 1961. Thus even in the eyes of God Anna became Marquise Casati Stampa di Soncino.

What kind of marriage did Camillo and Anna have? The true nature of their relationship came to light only after the murders. If anyone knew about or participated in their curious ménages, it had been kept secret.

The apartment on Via Puccini occupied two stories, the fourth and fifth floors, of the building. Its entrance was on the fourth floor, which also had the bedroom, a dressing room with a bathroom, and a den. The marquis' desk stood in a corner of the latter. The fourth floor also had a guest room, game room, and a room for servants. The upper floor had a large reception room, dining room, other servants' quarters, an aviary, and a room lined with Camillo's hunting trophies, all carefully stuffed and hung on the walls. These included not only birds, but also foxes, deer, roebucks, and wild boars. A locked gun case stood in one corner, full of well-oiled, shiny shotguns ready for use.

On August 30, 1970, the day of the crime, police officer Domenico Scali was one of the first to enter the apartment, and described what he saw in an interview: "The first body I saw was Anna Fallarino's. It looked as if she were still alive, sitting on a sofa with her legs crossed on a footstool. Her hands were in her lap, and her face looked serene. The part that was wrong was the dark bloodstain on her blouse. Near her, next to the sofa, was the young Minorenti. He was lying curled up on the floor, and wearing a light sweater and trousers. He was half-hidden behind a small table that he'd tried to use, it seems, as a last means of defense. Going farther in I saw the third body, that of the marquis. It wasn't a pretty sight; half his head had been disfigured by the shotgun blast. The gun, a Browning twelve-gauge rifle, was lying abandoned on an armchair. He must've used that chair to hold the rifle under his chin."

Valerio Gianfrancesco, the police commissioner who led the investigation, remembered, "There wasn't a lot of blood in the room, although there was the macabre detail of the marquis' ear hanging from a picture frame; it had been blown there by the bullet. One of the woman's breasts was protruding from the tear a bullet made in her clothes. Some white, thick substance was oozing from the wound, and I couldn't figure out what it was. I called over the medical examiner, an old friend of mine, to have a look at it. 'Don't worry,' he said, 'it's only silicone.' I couldn't believe it—it was the first time I'd seen anything like it."

Anna Fallarino was one of the first Italian women to get breast implants, an operation still completely unheard of at the time. The more important discovery the commissioner made, however, was Camillo Casati's diary. "It was in the desk of the study where the crime took place. It was a diary the size of a file folder, bound in green leather, and written in Casati's neat handwriting. It was an important discovery—together with the photographs it allowed us to reconstruct the events leading up to the crime, and thus to explain what had happened. But it was also a delicate discovery, something to be handled tactfully because of the names it contained and the details of certain accounts that were a good deal more lurid than the versions published in the newspapers."

With an almost maniacal precision and richness of detail the marquis had chronicled his wife's sexual encounters with workmen, soldiers, lifeguards, and waiters—encounters he himself had arranged, and sometimes paid for. This behavior began the very day they were married, right in the hotel where they spent their wedding night. When a waiter brought champagne to their room, the marquis left the door to the bathroom where Anna was showering ajar. At first the man didn't understand what was happening, but then he caught on and went in. That was the nature of their relationship, from that night on, for eleven years. "Today Anna made love with a lad so effectively that even at a distance I could share in the joy." "Today Anna met an airman. He was young and exceedingly handsome. It was a fantastic encounter. Anna was happy, and participated with great intensity." "We went to the beach at Fiumicino, and a lot of men were looking at her. Together we chose a young man. He was fulfilling, and we paid him 30,000 lire." "We were super-nude at Fiumicino. Anna was beautifully laid out, relaxing. Later a new airman passed by . . . totally divine." "I like it when you're in bed with someone else, I feel like I love you even more." "Today Anna made love to a soldier. It cost me 30,000 lire, but it was worth it." In addition to the diary, investigators found dozens, even hundreds of photographs that showed Anna nude, sometimes in poses meant to be artistic, sometimes just obscene, but always focused on the details you might easily guess.

Camillo's particular mental process, quite simple and not so uncommon, was explained this way by the psychiatrist Emilio Servadio, "It's called voyeurism, and it's the desire to be a witness, to look on, to observe. An accentuation, in other words, of what a famous American scholar called 'the visual stimulus.' It's a phenomenon that develops early, because there are children who, at a certain age, develop a curiosity that resolves itself in the need to see, to know, to watch. If this tendency is not overcome in their psychosexual development it can remain an important part of the adult's sexuality, and the adult will then exhibit a morbid desire to watch other peoples' sexual activities." These individuals, Professor Servadio continued, also have a heightened inclination toward masochism, especially the type called "moral masochism."

Even with this psychological explanation, we might ask why this man, who for eleven years had fed his habit with such evident satisfaction, so suddenly rebelled against a situation he'd created for his own pleasure. Servadio's answer to this was, "the key to the puzzle, and for me the solution to this case, is this: the masochist, contrary to what we may think, is not an individual who allows himself to be mistreated *ab libitum*, at the mercy of someone else's whims and desires. The masochist is always the director, always in control of the situation. Let's trace the term back to its roots: Leopold von Sacher-

Masoch, who gave this perversion its name, wrote to his lover, Wanda von Dunajew, 'I am coming to you at that hour. You will be dressed in a pair of high, black boots, and you will have a whip. You will say to me, "Kneel, slave, because I am your queen."' He wrote it, so he was in charge of the script. If at any point his partner forgot her role and didn't whip him enough, Masoch would react horribly. That's what he did, in effect, when he tried to strangle his wife upon finding her in a situation he hadn't planned."

It was something new in the routine that finally broke the pattern of behavior the Casati couple had created. After ten years of taking men to please her husband, Anna—perhaps even as a sign of her love for the marquis—for the first time chose a partner on her own, and then fell in love with him. She didn't just copulate with Massimo Minorenti, as she had with the others—she made love to him.

They had met at a party and begun seeing one another. One afternoon they went together to a hotel in the area around the Viale Liegi. These were brief meetings, and were Anna's first in secret after all the men she'd had in front of her husband.

If it's relatively easy to clarify Camillo's motivations, Anna's are much more difficult to explain. Why did she play such a game, right from the first night they were married? Was there some explicit agreement between them, or did they understand one another without a need for words? If he was a voyeur, was she, in the clinical sense, an exhibitionist? We don't know the answer to these questions, and Professor Servadio's opinion here seems more debatable: "It seems evident to me that it also gave the woman pleasure, in addition to the social and economic advantages she gained by allowing her husband to use her like that. Furthermore, it's been shown that the same masochistic or sadistic components are more common in women than in men. Thus it's entirely possible that she took direct pleasure from the turbid, abnormal situations her husband placed her in. Let's take the fact that she was photographed nude, in lascivious poses—this is a part of that disposition to perversion which women are more prone to than men."

If it was a matter of social and economic advantages, Anna had already guaranteed them by marrying the marquis. His first wife's settlement was substantial, and hers could have been even bigger—a mutual break up wasn't in the marquis' best interest. On the other hand, there are testimonies of the two servants, Felice and Oliviera, that mentioned they heard the couple fighting and yelling, saw Anna crying, and heard her, at least once, vent. On that occasion she transformed from the marquise back into the poor girl from Amorosi, exclaiming, "It'd be better to eat onions and bread and live like a bum where I came from than to accept the rules of this corrupt world, full of people who make me sick. If this continues, one day or another I'll toss it all to the wind and go back home."

This was one aspect of Anna's personality and the tone of the whole affair. The other, almost diametrically opposed aspect, belonged to the woman who allowed herself to be photographed nude hundreds of times—and in such immodest poses—and to be had dozens of times by the first stranger who passed by. How could she have done all that if she didn't also have some natural propensity for such erotic games, or, more crudely, such perversions? Perhaps, though, she did it because she nursed some kind of bottomless unhappiness deep down.

Speaking of perversions, Sigmund Freud had an opinion that gives us something to think about. "The omnipotence of love," he wrote, "never reveals itself as strongly as it does in its own aberrations." It's precisely this "omnipotence" that takes such a high toll because, as Franco De Masi explained in an essay on perversions published in his book *I concetti del male*, it manifests itself "by transforming the beloved into an object." He believes, and perhaps he's right, that a "pervert" is simply someone who acts on what most people only fantasize about (similarly, Georges Bataille claimed, "The perverse is nothing more than an excess of what we are"). But this is exactly the difference and, if true, also the premise of this tragedy. Franco De Masi and Leopold von Sacher-Masoch confirm the same thing: perversion is governed by its own precise rules, one of which is the objectification of the loved one. At the very instant Anna began to choose and decide on her own, abandoning her role of the "object," she broke the rules, and the tragedy was set into motion.

Anna wrote to Massimo from the island of Zannone, "I'm really sad. Usually I really love this island, but this year I hate it. . . . I think a note from you would make me happy. If you can, type the envelope and put the return address as Sartoria Botti (my dressmaker), Corso Italia 21, Rome. Now I need to leave you, Camillo is coming back in. I send you a big hug, your Anna." When she was taken on the sand of Fiumicino in front of her husband, Anna was complicit in a ribald game. Here, instead ("I need to leave you. Camillo is coming back in"), we have a classic "betrayal," the woman acting like an archetypal Emma Bovary. This happened in the spring of 1970. A few days later, she wrote again, "My only love, I am writing while Camillo is sitting comfortably in his armchair listening to the radio. What can I tell you more than I adore you so, so, so much? I think with such excitement about the time we can be together again, we two alone for a week or even just a day, all to ourselves. Bye, my great love." This is sheer Bovarism.

At the same time, or shortly afterward, Camillo realized what was happening and noted, bitterly, in his diary, "What a delusion. I wish I were dead and buried. How disgusting, how nasty. It makes me sick—that's what Anna gave me, sickness. Really, losing her head for a young man as absolutely insignificant as Massimo, who, if he didn't have such nice hair as a disguise, would be a total nobody." A nobody or not, Massimo was a handsome lad—part loafer, part playboy, he was a political science student who hadn't taken a single exam. He frequented nightclubs, took part in the neo-Fascist youth movement, and put on the affected airs of a professional poker player, even though he usually lost and had to sign countless IOUs. In compensation, though, he had some luck with the ladies, as is proven by the relationship he had with Lola Falana, an Afro-Italian dancer who had a fair amount of success on television. It seems his ambition was to open a car dealership, or maybe a nightclub. These were things he was familiar with, and he thought he could do it with Anna's help (and, of course, Camillo's). But by breaking the rules of the game he also took a risk. He certainly would have been more careful had he not also been so emotionally involved.

Anna essentially tried to beat her husband at his own game. She didn't hide her affair with Massimo and hoped, instead, to pass it off as a variation on their activities. She didn't allow him to watch when they made love, but told him about it, "Anna had her lover and one of his friends to dinner, she told me. But I think she usually hides about eighty percent of it from me. What a shame!" Since he couldn't expect traditional faithfulness from his wife, Camillo at least expected her to be faithful to their rules, and give him a detailed report of her encounters. He wrote in his dairy, "Anna has completely failed me, but my illness binds me to her. I can't sleep, even though I want to so much. But how can I when she tells me 'I will keep the phone close by until I go to sleep' and then she makes a call, receives another, then makes one more, and tells me nothing, and all the while I'm in the den tormenting myself? . . . I can't take this situation anymore. I really want to leave her, but I can't do it." A few days later, he added, "I'm slowly dying on the inside; I've lost everything. . . . I can't take this anymore."

He knew. She was aware of how depressed Camillo was, and saw the rancor pent up inside him. Perhaps to approach him, or to distance what she felt as a threat, she agreed to go with him to Fiumicino on August 26, four days before the end, and have sex in front of him with a passing soldier.

On Saturday, August 29, the marquis was in Valdagno, guest of his friends the Marzottos at a hunting party. He called home several times to speak with Anna. She told him she was having dinner with Massimo and another three friends. During the last call, at midnight, she admitted they'd all left except Massimo and his friend Aurelio. Camillo suspected that the former would spend the night with his wife, and he threatened to return to Rome and kill them. The Marzottos said that after that conversation Camillo went to bed upset. But things turned in a different direction. Anna, Massimo, and Aurelio guessed that Camillo was about to break. The marquis seemed beside himself; on the telephone he intimated they should leave the house, called Massimo a pimp, and set a date with his wife for the following day, saying he needed an explanation. Frightened, Anna and the two young men asked to stay the night with a fourth friend. At eleven o'clock on Sunday morning the marquise called a cousin of hers, an assistant police chief in Naples, and asked him to come with her for the meeting with her husband, but he refused. In a flurry of chaotic events, Massimo called a lawyer he knew and briefly described the situation to him. His advice made good sense, and he suggested to them that they not show up. But Anna, now terrified, wrote Camillo a note of near surrender, "Please forgive me if I've made a mistake. I promise to break it off immediately with Massimo and come back to you as before." A servant was responsible for delivering it to the marquis as soon as he set foot in the house.

That was at six thirty on Sunday afternoon. A servant called Anna from the house on Via Puccini and told her the marquis had returned and was waiting for her and Massimo as they had agreed. Hesitating, she asked to speak directly with her husband. He seemed calm on the phone, and reassured her by saying he only wanted to clarify the situation. While Anna and Massimo made their final plans with two friends who would go with them to the apartment, Camillo called his butler and ordered him to admit his wife and her companion, then close the door and not disturb them for any reason whatsoever.

At about seven Anna and Massimo arrived at Via Puccini in a Fiat 500; Massimo's friends followed them in a Rover. Meanwhile, Camillo was sitting at his desk writing this note, "I die because I can't stand that you love another man. I need to do what I am doing. Forgive me. And come sometimes to visit me." He put the note in an envelope and wrote "Anna" on it. The two cars were coming up the Lungotevere as Camillo unlocked the gun case and chose the Browning twelve-gauge rifle, loading it with five cartridges. The cars arrived at Via Puccini. Anna and Massimo got out, while their friends stayed in the Rover to wait for their return.

We don't know how the tragedy's prologue played out, but it was brief. If Camillo was thinking about killing himself, perhaps in front of Anna and her lover as his last note suggests, he quickly changed his mind. Maybe it was rage that blinded him, or perhaps the words they exchanged in the quiet of the den convinced him that Anna had lied, that nothing could be as it was before, that he had definitively lost. The first bullets were for his wife. The marquis was a good shot, and in any case couldn't have missed at such short distance. Two shots were fired, hitting her in the arm and chest. She was sitting in an armchair, and there she remained, thunderstruck. Even this detail had a certain importance. Massimo tried to flee, running to leave the room. A bullet struck him in the back, and either right before or immediately afterward he tried to use a little table as a shield. The second bullet, however, hit him directly in the head. Now crazed, Camillo approached Anna and from a few steps away shot her in the throat. He'd emptied the first five rounds, and then loaded two more shells into the rifle. Wedging the butt of the rifle against the back of an armchair, he put the barrel against his throat, pulled the trigger, and his head exploded along with the cartridge.

The two friends waiting in the street heard the shots and the sound of breaking glass, and decided to go up and ring the doorbell. The servants, too, had heard everything, but when the men asked to go see what was happening, the domestics said they had strict orders—they weren't to enter the den for any reason. It was about eight o'clock, and the three inside were already dead. The two friends went back to the street, and one of them called Anna's sister at Rocca di Papa, a town just south of Rome, telling her what they feared had happened. She immediately left for Rome, and when she met them in Via Puccini it was nine-thirty. All three went back upstairs, but the butler couldn't be convinced to do anything. Only after they insisted did he finally decide to open the door.

We already know what they saw inside, and also know, or at least can imagine, what followed—the doctor, the ambulance, the police, the investigation, the morbid curiosity fed by the photos and indiscretions (in the following days local newspapers increased their print runs by five hundred thousand copies), and the many unanswered questions. Did Massimo know about Anna's double life? Did she really think she could start over with a man sixteen years her junior? Was her relationship with Camillo consensual or forced? If the marquis had chosen suicide, what pushed him to murder instead? No one had any answers to these questions back then, and they're even more difficult to answer today. As is almost always the case with love affairs, the secrets the three of them shared were buried along with them.

Their story, however, has an afterword worth telling. A few weeks after the massacre the notary Carlo Pantalani made public the terms of Marquis Casati Stampa's will. It read, in part, "I name my wife, Anna Fallarino, my heir. I married her in church on June 21, 1961, and she made all the years she was with me happy ones. To my daughter by Letizia Izzo, Annamaria, I leave the child's due portion, plus 100 million lire in insurance, and the painting of the Madonna and Child." Anna's relatives challenged the document, assuming that if their relative died even a second after her husband, then the Casati Stampa estate would go to them. They were represented in this delicate matter by Cesare Previti, a lawyer born in Reggio Calabria in 1934 and a neo-Fascist sympathizer like his father, Umberto. He was an expert in commercial law, and a good friend of Anna's sister. The coroner's report, however, established that Anna had died instantly from her wounds, and as a consequence the marquis' heir was the daughter by his first marriage, Annamaria, born in Rome on May 22, 1951. Juvenile court entrusted the girl to a guardian until she reached legal adulthood. At this point Previti, the Fallarino family lawyer, called Annamaria and offered his services to her. Shocked by the tragedy, she accepted. Her maternal aunt and only living relative, Emilia Izzo, asked the court to name her guardian of her underage niece. In front of the judge, however, Annamaria declared that she didn't want to be entrusted to her aunt, and instead chose Senator Giorgio Bergamasco (born in Milan in 1904 and a member of the Liberal Party). The Milanese magistrate, Antonio De Falco supported her, ignoring the article in the civil code that governs the naming of guardians, stipulating that they should "preferably be the minor's ancestors, or at least his or her close relatives or in-laws." Previti remained her assistant guardian, as her lawyer and representative in any conflict-of-interest with the guardian himself.

Shaken by the loss of her father and the circumstances of his death, and bewildered by her legal troubles and the media assault, Annamaria left Italy. She moved permanently to Brasilia, Brazil, but only after marrying Pier Donà Dalle Rose. The young marquise eventually reached adulthood and was emancipated from her guardian. Bergamasco, now a minister in Andreotti's cabinet, was given her power-of-attorney with broad authority, and Previti stayed on as her attorney. Pressed by overdue and inheritance taxes, Annamaria asked Previti to sell the villa and grounds at Arcione, but specifically excluded the furniture, paintings, library, and surrounding farmland. In the spring of 1974 the attorney called Brasilia with the triumphant announcement of having made "a real deal." He'd sold the villa in its entirety, complete with the paintings (from the fifteenth and sixteenth centuries, as well as a magnificent portrait of Anna Fallarino by Pietro Annigoni, which critics deemed an exceptional work), the library (with its ten thousand volumes of valuable antiquarian books), the furniture, and the immense park, all for 500 million lire. From distant Brasilia Annamaria couldn't have known that the much-vaunted figure was only what one might pay for a nice apartment in the center of Milan.

A few days later the purchaser, real-estate developer Silvio Berlusconi, took up residence in the villa. He didn't immediately pay the agreed upon 500 million lire, but instead made comfortable annual payments that corresponded to Annamaria Casati's financial deadlines as well as her need to meet her deceased father's numerous outstanding debts. The Arcione property, which Berlusconi had taken possession of in 1974, officially remained Annamaria's, leaving her responsible for property taxes on it. In the act of sale, dated October 2, 1980, the villa was described as "a residence with adjacent farm buildings and land used for a variety of purposes." Shortly afterward, that "residence," which had cost 500 million lire, was deemed by the Cariplo bank an adequate collateral for a loan of 7 billion, 300 million lire.

Other upsetting episodes could easily be included now, but then this would no longer be the Roman story we've been following from the 1950s, turning instead into a lurid tale of twenty-first-century Italy, so it seems appropriate to end it here.

---

1. Cesare Pascarella, *Tutte le opere* (Milan: Mondadori, 1955); no English translation of this volume has been published. Carducci's comment appeared in a review published in the periodical *Nuova Antologia*, July 1886.
2. Italo Calvino, *Invisible Cities*, trans. William Weaver (New York: Harcourt Brace Jovanovich, 1972), 11.

XIV

LIFE BEYOND THE WALLS

THE VIA DI PORTICO D'OTTAVIA is one of the most suggestive and memory-filled streets in Rome. Its southern end faces the river and Ponte Fabricio, also called the "Quattro Capi" Bridge after the ancient milestones decorated with four faces at each corner, and in more ancient times as the *pons Judaeorum*, or Bridge of the Jews. There, on the right, is the small church of San Gregorio della Divina Pietà, a name derived from the legend that Saint Gregory the Great was born nearby. Despite its eighteenth-century facade, the building itself is much older. Its most interesting feature is the inscription over the doorway with a passage from Isaiah (65:2-3), written both in Latin and Hebrew: "All day long I have held out my hands to an obstinate people, who walk in ways not good, pursuing their own imaginations—a people who continually provoke me to my face." The church of San Gregorio stood just outside one of the gates to the Jewish ghetto, and was used for the forced sermons meant to convert the "wretched Jews" to Catholicism. Four or five times a year the Jews of the ghetto were escorted to the nearest church (either San Gregorio, Sant'Angelo in Pescheria, Santa Maria del Pianto, or one of several others) to listen to preachers who tried to convince them to abandon their religion. Those who didn't want to attend the religious services had to pay a fine, and anyone caught sleeping during the sermon was roused by a lash of the whips wielded by the Swiss Guards keeping watch.

A few steps down the street, between the church of Sant'Angelo and the Theater of Marcellus, the road widens into a broad plazalike space. A stone tablet mounted on the wall of an old building marks this as the spot were the Nazi trucks waited, on October 16, 1943, to haul away Roman Jews, an infamous page in the history of Nazi

Fascism I'll return to later. A bit farther along is a majestic arch framing a large portal flanked with columns. The arch is all that remains of the ancient Portico of Octavia, and the door is the entrance into the church of Sant'Angelo in Pescheria, also called Sant'Angelo *in foro piscium*. The street signs note that the Via del Portico d'Ottavia used to be called the Via della Pescheria.

The church's ancient foundations date back perhaps as far as the reign of Pope Boniface II, around 530, or of Stephen II, around 770. One of these popes had it built in the ruins of the portico, using the ancient monument's grandiose propylaeum as the new church's pronaos. The portico was a gigantic square construction decorated with over three hundred columns that Emperor Augustus had built in 33–23 BC in memory of his sister, Octavia, over a smaller pre-existing structure. In addition to serving as the public entrance to the nearby Theater of Marcellus, the portico was a meeting place, and enclosed two temples, two libraries (one Greek, the other Latin) and numerous works of art, including a bronze statue of Cornelia, matron of the Gracchi family and the first woman in Rome to have a statue erected in her honor (Cato thought this an intolerable gesture and vehemently protested, but in vain). The magnificent statue known as the *Medici Venus* was also found in the ruins of the portico, and gives us a good idea of the high-quality art treasures it contained.

The church of Sant'Angelo is famous not only for its unique location, inside an ancient monument, but also for a famed historical event. In 1347, on the eve of Pentecost and after long prayer, Cola di Rienzo set off from here, sword in hand and to the tolling of the church bells, to capture the Capitoline Hill and restore Rome to the grandeur of the ancient Republic. A few meters to the right of the church a small, elegant seventeenth-century facade embellished with stucco decorations marks the entrance to the Oratory of Sant' Andrea dei Pescivendoli.

Before moving on to the other surprises that await us in this neighborhood, you might understandably be wondering why so many places here refer to fish—the terms *pescheria* and *pescivendoli*, as well as others, all derive from the word *pesce*. The real reason is the most predictable one; the fish caught in the river, as well as those brought up the Tiber from the Tyrrhenian Sea, were unloaded by night on the banks of the Isola Tiberina. At dawn the fish market opened, selling both wholesale and to individuals. The fishmongers used slabs of marble taken from nearby temple facades as display counters, a long-standing practice visible in late nineteenth-century photographs of the market.

Farther down the street, at 25 Via del Portico d'Ottavia, there is an extraordinary example of a shop where fragments of ancient monuments were reused as building material. The doorjambs and entablature are finely worked ancient Roman marbles, and the wall around them was originally part of the thirteenth-century Torre dei Grassi, a tower that belonged, not surprisingly, to a family of fish-mongers. Thus we have a working, twenty-first-century shop in a medieval building decorated with first-century marble—a layering of history possible only in Rome. Continuing along, two extremely narrow parallel streets lead off the right side of the Via del Portico d'Ottavia—the Via Sant'Ambrogio and Via della Reginella. These tight spots give us a good idea of what the ghetto was like before the old, insalubrious neighborhood was razed and almost completely rebuilt according to the plans of a project begun in 1888.

Passing by the two little streets we come to a corner building constructed at roughly the same time Columbus discovered America. This residence is known as the Casa di Lorenzo Manilio or Casa dei Manili. Its enlightened owner wanted to decorate the facade of his house with marble fragments of finely carved Latin and Greek inscriptions. He wanted to contribute to an urban renewal by embellishing his house *ad forum Judaeorum* (in the Jewish ghetto) with Roman sculptures, including a funerary relief with four portrait busts and another relief of a lion attacking a deer. The overall effect is a touching testament to Manilio's dedicated humanism.

Just around the corner is the Piazza Costaguti and a small eighteenth-century chapel known as the Tempietto of Carmelo, another place designated for the coercive sermons intended to convert Jews. The Via del Portico d'Ottavia then ends in a wider stretch of road that corresponds to the ancient Piazza Giudea, a square immediately outside another of the gates that enclosed the segregated space of the ghetto. The rather drab sixteenth-century fountain here was designed by Giacomo Della Porta, and not far away, in the Piazza Mattei, is the graceful Turtle Fountain, which is also by Della Porta and is one of the city's most famous fountains.

An irregular space called the Piazza delle Cinque Scole opens to the left; its name refers to the five synagogues that once stood in the ghetto: the Temple, Sicilian, Castilian, Catalan, and New Synagogues. There is a lot to notice in this square, beginning with the steep, dark little hill called the Monte dei Cenci, shaped by underlying Roman ruins, that closes one end of it. The space is also defined by the unfinished church of Santa Maria del Pianto, dedicated to a fresco of the Madonna in an aedicule of the Portico of Octavia which is said to have shed tears over a murder committed right in front of the painting.

Ferdinand Gregorovius found it particularly appropriate that there was a church dedicated to a weeping Virgin at the edge of a neighborhood marked by the humiliation imposed on its inhabitants. In his major book of 1853 there's a vivid description of the miserable spectacle that was the mid-nineteenth-century ghetto:

> Walking down one of the streets of the ghetto we come across Israello working hard in front of his dilapidated house. The Jews sit on their stoops or just outside them, in the alleyways, where there is a little more light than penetrates their damp, smoky rooms. They sort out rags and sew. It is impossible to describe the chaos of rags that accumulate there. It is as if the whole world has been pulled into pieces and now lies at the feet of the Jews. There are heaps of them, of every manner and colour of material, in front of the doors: gilt fringes; pieces of silk and velvet brocade; fragments of red, light and dark blues, yellow, white, and black; and old, torn, stained cloths. I have never seen so many old things. The Jews could dress up all of creation as harlequins. They sit there now, adrift in that sea of rags, as if they are searching for some sort of treasure, or at least some little snippet of gold brocade.[1]

To talk about the Roman ghetto is to talk about the oldest Jewish community in the West. Its people survived centuries of persecution and misunderstanding, dominated first by the ancient Romans, followed by medieval, inquisitorial, papal, and finally Nazi Fascist oppressions. For generations the ghetto was a concentration of people compressed by insurmountable barriers, characterized by great heroism alongside the basest degradation imaginable. It was an amazing symbol of the human ability to adapt to the most extreme living conditions. For centuries the Jews of Rome lived on these four streets, narrow as the hold of a ship, amid a pervasive and unbearable stench. Forced to suffer privations they were forbidden to alleviate, they were persecuted for the sake of alternating advantages—political, religious, and sometimes merely capricious—to benefit various popes.

The first documented presence of Jews in Rome dates back to 159 BC, when an embassy sent by the Israelite general Judas Maccabeus arrived to negotiate an alliance with the government. With some reluctance and ambiguities the pact was finally concluded, making Jews the first Eastern people to sign a treaty that recognized them as the (near) equals of the greatest imperial power of the day. In the Republican and Imperial periods of Roman history the relationship between the Jewish community and city authorities had highs and lows, but even in the worst times it never sank to outright persecution. There were frictions and misunderstandings, like the one over ritual circumcision, which the Romans confused with castration and therefore wanted to ban. There were also, of course, wars. Pompey the Great conquered Jerusalem in 63 BC, and about a century later, in 70 AD, Titus sacked and destroyed the Temple of Solomon, an act that signaled the end of the Jewish nation, which was only resurrected from its ashes in 1948, nearly two thousand years after it had first disappeared. The disastrous sacking of the temple was interpreted as divine justice wrought by the Roman armies on the Jews for killing Christ. The spoils of war Titus brought back to Rome from Jerusalem became the foundation of the Imperial capital's largest museum collection. A relief panel in the Arch of Titus records the despoiling of the temple and the theft of the sacred menorah. This treasure stayed in Rome until the barbarian kings Alaric and Gaiseric sacked the city and stole it.

The relationship between the Jewish community and the Roman emperors also had its ups and downs, but the Jews were generally treated with the same tolerance Romans granted most foreign religions. Their relationship with Julius Caesar, for example, was excellent; he defended their rights and even allowed them to rebuild Jerusalem's city walls after they'd been partially destroyed during Pompey's siege. In his *Lives of the Caesars*, Suetonius wrote that upon Caesar's death, in 44 BC, "at the height of the public grief a throng of foreigners went about lamenting, each after the fashion of his country, above all the Jews, who even flocked to the place for several successive nights."[2]

One of the most important documents to survive from the ancient Greco-Roman world was penned by a Greek historian known by the Romanized name Dio Cassius. It's interesting to note, reading his *Roman History*, which single characteristic of the Jewish religion particularly struck him: "They are distinguished from the rest of mankind in practically every detail of life, and especially by the fact that they do not honour any of the usual gods, but show extreme reverence for one particular divinity. They never had any statue of him even in Jerusalem itself, but believing him to be unnamable and invisible, they worship him in the most extravagant fashion on earth. They built to him a temple that was extremely large and beautiful, except in so far as it was open and roofless, and like-wise dedicated to him the day called the day of Saturn [the Sabbath, Saturday], on which, among many other most peculiar observances, they undertake no serious occupation."[3] With extraordinary acuity, Dio Cassius encapsulated the intellectual abstraction of Jewish spiri-tuality into two words—unnamable and invisible. Tacitus arrived at the same conclusion in his *Annals*, remarking, "the Jews have purely mental conceptions of Deity, as one in essence. They call those pro-fane who make representations of God in human shape out of per-ishable materials."[4] It would be hard to find a starker contrast to the sumptuousness of Roman religion, in which statues of the gods were erected, covered with garlands, and brought very earthly offerings. It's not surprising that in the frenzy of their religious ceremonies the simulacrum, rather than the god, was often worshiped. This pagan characteristic recurs, to a certain extent, in Christianity, especially in some of its gaudier manifestations.

On the whole Jews succeeded in maintaining a dignified rela-tionship with the Romans, barring just a few sanguineous excep-tions. It was only with the advent of Emperor Constantine's reign, in the fourth century, that edicts began to label them a base, bestial, and perverted sect.

Papal attitudes toward the Jews were inconsistent. Gregory the Great, who reigned from 590 to 604, ruled with a balanced toler-ance. Following the great tradition of Roman law, he declared, "Just as no freedom may be granted to the Jews in their communities to exceed the limits legally set for them, so they should in no way suf-fer through a violation of their rights."[5] Other popes were less tolerant, and a habit developed—one that would prove hard to break—of disparagement and persecution.

Among the copious documentation of their condition, some of which we'll return to shortly, I want to highlight an eloquent sonnet by Giuseppe Gioacchino Belli, dated May 4, 1833, which describes with brutal frankness an outrageous custom of the time. The title of the poem is *L'omaccio de l'ebbrei,* a play on words between *omaggio,* an homage (as this piece is, after all, a tribute), and *omaccio*—a bad man. The poet was referring to a custom also described by Massimo d'Azeglio in his book *Miei ricordi (Things I Remember):* "On the first day of Carnival there was a noteworthy ceremony at the Capitoline. The Senate met, and the Senator was seated on the throne. The Chief Rabbi, accompanied by a delegation of Jews from the ghetto, came forward and kneeled before him. The Rabbi then made a speech full of humble declarations of devotion and subjection to the people elected to the Roman senate. Once the address was finished, the Senator extended his foot and kicked the Rabbi, who backed away, expressing his gratitude."[6] This is how Belli described that tradition in his verses:

I wanna tell you a little tale, I do:
In Rome, on the first day of Carnival,
The Jews go into one of the halls
Of the Magistrates at the Campidoglio;

And once they've paid a heavy tribute
To ransom themselves from an old imbroglio,
The Grand Rabbi weaves a pretty speech
of chatter with a moral woven in to boot.

The moral's that the whole ghetto
Swears allegiance to the Laws 'n' acts
Of the Senate and the Roman People.

Then, of those three powder-wigged old toads
The most senior big-wig
Gives 'im a kick and answers: "Go!"[7]

Nevertheless, in every epoch of the city's history there were Jews who managed to achieve economic success despite the difficulties they faced. This was particularly true in the trade and importation of highly coveted items from the East. The large synagogue discovered in excavations at the old port city of Ostia Antica revealed a sizeable local community active in maritime trade. Other Jews became bankers and often rose to the level of financing papal enterprises just as they had, years before, provided the capital for imperial campaigns. The management of Tiberius's family businesses, for example, had been entrusted to the heads of the Alexandrine Jewish community. But these were rare exceptions, and the vast majority of Roman Jews, originally ensconced in Trastevere, worked as small-scale artisans, merchants, and itinerant peddlers; there were a few painters among them, and even actors. One such actor, Aliturno, introduced Josephus Flavius, author of several books on Jewish history, to Nero's wife Poppea. The Roman poet Juvenal wrote about Jewish women who earned their living by interpreting dreams. Literary texts, funerary inscriptions, and a few precious documents portray an industrious community, rich in ingenuity, fairly well integrated, and welcomed with tolerance throughout the ancient city—only rarely were Jews treated with open hostility or ridicule.

The relationship between the Church and Roman Jews began to worsen after the Protestant Reformation. The spread of Lutheranism in Europe forced the pope to take strong repressive actions. Pope Paul III (Alessandro Farnese) officially recognized the counter-reformation Society of Jesus—the Jesuits—in 1540. In 1542 he instituted the supreme inquisitorial tribunal of Rome, also know as the Holy Office of the Inquisition, and nominated the austere cardinal Gian Pietro Carafa to preside over it. In 1553 Church authorities ordered that the Talmud be destroyed on the Jewish New Year in the Campo de' Fiori in a bonfire stoked with other Jewish books, beginning with religious titles. This was the beginning of a dark period destined to last a long time.

In May 1555 Carafa rose to the papacy as Paul IV, and things grew decidedly worse. The Venetian ambassador described him in his first dispatch after the election as a man with "a violent and fiery temperament . . . he is impetuous in dispatching his business, and he doesn't want anyone to contradict him." The pope published the index of banned books in 1559, and it even included parts of the Bible and some texts by Church Fathers. The Inquisition quickly became his favorite court of law. On July 17, 1555, less than two months after he was elected, the new pope issued a bull, *Cum nimis absurdum*, which was a heavy blow to the Jews and officially confined them to the ghetto:

> Both in Rome and other cities in the lands that belong to the Roman Church, all Jews must live together exclusively on one street, or, if this is impossible, in two or three or four as necessary. These spaces must be contiguous and easily distinguished from the places Christians live . . . [and] they must have only one ingress and exit.

The first Italian ghetto was established in Venice in 1516; forty years later Paul IV's bull turned it into an institution governed in every smallest detail by strict laws. The exclusion of the Jews not only forced them into ghettos, but also required they wear a glaring sign of identification, which served the double purpose of making them recognizable and perpetuating their public humiliation (a lesson the Nazis diligently applied later on):

> Men and women alike will be obliged to wear an easily visible hat, or some other obvious sign. It should be blue, and will prevent the Jews from hiding and otherwise pretending. No one may be exempted from this requirement for any reason, including the pretense of high rank, the importance of his title, or any privilege, nor may he acquire any dispensation or exemption.

The Roman ghetto was separated from the rest of the city by a high wall commonly known as the "serraglio," "cloister," or "Jewish jail." The five main access gates were built in 1603, and were shut an hour after sunset each evening between Easter and All Saints' Day, two hours after sunset for the rest of the year. They were opened again at dawn, at the first stroke of the morning bells. The scarcity of space within the gates (about seven acres) and a growing population meant that the ghetto's buildings were built ever higher and the area of each home was reduced; it wasn't unusual to have one or two families share a single room. The narrow streets, barely graced by sunlight, made the area unhealthy. Making the situation even worse was the fact that the buildings facing the Tiber, not yet contained by its current embankments, were repeatedly flooded, both by rising water and whatever was backed up and poured out through the storm sewers. Ghetto families eked out livings as small-scale artisans (leather tanners, haberdashers, and cobblers) or as merchants specializing primarily in fabrics (sometimes rags) but also wine and grain. Two of the few careers papal law permitted them were dealing in second-hand items and money lending.

The area chosen to contain the Jews is now outlined by the Lungotevere, the Via del Portico d'Ottavia, and the Piazza delle Cinque Scole. For three centuries life in the Roman ghetto bustled in the narrow roads and alleys of this area. The neighborhood's main street—its version of the Corso—was the Strada della Rua, which corresponds to what is now the Via Catalana. The ghetto eventually did increase in area over the years as the number of residents grew, and the number of gates rose to a total of eight. As Paul IV's ordinance made clear, this area was designated as the Jewish ghetto in part because the river offered a natural boundary, but also because a number of Jewish families, originally living in Trastevere, had moved across the river and settled near the Isola Tiberina. Only a few Christians had to be removed to make the population of the neighborhood homogeneous. From a commercial point of view the area also offered some strategic advantages. By the end of the war between the Goths and the Byzantine Empire in the middle of the sixth century, a conflict fraught with plundering and sacking, the city had retreated to the places where its first settlements had begun, such as the lowlands between the Isola Tiberina and the Capitoline Hill. This stretch of river allowed for the unloading of cargo, some of the abundant ruins nearby were transformed into residences, and a market on the Capitoline Hill stimulated the local economy. The future site of the ghetto was also ideal from a logistical point of view; the large fortified remains of the Theater of Marcellus marked its southeastern boundary, what remained of the two imposing porticos (dedicated to Octavia and Philip) lent themselves to multiple uses, and the ruins of various temples served as quarries for building material. Its location halfway between the river and the Capitoline market also made it convenient for financial and commercial activities.

The periodic issuance of various papal ordinances imposed severe restrictions on the community. Jews were prohibited from having Christian nursemaids or servants, and Jewish doctors were not allowed to treat Christians or be respectfully called *dominus* by them. It was also illegal for them to work in public on Sundays or operate any business except for selling used goods (*strazziariae seu cenciariae*—literally "tearing up their rags," or hawking second-hand wares). Jews weren't allowed to own property, and even had to pay rent for their ghetto homes to Christian landlords or the government. They could make loans, and occasionally buy and sell jewelry. These loans ranged from small sums lent at interest for the needs of individual families to large-scale financial operations.

An incident involving an ancestor of the painter Amedeo Modigliani illustrates how this financial world worked and what the limits on the Jews were. This branch of the Modigliani family moved to Rome, attracted by the lively commerce there, and Amedeo's ancestor was a well-to-do man, perhaps a banker, but more likely the owner of a pawnshop. He had one important client, a cardinal in financial distress whose situation was resolved with such mutual satisfaction that Modigliani imprudently thought he might challenge the papal ban on owning property by investing his earnings in a vineyard on the slopes of the Alban Hills. Upon finding out about this the Curia ordered the "insolent Jew" to divest himself of the vineyard, and threatened him with heavy sanctions. Having saved a prince of the Church was clearly not enough to warrant purchasing a piece of property. Modigliani obeyed, but shortly afterward moved his family to Livorno, which (along with Pisa) was the only Italian city never to expel or segregate its Jewish population. Modigliani's descendant Amedeo was born in Livorno in 1884.

Large-scale banking operations were obviously quite different from the business Modigliani was in, and for centuries before the relationship between the two communities deteriorated these financial dealings went smoothly. This was especially true throughout the medieval period, but, interestingly, there was still a Jewish banker at the Vatican during the reign of fickle Pope Clement VII (Giulio de' Medici) from 1523-1534. This banker, Daniele da Pisa, was one of the most influential men of his day, and even earned the honorary title *mercatores romanum curiam sequentes*. He enjoyed several rare privileges, including tax exemption from all customs duties throughout the Papal States.

Loans at this level were sometimes handled directly, but more often they went through Florentine intermediaries with ties to the Curia, who then arranged to partner with one or two *judei de Urbe*, the Jewish financiers in Rome. As Ariel Toaff noted in his essay "The Jews of Rome," "the Roman Curia turned to the Jewish bankers of the city to keep control of the local banking sector, in such a way as to manipulate the political levers of the city." Shared interests, which at times were remarkably close, reinforced ties between Roman bankers and the Curia, creating strong business connections between them. A loan to the city of Todi, for example, called for that city's government, should it fail to live up to the terms of the agreement, to pay a large penalty, half of which would go to the *judei de Urbe*, half to the Roman Curia. One of the most enterprising of the Roman Jewish banking firms, owned by Fosco della Scola, made loans to a number of communities in the Papal States, including the Sabine territories, the Duchy of Spoleto, Perugia, and the marches of Ancona.

The mid-sixteenth-century ghetto and accompanying institutions embittered these business relationships, but the crisis in the Roman Jewish community had actually begun some time earlier. The second half of the fourteenth century was marked by a severe economic downturn following the devastating outbreak of the Black Plague, an event vividly recounted by many authors, including Boccaccio, and Rome was hit particularly hard by this crisis. The plague, accompanied by famine, floods, an endemic state of anarchy, and widespread violence, reduced peoples' ability to make their living there and convinced many of them to leave and seek their fortunes elsewhere. That terrible century was also marked by a religious schism in the West (1378), which had a lasting impact on the Church, and the brief but significant career of Cola di Rienzo.

Cola was born "amid the Jews," in the Via della Fiumara, a lane destroyed when the quarter was rebuilt in the nineteenth century. There's a plaque in the Via di San Bartolomeo dei Vaccinari, named after an ancient church frequented by leather tanners, that tells us the Roman Tribune was born somewhere nearby. It's just behind the church of San Tommaso de' Cenci, a few steps from the old synagogues. The extraordinary *Life of Cola Di Rienzo*, written by an anonymous author, is one of the most important texts to survive from the Middle Ages; written in a vivid style, it offers a ruthless portrait of a city plagued by violence.[8] According to its unnamed author, "Cola di Rienzo was of humble origins. His father was an innkeeper, and his mother, Maddalena, made a living washing clothes and carrying water. He was born in the district of Regola and raised by the river, among mill workers, on the street that goes through Regola to the church of San Tommaso, in front of the temple of the Jews."

His humble beginnings weighed on him so much that even as a boy he pretended he was the illegitimate son of Emperor Henry VII. Stubborn, ambitious, and obsessed with the vanished glory of Rome, "he loved to tell stories about how great Julius Caesar was. He spent long days looking at the marble reliefs that lay around Rome, and was the only one who knew how to read the ancient inscriptions."

Cola managed to get an education and became a notary. Shortly after his thirtieth birthday he was sent to Avignon as ambassador to Pope Clement VI (Pierre Roger) to beg him to return to Rome. The pope refused—the city was too troubled and its political situation too uncertain, poisoned as it was by continuous fighting among the baronial families. The pope was nonetheless struck by the ambassador's eloquence, and sent him back to Rome with the title "Notary of the Capitoline Chamber." This was the first step in a brilliant political career—perhaps too brilliant. Cola envisioned a humanistic utopia; he wanted to restore the ancient glory of the city and make Rome once more the world's capital.

To realize his dream Cola first had to subdue the barons, especially the Colonna family, who fought amongst themselves for power and tore each other to pieces in the process. He also needed allies, including the Jews, and made a spectacularly ruthless gesture to win their favor. Several killers, who'd been convicted four years earlier for killing a Jewish banker and his wife in Perugia, were still languishing in prison, almost forgotten. One of the first things Cola did when he came to power was to order their execution, offering "justice" to the Jewish community and thereby garnering their support. When it was time to ring the bells of Sant'Angelo in Pescheria as Cola marched to the Capitoline Hill, it was a Jew who did it; in the voice of a contemporary witness, "The bells of Santo Agnilo Pescivennolo rang for a night and a day. A Jew rang them."

Yet there was something wrong with Cola's notion of state, and this became glaringly clear in the majestic ceremony he held on August 1, 1347, to have himself declared Tribune of Rome, assuming the high-sounding and rather ridiculous title of *Candidatus Spiritus*

Sancti miles, Nicolaus severus et Clemens, liberator Urbis, zelator Italiae, amator orbis et tribunus augustus. He orchestrated opulent and elaborate ceremonies, processions, and banquets throughout the city, and became a daily spectacle himself, always donning splendid new fashions, resembling a reincarnated Nero. Cola was so carried away by his own performances that his contemporaries saw him as a veritable "Asianic tyrant."[9]

The pope grew uneasy in the face of Cola's antics, and the cities of Central Italy (which he hoped to federate) greeted his project warily. His plans failed. The Colonna family fomented a rebellion, and, his theatrical eloquence notwithstanding, Cola was forced to flee in 1350. He returned in 1354, in a pathetic attempt to retake the reins of government, but he couldn't even count on the support of the Jews, who'd since discovered how unrealistic his political ideals were. He became arrogant, unreasonably cruel, and capricious; the weaker he proved to be, the more persistent his delusions. When the Capitoline was stormed in an uprising, he decided to die, weapon in hand like the hero of an ancient bas-relief, in the manner of a majestic and imperial man. But he was also a mere mortal, and feared death as much as the next guy. He disguised himself, shaved off his beard, stripped himself of the symbols of his office, and hid his features by carefully blackening his face. Near the small apartment where the porter slept, he went in and took a cloak of rough cloth, like something a shepherd from Campania would wear, and put on the plain cloak.

This shepherd's disguise did him little good. Cola was recognized and dragged to the spot where justice was meted out, a fateful place inhabited by nothing but silence, where no one dared touch him. This incredible scene lasted for an entire hour—Cola stood silent, arms folded, surrounded by an enormous crowd of men who wanted to kill him but didn't yet dare, until someone named Cecco dello Vecchio grabbed a sword and stabbed him in the belly. As if a spell had been broken, a hail of blows followed the first strike, and his body was pierced a hundred times, ending up like a sieve. He was beaten, bound by his feet, and horribly mutilated. The mob hung his corpse from a balcony for two days and a night; people heaped abuse on it, and youths pelted it with stones. His body was then dragged once again through the streets, this time to the Mausoleum of

Augustus, where all the Jews had gathered. There they lit a fire with dry paper, and his body set atop it all. He was fat, so his corpse burned easily. The Jews stayed there, busy, overheated, with sleeves rolled up. They poked at the paper so it would burn. Thus the body was completely burnt and reduced to mere ashes. The Jews were among the Romans most betrayed by Cola's broken promises, and the macabre fury with which they burned his body, isn't all that surprising.

For many decades—centuries, really—the Jewish community in Rome experienced economic ups and downs, and its relationship with the Curia was characterized by a formal respect that masked mutual mistrust. Their considerable financial dealings, as we have seen, caused both sides to act cautiously and cooperate with one another. The papal physicians, too, were often Jewish, and because the pope entrusted his health to a Jewish doctor, he also often made his physician governor of the Roman community, since the man's professional prestige might help him govern better. Like any other, the Jewish community also had prolonged and intense internal debates, and there was fierce competition for the official positions of power. It also unequivocally refused to harbor refugees from other countries, including those who came from Spain after Queen Isabella's expulsion of all non-Catholics in 1492 (the same queen who gave Columbus the ships he needed to sail to the New World).

According to Ariel Toaff the intellectual climate of Rome's fifteenth-century Jewish community was "depressing, and got no better in the following centuries." The final blow came when the city was sacked by Imperial troops in 1527. This traumatic event was followed by a general downturn in the economy that soon proved catastrophic, as recorded by David de Pomis, a learned doctor in Spoleto (originally from Rome):

> In the year 5287 [1527] fine gold disappeared opening the way for a baser metal. When the lansquenets sacked Rome, that powerful and famous city, the Imperial soldiers took everything we had, forcing us into bankruptcy.

Pope Sixtus V (Felice Peretti), who ruled from 1585–1590, was among the most open minded of the late-sixteenth-century popes. He was also one of the few who really paid attention to the city's living conditions, clearing new streets and improving conditions in the countryside. He allowed the Jews to pursue whatever craft or career they wanted, exempted them from wearing distinctive badges, and allowed them to build schools and synagogues as necessary. After his reign, however, things again went sour. No hint of change came until the eighteenth century, and even then there were still many contradictions in the treatment of the Jews. In 1791, French Jews were the first in Europe to be emancipated from their ghettos, and the Roman community began to have a glimmer of hope. Unfortunately, the whole of Rome—not just its Jews—suffered from the rapid and chaotic chain of events in 1798–1799. Pope Pius VI (Giovanni Angelo Braschi) fled the city as Napoleon's army approached, and was then deported across the Alps. French troops invaded the city, and a short-lived republic came and went. Napoleon established an Israelite Consistory, but did little else for the Jews—he didn't want to offend the pope, as he'd later need his help to be crowned emperor.

The consistory didn't last long. The Congress of Vienna and restoration of the papacy in 1814–1815 brought the pope and his absolute power back to Rome. For the Jews this meant an anguishing return to the ghetto. Pius IX (Giovanni Mastai Ferretti), who rose to the throne in 1846, experimented at first with more liberal policies. He abolished the forced homage performed atop the Capitoline, and ended required sermons, although this had little real impact. More importantly, he ordered that on the evening of April 17, 1848— Passover—the gates of the ghetto, which had had been closed every evening for about three centuries, be demolished; even this didn't last long. After the brief interlude of the Roman Republic (discussed in Chapter XII), Pius IX returned to Rome profoundly changed. He took back the reins of government embittered by the trauma he'd endured, worried about the future, and disgusted by freedom of thought and the other trends he believed represented an intolerable dissolution of morality. He'd suffered through the unification of Italy, and now seemed unable to suffer the Jews, who he began to humiliate and treat harshly. Even if the gates of the ghetto could no longer be closed, he reinstated the ban on owning real estate, investing in mortgages, and doing business with Christians. He also imposed the payment of tributes and reinstated the practice of forced baptisms.

A serious incident occurred over this last imposition. At eight o'clock in the evening on June 20, 1858, five policemen and a monk of the Inquisition burst into the home of the Mortara family in Bologna and kidnapped Edgardo, their six-year-old boy. The authorities claimed Edgardo had been baptized two years earlier, by a Christian servant named Anna Morisi, when he was gravely ill. The boy was brought to Rome, where he was placed in the Institute for Neophytes, given a Catholic education, and later became a priest. This case caused great uproar, and influential individuals and representatives of foreign governments protested against the violent act. Young Edgardo was taken through the poorest and dirtiest streets in the ghetto to see the sad fate he'd escaped. Every Jewish community in Italy protested—except the Roman community, for clear reasons of political prudence. But abstaining from the protest still wasn't enough to shelter it from the pope's fury. On February 2, 1859, and for about six months after the fact, a group from the Roman community held audience with the pope. The secretary of the delegation, Sabatino Scazzocchio, had just finished his opening remarks when the pope attacked him, "Yes, yes, you gave a lovely demonstration of your faithfulness last year when you threw all of Europe into turmoil over the Mortara case." The secretary tried to reply, but the pope, now furious, interrupted in ever more acerbic tones: "You, yes you, poured oil on the fire and fanned the flames . . . this was your gesture of appreciation for all the benefits you have received from me. Be careful, I can still hurt you, and hurt you very deeply. I could force you to go back into your hole . . . but such is my goodness, and so strong the piety I feel for you, that I forgive you, indeed I must forgive you."

Abraham Berliner reported these words in his *Geschichte der Juden in Rom* (History of the Jews of Rome), based on notes taken at the time by one of the participants at the audience.[10] He added that the pope, who quickly regretted venting his anger, turned to his chamberlain once the meeting was over and spoke "flattering words about Secretary Scazzocchio in a voice loud enough that the delegates, who were already out in the hall, could hear him."

Even during the audience the tone calmed considerably, mostly because the delegates behaved cautiously and waited for their chance to speak, and the pope avoided using such abusive language in later meetings. On the other hand, Pius IX never missed the chance—at any encounter with a Jew, albeit in milder terms—to reassert his disapproval of the sin of a people he considered guilty of deicide. One example occurred on May 29, 1868, when delegates from the Jewish community visited the pope to thank him for the eleven silver medals awarded to Jewish doctors in recognition of their selflessness during the cholera epidemic. The pope answered them, "He who elevates us with his wonders can also bring us down. He can illuminate your mind so that you honor the pope as a sovereign and pastor, but only He, only God, can work the miracle of your conversion."

The Jews of Rome had to wait until they became part of the Kingdom of Italy for full recognition of their rights. On October 13, 1870 (twenty days after the city was taken), two of them, Samuele Alatri and Settimio Piperno, were named city councilors, and another nine were elected to the national parliament. The Kingdom of Italy granted Jews full citizenship, and they could also now work as university professors, magistrates, and officials, and became some of the most influential leaders of the new country. They could also serve in the military; Jews had already fought with the *Garibaldini* to defend the Roman Republic in 1849, and later they were among the troops that disembarked in Libya in 1911 and fought in the trenches of World War I.

In 1885 the houses of the Jewish ghetto began to be demolished. This was part of an urban renewal effort accompanied, it must be said, by rampant real-estate speculation—as common in Rome as anywhere else, if not worse. Wider streets and dignified residences took the place of the unhealthy, humble dwellings that had been there before. In 1904 the new Jewish Temple on the Lungotevere de' Cenci was completed; designed by architects Osvaldo Armanni and Vincenzo Costa in a style reminiscent of Assyrian and Babylonian art, the synagogue, with its cloister cupola set on a square drum, immediately became a prominent part of the Roman skyline. Some of the decorative elements from the older temples were preserved in its interior—including the seventeenth-century benches and niches made by Roman marble cutters and the Ark, which came from the Castilian synagogue. Today the synagogue also holds exhibitions about Rome's Jewish community.

This peaceful coexistence lasted for thirty years, and many Jews abandoned the ghetto, moving to other parts of the city. It all came to an end when Benito Mussolini, head of government and the Fascist

Party, broke the truce with one of his most shameful pieces of legislation—the racial laws of 1938. Why did Mussolini stain his record with such a crime, and what was his political rationale? Historians agree that Hitler put no direct pressure on him, even if in Germany the social marginalization of Jews had become widespread after the Nuremberg laws of 1935.

The Fascist leader perhaps thought it would be useful to create the specter of an "enemy" to help consolidate his regime, and profited from an anti-Semitic current that had begun to move across Europe— not just in Nazi Germany, but also in Austria, Poland, Hungary, and Romania. An anti-Semitic campaign was launched in Italian newspapers and "specialized" journals that republished, among other things, the famous *Protocols of the Elders of Zion* in 1937. It was accompanied by a preface by Julius Evola, a phony sensationalist historian used by the regime to nourish a hatred most Italians didn't really feel. But creating a "Jewish enemy" out of thin air served other purposes as well, including distracting public attention from colonial enterprises that had resolved none of the country's many problems. Suggestions of Italians' "racial purity" also helped combat the danger of mixed marriages between soldiers and colonial subjects. A very harsh law promulgated in 1937 made it punishable by three, four, or even five years in prison for an Italian citizen in the "territories of the Kingdom or the colonies to have a conjugal relationship with a subject of Italian East Africa."

On July 13, 1938 the *Manifesto della razza* (Manifesto of Race), a theoretical basis for claiming the existence of an "Italian race," was published, and Mussolini was apparently one of its editors. The text, presented as a "manifesto of racist scientists," was signed by a group of "Fascist scholars" who proclaimed:

> The present population of Italy is of Aryan origin, and its civilization is Aryan. . . . It is only legend that a huge number of people emigrated here in historical times. . . . A pure Italian race exists. . . . This proposition is based on the pure blood relationship that unites today's Italians with past generations and millennia of the Italian people. . . . The time has come for Italians to declare themselves openly racist.

The manifesto's concluding lines were explicit: "Jews do not belong to the Italian race." On October 6, 1938, the Grand Council of Fascism (the same council that, five years later, toppled Mussolini's reign) issued a "Declaration on Race"; it was a preview of the provisions that became law on November 17, 1938:

> Marriage between any Italian man or woman and a member of non-Aryan races is forbidden; Jews shall be expelled from the National Fascist Party; Jews may not own or direct any kind of business, nor own more than 120 acres of land; they are excluded from military service; they will be removed from public sector jobs and schools in the Kingdom; there will be special regulations for the right to practice professions . . . .

Enzo Collotti, in his *Il fascismo e gli ebrei* (*Fascism and Jews*),[11] explored the hypothesis that Mussolini's behavior was influenced by psychological components: "He must have had the need, as he approached the politics of the Third Reich, to rid himself of a sense of inferiority. . . . Uncovering the Roman origins of the Italian people, he was convinced that 'we are Mediterranean Aryans, pure.' . . . He stoked a campaign of hatred against the Jews even though he was perfectly aware of what was happening in Germany. He knew exactly what the implications of persecuting the Jews were, and embraced even the most brutal aspects of that policy."

And there was no shortage of brutal aspects: first came humiliation, misery, and exclusion from normal public life; then, after September 8, 1943, open persecution by the Nazis; the culmination arrived on Saturday, October 16, 1943, with the dramatic sacking of the Roman ghetto. On this day 2,091 Jews—including women, the elderly, and children—were rounded up, loaded onto armored cars, and sent to the gas chambers of Auschwitz and Birkenau. That tragic day is reconstructed in a splendid short story by Giacomo Debenedetti titled *16 ottobre 1943*.[12]

The roundup's sinister preamble had already occurred. On the evening of September 26 the presidents of the Roman Jewish community and the Union of Jewish Communities were called to the German Embassy, where the SS Lieutenant Colonel Herbert Kappler, speaking with a feigned affability to mask his terrible ferocity, declared the Jews of Rome guilty on two accounts: first as Italians, for the betrayal of Germany; and second as Jews, members of the racial archenemy of all Germans. The German government then demanded a tribute of fifty kilos of gold to be delivered by eleven o'clock on the morning of September 28. They had thirty-six hours to gather over one hundred pounds of gold. In the event they should fall short, two hundred Jews would be rounded up and deported to Germany. When the representatives of the Jewish community asked if gold might be combined with cash, Kappler replied that he wouldn't know what to do with banknotes and, in any case, he could easily have cash printed as necessary.

In the short time available a strong solidarity developed both in the Jewish community and with many non-Jewish Romans. According to Debenedetti, "The collection area was established in one of the community's offices. The police precinct, which had finally begun to listen to us, provided regular patrols and extra security. A flood of people began to arrive, and it was remarkable. A trustworthy person was sitting at a table; next to him a goldsmith tested the offerings, and another weighed them." Even the Vatican was moved, officially announcing that it had fifteen kilos of gold available should it be needed.

The amount demanded (and a bit extra) was collected and delivered on time, despite the Germans' last-minute trick of making one of the ten five-kilo packages of gold disappear. There was no need of additional help to fulfill this task, but even their adherence to Kappler's orders didn't save the Roman Jews from the October 16 roundup.

It began at dawn on an autumnal day, drenched and slippery with rain. Shootings, breathless screams, lugubrious shouts, and doors kicked in with the butts of rifles resounded through the neighborhood's streets—sounds of the roundups Rome has experienced so many times throughout its history. At five thirty in the morning almost four hundred German soldiers commanded by fourteen officers and noncommissioned officers—Italian Fascists were considered untrustworthy (in this case, rightly so) for this operation—were mobilized to hunt down the Jews. A hundred soldiers surrounded the ghetto, and the others were set loose to cover addresses outside the ghetto that had been identified with the help of Raffaele Aniello and Gennaro Cappa, two Fascist police officers. According to Debenedetti's account:

A mix of screams and shouts reached the Via del Portico d'Ottavia: Mrs. S. appeared at the corner where the Via Sant'Ambrogio meets the Portico. It's true that they took everyone, really everyone, worse than you can imagine. The families that had been rousted passed down the middle of the street in single file line, straggling a little. There was an SS soldier at the head of the line and one behind. Guarding the little groups, they kept them more or less in line, and pushed them forward with the butts of their machineguns, even though no one put up any resistance other than cries, moans, pleas for mercy, and bewildered questions.

Successive roundups yielded more Jews. In the end 1,067 men, 743 women, and 281 children were taken. These poor souls were loaded into an armored convoy that left Rome on Monday, October 18, at five after two in the afternoon, and arrived at Auschwitz at eleven o'clock Friday night, the 22nd. The prisoners—exhausted, thirsty, and in some cases dying—stayed locked in the trucks until dawn the next day, exactly a week after they'd been captured.

The troops who carried out this terrible task were sent to Rome expressly for that purpose, and some of the truck drivers took advantage of the opportunity to see Saint Peter's. While the soldiers, wholly unconcerned about their human cargo, took in the basilica's majesty, cries and pleas to the pope to intervene, to help them, came from inside the vehicles. Then the trucks started off again, and even that last hope was lost. There was no reaction from the pope, despite the fact that the crime took place almost "right under his window," as the German ambassador to the Holy See, Ernst von Weizsäcker, wrote. On the 28th he sent a telegram to his ministry, satisfied that "the pressure on him notwithstanding, the pope was not moved to issue any protest against the deportation of Rome's Jews."

I'd like to cite two brief episodes from Debenedetti's story that document, with the ruthless clarity details can often convey, the mood of that day, and what a major role the capriciousness of chance played in those hours. One tells of a young man who went for a coffee before he was dragged off with the others:

With a sort of a timid and tired smile he asked the man making the coffee, "What will they do with us?" These poor words are among the few left behind by the people as they left, and in them we hear the voice of someone who has returned for a moment to our regular, everyday life. He was among us, but our normal life was no longer his, and he had already entered a new, dark, terrible existence.

The second episode is even more touching in the horror it evokes:

> Another woman thought she was safe by then. They had already taken her husband away; he had been hiding in the water cisterns. She and her four children, two of whom had diphtheria and high fevers, were fleeing and had gotten as far as Ponte Garibaldi. She saw a truck pass carrying her relatives, and let out a cry. The Germans pulled up beside her, seizing her and her children. An "Aryan" intervened and managed to save one of the girls, protesting that she was hers, but the child began to cry because she wanted to be with her mother, and she too was taken away.

Of the 2,091 deported, only seventy-three men and twenty-eight women returned alive, and all of them profoundly scarred by the inhuman experience of the death camps. On March 23, 1944, another seventy-five Roman Jews were shot to death, along with another 260 innocents, at the Fosse Ardeatine.

The most recent tragedy staged in the Roman ghetto happened five minutes before noon on Saturday, October 9, 1982. It was Shemini Atzeret (Hebrew for "eighth day of assembly"), following the seven-day celebration of Sukkoth, or Feast of the Tabernacles. The faithful were leaving the synagogue through the small iron gate onto the Via Catalana. A young man of Middle-Eastern appearance stopped on the sidewalk across the street, put his hand into a bag, smiled, and threw a grenade. Many fell, and then came a burst of machine-gun fire from about a dozen attackers. The police arrived immediately, but the terrorists managed to get away. The only commando successfully identified was Jordanian-Palestinian Osama Abdel Al Zomar, who was later condemned to life in prison by an Italian court. In the meantime, however, he'd taken refuge in Greece, and the Greek government refused the plea for his extradition. Sometime in late 1988 he boarded an Olympic Airlines flight from Athens to Tripoli and vanished into thin air.

The morning of the attack thirty-five people were wounded and one died, a three-year-old named Stefano Tachè, the first victim of anti-Semitic violence in Italy since the defeat of Nazi Fascism in 1945.

1. See also Ferdinand Gregorovius, *The Ghetto and the Jews of Rome*, trans. M. Hadas (New York: Schocken Books, 1948).

2. Suetonius, *Lives of the Caesars* (London and Cambridge, Mass.: Loeb Classical Library, 1913), 117.

3. Dio Cassius, *Roman History* (London and Cambridge, Mass.: Loeb Classical Library, 1914), 128–29.

4. See also Tacitus, "The History," in *The Complete Works of Tacitus*, ed. M. Hadas, trans. A. J. Church and W. J. Broadribb (New York: Modern Library, 1942).

5. Solomon Katz, "Pope Gregory the Great and the Jews," in *Jewish Quarterly Review*, no. 24 (1933), 120–21.

6. See Massimo d'Azeglio, *Things I Remember* (Oxford: Oxford University Press, 1966).

7. This sonnet, previously unpublished, appears here in a translation by Daniel Seidel.

8. See the English edition of *The Life of Cola di Rienzo*, trans. J. Wright, ed. A. M. Ghisalberti (Toronto: Pontifical Institute of Mediaeval Studies, 1975).

9. "Asianic" is used here in the stylistic sense, referring to the opposing Asianic and Attic styles of rhetoric in ancient Roman public speeches.

10. See Abraham Berliner, *Storia degli Ebrei di Roma* (Milan: Rusconi Editore, 1992), originally published as *Geschichte der Juden in Rom* (Frankfurt am Main: J. Kaufmann, 1893).

11. Enzo Collotti, *Il fascismo e gli ebrei. Le leggi razziali in Italia* (Rome and Bari: Editore Laterza, 2003).

12. Giacomo Debenedetti, *16 ottobre 1943* (Turin: Einaudi, 2001).

XV

THE TWENTIETH ANNIVERSARY
THAT NEVER WAS

In a curious corner of Rome there's an extraordinary model of
the city as it appeared around the reign of Constantine, in the fourth
century AD. It's enormous—the rectangular platform beneath it has a
diagonal of 15 meters—and the city's principal buildings are skillfully
reconstructed, with circuses, theaters, baths, basilicas, triumphal
arches, columns with spiral bas-reliefs, fora, and broad expanses of
residential neighborhoods. The model is viewed from a balcony,
giving us a bird's-eye view of the ancient capital and a sense of the
monuments, now mere ruins, in their original urban context. It's surprising to see that some parts of the city—the Via del Corso, Via del
Babuino, and the Archeological Promenade, for example—are still
more or less the same as they were seventeen centuries ago. Many
marvels of engineering are plainly visible, including the 19-kilometer
circuit of city walls, the many watchtowers, and the long course of
the Claudian Aqueduct as it crosses the city from east to west, bringing water to the imperial palaces; the last arches of this impressive
construction are still visible, just within the city walls, along the Via
di San Gregorio.

The model is strikingly beautiful, and helps us understand the
grandeur of the ancient city, orient ourselves within it, and see how
much of the ancient *Urbe* remains in present-day Rome. Created in
1937, the model is now in the Museum of Roman Civilization in
the quarter called EUR (an abbreviation of *Esposizione Universale di
Roma*, the Universal Exposition of Rome), which also has a stunning
planetarium with an equally spectacular vision of the skies above us.

Paradoxically, this vision of ancient Rome is located in the capital's newest neighborhood. It's not that other building complexes

weren't constructed after it—on the contrary, postwar Rome literally exploded in every direction—but EUR nevertheless remains the greatest achievement of twentieth-century Italian urban planning. It was carefully designed by some of the best architects of the day to house the 1942 expo, a huge fair intended to celebrate the twentieth anniversary of the "Fascist revolution" of 1922. The area was originally to be called E42—as in "E" for exposition, and 42 for the celebration's date. Hitler had assured Mussolini war wouldn't break out before then, and the Italian dictator trusted him. Instead, Hitler invaded Poland on September 1, 1939, and one of the many things wiped out by the invasion was Mussolini's exposition.

Mussolini first conceived of the exposition in 1935. Planned for 1942, it was to follow Paris's 1937 expo and New York's 1939 World's Fair. It differed from the others in that the monumental buildings erected for it were meant to be permanent—not just pavilions of ephemeral material rigged to last a few months, but robust buildings of stone or reinforced concrete with solid facings. They were also designed as the core of a new neighborhood planned southwest of the city's ancient center, halfway between it and the sea. It was a nice idea in its own way, if only because it so strongly anticipated later concepts of regional decentralization. EUR was also envisioned at a time when no one had a clue of how intense and chaotic automobile traffic would become after World War II. Creating a new neighborhood planned as a magnet for businesses and residents in the open countryside meant enlarging the city, drawing Rome out from the narrowness of its seventeenth-century streets and freeing it from the overcrowding bound to intensify over time. The plan was to "decentralize" the city's historical center, shifting it toward the periphery.

The project basically failed, and not just because of the war. It was a failure because postwar urban development was like a vortex, growing in concentric circles like an oil stain on pavement, leaving the center at the center—with all the consequences (of traffic, circulation, and movement through the city) Romans now know all too well. But even if it was a failure, a glimmer of what EUR could have been is still easy to see, and becomes even more evident as the passage of time transforms it into urban history.

For those who really want to see EUR, rather than just look at it, a good starting point would be the Palazzo degli Uffici, on Via Ciro il Grande. It was the only building completely finished, furnishings and decorations included, before war broke out. The inscription across its imposing facade reads, "La Terza Roma si dilaterà sopra altri colli lungo le rive del fiume sacro sino alle spiagge del Tirreno" (The Third Rome will expand across other hills, along the banks of the sacred river, all the way to the beaches of the Tyrrhenian), and verifies Mussolini's intention of pushing urban development toward the southwest. In front of the building's colonnade is a fuguelike series of eighteen basins with black-and-white mosaics designed in 1939 by Gino Severini, Giovanni Guerrini, and Giulio Rossi; it represents a mixture of myths about "Roman spirit" and other narratives dictated by Mussolini. Their depictions are quintessentially Fascist in content: the destruction of Carthage; Roma, goddess of the seas; Flora; Time; Victory; but also include scenes of Italic youths, land reclamation, construction projects, and so on. The mosaic cycle comes to an end at Fausto Melotti's figure of a nude youth leaning on a club. Its proposed title was *Si redimono i campi* (*The Fields are Redeemed*), and was conceived not as an isolated sculpture, but a group of three figures, with the youth accompanied by a woman and child. All three statues were ready, but only the first was installed in its intended location; the train carrying the other two ran into a bombing raid and was turned around. These other two figures are now in Versilia, a costal area in northern Tuscany, in the warehouse studio where they were created.

The wall-sized travertine bas-relief in the building's entrance is also striking. Publio Morbiducci designed it in 1939, drawing inspiration from the Roman tradition of historical reliefs like those that spiral up the columns of Trajan and Antoninus Pius. It represents the history of Rome through its building projects: from the furrows Romulus traced with his plow to the great projects of Julius Caesar and the Roman Empire; from the destruction of the Temple in Jerusalem (the Fascist Racial laws had been passed the previous year) to the erection of the obelisk in Saint Peter's Square; from the construction of E42 (represented by its best-known icon, the Colosseo Quadrato, or Square Coliseum, as the Palace of the Civilization of Labor is almost affectionately called) to an image of Mussolini on horseback standing warriorlike in his stirrups. The anecdote of the bronze statue of a young athlete next to it is also interesting. His arm is raised in a so-called Roman salute, and its sculptor, Italo Griselli, meant it to be a portrayal of the *Genio del fascismo*, the Spirit of Fascism. After the war the athlete was fitted with simple boxing gloves in an attempt to modify the meaning of his gesture, and he is now called *Genio dello sport*, the Spirit of Sports.

This building's furniture would look right at home in a museum of decorative and applied arts. Many of the original pieces survived the war and the successive occupations, beginning with the Germans, followed by the Americans, and finally the refugees from the Dalmatian coast temporarily housed here. The furnishings include beautiful exhibition tables designed by Guglielmo Ulrich, solid-glass balusters along the grand staircase, marble door frames, rare wooden doors and floors, intarsia decorations on the walls, and elegantly functional aluminum door handles designed by Gio Ponti. In one of the reception rooms on the second floor an entire wall is decorated with a splendid mural painted by Giorgio Quaroni in 1940; it's yet another representation of the founding of Rome, envisioned here under the protection of a goddess draped in a rich red mantle.

Even the building's basement has a few things worth seeing: five enormous bronze heads, two of King Vittorio Emanuele III, three of Mussolini. Both men are represented with and without helmets, and with varying degrees of realism in their features. A few rooms down there's a space with a reinforced concrete ceiling used as a bomb shelter during air raids. It's heart-wrenching to see, but worth the visit, as it's an emotional reminder of what it was like to live with the constant threat of ever more frequent bombing raids as the war worsened.

The Viale della Civiltà del Lavoro ends at the Palace of Italian Civilization, better known as the Palace of the Civilization of Labor or, as mentioned earlier, the Square Coliseum. This dazzling cube has become the icon of EUR, but has also occasionally been used as the logo of Italian architecture in the first half of the twentieth century. Built between 1938 and 1943 by the architects Giovanni Guerrini, Ernesto Bruno La Padula, and Mario Romano, this massive building is faced entirely in travertine and stands atop a podium with a particularly imposing staircase on its west side. The four facades are identical, sheer, and free of any ornamentation, cornice, or stringcourses. It's pure geometry, verticality, and volume—a metaphysical abstraction that has been associated (and not by mere chance) with the paintings of Giorgio de Chirico. Each facade is six stories tall, and each story has nine rounded arches—for a total of 216 arches on the building's four facades, representing nothing beyond the void they've created in the travertine's solid mass. On the front is an inscription as famous as the building, with a phrase that has been imitated and parodied in countless ways: "Un popolo di poeti di artisti di eroi / di santi di pensatori di scienziati / di navigatori di trasmigratori" (A people of poets, artists, heroes / saints, thinkers, scientists / navigators, travelers). Four groups of figures representing the Dioscuri (Castor and Pollux) stand at each corner of the podium. They were sculpted by Publio Morbiducci and Alberto Felci and were based on the ancient *Horse Trainers* sculpture in the Piazza del Quirinale. The ground-floor arches have twenty-eight statues that personify the arts, crafts, and values—music, astronomy, history, physics, handicrafts, heroism, the spirit of the military, and so on.

The basilica of Saints Peter and Paul, designed by the architectural office of Arnaldo Foschini, is another notable building, erected on high ground, making it highly visible. It has a square layout, and its cupola—32 meters in diameter, making it the second largest dome in Rome after Saint Peter's—was cast in reinforced concrete. It's a lovely church, and one of the most successful and appropriate examples of more recent sacred architecture. Postwar churches built in Rome have generally been quite modest, and sometimes embarrassingly ugly, as if sacred architecture had lost the ability to represent itself after so many centuries of glory.

Another noteworthy building, originally called the Palace of Receptions and Congresses, faces the Square Coliseum and is the masterpiece of architect Adalberto Libera (1903–1963), a major proponent of rationalism and designer of Curzio Malaparte's villa on the island of Capri. The construction of this congress center was interrupted by the war, but started up again in peacetime, and the building was completed in 1954. Even though the original architect didn't approve all the changes made to his design, the building, with its unusual sail vault, is nevertheless one of the most significant examples of twentieth-century Italian architecture. There are two symmetrical entries on opposite sides of the structure that allow access to different parts of the building (the areas for receptions and congresses, respectively). Everything is coordinated and happily harmonious—the fourteen granite columns without capitals, the tall windows, Achille Funi's frescoes (unfortunately unfinished), and the grandiose interior space, whose vastness, according to some calculations, could enclose the entire Pantheon.

The Palazzo della Luce, or Palace of Light, was planned to stand in the middle of the Via Cristoforo Colombo (originally named the Via Imperiale), on the hilltop now occupied by the sports arena. It was never built, but the design description tells us it was to be, "a fantastic vision made only of glass, light, and water: it will be a radiant beacon above the entire Exposition, and with its modern contents and technologies will be one of its most unusual attractions." The plans for a large, futuristic arch designed by Adalberto Libera to symbolize peace and universality were also abandoned before construction. The arch was to include an incredible 200 linear meters of lighting (later extended to 320), and would have been 103 meters tall at its highest point. Set against the horizon toward the sea, the arch would have crowned the whole of the exposition complex. Libera rejected the idea of building it in reinforced concrete, and considered using aluminum, although he had to give up on that plan because of insurmountable technical obstacles.

These are just a few summary notes; EUR is there for all who might want to see it (and I mean *really* see it). Its enormous buildings survived the terrible events of the war and immediate postwar period—survived, we might say, their own troubled histories—including the ups-and-downs of their planning and construction, in which technological and practical difficulties were added to by political necessities and personal rivalries.

Right after Mussolini had the grand idea of holding a universal exposition in Rome to highlight Italian culture, he immediately had to face the question of where to put it. The Villa Borghese was considered, as were the Janiculum Hill and the Foro Italico (then called the Foro Mussolini) toward the Milvian Bridge, north of the city center. The idea of building it on the southern edge of town took root slowly, and was initially promoted by Virgilio Testa, Secretary General of the Governorship of Rome and a proponent of pushing urban development toward the Tyrrhenian Sea. Places like the Magliana neighborhood and Lido di Ostia were considered, but in the end the Tre Fontane area—supposedly named for three fountains—was selected, in part for logistical reasons. The industrialist Vittorio Cini described the site in a report sent to Mussolini in November of 1936: "The area to the left of the Via del Mare sits on high ground around the Ponte della Magliana, between the eucalyptus woods of Tre Fontane and the Rome-Lido railway line. This land is about 30 or 40 meters above sea level, and thus dominates the Tiber Valley with a variety of graceful sites that offer picturesque and panoramic views. It also offers practically unlimited possibilities for urban development toward the sea."

The little-known history of this part of Rome is extraordinarily interesting because it represents a cross section of the layered religious and military events that formed the city. The valley of Tre Fontane, including a tract of about 250 acres of land along the Via Laurentina, has had several names over time. In ancient times it was called *Ad aquas salvias*, probably because of a spring or bath complex there. According to legend, this is also the place were Saint Paul was decapitated. The blow of the sword was so powerful that his severed head bounced three times, and each time it touched the ground a spring appeared—the first was hot, the second warm, and the last cold. Three small structures were built in the fifth century, each with a fountain in it, giving the area its later name. Shortly afterward a group of Greek monks particularly devoted to the relics of Saint Anastasius, a Persian martyr, founded a monastery here in his name. Subsequently the remains of the Spanish martyr Saint Vincent were also interred at the monastery. After the year 1000 a group of Cistercians, the order founded by Saint Bernard of Clairvaux, occupied the monastery, which was abandoned at the time. The repopulated abbey grew wealthy enough to acquire properties in the hills south of Rome, around the Castelli Romani, including Nemi, which served as a retreat for the monks during the hot summer months. When Tre Fontane was again abandoned, stagnant water made the terrain swampy, and the area became infested with malaria. In 1868, Pius IX ordered a community of French Trappists to take up residence in the old monastery; they undertook large-scale land reclamation projects and planted vast plots of eucalyptus trees, laying the seeds of the forest still there today.

Of all the churches around the abbey the most striking, if not the most beautiful, is Santa Maria Scala Coeli, built in the late sixteenth century by Giacomo Della Porta on the site where 10,203 Roman soldiers who converted to Christianity were supposedly martyred by Emperor Diocletian. The church was named for a vision Saint Bernard had: after praying for the salvation of a sinner's soul, he saw a long staircase and the same unfortunate soul ascending it as the Madonna waited at the top, blessing him. An underground chapel dating back to the twelfth century was consecrated in honor of this event.

Mussolini attended the site inspection himself, and on December 15, 1936, Tre Fontane was approved as the site for E42. Giuseppe Pagano, Marcello Piacentini, Luigi Piccinato, Ettore Rossi, and Luigi Vietti—the same group of architects who planned the new campus for the University of Rome—were commissioned to oversee the project. Their earliest designs reveal their indebtedness to the plans for the royal chateau at Versailles, designed by the major French architect André Le Nôtre (1613–1700). The first drawings for E42 included a large entry plaza on the side of the development closest to the city center, to be called the Imperial Gate; a network of streets laid out following the Roman grid system, based on two principal intersecting axes, the *cardus maximus* and the *decumanus maximus*; a lake at the center of the project; and a gate leading to the sea, the Porta del Mare, on the side opposite the Imperial Gate. The lustrous Square Coliseum would rise from a hilltop with a panoramic view over the Tiber Valley, forming an ideological and scenographic pair to the basilica of Saints Peter and Paul, the valley's second dominant structure. E42 co-opted the dual symbolism, Catholic and secular, established in the ancient city center by the Coliseum and Saint Peter's. The project as a whole is characterized by its rationalism and rigorous use of geometry, both in its general layout and the designs of individual buildings. The development was also meant to be clearly different from the Renaissance city, as well as its early-twentieth-century neighborhoods, with their winding, narrow streets. The sense of rigor was underscored by the use of "modern" materials like glass and aluminum which, like travertine, meant the exteriors of the buildings would generally be light in color.

During the Fascist period the ongoing conflict between modernity and tradition in architecture often took on truly bitter tones. E42 expressed the idea of a rationally defined city without ceding any ground to the increasingly predominant International style.

Marcello Piacentini, the chief designer, succeeded in creating a balance between classical models, the qualities of the ideal city as described by Leon Battista Alberti and Leonardo da Vinci, and the monumentality the regime so desired. Renaissance theories of the ideal city were characterized by rigorous symmetry and a rational relationship between buildings and the surrounding urban spaces. The famous painting *Ideal City*, by an unknown Central Italian artist and now in Urbino, is a perfect example of what those spaces were meant to look like. The qualities of purity, harmony, and balance were essential; solids alternated with voids, as did straight and curved lines, and churches and palaces, forming a whole that became both exemplar and canon. E42 was the only modern attempt to re-create these ideas.

Motifs from classical architecture were then thrown into the mix; they included the two exedras (now the corporate headquarters for the INA and INPS companies) at opposite sides of the Imperial Gate, and the tall colonnade across the facade of the Museum of Roman Civilization. The large square at EUR's center (now called the Piazza Guglielmo Marconi) recalls the fora of ancient Roman cities, as well as Greek cities' agora.

The regime's architects were excellent at their jobs, and already had accomplishments like the University's Città Universitaria, the Foro Mussolini, and Cinecittà—all Fascist projects—under their belts. The architect and urban planner Enrico Guidoni noted that these earlier projects, although created to serve different ends, demonstrate "the success of a formula based both on artistic form and the persuasive force of representation." E42 was conceived as a representation; it was to be the stage of an exhibition designed to show the rest of the world the design capabilities and dynamic capacity of Mussolini's Italy.

Yet all twentieth-century dictators used architecture as an instrument of political propaganda. Hitler did it through his talented architect Albert Speer, whose projects were derived from neoclassical rhetoric. He constructed the monuments of National Socialism, and the Nuremberg Parade Grounds, inaugurated in 1935, are one of the most important examples. Leni Riefenstahl made a documentary, titled *Triumph des Willens* (*Triumph of the Will*), about the 1934 Nazi party congress using Speer's unfinished parade grounds as a backdrop; two years later she also filmed the 1936 Berlin Olympics with sinister perfection. Hitler strongly believed in the exemplary and admonitory value of "his" architecture, both for Germans and the rest of the world. He made this clear in a 1937 interview published in the architectural journal *Baubilde*: "National Socialism, which beyond its original societies represents the biggest collective of peoples and nations ... prefers public buildings to private ones. And as the demands the state makes on its citizens grow larger, it must in turn appear that much more powerful in their eyes." Had Mussolini pondered the threatening subtext of this discussion of architecture, rather than just the political manifesto in *Mein Kampf*, he might have avoided the unspeakable tragedies he caused both the Italian people and himself.

Those, however, were the ideological guidelines, and the E42 project pointed in the same direction. In the years leading up to the war, the two future Axis allies would scrutinize each other based on their respective building projects. Having won thirty gold medals to the twenty-five won by the United States, Germany dominated Berlin's 1936 Olympics, and did so against an unprecedented backdrop. Rome was booking itself as best candidate for the 1944 Games (the 1940 Games were canceled because of international events), and Mussolini was already planning an entire Olympic city at Ostia.

Meanwhile an ingenious public relations campaign for the upcoming exposition was launched, and baptized the "Olympics of Civilization." If the Germans had dominated on the playing fields, Rome made clear its intention of winning on the larger stage of intellectual achievements. Hitler got a hint of this during his 1938 visit to Rome, when Mussolini showed him a series of spectacular projects, including the *ex novo* construction of Ostiense Railway Station.

E42 was a piece of this larger picture, and also an integral part of the imperial airs Fascist Italy assumed after its campaigns in East Africa. Giuseppe Pagano, architect, urban planner, and director of the architectural magazine *Casabella*, wrote, "When Rome finishes this city, so boldly aimed at the future, it can take pride in its traditions and consider modern architecture the concrete expression of a renewed Italy." Mussolini was not alone in seeing these new constructions as useful instruments of propaganda, and his shrewdest architects were fully aware of the political value of what they were planning.

Most of the E42 designs involved permanent structures meant to last and be used for the fair. In a press conference given in January of 1937, Vittorio Cini, commissary of the project's supervisory board, said that the exposition need not be (as was so often the case) "an end in itself . . . but rather can contribute to resolving important urban planning problems." In late 1938 Plinio Marconi published an article in *Illustrazione Italiana* claiming, "What distinguishes [this exposition] is its practical basis and the lasting quality of its urban plan." Piacentini himself repeated this idea in a 1938 article in the journal *Architettura*:

> The urban plan of E42 has its own particular character, which differentiates this exposition from those all over the world that have come before it. The plan of this great exhibition of civilization, which Italy will offer on occasion of the twentieth anniversary of Fascism, goes hand in hand with the plan for a new and monumental quarter of Rome, capital of the Empire . . . The piazzas and streets, with their underground fittings, paving, sidewalks, trees, and lighting will be fixed and definitive. The parks, gardens, fountains, staircases, and decorations (sculptures, mosaics, bronzes) will be permanent, as will the large lake with its waterfalls, jets of water, porticoes, and terraces. A large number of the buildings will also be permanent.

This permanence was not really as novel as was claimed. The architectural historian Ezio Godoli has observed that the tendency to use an exposition to build something useful for the city was fairly common; this was true in Paris, for example, although the permanent buildings constructed there were largely intended as exhibition halls or museums. The Grand and the Petit Palais were built for the expo of 1900, and the Pont Alexandre III, which crosses the Seine directly in front of them, was also constructed for the same event. The Palais du Trocadéro, across the river from the Eiffel Tower, was built for the expo of 1878. (A noteworthy photograph taken in 1940, just after the Nazi arrival in Paris, depicts Hitler posed on the esplanade in front of the building with the tower as a grand backdrop.)

A precedent for building permanent fair structures also existed in Italy. A number of buildings went up in Rome in 1911, on the occasion of the fiftieth anniversary of the Kingdom of Italy, which were also important for the city's development, including the high bridge crossing the Viale del Muro Torto, connecting the Villa Borghese and the Pincio; the new plan for a neighborhood called Vigna Cartoni, where the Piazza Don Minzoni and Viale Bruno Buozzi now stand; the National Gallery of Modern Art in the Valle Giulia; numerous national academies of fine arts, all of which still exist and lend a pleasantly cosmopolitan feeling to that part of Rome; the development of apartment buildings and houses along the Lungotevere delle Armi, between Ponte Risorgimento and Ponte Matteotti (which won a national award for architecture); and plans for the Mazzini neighborhood, including the star-shaped Piazza Mazzini, a smaller version of the Place d'Etoile at the head of the Champs Elysées in Paris. These new constructions also included Ponte Risorgimento (originally called Ponte Flaminio), the first single-span bridge to cross the Tiber, designed by the French engineer François Hennebique (1842–1921), a pioneer in the use of reinforced concrete.

The 1911 expo resulted in several significant permanent building projects. No neighborhoods were built from scratch, as EUR later was, but it did establish the infrastructure for several neighborhoods set up shortly afterward. We can also see from examples in Barcelona, Cologne, Brussels, and New York that the decision to make E42 a real opportunity for large-scale urban planning was part of a broader trend in the 1930s.

But Fascist Italy was facing a problem other nations hadn't; on October 3, 1935, Italian troops commanded by Pietro Badoglio and Rodolfo Graziani invaded Ethiopia, launching a war that lasted seven months. Large-scale bombing raids and poisonous gas attacks were used to quell indigenous resistance. Badoglio took Addis Ababa in May of 1936, and on the ninth of the same month Mussolini proclaimed the foundation of the Italian Empire from the balcony of the Palazzo Venezia in Rome. Ethiopia became part of Italian East Africa, which already included Eritrea and Somalia. Just after the invasion the League of Nations imposed economic sanctions on Italy, a move driven largely by Britain, which wasn't interested in seeing a greater Italian presence in East Africa. The effects of the sanctions were largely mitigated by the United States and Germany, which continued to sell industrial products and raw materials to Italy. They did cause some problems, and for EUR this meant a scarcity of building and finishing materials. The competition outlined for the Palace of Italian Civilization was explicit, for example, when it said that the building would have to be constructed "in large part with local building materials, permitting only the most essential use of iron, and in compliance with the directives intended to establish national self-sufficiency."

Given the scarcity of valuable raw materials locally, such as iron and oil, the directives meant that competing architects had to use their imaginations in employing other products available domestically to reduce Italian dependence on imported materials. This meant that the majority of buildings in E42 were built of reinforced concrete and then faced with more precious materials. In addition to travertine, which was available in large quantities from quarries (still in use today) in Tiburtina, to the east of Rome, they used wood substitutes, including fiberboard and masonite, as well as glass, ceramic glass paste, reinforced concrete with glass tiles to create translucent surfaces, linoleum for flooring, and artificial marble made from plaster or concrete mixed with other materials. Aluminum alloys were also widely used; considered "young and modern" metals, they ultimately represented the regime's sought-after self-sufficiency.

The fact that Tre Fontane wasn't uninhabited terrain was another obstacle for the grandiose EUR plans. The land was mostly divided into small plots with underground tunnels, wells, and tufa and pozzolana quarries, as well as rudimentary housing not unlike the primitive huts in the recently conquered colonies—indeed, these hovels were derogatorily called "Abyssinian villages." Like East African huts, they sheltered the poorest peasant and working-class families, who lived in dire circumstances. In its quest for an imperial image, Fascist Italy obviously couldn't tolerate their presence, and Mussolini ordered that the "deplorable inconveniences" be removed as quickly as possible. In a note dated June 1937, he ordered, "by July 15 these shacks must be gone from the site of the exposition, which will soon be overrun by workmen and engineers from all over Italy and abroad. In the next fifteen days ten or fifteen masonry hovels [for the displaced inhabitants] can be built somewhere else."

Resorting to this solution, Mussolini repeated a tactic used before. In the early 1930s large sections of the city's historical center had been demolished, and this involved moving huge numbers of people from areas like those around the Roman Forum and the Piazza Augusto Imperatore. These forced transfers gave rise to the so-called *borgate ufficiali rapidissimi*, impromptu developments that were essentially improvised towns of very basic blockhouses—San Basilio, Gordiani, Tor Marancio, Pietralata, and others. This was meant to be a temporary solution, but in the end (as so often happens) it became permanent. *Borgate* became a pejorative term for large sections of the city's suburbs, and after the war they were used as sets for many of the neorealist films. Pier Paolo Pasolini recorded the tragedy evident in these areas, and at the same time elevated them to a state of almost literary dignity.

The end of rent control in 1930, and the large number of evicted tenants that followed, forced another wave of people into the *borgate*. The same thing had happened during preparations for the 1911 celebrations. The area of the city that later became Prati, for example, was completely emptied, creating a wave of evacuees who found shelter in the hovels around Porta Metronia and along certain sections of the Aurelian walls. A bit more recently, people were again displaced as preparatory work was carried out for the 1960 Olympic games in Rome.

But getting back to E42, a census was taken that counted about eighty shacks in the area. Some were used to store farming equipment or chickens, but others were actually improvised residences that housed twenty-four families, for a total of 102 people. Pietro Colonna, governor of Rome at the time, explained in a report to Mussolini that many of these people "cultivated small plots of land to supplement their wages." Driven by some humane sense, or perhaps worried about the civil disorder forced evacuations might cause, Colonna added, "in the case of immediate evictions, these twenty-four families will likely find themselves deprived of their livelihoods . . . inasmuch as they will no longer be able to count on the small parcels of land that now sustain them. . . . If Your Excellency believes it necessary that they be cleared in July, this administration will seek the least damaging provisions to accomplish this." Mussolini read the report, thought about it, then made a nervous annotation with red pencil in the margin, "Tend to it! M."

Collateral projects were tied to E42, and one of the most important was the excavation of Ostia Antica. The Tyrrhenian Coast, including the area around the mouth of the Tiber, had for centuries been as plagued by malaria as the more famous Pontine Marshes to the south. Everyone knew that the predictably impressive remnants of Ostia, the ancient port of Rome, had been buried for centuries. There had been some excavations at the site, but they weren't systematic, and bureaucratic inertia, the large number of competing plans, and a lack of funding had delayed any real exploration of the ruins at Ostia.

Dante Vaglieri, Superintendent of Antiquities, was the first to tackle the excavation of Ostia in any modern, systematic way. Although a rather rotund and somewhat ridiculous figure, this scholar from Trieste was both a gifted Latinist and a tenacious worker. With the tools of the day (essentially a pick and a shovel), Vaglieri undertook the first real excavations there in 1907. When he died, in April 1913, the excavations continued under the direction of other capable archaeologists, including Italo Gismondi and Guido Calza. Funding remained scarce, however, and as a consequence the excavators' finds were a bit thin.

Simultaneously with the start of work on E42, in 1937, some serious attention was finally paid to Ostia. Calza presented a "complete and organic plan for all the work involved in the excavations at Ostia," including the restoration and restructuring of the ruins themselves. The excavation, he wrote, will focus on "an area of about 45 acres, which is more than has been uncovered in the last twenty-five years of digging (a total of 38 acres). The city's walls contained an area of about 120 acres, and so at the end of the excavation we will have uncovered almost two-thirds of Ostia Antica."

Over a period of four years, from 1938 to 1942, he worked on an area of about 400 by 300 meters; 60,000 square meters of it were excavated between March 1938 and June 1939, a task that included moving 22,000 cubic meters of dirt almost literally by hand. Through their efforts, Calza and Gismondi uncovered one of the great vestiges of antiquity, its ruins almost as significant as those of Pompeii. A *Corriere della Sera* correspondent named Alberici commented on the results of the excavation in one of his articles, "A visit to Ostia Antica is an amazing experience; its vastness and buildings are an extraordinary surprise, as are the solemnity of the ruins and the sincerity with which they represent the Roman spirit."

Rome's ancient port has an extraordinary history. Augustus endowed the original settlement, which dated back to the reign of Ancus Marcius, the fourth legendary King of Rome, with a theater, a forum, and an aqueduct. Two ports were later built there, first by Claudius, then Trajan, and they enhanced Ostia's importance as a place for the sorting and storage of goods shipped on to Rome. The numerous and spacious warehouses (*horrea*) testify to this role. Because of silt deposits, by the beginning of the fifth century the branch of the Tiber that flowed through Ostia was no longer navigable, and vast parts of the city (which at its height reached a population of about fifty thousand people) were apparently abandoned. It's also hard for those who visit Ostia Antica today to imagine that it once stood at the edge of the sea; the silting in of the river has steadily pushed the coast line almost two kilometers out, and the course of the river itself also changed over time, moving away from the northern side of the settlement.

Unlike Pompeii, in Ostia there aren't any shadows of human presence to perpetuate the sense of a great tragedy. What remains are the ruins of numerous public buildings, houses, and shops, as well as streets and squares that document life as it once was. Several guidebooks to Rome (the Italian language *Red Guide* issued by the Touring Club of Italy is the best, and innumerable English language guides now exist) enumerate the remarkable monuments at Ostia, but I'd like to mention a few of them here, even if just to repay a personal debt. It was here that a particularly enlightened high school teacher introduced me and my classmates to the beauty of Latin poetry. Two or three times he took the class to the ancient theater at Ostia, where we studied Horace's satires, and the most talented students read a few verses aloud. Even the less gifted understood they were seeing the pure grandeur of life, or at least an echo of it. A few of the most resounding verses of those compositions still ring through my head, even after so many years, thanks to those warm, sunny mornings among the ruins.

The grandeur of the theater, rebuilt several times and greatly restored in the modern period, remains largely unchanged, even in its ruinous condition. The stage's columns, the steps of the *cavea* (which have been partially restored), and the remaining ambulatories all speak clearly of the prominent place theater held in Roman society and culture.

The Baths of Neptune are another remarkable nearby monument. Built during the reign of Emperor Hadrian (117–138 AD), they stand just to the right of the theater. There are at least two beautiful mosaics there worth admiring: one represents Neptune and Amphitrite; the other, on the east side of the baths, depicts the four winds and the four provinces that supplied Rome with grain (Sicily, Spain, Egypt, and Africa). Close by is the House of Cupid and Psyche, named for the statue of the divine lovers found there, now on exhibit in the local museum. This domus is a relatively recent structure, dating back only to the fourth century (Aurelian's reign). Its owners must have been rich, because they decorated their home with colored mosaics, vibrant wall marbles, and enjoyed the luxury of a verdant indoor garden.

The well-preserved Mithraeum of the Seven Spheres stands just to the left of the theater. The cult of the god Mithras, whose origins are buried deep in the ancient history of Persia, was so important that in the years before the Christian era it became the most popular alternative to Rome's state religion. Widely practiced in the capital, where it arrived from the Greek world, Mithraism also spread to the northern provinces (Mesia, Dacia, Pannonia, Germania, and Britannia), carried abroad by soldiers and slaves. Like many Eastern religions, Mithraism involved mysterious initiation rites and secret rituals. Its sanctuaries, called Mithraea, were always underground, to symbolize the cave where the god was born. Mithras was the protector of rights and contracts, as well as patron of livestock and righteous men, to whom he promised eternal salvation. The central ritual of the cult was the sacrifice of a bull (be it actual or symbolic), whose death was supposed to encourage life and universal fecundity. Subduing the wild bull also represented the victory of order over chaos and barbarity. The culmination of the rite was a collective meal of bread and water, or perhaps wine. Some Mithraea had sanctuaries beneath the main room called *fovea sanguinis*, or blood pits, which were probably used for some sort of baptism in the blood of the sacrificed bull that drained down through special conduits.

At the end of his time on earth, Mithras ascended into heaven with the help of the Sun, and from the heavens he continued to protect human beings. The annual festival to mark his birth fell around the winter solstice—in other words, close to December 25. Even though a number of Roman emperors tolerated Mithraism, it never became an official religion of the state. It did enjoy a vast following, and included soldiers, but essentially drew from the lower strata of society—slaves, freedmen, workmen, artisans, and small-time merchants. These were the same ranks that, moved by similar religious needs, became interested in the other great monotheistic religion of the time, Christianity. Indeed, Mithraism represented its most direct and dangerous competition. The French historian Ernest Renan put it this way:"If Christianity had somehow been stopped in the course of its expansion by some fatal disease, the world would be Mithraic."

There are certainly indisputable similarities between the two religions, both in their inspiration and the miraculous events on which they are constructed, and it has even been suggested (albeit without any documentation) that Mithras was born of a virgin. It's true, though, that the two communities viewed one another with suspicion and even fought amongst one another. Beginning in the third century Christianity absorbed some aspects and rituals of the cult of Mithras, and finally gained the upper hand over it, first under Constantine, and then definitively under Theodosius the Great (347–395) who persecuted any and all expressions of paganism, from visiting temples to the cults of the household gods, making Christianity the official state religion and in the process transforming the Church into a temporal as well as spiritual power.

The widespread presence of Mithraism in Rome is demonstrated by the large number of Mithraea throughout the city. In addition to the one beneath the church of San Clemente, I can also point to the one below the small church of Santa Prisca, on the Aventine Hill. Visitors enter through a narrow passage, and it's one of the few that still has some of the original fresco decorations representing the seven steps of initiation for the faithful, a procession in honor of Mithras, and the sacrifice of the bull.

So what effect does EUR have today? The Austrian writer and adopted Roman Ingeborg Bachmann defined it "an empty and macabre complex of buildings." Perhaps the place wasn't yet finished, or perhaps its architecture seemed too far from the forms, style, and fullness of the baroque style foreigners have come to expect in Rome. What I like about EUR is its sense of the metaphysical (Michelangelo Antonioni used it for his 1962 film *Eclipse*), even if it's now a little tarnished by traffic and advertising posters. Its avenues, boulevards, and the impression of the ideal city set by its orthogonal intersections remain crisp and clean, even though life has left its marks on them, humanizing their outlines and smoothing their corners where the predominant white of the travertine is tempered by the vivid green of the gardens, the cerulean blue of fountains and waterfalls, and the multicolored cars passing by.

The architects who designed the complex were aware both of classical models and the most recent twentieth-century experiments. They knew how to appreciate the Renaissance's legacies, and were capable of using its harmonic sense of symmetry and proportion, the rich legacies left to all arts.

EUR is also one of the few largely secular places in a city profoundly wrapped up in the presence of religion over so many centuries. Only twice in Rome has anyone built a neighborhood where the secular prevails over the religious; the first time was when the *Piemontesi* built the Macao neighborhood around the Piazza Indipendenza, and the second time was the Fascists' construction of EUR. Rome is Rome—there's no questioning that—but E42 remains the greatest attempt by extraordinary architects to bring the city to more closely resemble other important European cities.

But bringing it closer doesn't mean making it the same. We need only detach ourselves for a moment from the almost abstract geometry of EUR, abandon its avenues and take a stroll through the surrounding areas, and we run into some of the marvels mentioned in this chapter, from the monastery of Tre Fontane to the excavations at Ostia Antica. This contiguity, these temporal short circuits, this instant flight through the centuries occurs only in Rome with such extraordinary frequency and impact; this is a privilege to remember a bit more often, and perhaps this book can help us do just that.

ACKNOWLEDGMENTS

In the two and a half years it took to write these pages I've incurred numerous debts to many kind and knowledgeable people who, whether in person or through their work, have offered me their suggestions, information, and time.

I would like to extend thanks to my principal collaborators; for starters, I'm grateful for the help of two experts on all things Roman, Claudio Rendina and Armando Ravaglioli, as well as my friend Giorgio Ruffolo. Aurelio Urciuoli, Maria Rosaria Coppola, and Bruno Tobia provided generous consultation on my research of the Vittoriano. Giuliano Capecelatro and Laura Biagiotti, curator of the Fondazione Marco Besso, were my guides to seventeenth-century Rome; Giorgio Bouchard, Sergio Lepri, and Antonio Thiery led me through the Roman Republic of 1849.

My research of witness accounts and documents of the attack on Via Rasella and subsequent massacre at the Fosse Ardeatine was facilitated by Robert Katz, Alessandro Portelli, and Gerhard Schreiber. I was able to reconstruct the world of Cinecittà thanks to Flaminio Di Biagi, Tullio Kezich, Dino Risi, and Mario Verdone. For the interpretations of Michelangelo's *Moses* I'm indebted to Antonio Forcellino's studies. Vincenzo Cerami, Irene De Guttry, and Giuseppe Fiori helped me understand 1960s Rome and the Casati scandal. The suggestions of Cesare D'Onofrio, Cristina Nardella, and Giovanni Maria Vian—as well as their published works—were essential to my exploration of Rome in the High Middle Ages.

Abraham Berliner, Enzo Collotti, Ruth Liliana Geller, Stephanie Siegmund, and Ariel Toaff illustrated the stories and history of the Roman ghetto for me. The archaeologists Ida Sciortino and Laura Vendittelli helped me see many of the city's monuments in the right perspective, as did Dr. Francesca Balboni for the Roman Fora. For information on the church of San Clemente and all that lies below it I'm grateful to Don Giacomo Saladino, and Father Morris Fearon described the frescoes and history of the Santi Quattro Coronati to me with supreme competence. Renzo Ferri, Fabio Grisanti, and Ida Viola all helped with information about EUR and its extraordinary history.

All of these suggestions came together thanks to the invaluable help of Nicoletta Lazzari and Pier Angela Mazzarino, who edited the text. I'm also grateful for the generous assistance of Anna Ramadori in Mondadori's Rome office, and Marco Ausenda and Julie Di Filippo at Rizzoli International Publications in New York. Additional thanks to Umberto Eco and Alexander Stille; and to Alta Price, Lawrence Jenkens, and Daniel Seidel for their linguistic sensitivity.

I extend heartfelt thanks to all, with the recognition that any errors or misunderstandings are mine alone—and I'd be grateful to anyone who might point them out for potential future editions.

PHOTOGRAPHY CREDITS

Andrea Alteri: Palazzo degli Uffici, EUR

Archivi Alinari, Florence: Tomb of John Keats; aerial view of the Baths of Cara-calla; the tomb of Cecilia Metella; the excavations at Largo di Torre Argentina; the Roman Forum; Porta Latina; Porta San Sebastiano; the Theater of Marcellus; views of daily life (a sandal maker at work and a woman hanging laundry); the Torre dei Conti; the Torre delle Milizie; the Torre della Scimmia; the courtyard of the church of Santi Quattro Coronati; Sala dei Santi, Vatican Museum; Pinturicchio, detail of a painting depicting Lucrezia Borgia as Saint Catherine; Sala del Credo, Vatican Museums; Pinturicchio, *The Resurrection*; a Fascist ceremony of the Altar of the Nation; three horsemen; a country festival; the Villa Il Vescello; and a view of a street in the Jewish Ghetto.

Archivio Bruni/Gestione Archivi Alinari, Florence: Mussolini visiting a film set at Cinecittà; women walking in front of a shop in the Campo dei Fiori.

Archivio Centrale dello Stato, Ministero per i Beni e le Attività Culturali, Rome: Ettore Muti's *Buen Retiro*.

Bridgeman—Archivi alinari, Florence: Caravaggio, *Death of the Virgin*; Tomb of Pope Julius II; and cloister of the church of San Pietro in Montorio.

The Bridgeman Art Library: Vincenzo Camuccini, *Death of Julius Caesar* © Museo e Gallerie Nazionali di Capodimonte, Naples, Italy/The Bridgeman Art Library; Interior view of the Main Altar of San Clemente, Rome © Bridgeman Art Library, London/The Bridgeman Art Library Nationality.

Centro Documentazione Mondadori: Camillo and Anna Casati; and Massimo Minorenti.

Fototeca Storica Gilardi, Milan: Men rounded up by the Nazis after the attack in Via Rasella; bodies of those massacred at the Fosse Ardeatine; "Il Diario della Marchesa Anna Casati Fallarino;" and the Nazi roundup in the Jewish Ghetto.

Istituto Luce/Gestione Archivi Alinari, Florence: Ettore Muti; the actress Anita Ekberg; first take of the film, *Scipione l'Africano*; four middle class women convers-ing; and a truck carrying some of the Jews deported from the Roman Ghetto.

Olycom, Milan: Detail of the Baths of Caracalla; interior of the Tomb of Cecilia Metella; the Aurelian Walls of Rome; nave of the church of San Pietro in Vincoli; view of Rome from one of the terraces of the Vittoriano; the Vittoriano; and Gino Coppedè's so-called House of the Fairies on the Via Tagliamento.

Raffaelle Bencini / Archivi Alinari, Florence: Caravaggio, *Martyrdom of Saint Matthew*; Caravaggio, *Conversion of Saint Paul*; and Caravaggio, *Crucifixion of Saint Peter*.

Remo Casilli / Grazia Neri: Tomb of Antonio Gramsci.

Team / Archivi Alinari, Florence: Entrance to Cinecittà.

© 2005 Foto Scala, Florence: Caravaggio, *Madonna di Loreto*.

All other photographs are property of the author.

INDEX OF NAMES AND PLACES